EVOLUTION AND ETHICS

EVOLUTION AND ETHICS

*Human Morality in Biological
and Religious Perspective*

Edited by

Philip Clayton and Jeffrey Schloss

WILLIAM B. EERDMANS PUBLISHING COMPANY
GRAND RAPIDS, MICHIGAN / CAMBRIDGE, U.K.

Wm. B. Eerdmans Publishing Co.

255 Jefferson Ave. S.E., Grand Rapids, Michigan 49503 /
P.O. Box 163, Cambridge CB3 9PU U.K.

Printed in the United States of America

09 08 07 06 05 04   7 6 5 4 3 2 1

Library of Congress Cataloging-in-Publication Data

Evolution and ethics: human morality in biological and religious perspective /
    edited by Philip Clayton and Jeffrey Schloss.
        p.   cm.
    Includes bibliographical references and index.
    ISBN 0-8028-2695-4 (pbk.: alk. paper)
        1. Ethics, Evolutionary.   2. Evolution (Biology) — Moral and ethical aspects.
    3. Biology — Religious aspects — Christianity.   I. Clayton, Philip, 1956-
    II. Schloss, Jeffrey.

    BJ1311.E95   2004
    171′.7 — dc22

                                                                    2004047241

www.eerdmans.com

Contents

II. Religious and Evolutionary Ethics — Are They Compatible?

III. The Ethics of Evolution: Theological Evaluation and Critique

Preface

This book is far more than a random collection of papers that happened to have been presented at a conference somewhere. The majority of the authors spent four weeks in residence together at Calvin College during a recent summer, engaged in intensive study and debate concerning the core questions of this book. We are grateful to the John Templeton Foundation, without whose generous funding this collaborative project would not have been possible, and to the Seminars in Christian Scholarship program of Calvin College, which hosted this research consultation, especially to Susan Felch, its Director, and to Anna Mae Bush, Kara Vandrie, and their staff.

With the financial assistance of the Templeton Foundation, we were able to bring in leading figures in the field for extended discussion and debate. The in-depth interactions that took place over the summer with the scientists Richard Alexander, David Sloan Wilson, and Malcolm Jeeves, and with the theologians Niels Gregersen and Kevin Vanhoozer, were a testing ground for the proposals made in this volume. Each paper was then presented and critiqued at a major conference at Calvin College in November, 2002. Joining us as keynote speakers at the conference were Larry Arnhart, Christopher Boehm, Thomas Lewis, Peter Richerson, and Holmes Rolston III. All but one of their papers have been added to this summary of the project's conclusions. In addition, we have been able to include papers by Michael Ruse, Joseph Poulshock, and David Lahti, which were written expressly for this volume, since their research results bear directly on the "evolution and ethics" debate.

Not all of the papers written by members of the core research group were focused directly on the topic of this book, and so not all of their papers could be included in this volume. Each core participant, however, has contributed substantially to these published results through his or her research, ideas, criticisms, and comments. We gratefully acknowledge our intellectual and personal debt to these other colleagues: Stacey Ake, Dan Brannan, Eduardo de la Cruz, Alvin Plantinga, Richard Weikert, and Doug Vakoch.

During four years of working together on this project I have come increasingly to respect the level of scholarship in both biology and theology brought by my co-organizer and co-editor, Jeffrey Schloss. Without his unparalleled sense for the tensions between these two fields, but also for the exciting opportunities for integration that they present, this project would not have achieved the significant results that it has. Finally, the heavy burden of turning a wide-ranging research project into a coherent book was carried in large part by my assistants Kevin Cody and Andrea Zimmerman, to whom I express my deep appreciation.

PHILIP CLAYTON
Claremont School of Theology
May 2004

INTRODUCTION

Evolutionary Ethics and Christian Morality: Surveying the Issues

Jeffrey P. Schloss

MacDuff: What? All my pretty Chickens, and their Damme
at one fell swoop?
Malcomb: Bear it like a man!
MacDuff: I shall do so: But I must first also feel it as a man.

Shakespeare, *Macbeth*, act 4, scene 3

Over the last 150 years many Christians have viewed evolutionary theory as attempting to slay cherished elements — "all our pretty chickens" — of theological and moral belief. Indeed, not only Christians but also evolutionary theorists themselves have asserted this, both historically and currently (T. H. Huxley [1894] 1989; Dewey [1909] 1988; J. Huxley 1960; Rachels 1990; Dennett 1995; Dawkins 1997 and 2003). In the face of this conflict, exhortations to engagement are common, in a sense urging us to "bear it like a man!"

Understandings of what is entailed by proper engagement vary wildly, though. For some, it means beating back the evolutionary enemy, especially along the front lines of ethical conflict (Johnson 1998 and 2002; Hunter 2001 and 2003; Wiker 2002; Morris 2000). For others, it means coming to see there is no real battle (Pope 1994; Gould 1999; Miller 1999). For others still, it means recognizing the conflict is real, but theology can be enriched by making concessions of territory that was not properly managed to begin with, or modifications to our maps of terrain inaccurately surveyed: "the challenge by Darwin to theology . . . may prove to be not so much peril as gift" (Haught 2000, 46; cf. P. Williams 2001; Hefner 1993). The premise of this volume is that before we decide what it means to "bear" the issue with dignity, we must first "feel" it with integrity. We must openly survey the issues before advocating a response.

Just what are the "issues," then? The tension between evolutionary theory and Christian belief is often viewed as the most recent (and also long-

1

standing) instance of defensive posturing by religion in the face of advancing scientific understanding, which has progressively overrun outposts of belief in the supernatural by the firepower of naturalistic explanation (White 1955; Dennett 1995; Dawkins 2000 and 2003). But this is simultaneously saying too much and too little. It is saying too much, not only because this warfare account of science and religion itself is hyperbolic and over-generalized (Brooke 1991; Brooke and Cantor 2000; Lindberg and Numbers 1986 and 2003), but also because the most serious and widespread Christian resistance to evolutionary theory has never really centered on defending particular supernatural accounts of how creation occurred. Rather, it has involved fundamental beliefs about what *kind* of creation we have. Indeed, the issue has appeared to be whether the cosmos can properly be conceived of as a creation at all, or for that matter, as a cosmos rather than a chaos, where the reality of nature and humanity's place in it is grounded in and reflective of coherent moral purpose.

So here is where generic science-religion skirmish accounts say too little. On the face of things, particularly when it comes to matters of ethics and human purpose, we seem to be dealing with two profoundly different meta-narratives in evolutionary naturalism and Christian theism (Wilson 1978; Rachels 1990; Smith 2003). Western theism has traditionally affirmed a transcendent creator of and purpose to life, which the design of the cosmos manifestly, even jubilantly, testifies to; and it has embraced the conviction that human beings, fashioned in the Creator's image, are specially suited to apprehend and cultivate that purpose, in a moral vision of self-giving and unconditional love. Philosopher James Rachels (1990, 5) is by no means alone in pointing out that, in contrast to the traditional Western view, "Darwin's great contribution was the final demolition of the idea that nature is the product of intelligent design," and that evolutionary theory "undermines the idea that man is made in the image of God. . . . The idea of human dignity turns out, therefore, to be the moral effluvium of a discredited metaphysics." In an essay that explores the issue of incommensurability between evolutionary biology and the Christian love command, Michael Ruse (1994, 5) cautions that "those who are worried about the clash between science and religion have good reasons for their worries."

Is this true? We want to ask if this is an accurate description of tension between essential, or even appropriately representative, conceptual positions in evolutionary theory and Christian theology. And, to whatever extent it is accurate, can there be integrative advance without doing violence to each tradition by accommodation? We are not starting with answers to these questions. If this volume engages the audience we are hoping for, readers will already be responding divergently. Some may be impatient with beginning this chapter by the rhetorical invoking of an ostensible "straw man," stuffed with unnecessarily dichotomized depictions of polar positions. Others may recognize that these positions have thoughtful and highly influential advocates and are not mere distortions resulting from conspiratorial paranoia; they will therefore eschew even exploring "peace, where there is no peace." Our goal is to begin tentatively, not out of noncommittal diplomacy, but out of exploratory humility. Therefore contributors to this volume bring a wide spectrum of backgrounds and positions, including those of evolutionary biologists, human behavioral scientists, philosophers, and theologians from atheistic, agnostic, and a variety of Christian traditions. The editors themselves bring differing disciplinary and integrative perspectives.

Differences notwithstanding, this volume reflects five shared commitments. First, we are not debating whether evolutionary theory is necessary to understanding the history of life. Second, we reject what amounts to the ancient error of gnosticism, and affirm the notion that human moral understanding must take account of human biological embodiment. Third, we are quite open to discussing the extent to which evolutionary theory furnishes a sufficient, or at present even concretely demonstrable, descriptive account of human morality. Fourth, while we agree that biology must inform moral understanding, we are committed to debating arguments that biology can justify ethics, and, on the other hand, claims that some naturalistic accounts actually weaken ethical justification. And fifth, we are persuaded that the more serious these differences, the more important it is to address them by rigorous and civil intellectual discussion within the academic community, not by inbred polemics lobbed into the political domain.

I want to do two things in the rest of this introduction. First, I want to amplify and nuance this general notion of differing evolutionary and theological meta-narratives as they apply to ethical issues. My goal will be largely descriptive rather than evaluative, so that other authors in the volume can argue whether differing perspectives are congruent, complimentary, or conflictual. Second, I want to map the terrain of theoretical relief *within* rather than *between* scientific and theological understandings of evolutionary ethics, emphasizing three major areas of controversy within the disciplines that serve to structure this book. As we will see, many points of debate do not represent intrinsic conflict between science and religion but long-standing ambiguities within each.

General Considerations

Evolutionary theory raises a series of issues for ethics, along a continuum of increasing specificity that is reflected in progressive topical emphases of this volume. First, and most generally, is the issue of naturalism and morality. Of course, there exists long-standing debate that is not necessarily wedded to either evolutionary or theological ideas, about whether naturalism is compatible with realist meta-ethics or justifiable normative ethics. These concerns have received substantially more attention in the wake of Darwin's theory, and especially since the development of evolutionary and sociobiological theories of moral capacity (Nitecki and Nitecki 1993; Maienshein and Ruse 1999; Bradie 1994; Farber 1994; Thompson 1995). In addition to these philosophical questions, there are theological questions raised by naturalistic approaches to ethics. How do we understand God's role in the revelation of morality, in the conviction of moral failure, and in empowering change? More generally, in the context of a purportedly seamless naturalistic ontogeny of the world, what can it mean to say that nature, or human nature, is fallen, or in need of redemption? And how would such redemption occur, moreover — what would distinguish it from simple maturation or development? Several authors in this volume take on these themes.

Beyond the question of ethical naturalism, though, are issues related to what *kind* of naturalism Darwinian accounts of ethics entail. Here the series of issues becomes progressively more linked to the distinctives of evolutionary theory. First is the issue of determinism. The question of whether there can be both determinism and moral responsibility clearly has a long, pre-Darwinian pedigree of theological and philosophical debate. While contemporary evolutionary and sociobiological theory exhibits a range of positions on biological determinism (Gould 1977; Wilson 1975 and 1978; S. Rose 1982; H. Rose and S. Rose 2000; Pinker 1997 and 2002; Alcock 2003; Dennett 2003), this tends to reflect differences in evaluating genetic and environmental determinants of behavioral phenotype, rather than a wide divergence on the issue of human freedom. Moreover, although evolutionary theory itself underspecifies predictions of particular behaviors, population genetic models almost uniformly assume a determinative relationship between genes and behaviors like altruism or cooperation, and evolutionary approaches to behavior understandably seek to describe constraints and central tendencies in prescriptive terms. Daniel Dennett (2003) argues for complete determinism — only one future is possible from any present — while attempting to make a case for the evolutionary emergence of moral responsibility.

Next is the issue of evolutionary reductionism, that is, to whatever extent things are or are not causally determined, what level of description is necessary to give an account of relevant causes? Recent discussions of hierarchical selection notwithstanding, most of the various contemporary accounts of ethical evolution tend to be particulate or causally reductive. Traditional sociobiological approaches boldly assert the reductive teleology of the gene: "an organism is just a gene's way of reproducing itself" (Dawkins 1976; Wilson 1975); or even, "your mind works in the service of your gonads" (Wright 1994). What is significant here is not the determinism but the reductive reconceptualization from organism as agent to organism as instrument. The loss of agency, at organismal not to mention mental levels, has profound implications for understanding morality.

This tension persists in more recent elaborations of moral evolution. Multilevel selection theory has posited a structural hierarchy of instruments (or vehicles) in the form of groups of organisms but still affirms the particulate telos of genetic replication. Dual inheritance or functional hierarchy theory argues that for humans (and so far, this is suggested only for humans) there is, in addition to genes, a nonmaterial, ideational source of replicating information — the meme (Durham 1991; Plotkin 1993 and 1997; Blackmore 1999). But note, it is still atomistic: "A mind is just a meme's way of replicating itself" (Blackmore 1999). While there are some interesting holistic accounts of organismal and mental evolution (Oyama 2000; Deacon 1997), current Darwinian approaches to morality tend to be ambivalent about or dismissive of agency. Thus, even if we escape naive determinism, that doesn't get us as far as moral agency or self-determination. In fact, an opportunity explored by several contributors to this volume involves the important and under-examined issue of emergence and mental causation in relation to evolutionary ethics.

Third, and yet more tightly coupled to evolutionary concerns, is the issue of functionalist accounts of ethics. A general issue here involves questions of whether a functional explanation of a belief — in God, an ethical principle, or freight trains, for that matter (Ruse 1994) — subverts rationale for the truth of that belief, and also whether a functional account of ethical precepts subverts its normative demand by, for example, making it a means rather than an end. This is the stuff of current debates over evolutionary ethics (Nitecki and Nitecki 1993; Farber 1994; Richards 1999; Woolcock 1999; Harms 2000; Joyce 2000; Casebeer 2003). But beyond these questions, and also an important focus of this book, is the fact that traditional Darwinian explanations entail a particular *kind* of functionalism, which has implications for specific altruistic moral tenets in Christianity and other religious traditions (Ruse 1994; O'Hear 1997).

Like all behavior, human ethical behavior is viewed evolutionarily as "the circuitous technique by which human genetic material has been and will be kept intact; morality has no other demonstrable ultimate function" (Wilson 1978, 167). This fitness-enhancing functional distinctive raises the question of altruism, one of the major themes of this book. While altruism or self-relinquishing love or other-regard is not the sole focus of human moral systems, it is arguably the central focus of religious morality (Hare 1997; Grant 2001; Smith 2003). And yet, the operation of natural selection via reproductive self-interest is virtually universally recognized as constituting at least a problem, if not a nonnegotiable impediment, for the origin and maintenance of genuine altruism, not necessarily in terms of motivations, but in terms of behavioral consequences. "If natural selection is both sufficient and true, it is impossible for a genuinely disinterested or 'altruistic' behavior pattern to evolve" (Ghiselin 1973, 967). Contributors to this volume include prominent and provocative scholars with very different approaches to this issue.

At this point I want to attend to three areas of inquiry in evolution and ethics that will structure discussion in this volume. The "evolution of ethics" entails descriptive theories of the biological origin and/or functional maintenance of ethical capacity or norms. "Ethics from evolution" is the philosophical attempt, sometimes referred to as evolutionary ethics, to provide meta-ethical justification or derive normative ethical principles from evolutionary theory. Finally, the "ethics of evolution" involves questions about the ethical implications of the evolutionary process itself, and indeed about the moral nature of the universe. In particular, Darwinian understandings of nature have been viewed as both dramatically exacerbating the problem of natural evil (T. H. Huxley [1894] 1989; Oates 1988; G. C. Williams 1988 and 1993; Dawkins 2003) and also as contributing to a natural theodicy (Miller 1999; Haught 2000). The underlying issue is whether, and if so in what ways, evolutionary process may be seen to reflect cosmic moral purpose or the goodness of God. Because the first of these three themes is the dominant one in this volume, I will devote the larger part of this introduction to describing it.

Evolution of Ethics

There are two different but related questions in attempts to explain the evolutionary origin of human morality. The first, analogous to meta-ethical questions in philosophy, concerns the origin of ethical systems in general — the human capacity, indeed the universal inclination, to believe there is something "out there" that makes a normative demand upon behavior. The second, similar to philosophical questions of normative ethics, involves the question of whether there is an evolutionary basis for the particular content of ethical systems, that is, specific moral beliefs or norms. Evolutionary theories *of* ethics are descriptive rather than prescriptive; they posit natural causes for ethical capacity or particular moral beliefs, but do not in themselves purport to provide justification.

Evolution of Ethical Capacity

With respect to the first question involving the evolutionary origin of ethical systems or the capacity for moral judgment, we need to say something about what it is that is in need of an explanation. Morality constitutes a particularly interesting evolutionary question, not only because ethical systems urge specific behaviors that sometimes appear contrary to reproductive self-interest (see next section below), but also because ethical judgment involves choosing behaviors by criteria that are understood to exist independent of the inclinations of the actor. In his sociological study of the universal moral structuring of human culture, Christian Smith (2003) describes morality as "an orientation toward understandings about what is right and wrong, good and bad, worthy and unworthy, just and unjust, that are not established by our own actual desires, decisions, or preferences but instead believed to exist apart from them, providing standards by which our desires, decisions, and preferences can themselves be judged" (Smith 2003, 8).

Although referring to good and bad itself may be question-begging, the above approach reflects two salient features of human moral capacity (Taylor 1989) that stand out as needing evolutionary explanation. First, the demand of ethical norms is understood or felt to be categorical: what is moral is so regardless of personal desire, and it is not understood as merely one among many optional strategies for life enhancement (Bellah et al. 1996). Second, our experience of the moral life involves not just the evaluation and selection of behaviors independent of, and sometimes even in opposition to, personal desire, but it also includes a distinctive kind of desire — secondary desire (Taylor 1985) or meta-affection (Schloss 2000) — that entails the "desire for right desire" (Schloss 2002b; Hare, this volume).

Evolutionary accounts of moral capacity address questions of *why* this capacity exists (in other words, what adaptive role it might have), and also *how* it came about (in other words, what proto-moral capacities were modified, and in what selective environments, to account for its phylogenetic and cognitive origin)? Although occasionally conflated, these two specific questions are not identical. There are two broad traditions that take differing approaches to these questions.

The non-adaptationist approach does not address the why question, because it does not view human morality as a biological adaptation at all but rather as a "spandrel" (Gould and Lewontin 1979) or by-product of interaction between other cognitive capacities that are adaptive. Ayala (1995, 1998) views morality as an incidental consequence of three other, adaptive cognitive abilities: the abilities to anticipate behavioral consequences, to evaluate options as more or less desirable, and to choose between behavioral alternatives. "We make moral judgments as a consequence of our eminent intellectual abilities, not as an innate way for achieving biological gain" (Ayala 1998). Even if Ayala's account is correct, however, it only addresses why moral judgments are possible, but does not account for the striking situation that they actually exist, and exist universally in human societies: it addresses the necessary but not sufficient cognitive preconditions for human morality (Smith 2003). Other by-product accounts of human meta-cognition offer more detailed proposals for the inveterate human inclination to believe in normative, transcendent realities (Boyer 2001; Hinde 1999 and 2002). One general question raised by spandrel or by-product approaches is how it is that an incidental feature exerts such ostensibly central and determinative influence on human behavior.

In part because of this, functionalist perspectives on moral evolution view human ethical capacity as a distinguishing and crucial biological adaptation of human beings. There are several different but not incompatible approaches here. One approach emphasizes human morality as a cognitive adaptation for behavioral flexibility. Unlike organisms with a relatively small repertoire of rigidly determined behaviors, the extensive range of behaviors open to human beings requires a parsing mechanism to help us choose among behavioral options that are too varied to computationally assess (Ruse 1994; Casebeer 2003). At first blush (no pun intended), this may sound like a general theory of emotions, which also can be viewed as prescreening mechanisms to reduce cognitive load — "somatic markers" (Damasio 1995) or "postcards from our genes, [which] inform our intelligence what to learn and think about" (Plotkin 1993).

So why do we have morality if we already have emotional value markers — disgust, pleasure, fear, attraction — for behaviors, internal states, or environmental conditions with significant reproductive consequences? The proposal is that our emotional inclinations themselves have become so varied and at times ambiguous, perhaps as a result of conflicting legacies of selection (Boehm 1999), and the cultural environment that helps mediate emotional responses changes so rapidly (Plotkin 1997), that moral capacity serves as a meta-affective evaluator of behavioral motivations. Darwin himself proposed such a role for conscience, which he argued was pained when one chose between conflicting desires, electing to satisfy a desire with shorter- rather than longer-term fulfillment (Darwin [1871] 1981). Ruse (1986) takes this a step further by suggesting a role for moral tradition or specific ethical beliefs as a "backup mechanism" to promote behaviors with crucial adaptive significance, since emotional inclinations alone can be frail or contradictory. For example, instances of child abuse, and even the interior experience of most parents, reveal that affections for parental care need to be supplemented with cognitive beliefs that it is wrong to treat children in certain ways. In the movie *Lawrence of Arabia,* when a visitor is impressed by the compassion of Lawrence, his conversation partner cautiously remarks, "For Lawrence, mercy is a passion; for the Prince, it is a convention. Judge for yourself, which is the more reliable of the two." Within a few months, Lawrence was shouting, "Take no prisoners!"

Mercy to enemies is one thing, but why would crucial adaptive behaviors like parenting need a cognitive moral "back-up" at all? Which is to say, why would human motivations for behaviors essential for reproductive success be conflicted? Moreover, the account of conscience as entailing guilt over past choices, or of morality as helping us choose between alternative inclinations, is certainly part but not all of the human moral experience. It also entails the sense of mandate to choose behaviors we do not feel inclined to at all, or the positive desire to reform desires. These are questions that meta-cognitive theories of morality may have resources to address, but have not yet fully engaged (Schloss 2000). Several authors in this volume take on these issues.

Another functionalist approach views human morality as an adaptation for cooperation within social groups. Some accounts view it as an individual adaptation to the challenges of social exchange within groups that, unlike other primate groups, may be too large to keep track of the history of reciprocity with each individual. Richard Alexander (1987) suggests that morality allows for "indirect reciprocity," where reputations for faithful cooperation or defection, founded on moral judgments, mediate inclusion in the cooperative matrix. Other accounts view morality as a group adaptation, perhaps promoted by inter-group competition. Darwin suggested such a role for morality (Darwin [1871] 1981) along with his thoughts on conscience. In a similar vein, Christopher Boehm (1999) has a proposal that integrates morality as promoting intra-group cooperation, and also as overseeing motivational ambivalence arising from conflicting legacies of individual and group selection. Although individual and group selection approaches are often presented as fundamentally oppositional, both emphasize the nature of morality as an adaptation to life in social groups, one that promotes an intensiveness or extensiveness of cooperation exceeding that of nonhuman primates.

Evolution of Ethical Norms

The issue of cooperation brings up the crucial theoretical question in evolutionary theories of ethical norms, and in fact a profound question for biological theories of behavior in general: the question of altruism or cooperative sacrifice. Of course, the issue of sacrificial love is also of paramount importance to religious understandings of morality. In the Christian tradition, it is considered the ultimate telos of human existence, the summation and fulfillment of all moral obligation. For evolutionary biology, it constitutes a "central theoretical issue" (Wilson 1975; Holcomb 1993), inasmuch as it has entailed a quandary needing explanation. Why so? Darwin himself recognized that an exclusively other-benefiting trait "would annihilate my theory, for such could not have been produced through natural selection." And yet, it appeared that the world in fact did contain such traits, from sterile, other-serving castes in social insects to manifold instances of ostensibly self-relinquishing altruism in human societies.

We had to wait a century for two theoretical breakthroughs that cast new light on the issue of altruism. First was a reconceptualization of fitness that accompanied the synthesis of selection theory and genetics. Fitness could now be construed as a property of genes, not individuals, and therefore it could be advanced not just through direct progeny but also through the reproductive success of genetically related kin who share genes. In his development of inclusive fitness theory — which turned out to solve the social insect dilemma — William Hamilton (1964) reasoned that a sacrificial behavior could be established if the cost to the actor was less than the benefit to the recipient, times the degree of genetic relatedness ($C \leq B * R$).

Second, using an analogous cost/benefit logic to explain sacrifice outside of kinship boundaries, Robert Trivers (1971) argued that sacrificial behaviors could be selectively established if the cost to the actor was less than the benefit of a future compensatory return, times the probability of receiving such a return. He termed this phenomenon "reciprocal altruism." While this sounds like an oxymoron — after all, altruism is precisely not reciprocity — the idea is that such behaviors are not strictly and immediately reciprocated, as in typical cases of mutualism. Rather, individuals make genuinely costly investments in others — but only in those particular others with whom the net balance of trade is likely to be positive in the long run. Reciprocal altruism, therefore, typically requires long-lived organisms with sufficient cognitive capacity to recognize other individuals and keep track of cooperative relationships.

These powerful insights have been immensely successful in making sense of previously puzzling sacrificial behaviors, and formed the basis for the sociobiological revolution — the comprehensive attempt to explain social behavior in light of evolutionary theory (Wilson 1975; Dawkins 1976). In its initial triumphalist zeal, sociobiology ambitiously asserted that all human social behavior could be explained by these two processes, and hence could be reduced to "nepotism and favoritism." In more recent years, however, it has been acknowledged that things are considerably more complicated than that. In what E. O. Wilson calls the scandal of mammalian biology, human beings manifest an unusual degree and scope of cooperation: we invest in others outside the boundaries of kin and crony, and do so at significant personal cost. This is where theories of the evolution of cooperative moral norms come in. There are three primary approaches: individual selection, group selection, and hierarchical selection accounts.

A primary architect of individual selectionist accounts of morality, Richard Alexander (1987) advanced the notion of indirect reciprocity, utilizing a modification of the Hamiltonian cost/benefit calculus. As mentioned above, indirect reciprocity theory argues that in human beings — the only primate living in groups too large to keep track of personal relationships — reputation for being a faithful reciprocator mediates inclusion in the cooperative matrix. Morality is an adaptation to large group size that provides the rules for accruing resources in one's reputational bank account. Conscience serves as a "reputation alarm" that goes off when one is behaving in a way likely to erode principal (Alexander 1987). Thus in humans, and perhaps only in humans, individuals exhibit sacrificial cooperation with others who will never repay the favor. But here is where the theory specifies not only moral capacity but moral norms. Humans should affirm cooperation only so long as the cost of the sacrifice is less than the benefit of an indirect compensatory return from someone else, times the increased likelihood this will happen from reputational enhancement. According to indirect reciprocity theory, we're as unselfish as it pays to be; we're as selfish as we can get away with.

Cynical implications notwithstanding, indirect reciprocity does make sense of, and successfully predicts, many aspects of human moral systems. But there are also explanatory limits. Virtue may be its own reward, but virtue consciously pursued for reward's sake strikes most people as suspiciously unvirtuous; thus humans are on vigilant lookout for hypocrites whose goodwill is intentionally tied to the rate of reputational return. Moreover, human group sizes are often so large that we need to make decisions about cooperating with others whose reputations we don't know. Enter signaling theory, which suggests that individuals develop costly or hard-to-fake, often involuntary displays that reliably convey cooperative disposition. Indeed, consciousness is understood by some evolutionary biologists primarily as an adaptation for defensively inferring the interior state of others, "a game of life in which the participants are trying to comprehend what is in one another's minds before, and more effectively than, it can be done in reverse" (Alexander 1987). As a complement, the uniquely neotonous and hairless human facial morphology is a highly effective stage for emotional display. Recent experimental work has confirmed the connection between involuntary facial signals and altruistic dispositions, and has revealed that people indeed have a fascinating ability to make accurate inferences from facial information (Brown et al. 2003).

So is the very best strategy for cooperative inclusion to be a genuinely good person? Groucho Marx quipped, "Honesty and fair-dealing is the way to succeed — if you can fake that, you've got it made." Then perhaps the best strategy is to fake being real. But the best, perhaps the only way, to "fake" an involuntary display is to be sincerely though erroneously convinced of one's good intentions. Self-deception theory, the last refinement in the individual benefit line of argument, suggests that human cognition is structured with a bias toward overestimating one's own virtue and concealing one's ultimately self-serving motives from self-conscious recognition. The most effective fitness-maximizing strategy is not intentional hypocrisy but entirely sincere, though self-deceived, professions of beneficence. Indeed, believing you believe the New Testament love command has been described as the most effective strategy for manipulating others to your own benefit (Cronk 1994).

Oscar Wilde observed that "sentimentality is the desire to have the pleasure of an emotion without the willingness to pay its price." Sociobiological elaboration of individual benefit approaches end up positing this as a biological adaptation. If this theory *is* correct, and that is all there is to cooperation and human morality, it would appear that "No hint of genuine charity ameliorates our vision of society, once sentimentalism has been laid aside. What passes for cooperation turns out to be a mixture of opportunism and exploitation" (Ghiselin 1974).

There is disturbing but undeniable truth to the above perspective. But this is nothing new to moral and religious traditions, which have a rich legacy of recognizing and prophetically confronting the threat of sanctimonious self-deception. The question is, can the moral reform and religious prophetic traditions themselves be deconstructed as the grandest self-deception? There is an empirical implication of this question. If individual reproductive benefit were the only source of human moral beliefs and cooperative behavior, we would expect rhetorical affirmations of altruism to be largely uncoupled from genuinely sacrificial behavior. But this does not appear to be entirely the case. Therefore, in recent years, unifactorial explanations involving individual selection have been supplemented with theories invoking different levels of genetic selection (Richerson and Boyd 1999; Sober and Wilson 1998; Boehm 1999) and nongenetic or cultural evolution (Durham 1991; Plotkin 1993 and 1997; Cronk 1999), which significantly expand the evolutionary moral domain.

Group or multilevel selection theory holds that genes for altruism can be selected if the within-group decrement to fitness of the altruist is less than the between-group enhancement. This approach has the benefit of explaining genuinely sacrificial behavior on behalf of group members. The "dark side" of group altruism, however, is intergroup conflict (Sober and Wilson 1998). Group selection of altruistic morality does not explain norms for enemy love, and in fact is driven by out-group hostility.

Yet another approach is to posit not just that selection operates on structurally scaled levels of replicators, transmitted from assemblages of chromosomes to individuals to groups and so on, but that there is a nested hierarchy of replicators themselves — material and ideational, genes and memes (Durham 1991; Plotkin 1993 and 1997). This provocative account, suggested only for humans, provides a unique route by which human behavior is influenced not only by genetic information but by extra-somatic, cultural information that is not reducible to, and may under some circumstances countervail, genetic constraints (Dawkins 1976; Plotkin 1997; Lopreato 1984; Blackmore 1999). This dramatically widens the scope of possibility for both altruistic moral norms and actual behaviors. It does so, however, at an explanatory cost (Schloss 2003). Some criticize this as entailing a return to gnostic dualism, placing altruistic morality outside of human biological nature, rather than being a fulfillment of it (Midgley 1994; de Waal 1996). Others suggest that this accommodation, made necessary by the inability of evolutionary theory to explain altruistic morality, itself is not meaningfully founded on evolution (Smith 2003). There are, however, a variety of accounts that integrate group selection and cultural evolutionary approaches in ways that attempt to avoid these criticisms (Richerson and Boyd 1999; Boehm 1999).

Emerging revisionist accounts present a more nuanced but ambiguous picture of human nature, one that entails deep ambivalences that reflect contrasting legacies of individual and group selection (Boehm 1999) and tensions between biological and cultural (even religious) influence. Interestingly, these developments over the last decade or so mirror debates about the conflictedness and transformability of the human capacity to live up to altruistic morality, that which theology has been wrestling with for centuries. Indeed, recent "camps" in evolutionary thought in many ways mirror longstanding polarities in Augustinian vs. Thomistic, and Reformed vs. Wesleyan, theology (Schloss 2002a). Several authors in this volume explore these themes.

Ethics from Evolution

While theories of the evolutionary origin of ethics are strictly descriptive, their existence raises philosophical questions about whether evolution can justify ethical demands or inform ethical norms, whether attempts to do so commit the naturalistic fallacy (Hume [1738] 1911; Moore 1903), or, indeed, whether a fully naturalized evolutionary account of morality actually subverts ethical justification.

I will briefly mention two lines of inquiry that represent axes on the intellectual landscape occupied by various contributors to this volume. The first involves issues of meta-ethics. One question here is whether evolutionary explanations of morality necessarily entail ethical anti-realism. For example, Ruse (1995) and Joyce (2000) argue that they do; Richards (1986, 1999) and Rottschaeffer and Martinsen (1990) argue that they do not. (See Harms 2000 and Woolcock 1999 for critiques.) None of the contributors to this volume makes a case for anti-realism.

Another question more central to this book involves what implications theories of moral evolution have for ethical demand. Ethical anti-realism notwithstanding, Ruse (1986, 1995) argues for an evolutionary justification of ethics. Richards (1999) argues for an evolutionary justification of ethics and ethical realism, as does Arnhart (1998, and this volume). Traditional criticisms of fully naturalized ethics have argued that it commits the naturalistic fallacy, or entails the unjustifiable "attempt to derive an is from an ought." The claim is that descriptive accounts of how things are do not provide adequate warrant for normative determinations of how things should be (Midgley 1994; Woolcock 1999). Several recent proposals for evolutionary ethics squarely acknowledge and attempt to respond to this criticism (Ruse 1995; Richards 1999; Harms 2000; Joyce 2000), primarily on the basis of the particular kind of functional "is-ness" entailed by evolutionary biology. This raises an interesting question, which is a focus of several contributors to this volume: Even if we can infer an ethical demand from a natural description without logical error, would there be moral peril in doing so, since we would be reducing ethical demand, in other words, tailoring our sense of what should be to fit the evolutionary account of what is (Grant 2001; Schloss 2002a; Hare, this volume)? A complementary peril could be involved in inflating our understanding of natural capacity to meet demand (Ruse 1994; O'Donovan 1994; O'Hear 1997). These questions involve the general issue (discussed — and debated — long before evolutionary theory) of how morality calls us to be what we may not yet be, and perhaps what we cannot be without divine assistance (Hare 1997; Grant 2001). But they also involve specific and nuanced questions about the ways contrasting versions of evolutionary theory may present differing pictures of both what is humanly possible and what is morally necessary.

This raises the second line of inquiry, also a focus of this volume, which involves questions of normative ethics and the attempt to derive specific ethical principles from evolutionary theory. While basing specific moral norms on evolutionary theory may raise the above-described questions about grounds for understanding a moral gap between who we are and who we should be, it also harbors profound potential for positive integration with theological understandings of creaturely embodiment. When Mary Midgley (1994) remarks that love should be understood as a fulfillment of rather than an imposition on human nature, she reflects an ancient scriptural (and Thomistic) perspective that the moral law is rooted in who we are, not in arbitrary demands of who we should be, gnostically uncoupled from creation: "the Sabbath was made for man, and not man for the Sabbath." Indeed, not only is *moral behavior* understood as fulfilling our created nature, but wisdom or *moral prudence* requires appropriate understanding of the challenges and limits posed by that nature (Midgley 1980). Moreover, the moral graces of forgiveness and transformation hinge on the interplay of fulfillment and failure, rooted in our natural capacities and desires. As the psalmist affirms, "As far as the east is from the west, so far has He removed our transgressions. . . . For He knows our frame; He is mindful that we are but dust" (Ps. 103:12-14). One of the theologically valuable contributions biology can make is to enhance the understanding of "our frame." By the same token, theological understanding can illuminate ways in which biological explanation is incomplete. And on a broad and highly varied scientific landscape, it may provide a perspective for assessing how some positions reflect ideological precommitment in addition to scientific conclusions.

Along these lines, several authors in this volume explore the relationship between evolutionary biology and natural law theory. Among these is Larry Arnhart, who argues (1998, and this volume) that what is right is what fulfills fundamental, evolved human desires. Richards (1999) points out that one would need a principle to adjudicate between conflicting desires, and he suggests the good of the group. But, one might ask, why this principle, which can be critiqued as being no less arbitrary than utilitarianism or hedonistic individualism (Woolcock 1999)? Moreover, inferring moral norms from biological desires has been criticized on the basis of the reduction of ethical demand this entails; in other words, if specific moral norms are ultimately justified by desire, how can specific desires be categorically assessed and justified by morality (Hare 1997; Taylor 1989; Smith 2003)?

In a recent naturalistic approach that acknowledges these criticisms and opens up new ground for exploring normative ethics on the basis of evolution, William Casebeer (2003) agrees that desires are not an adequate input, much less justification, for ethical norms, because they are an imperfect marker of either personal fulfillment or biological success. Evolved desires are not optimal, and even if they were at one time, variation in the environment, especially the rapidly changing cultural environment, makes them an unreliable guide for the "good." We have deep desires that do not result either in our own fulfillment or the welfare of others. Instead, Casebeer suggests a return to Aristotelian notions of proper function, informed by evolutionary perspectives on organismal homeostasis. Morality helps us identify and avoid pathological desire.

Schloss (2002b) makes a similar point, observing that some moral teaching, particularly in a number of wisdom traditions, sounds less like moral commandments than it does like descriptions of how life works, along with counsel for personal flourishing. "Choose good, that you may live" is a repeated refrain in Deuteronomic moral teaching. More specifically, "He who clings to his life will lose it; he who loses it will preserve it" is the gospel's view of the way life works. The irony is that while virtue may entail reward, to be virtue, and to result in reward, it cannot be chosen *for* reward: it is self-relinquishment rather than self-seeking, which results in flourishing selfhood. Nearly all the authors in this volume explore — from varied starting points and with different conclusions — the relationship between evolutionary theory and a moral vision of deep other regard.

Ethics of Evolution

Finally, evolutionary theory is necessarily attended by ethical questions about the evolutionary process itself, or the moral nature of the universe. This is the case in two ways. First, evolutionary theory relates to questions of redemption and eschatological hope. Is there an intimation of purpose that is suggestive of or, on the contrary, in need of eschatological promise (Polkinghorne and Welker 2000; Schloss 2002b; Polkinghorne 2003)? Second, many believe that evolution dramatically exacerbates the theodicy problem (T. H. Huxley [1894] 1989; G. C. Williams 1988 and 1993; Haught 2000; Dawkins 2003). In fact, this involves not just the issue of divine benevolence but also the question of whether nature itself can be viewed as good in any meaningful sense. Darwinian theory raises this issue in three ways. In the first place, what is viewed as natural evil is not only primordial in time but also central in function: it is the driving force of creation (Oates 1988). Second, natural goodness or beneficence is at best constrained by a Darwinian leash, at worst nonexistent (G. C. Williams 1993). Third, the evolutionary process itself is fundamentally disteleological. Nature lurks, in the famous words of Tennyson, "in some wild poet, when he works without a conscience or an aim." Huxley himself argued that the cosmic process of evolution did not conform to, in fact was opposed by, human moral principles. (For a rejoinder to this view, see Dewey 1988.) Thus David Oates concludes, "For followers of Darwin, the traditional 'problem of evil' was turned on its head: evil could henceforth be assumed; the problem became, the problem of goodness" (Oates 1988).

In one sense, we are back to where we began, with ostensibly conflicting scientific and theological meta-narratives. But not so fast. The above accounts are only one version, perhaps an ideologically influenced interpretation, of evolutionary theory. New scientific approaches or traditional religious understanding may expose the illusory attractiveness of oversimplification (Lash 1995). It is also possible that there is truth here, which needs to inform and enrich theology (Haught 2000). Most evidently, the engineering notions of nature's design and the romantic idealizations of nature's goodness that informed natural theology historically have been appropriately corrected. More deeply, the dramatic turmoil of the evolutionary process may compel us to consider, or recover, a vision of pathos in the artistry of creation. Christian theology would not agree that the divine poet "works without a conscience or an aim," but he may be no less wild than Tennyson, or evolution, suggests. And the deep time and profound historical constraint entailed in the evolutionary process may provide a metaphor, if not an actual stage, for the drama of God's role in salvation history. Grace is not magic, and the drama of redemption is not a trick that instantaneously transmutes the world by divine alchemy, but rather a historically embedded process that both honors and redeems a cruciform nature, where death is the down payment for renewed life. Scientific descriptions of nature may inform but not wholly determine our understanding, however: theology brings its own long-standing interpretive resources for the extraction of hope from the ore of natural ambiguity (Watts 2000; Schloss 2002b). Of course, all of these options are simultaneously possible.

Closing Comments

I want to close with brief comments on two ways that scientific and theological understandings of morality may each enrich each other. First, theology may graciously but persistently articulate what we know about the reality of morality by drawing on ways of understanding that come from outside the sciences. With no religious agenda, Frans de Waal (1996, 14) critiques gene-centric theories as dismissing what "many of us consider to be at the core of being human," and concludes that "a more cynical outlook is hard to come by." Mary Midgley (1994, 17) observes that "Darwinism is often presented . . . as a reductive ideology requiring us to dismiss as illusions matters which our experience shows to be real and serious." Now such assertions do not themselves advance, or even answer, scientific propositions; but they do remind us that there is unresolved tension between truth claims. Ironically, a good deal of religious thought has been so eager either to refute or to accommodate itself to Darwinian theory that it may have overlooked the opportunity, and responsibility, to keep us clear about mysteries that so far remain *unclear*. As Nicholas Lash eloquently suggests, "[Conflicts] arise when evolutionary science, having forgotten its 'fragmentary' character, expands into a comprehensive explanatory system. . . . Christian hope paradoxically 'enriches our knowledge' by protecting our nescience from illusion" (1995).

Second, as alternative scientific accounts for the evolution of morality and human purpose emerge, theology must take care to reflect on the entire landscape of scientific theory and not just a favored position or easy target; moreover, it can serve as a conversation partner in territory that it has spent much effort mapping. Quite interestingly, recent and fairly virulent debates in evolutionary theory reflect tensions that have been the long-standing object of theological debates and discussion (Schloss 2002a). For example, there is a rich legacy of theological reflection on questions of whether radical altruism represents an extension or a transcendence of natural affections, and whether morality entails a constraint, fulfillment, or transformation of human desires — points of deep ambiguity in the human experience that are represented in current and competing accounts of evolutionary ethics.

It would be presumptuous to suggest that religion should speak and not listen to science on the issue of ethics, and I want to propose that spiritual understanding may be both refreshed and advanced by contemporary evolutionary accounts of morality in at least two ways. First, notions of kin selection and reciprocal altruism constitute the most systematic explanation to date of the central tendency of moral affections, theologically regarded as expressions of common grace. Moreover, they provide a basis for inquiry into the groupish constraints on natural affection and the question of how to expand the domain of human beneficence in ways that all religions urge. Indeed, Jesus almost sounds like a sociobiologist in the synoptic gospel accounts that exhort us not to restrict our greetings or dinner invitations or lending to those who do the same in return. He seems to regard these behaviors as native defaults, observing that even Gentiles and sinners and tax collectors do the same. He might just as easily have commented that all social vertebrates do the same. Religious indifference to the very real constraints of biological embodiment in the name of moral transcendence is an intellectual presumption that subverts — rather than advances — love and genuine spirituality. As Pascal observes, "Man is neither angel nor brute. And the unfortunate thing is, he who would act the angel, acts the brute" (Pascal 1958, Pensée 358).

Second, notions of indirect reciprocity and self-deception constitute an unusually rich resource for understanding — and exposing — religious inauthenticity and the conditions that promote it. Religious profession uncoupled from genuine love has consistently been viewed as counterfeit spirituality in biblical and church tradition. Signaling theory provides a polarizing lens to examine behaviors that have been culturally reified as emblems of religious commitment, but which may mask self-serving and even exploitive personal orientations or social structures (Schloss 1996). This is precisely what the biblical prophetic tradition confronts in its criticism of mere lip service, or frequent exhortations to justice over religious ritual. Contemporary biological accounts provide a heuristically effective tool, which we have not yet developed the ability to disarm.

REFERENCES

Alcock, John. 2003. *The Triumph of Sociobiology.* Oxford: Oxford University Press.
Alexander, Richard D. 1987. *The Biology of Moral Systems.* Chicago: Aldine de Gruyter.
Arnhart, Larry. 1998. *Darwinian Natural Right: The Biological Ethics of Human Nature.* Albany: State University of New York Press.
Ayala, F. J. 1995. The difference of being human: Ethical behavior as an evolutionary byproduct. Pp. 113-36 in *Biology, Ethics, and the Origins of Life,* ed. H. Rolston III. Boston: Jones and Bartlett.

————. 1998. Human nature: One evolutionist's view. Pp. 31-48 in *Whatever Happened to the Soul?* ed. Warren Brown, Nancey Murphy, and H. Hewton Malony. Minneapolis: Fortress.

Bellah, R., R. Madsen, W. Sullivan, and S. Tipton, eds. 1996. *Habits of the Heart: Individualism and Commitment in American Life.* Berkeley: University of California Press.

Blackmore, Susan. 1999. *The Meme Machine.* New York: Oxford University Press.

Boehm, Christopher. 1999. *Hierarchy in the Forest: The Evolution of Egalitarian Behavior.* Cambridge, Mass.: Harvard University Press.

Boyer, Pascal. 2001. *Religion Explained: The Evolutionary Origins of Religious Thought.* New York: Basic.

Bradie, Michael. 1994. *The Secret Chain: Evolution and Ethics.* Albany: State University of New York Press.

Brooke, John Hedley. 1991. *Science and Religion: Some Historical Perspectives.* Cambridge: Cambridge University Press.

Brooke, John Hedley, and Geoffrey Cantor, eds. 2000. *Reconstructing Nature: The Engagement of Science and Religion.* Edinburgh: T&T Clark.

Brown, M., B. Palameta, and C. Moore. 2003. Are there non-verbal cues to commitment? An exploratory study using the zero acquaintance video presentation paradigm. *Evolutionary Psychology* 1:42-69.

Casebeer, William D. 2003. *Natural Ethical Facts.* Cambridge, Mass.: MIT Press.

Cronk, L. 1994. Evolutionary theories of morality and the manipulative use of signals. *Zygon* 29:81-101.

————. 1999. *That Complex Whole: Culture and the Evolution of Human Behavior.* Boulder, Colo.: Westview.

Damasio, Antonio. 1995. *Descartes' Error: Emotion, Reason, and the Human Brain.* New York: Avon.

Darwin, Charles. [1871] 1981. *The Descent of Man and Selection in Relation to Sex.* Princeton, N.J.: Princeton University Press.

Dawkins, Richard. 1976. *The Selfish Gene.* Oxford: Oxford University Press.

————. 1997. *Climbing Mount Improbable.* New York: W. W. Norton.

————. 2000. *Unweaving the Rainbow: Science, Delusion, and the Appetite for Wonder.* Boston: Houghton Mifflin.

————. 2003. *A Devil's Chaplain: Reflections on Hope, Lies, Science, and Love.* Boston: Houghton Mifflin.

Deacon, Terrence W. 1997. *The Symbolic Species: The Co-evolution of Language and the Brain.* New York: W. W. Norton.

Dennett, Daniel. 1995. *Darwin's Dangerous Idea: Evolution and the Meaning of Life.* New York: Simon and Schuster.

————. 2003. *Freedom Evolves.* New York: Viking.

de Waal, Frans. 1996. *Good Natured: The Origins of Right and Wrong in Humans and Other Animals.* Cambridge, Mass.: Harvard University Press.

Dewey, John. [1909] 1988. *The Influence of Darwin on Philosophy and Other Essays in*

Contemporary Thought. In *Collected Works: The Middle Works,* vol. 4. Carbondale: Southern Illinois University Press.

―――. [1972] 1989. Evolution and ethics. In *John Dewey: The Early Works, 1882-1989,* vol. 5. Carbondale: Southern Illinois University Press.

Durham, William H. 1991. *Coevolution: Genes, Culture, and Human Diversity.* Stanford, Calif.: Stanford University Press.

Farber, Paul Lawrence. 1994. *The Temptations of Evolutionary Ethics.* Berkeley, Calif.: University of California Press.

Ghiselin, Michael T. 1973. Darwin and evolutionary psychology. *Science* 179:964-68.

―――. 1974. *The Economy of Nature and the Evolution of Sex.* Berkeley: University of California Press.

Gould, Stephen J. 1977. Biological potentiality. In *Ever Since Darwin.* New York: W. W. Norton.

―――. 1999. *Rocks of Ages.* New York: Ballantine.

Gould, Stephen J., and R. D. Lewontin. 1979. The spandrels of San Marco and the Panglossian paradigm: A critique of the adaptationist programme. *Proceedings of the Royal Society of London* 205:581-98.

Grant, Colin. 2001. *Altruism and Christian Ethics.* Cambridge: Cambridge University Press.

Hamilton, William D. 1964. The genetical evolution of social behavior I. *The Journal of Theoretical Biology* 7:1-16.

Hare, John. 1997. *The Moral Gap: Kantian Ethics, Human Limits, and God's Assistance.* Oxford: Oxford University Press.

―――. 2001. *God's Call: Moral Realism, God's Commands, and Human Autonomy.* Grand Rapids: Eerdmans.

Harms, William F. 2000. Adaptation and moral realism. *Biology and Philosophy* 15:669-98.

Haught, John. 2000. *God after Darwin: A Theology of Evolution.* Boulder, Colo.: Westview.

Hefner, Philip. 1993. *The Human Factor: Evolution, Culture, and Religion.* Minneapolis: Fortress.

Hinde, Robert A. 1999. *Why Gods Persist: A Scientific Approach to Religion.* London: Routledge.

―――. 2002. *Why God Is Good: The Sources of Morality.* New York: Taylor and Francis.

Holcomb, H. R. 1993. *Sociobiology, Sex, and Science.* Albany: State University of New York Press.

Hume, David. [1738] 1911. *A Treatise of Human Nature.* Vol. 2. London: J. M. Dent.

Hunter, Cornelius. 2001. *Darwin's God: Evolution and the Problem of Evil.* Grand Rapids: Brazos.

―――. 2003. *Darwin's Proof: The Triumph of Religion over Science.* Grand Rapids: Brazos.

Huxley, Julian. 1960. The evolutionary vision. Pp. 249-81 in *Issues in Evolution,* ed. Sol Tax, vol. 3 of *Evolution after Darwin.* Chicago: University of Chicago Press.

Huxley, T. H. [1894] 1989. *Evolution and Ethics.* Princeton, N.J.: Princeton University Press.

Johnson, Phillip. 1998. *Reason in the Balance: The Case against Naturalism in Science, Law, and Education.* Downers Grove, Ill.: InterVarsity.

———. 2002. *Wedge of Truth: Splitting the Foundations of Naturalism.* Downers Grove, Ill.: InterVarsity.

Joyce, R. 2000. Darwinian ethics and error. *Biology and Philosophy* 15:713-32.

Lash, Nicholas. 1995. Production and prospect: Reflections on Christian hope and original sin. Pp. 273-89 in *Evolution and Creation,* ed. E. McMullin. Notre Dame, Ind.: University of Notre Dame Press.

Lindberg, David, and Ronald Numbers, eds. 1986. *God and Nature: Historical Essays on the Encounter between Christianity and Science.* Berkeley: University of California Press.

———, eds. 2003. *When Science and Christianity Meet.* Chicago: University of Chicago Press.

Lopreato, J. 1984. *Human Nature and Biocultural Evolution.* Boston: Allen and Unwin.

Maienshein, Jane, and Michael Ruse. 1999. *Biology and the Foundations of Ethics.* Cambridge, U.K.: Cambridge University Press.

Midgley, Mary. 1980. Rival fatalisms: The hollowness of the sociology debate. Pp. 15-38 in *Sociobiology Examined,* ed. Ashley Montagu. New York: Oxford University Press.

———. 1994. *The Ethical Primate: Humans, Freedom, and Morality.* London: Routledge.

Miller, Kenneth R. 1999. *Finding Darwin's God: A Scientist's Search for Common Ground between God and Evolution.* New York: Harper Collins.

Moore, G. E. 1903. *Principia Ethica.* Cambridge, U.K.: Cambridge University Press.

Morris, Henry. 2000. *The Long War against God: The History and Impact of the Creation/Evolution Conflict.* Green Forest, Ark.: Master.

Nitecki, Matthew H., and Doris V. Nitecki, eds. 1993. *Evolutionary Ethics.* Albany: State University of New York Press.

Oates, David. 1988. Social Darwinism and natural theodicy. *Zygon* 23, no. 4:439-54.

O'Donovan, Oliver. 1994. *Resurrection and Moral Order: An Outline for Evangelical Ethics.* Grand Rapids: Eerdmans.

O'Hear, Anthony. 1997. *Beyond Evolution: Human Nature and the Limits of Evolutionary Explanation.* Oxford: Clarendon.

Oyama, Susan. 2000. *Evolution's Eye: A Systems View of the Biology-Culture Divide.* Durham, N.C.: Duke University Press.

Pascal, Blaise. 1958. *Pensées.* New York: E. P. Dutton.

Pinker, Steven. 1997. *How the Mind Works.* New York: Norton.

———. 2002. *The Blank Slate: The Modern Denial of Human Nature.* New York: Viking.

Plotkin, Henry. 1993. *Darwin Machines and the Nature of Knowledge.* Cambridge, Mass.: Harvard University Press.

————. 1997. *Evolution in Mind: An Introduction to Evolutionary Psychology.* Cambridge, Mass.: Harvard University Press.

Polkinghorne, John. 2003. *The God of Hope and the End of the World.* New Haven: Yale University Press.

Polkinghorne, John, and Michael Welker. 2000. *The End of the World and the Ends of God: Science and Theology on Eschatology.* Harrisburg, Pa.: Trinity Press International.

Pope, Stephen J. 1994. *The Evolution of Altruism and the Ordering of Love.* Washington, D.C.: Georgetown University Press.

Rachels, James. 1990. *Created from Animals: The Moral Implications of Darwinism.* Oxford: Oxford University Press.

Richards, Robert J. 1986. A defense of evolutionary ethics. *Biology and Philosophy* 1:265-93.

————. 1999. Darwin's romantic biology: The foundation. Pp. 113-53 in *Biology and the Foundation of Ethics,* ed. Jane Maienschein and Michael Ruse. Cambridge, U.K.: Cambridge University Press.

Richerson, Peter J., and Robert Boyd. 1999. Complex societies: The evolutionary origins of a crude superorganism. *Human Nature* 10, no. 3:253-90.

Rose, Hilary, and Steven Rose, eds. 2000. *Alas, Poor Darwin: Arguments against Evolutionary Psychology.* New York: Harmony.

Rose, Steven, 1982. *Against Biological Determinism.* Schocken Books.

Rottschaeffer, W. A., and D. Martinsen. 1990. Really taking Darwin seriously: An alternative to Michael Ruse's Darwinian metaethics. *Biology and Philosophy* 5:149-73.

Ruse, Michael. 1986. Evolutionary ethics: A phoenix arisen. *Zygon* 21:95-112.

————. 1994. Evolutionary theory and Christian ethics: Are they in harmony? *Zygon* 29, no. 1:5-24.

————. 1995. Evolutionary ethics: A defense. Pp. 89-112 in *Biology, Ethics, and the Origins of Life,* ed. Holmes Rolston III. Boston: Jones and Bartlett.

Ruse, Michael, and Edward O. Wilson. 1993. The evolution of ethics. Pp. 308-27 in *Religion and the Natural Sciences: The Range of Engagement,* compiled by J. E. Huchingson. Orlando: Harcourt Brace Jovanovich.

Schloss, Jeffrey P. 1996. Sociobiological explanations of altruistic ethics: Necessary, sufficient, or irrelevent perspective on the human moral quest. Pp. 107-45 in *Investigating the Biological Foundations of Human Morality,* ed. James Hurd. New York: Edwin Mellen.

————. 2000. Wisdom traditions as mechanisms of homeostatic integration: Evolutionary perspectives on organismal laws of life. Pp. 153-91 in *The Science of Wisdom and the Laws of Life,* ed. William Brown. Radnor, Pa.: Templeton Foundation.

————. 2002a. Emerging evolutionary accounts of altruism: "Love creation's final law?" Pp. 212-42 in *Altruism and Altruistic Love: Science, Philosophy, and Religion in Dialogue,* ed. S. Post, L. Underwood, J. Schloss, and W. Hurlbut. Oxford: Oxford University Press.

————. 2002b. From evolution to eschatology. Pp. 256-85 in *Resurrection: Theological and Scientific Assessments,* ed. Ted Peters, Robert J. Russell, and Michael Welker. Grand Rapids: Eerdmans.

————. 2003. Evolutionary ethics. Pp. 285-87 in *Encyclopedia of Science and Religion,* ed. Wentzel Van Huyssteen. New York: Macmillan Reference.

Smith, Christian. 2003. *Moral, Believing Animals.* Oxford: Oxford University Press.

Sober, Elliott, and David Sloan Wilson. 1998. *Unto Others: The Evolution and Psychology of Unselfish Behavior.* London: Harvard University Press.

Taylor, Charles. 1985. *Human Agency and Language.* Cambridge, U.K.: Cambridge University Press.

————. 1989. *Sources of the Self.* Cambridge, Mass.: Harvard University Press.

Thompson, Paul, ed. 1995. *Issues in Evolutionary Ethics.* Albany: State University of New York Press.

Trivers, R. L. 1971. The evolution of reciprocal altruism. *The Quarterly Review of Biology* 46:35-39.

Watts, Fraser. 2000. Subjective and objective hope: Propositional and attitudinal aspects of eschatology. Pp. 47-60 in *The End of the World and the Ends of God: Science and Theology on Eschatology,* ed. John Polkinghorne and Michael Welker. Harrisburg, Pa.: Trinity Press International.

White, Andrew Draper. 1955. *The Warfare of Science with Theology.* New York: George Braziller.

Wiker, Benjamin. 2002. *Moral Darwinism.* Downers Grove, Ill.: InterVarsity.

Williams, G. C. 1988. Huxley's evolution and ethics in sociobiological perspective. *Zygon* 23:383-407.

————. 1993. Mother nature is a wicked old witch. In *Evolutionary Ethics,* ed. M. H. Nitecki and D. V. Nitecki. Albany: State University of New York Press.

Williams, Patricia. 2001. *Doing without Adam: Sociobiology and Original Sin.* Minneapolis: Augsburg Fortress.

Wilson, Edward O. 1975. *Sociobiology.* Cambridge, Mass.: Harvard University Press.

————. 1978. *On Human Nature.* Cambridge, Mass.: Harvard University Press.

Woolcock, Peter G. 1999. The case against evolutionary ethics today. Pp. 276-306 in *Biology and the Foundation of Ethics,* ed. Jane Maienschein and Michael Ruse. Cambridge, U.K.: Cambridge University Press.

Wright, Robert. 1994. *The Moral Animal: The New Science of Evolutionary Psychology.* New York: Vintage.

I. The Evolution of Ethics:
Scientific Perspectives

1. Evolutionary Ethics Past and Present

Michael Ruse

Forty years ago, evolutionary ethics was the philosophical equivalent of a bad smell. One knew that it was flawed through and through. At the level of directives, what philosophers call the "substantive" or "normative" level of ethics, it proposed and promoted problematic and even vile programs ranging from right-wing capitalism to the social policies of the fascist countries in the 1930s. At the level of justification, what philosophers refer to as "metaethics," it fell afoul of the grossest technical mistakes. It drove straight through the distinction that David Hume drew (1978) between matters of fact and matters of obligation (the is/ought dichotomy), and in so doing fell guilty of what English philosopher G. E. Moore had labeled the "naturalistic fallacy" (1903). If ever a way of thinking was discredited, it was evolutionary ethics or (as it was more traditionally known) Social Darwinism.

Things change in philosophy as well as in the real world. Today there is much enthusiasm for approaches that try to link morality to our evolutionary biology, and a realization that Social Darwinism has been given an unjustified bad reputation and deserves more credit. Far from being simply a vehicle for repressive or capitalist policies, Social Darwinism has often been used in support of practices that today would be cherished by people from all parts of the moral and social spectrum. It is the aim of this discussion to look briefly at this history, and then to take an equally brief glance at the state of play today. Others might then be encouraged to take the dialogue further.

Erasmus Darwin

Evolutionary thinking is a child of the eighteenth century, and right from the beginning it was entwined with directives for proper behavior. Indeed, with reason one might well say that the very justification of the evolutionary approach was that of providing support for moral directives (Ruse 1996). En-

thusiasts, to a person, were supporters of the notion or philosophy of progress — the belief that through human effort we can improve our lot and that
of our fellows — and they used the idea of biological progress (as they interpreted evolution) as an illustration and support of this idea. Typical was Erasmus Darwin, the grandfather of Charles Darwin. He saw the biological world
as an upward chain or escalator, with the primitive at the bottom and the
complex, the human, at the top. As he put it, life progressed from the monarch (the butterfly) to the monarch (the king).

> Imperious man, who rules the bestial crowd,
> Of language, reason, and reflection proud,
> With brow erect who scorns this earthy sod,
> And styles himself the image of his God;
> Arose from rudiments of form and sense,
> An embryon point, or microscopic ens!
>
> (Darwin 1803, 1; see also 295-314)

This progress is not just some unimportant fact; it is of direct relevance to
humans. Erasmus Darwin was a deist, believing in a God who works through
unbroken law; according to his understanding, then, God has so organized
things that there is upward progression. Now it is up to us to keep this going.
Darwin drew an analogy between the progress of culture and the progress of
biology, the one feeding into the other and then back again. This idea of organic progressive evolution "is analogous to the improving excellence observ-
able in every part of the creation; . . . such as the progressive increase of the
wisdom and happiness of its inhabitants" (Darwin 1794, 509). Darwin was a
member of the so-called Lunar Society, a group of inventors and businessmen
in the British Midlands in the late eighteenth century, and with them he
thought that ever-improving industry was the key to the overall improvement
of societal happiness, and that it is hence our moral obligation to keep the process going. God has done his bit; now it is up to us to do ours. Evolution, the
triumph of unbroken law, is the apotheosis of God's standing and worth. Everything is planned beforehand and goes into effect through the laws of nature. "What a magnificent idea of the infinite power of *The Great Architect!
The Cause of Causes! Parent of Parents! Ens Entium!*" (Darwin 1794, 509)

Erasmus Darwin and others of his age set the pattern for the future: a
progressivist form of evolution, linked to our need to promote this evolution
and to keep it going at the human level. The great evolutionist of the nineteenth century — the greatest evolutionist of all time — was Charles Darwin,
the author of the *Origin of Species,* the work in which he argued that ongoing

change is a function of a struggle for existence that brings on a natural selection of the fitter, thus leading to adaptations like the hand and the eye. As a matter of fact, in the *Origin* Darwin said virtually nothing about our species, other than to acknowledge that we are indeed part of the scenario. But in a later work, *The Descent of Man*, written some twelve years after *Origin*, Darwin turned full attention to *Homo sapiens*, arguing that we are as much a part of the natural evolved world as is any other species. Included in his discussion was an extended treatment of our human moral nature, although in fact then and for many years thereafter Darwin's discussion was somewhat of a sideline. In our own time, however, there has been renewed interest in what he thought, and why he argued as he did.

Herbert Spencer

Far more important in his time and for the century thereafter (even today in some circles) was Darwin's fellow Englishman and evolutionist Herbert Spencer. Spencer was an ardent progressionist. He saw such progress as a move from the undifferentiated to the differentiated, or (as he put it) from the homogeneous to the heterogeneous. "Whether it be in the development of the Earth, in the development of Life upon its surface, in the development of Society, of Government, of Manufactures, of Commerce, of Language, Literature, Science, Art, this same evolution of the simple into the complex, through successive differentiations, holds throughout" (Spencer 1857, 2-3). Everything obeys this law. Humans are more complex or heterogeneous than other animals, Europeans more complex or heterogeneous than savages, and the English language more complex or heterogeneous than the tongues of other peoples.

Spencer was also ardent for a social and moral program that in major respects drew directly on evolution: progress in biology, progress in society.

> We must call those spurious philanthropists, who, to prevent present misery, would entail greater misery upon future generations. All defenders of a Poor Law must, however, be classed among such. That rigorous necessity which, when allowed to act on them, becomes so sharp a spur to the lazy and so strong a bridle to the random, these pauper's friends would repeal, because of the wailing it here and there produces. Blind to the fact that under the natural order of things, society is constantly excreting its unhealthy, imbecile, slow, vacillating, faithless members, these unthinking, though well-meaning, men advocate an interference which not only stops the purifying process but even increases the vitiation — absolutely encourages the

multiplication of the reckless and incompetent by offering them an unfailing provision, and *discourages* the multiplication of the competent and provident by heightening the prospective difficulty of maintaining a family. (Spencer 1851, 323-24)

We must take care here, however, and unpack things rather slowly. In so doing, we start to see that simplistic readings of evolutionary ethicists have led to grave misunderstandings. (As noted, evolutionary ethics became known as Social Darwinism, obviously cashing in on the fame and authority of the author of the *Origin*. It would be far fairer to history were it known as Social Spencerianism.) The easy connection to draw focuses on the Darwinian claims about struggle and consequent selection, and then simply concludes that someone like Spencer was taking these ideas and transferring them to society; struggle and selection in society might be better known as laissez-faire, according to which there is brutal competition and some win and some lose. But in fact, although as the above passage clearly shows there were laissez-faire elements in Spencer's thinking, there was no simple connection (Richards 1987). On the one hand, although he discovered it independently, Spencer always downplayed selection. In fact, he thought that as one closes in on the upper echelons of the progressive movement, the struggle will fall away and become irrelevant. On the other hand, although he approved of struggle in society, Spencer was much against struggle between nations. He thought it inimical to free trade and against open competition. Here, to be candid, Spencer owed as much to influences of a Quaker background as to anything in biology. The point is not that evolution was irrelevant to Spencer's position. Nothing could be further from the truth. Rather, it was that Spencer's thinking was a complex package, with evolution and ethics more partners in a common picture than one leading directly to the other.

And this has always been very much the case for other evolutionary ethicists in Spencer's mold, whether they were influenced by him consciously (as tended to be the case in Anglophone countries, especially the United States) or whether they were working in parallel with him (as tended to be the case in countries like Germany, where people such as the morphologist Ernst Haeckel promoted "Darwinismus," a philosophy that owed little to Darwin himself and much to the socioeconomic visions of middle-class Germans under Bismarck). In many respects, evolution took on the role of a substitute secular religion (or, for some, an addition to their already-held Christian religion). One sees that, as always with religion, different people found in evolution very different stories and justifications for their moral imperatives — always progress at the back of the story, but very different ideas at the front

(Ruse 2000). To see this, rather than just a sequential history, let us look at three different areas of interest to evolutionary ethicists (and indeed to us today): politics and social policy, war and peace, and feminism.

Social Policy

Following Spencer, many of his keenest American followers promoted fairly libertarian social philosophies. The end-of-the-century American sociologist William Graham Sumner was notorious. "The facts of human life . . . are in many respects hard and stern. It is by strenuous exertion only that each one of us can sustain himself against the destructive forces and the ever recurring needs of life; and the higher the degree to which we seek to carry our development the greater is the proportionate cost of every step" (Sumner 1914, 30). After the Civil War, businessmen were keen Spencerians, and they certainly turned to his philosophy to support their selfish ways. But the story is complex. John D. Rockefeller, founder of Standard Oil, and Andrew Carnegie, founder of U.S. Steel, were followers of Spencer, but such men generally preferred to stress the positive side to laissez-faire (their own success) rather than its downside (the failure of others). They used their gains to build places that would further the upward rise of society — Rockefeller gave millions to the University of Chicago, and Carnegie supported the founding of public libraries. The latter in particular was very much in a Spencerian mode: free libraries were places where the poor but bright child — society's naturally fitter — could go and through hard work and self-discipline rise up in education and succeed in society (Bannister 1979).

Others had a very different philosophy. Alfred Russel Wallace, the co-discoverer of natural selection, was a socialist. He thought that the state can and should regulate people's lives for the better, and was motivated in his thinking by the early influence of the Scottish mill owner and socialist Robert Owen. Believing that selection favors groups as well as individuals, Wallace concluded that a state founded and run on socialist principles would be superior now as well as more prepared for the future than one which simply bowed before market forces (see Jones 1980). Similar sorts of reasoning led the Russian Prince Petr Kropotkin to anarchism. He believed that there is a natural sympathy existing between people (and animals) — "mutual aid." Coming from nineteenth-century Russia, a vast pre-industrial society where the chief threat to life lay in the elements, it seemed obvious that evolution must work for good and sympathy rather than for harm and competition. "The animal species, in which individual struggle has been reduced to its narrowest limits, and the practice of mutual aid has attained the greatest development, are invariably the most numerous, the most prosperous, and the most open to further progress. . . . The unsociable species, on the contrary, are doomed to decay" (Kropotkin [1902] 1955, 293). Likewise in the human species, Kropotkin thought that we have a natural tendency to help each other and that we should follow this tendency. To deny it or to go against it is not just unnatural but morally wrong and the quickest way to human decline.

War and Peace

Turning next to the issue of war, there were many — especially in Germany — who justified its existence and ongoing necessity in evolutionary terms. One writer, in a passage which admittedly perhaps owes as much to Hegel as it does to Darwin, claimed that war is "a phase in the life-effort of the State towards completer self-realization, a phase of the eternal nisus, the perpetual omnipresent strife of all beings towards self-fulfilment" (quoted in Crook 1994, 137). Even though not this enthusiastic, others saw it as "more or less normal for men at times to plunge back down the evolutionary ladder . . . to break away from the complex conventions and routine of civilized life and revert to that of the troglodytes in the trenches." Crook adds, "Man has always been a fighter and his passion to kill animals . . . and inferior races . . . is the same thing which perhaps in the dark past so effectively destroyed the missing link between the great fossil apes of the tertiary and the lowest men of the Neanderthal type. All these illustrate an instinct which we cannot eradicate or suppress, but can best only hope to sublimate" (143-44). Although in respects evolution was antithetical to many of his beliefs (especially about our simian origins and the closeness of Gentiles and Jews), Hitler — as could be expected — got in on the war theme. Indeed, there are times when Hitler sounds like the paradigmatic Social Darwinian: "He who wants to live must fight, and he who does not want to fight in this world where eternal struggle is the law of life has no right to exist" (quoted in Bullock 1991, 141).

On the other hand, there were many who used evolution to argue against war. Until the First World War changed people's thinking, there was a vigorous peace party in America, and much reference was made to evolutionary principles. Vernon Kellogg, professor at Stanford and popular writer on evolution, insisted constantly that the true way of the biological future — the way of progress — was one leading us away from conflict and fighting. The human being is a product of evolution. "And just as Evolution made him, with his need, a Fighter, and taught him War, so now, with the passing of this need, with the substitution of reason and altruism for instinct and egoism, Evolution will make him a Man of peace and goodwill, and will take War from him. And any man will find his greatest advantage and merit in aiding, rather than delaying, this beneficence" (Kellogg 1912, 140-41). Kellogg added, in an argument that was repeated by many, that war is biologically stupid because it means that the strongest and brightest and bravest are those most likely to be killed. This is as counter-productive as the farmer killing and eating his prize animals and breeding from the runts.

Feminism

Then there is feminism. As many have pointed out, Darwin himself does not wear well here. "Man is more courageous, pugnacious, and energetic than woman, and has a more inventive genius" (Darwin 1871, 2:316). In compensation, woman has "greater tenderness and less selfishness" (326). And so on and so forth. Others were even worse:

> The higher the animal or plant in the scale of being, the more slowly does it reach its utmost capacity of development. Girls are physically and mentally more precocious than boys. The human female arrives sooner than the male at maturity, and furnishes one of the strongest arguments against the alleged equality of the sexes. The quicker appreciation of girls is the instinct, or intuitive faculty in operation; while the slower boy is an example of the latent reasoning power not yet developed. (Allan 1869, cxcvii)

Males were thus considered life's natural winners while females were destined for lower things. To deny this was unnatural and immoral. Feminism was against nature and a recipe for disaster.

On the other hand, we find from some quarters exactly the opposite claims. Take A. R. Wallace. He held the view that human progress depends ultimately on female sexual selection. Men cannot be trusted with the future of our race. Fortunately, in days to come, young women will take over the reins, choosing as mates only those males with the highest moral and intellectual properties. Thus upward progress is guaranteed. "In such a reformed society the vicious man, the man of degraded taste or of feeble intellect, will have little chance of finding a wife, and his bad qualities will die out with himself. The most perfect and beautiful in body and mind will, on the other hand, be most sought and therefore be most likely to marry early, the less highly endowed later, and the least gifted in any way the latest of all, and this will be the case with both sexes" (Wallace 1900, 2:507). Apparently this will all lead to ever better and more harmonious human societies. With reason, you may complain that if Wallace truly thought any of this to be remotely possible — that young women in the future would freely mate with only the best of the male crop — he must have had his head in the clouds. But the fact remains that Wallace made his claims in the name of evolution. And if any nineteenth-century evolutionist deserves the label "Darwinian," it is he.

Neo-Darwinians

Politics, war, feminism — all three topics tell a similar story. In short, people took their prior prejudices — convictions, if you like — and read them into their evolutionism, and then read them right back out again as justified. Consider the analogy with religion. There is no doubt that many evolutionists consciously set out to provide an alternative to (or a supplement for) what they saw as exhausted myths of the past. Socially, evolution was to replace Christianity. It is also the case that believers are notorious for reading into their theology the ends they want to derive. Militarists find justification for war in Holy Scripture while pacifists find justification for their nonviolence. In the nineteenth century both abolitionists and slaveholders appealed to the Bible to support their opposing beliefs. And the same is true with feminism and other social issues like conservation. This is not to say that such theorizing is worthless, or to suggest cynically that nothing changes people's minds. It is to argue that the success and perhaps the weakness of Social Darwinism lay in its flexibility and its ability to adapt itself to changing circumstances and interests and needs.

This all being so, it would have been surprising indeed if the end of the nineteenth century marked the end of Social Darwinism. And it did not. The name fell out of favor because (rightly or wrongly) it got associated with the excesses of capitalism and militarism, but the ideas and the approach persisted. This is shown very clearly by three of the leading players in the era when Darwinian selectionism and Mendelian genetics were being forged together in the synthesis that became known as "Neo-Darwinism." In the early 1930s, the English population geneticist Ronald A. Fisher combined a belief in evolution with a very old-fashioned Anglican Christianity. He thought that evolution moves ever upward, and that this is the means that God has used to produce humankind. We have an entropy-reversing process that leads to *Homo sapiens*. So analogously, we humans have a task of improvement here on earth. "In the language of Genesis we are living in the sixth day, probably rather early in the morning, and the Divine artist has not yet stood back from his work, and declared it to be 'very good.' Perhaps that can only be when God's very imperfect image has become more competent to manage the affairs of the planet of which he is in control" (Fisher 1947, 1001). Fisher described a parallel between, on the one hand, faith and works, and, on the other, Lamarckism (the inheritance of acquired characteristics) and Darwinism (natural selection):

> There is indeed a strand of moral philosophy, which appeals to me as pure gain, which arises in comparing Natural Selection with the Lamarckian group of evolutionary theories. In both of these contrasting hypotheses living things themselves are the chief instruments of the Creative activity. On the Lamarckian view, however, they work their effect by willing and striving only; but, on the Darwinian view, it is by doing or dying. It is not mere will, but its actual sequel in the real world, its success or failure, that is alone effective.
>
> We come here to a close parallelism with Christian discussions on the merits of Faith and Works. Faith, in the form of right intentions and resolution, is assuredly necessary, but there has, I believe, never been lacking through the centuries the parallel, or complementary, conviction that the service of God requires of us also effective action. If men are to see our good works, it is of course necessary that they should be good, but also and emphatically that they should work, in making the world a better place. (Fisher 1950, 19-20)

What is our task here on earth? Fisher focused on eugenics. He feared that as culture develops, the upper classes (and hence the genetically superior) reproduce less and less. Hence, given the over-reproduction of those in the lower ranks, there is a biological degeneration and end to God's progress. It is our task to reverse this.

A little later, also in England, we find Julian Huxley, the biologist grandson of Darwin's bulldog Thomas Henry Huxley, promoting major state-financed works (like the Tennessee Valley Authority earth works) in the name of progressive evolution. "Evolution, from cosmic star-dust to human society, is a comprehensive and continuous process. It transforms the world-stuff, if I may use a term which includes the potentialities of mind as well as those of matter. It is creative, in the sense that during the process new and more complex levels of organization are progressively attained, and new possibilities are thus opened up to the universal world-stuff" (Huxley and Huxley 1947, 131). This has immediate moral implications. Although the state as such does not have more value than the individual, the individual only makes sense in the context of the state. "The individual thus has duties and responsibilities as well as rights and privileges, or if you prefer it, finds certain outlets and satisfactions (such as devotion to a cause, or participation in a joint enterprise) only in relation to the type of society in which he lives" (138-39). Above all, Julian Huxley wanted to stress the application of *scientific* principles and results in societal planning and its implementation. You must not leave things to chance or intuition, but rather should bring the trained scientific mind to bear on life's problems.

Finally, crossing the Atlantic, we see that Huxley's friend, the American paleontologist George Gaylord Simpson, wrote just after the Second World War when the Cold War was settling into its long winter and when in Russia the charlatan Trofim D. Lysenko was bringing disaster to biology and death to biologists. Simpson saw two major moral directives. First, we must improve and promote knowledge — knowledge in itself is a good thing. "The most essential material factor in the new evolution seems to be just this: knowledge, together, necessarily, with its spread and inheritance." This is not to say that only the production of knowledge is needed. There is also the obligation to spread the good word. "This ethic of knowledge is not complete and independent. In itself knowledge is necessarily good, but it is effective only to the degree that it does spread in a population, and its results may then be turned by human choice and responsible action for either good or evil" (Simpson 1949, 311). Then second comes personal responsibility, leading in turn to integrity and dignity: "it is good, right, and moral to recognize the integrity and dignity of the individual and to promote the realization or fulfilment of individual capacities. It is bad, wrong, and immoral to fail in such recognition or to impede such fulfilment." Simpson added: "This ethic applies first of all to the individual himself and to the integration and development of his own personality. It extends farther to his social group and to all mankind. Negatively, it is wrong to develop one individual at the expense of any other. Positively, it is right to develop all in the greatest degree possible to each within the group as a whole. Individuals vary greatly in other capacities, but integrity and dignity are capable of equal development in all" (315).

Edward O. Wilson

Finally in this too-brief survey, coming right to the present, we have the doyen of today's American evolutionists, the student of the ants and leading sociobiologist Edward O. Wilson. In respects he (like many before him) is much against traditional religion. Materialism or naturalism as represented by evolutionary thinking is to be the new "myth." It will beat the old religions if only because it will absorb them: "the final decisive edge enjoyed by scientific naturalism will come from its capacity to explain traditional religion, its chief competition, as a wholly material phenomenon. Theology is not likely to survive as an independent intellectual discipline" (Wilson 1978, 192). At the same time, Wilson sees his negativism about Christianity in a positive light, as clearing the way for something better. Like Spencer, a man whom he much admires, Wilson is an ardent progressionist. He writes, "the overall average across the history of life has moved from the simple and few to the more complex and numerous. During the past billion years, animals as a whole evolved upward in body size, feeding and defensive techniques, brain and behavioral complexity, social organization, and precision of environmental control — in each case farther from the nonliving state than their simpler antecedents did" (Wilson 1992, 187). There is but one conclusion: "Progress, then, is a property of the evolution of life as a whole by almost any conceivable intuitive standard, including the acquisition of goals and intentions in the behavior of animals." From this Wilson goes on to argue that we must strive to protect and preserve humankind and that the way to do this is by promoting biodiversity. In a world of plastic, humans would die literally as well as metaphorically. In his recent *The Future of Life,* Wilson is explicit: "a sense of genetic unity, kinship, and deep history are among the values that bond us to the living environment. They are survival mechanisms for ourselves and our species. To conserve biological diversity is an investment in immortality" (Wilson 2002, 133). Wilson himself has been much involved in the preservation of the Amazonian rain forests.

Anti-Progress

Did no one ever want to break from this way of thinking? Certainly there were those who doubted that progress is inevitable — even those who thought that progress would come to an end. The novelist H. G. Wells — a student of Thomas Henry Huxley — expressed these worries in his science fiction novel *The Time Machine.* In Wells's story, an inventor has created a machine capable of carrying him forward and backward in time. The inventor sets off in his time machine, out of interest moving forward in time rather than backward. The main stop he makes is in the year 802,201. Here he finds "The Sunset of Mankind." *Homo sapiens* has evolved into two separate species. There are the Eloi who live above ground, and the Morlocks who live beneath the ground. The Eloi are friendly, childlike creatures who seem to spend their whole days playing, without any thought of the future or of the need to provide for themselves, and without indulging in any intellectual work. Then the traveler discovers the terrible truth. The Eloi are kept as cattle by their subterranean neighbors, the Morlocks, who do all the work and provide all the food for those above ground. But just as the Eloi are in a very fundamental sense "degenerates," so also are the Morlocks. They capture Eloi, taking them beneath the ground to provide their food. The Morlocks truly are repellant creatures: "I lit a match, and, looking down, I saw a small, white moving creature, with large bright eyes which regarded me steadfastly as it retreated. It made me shudder. It was so like a human spider!" (101). Continuing, the traveler writes: "I felt a peculiar shrinking from those pallid bodies. They were just the half-bleached colour of the worms and things one sees preserved in spirit in a zoological museum. And they were filthy cold to the touch" (111). And yet, we have to accept that the Morlocks, no less than the Eloi, were descended from us: "gradually, the truth dawned on me: that Man had not remained one species, but had differentiated into two distinct animals: that my graceful children of the Upper World were not the sole descendants of our generation, but that this bleached, obscene, nocturnal Thing, which had flashed before me, was also heir to all the ages" (101).

Of course, one could still use a picture such as this as the base of (or at least the inspiration for) an ethical system. At the level of moral prescription, the effort must be less that of pushing forward and more that of seeing that we do not fall backward. But there were always some who doubted the progressiveness of evolution at all, and hence any attempt to use it as a basis for a moral life. One such was Thomas Henry Huxley, whose dark vision of life led him to argue that it is in opposing evolution that the true virtues lie (1893). More recently, the late Stephen Jay Gould was a major critic of progress and any philosophy based on it. (See especially 1981, 1988, 1989.) He considered this idea of a progress a false picture of history, which is truly one of randomness and chance and lack of any significant direction. Certainly, humans came last; if they had not, we would not be around now to tell the tale. But we are not the finest culmination of a directed process. Like everything else, we just happened. And the fossils of the Burgess Shale, Gould believed, show that this is so. There are all sorts of weird and wonderful forms, all now extinct with very few exceptions (one of which may be a vertebrate predecessor), and any one of these might have been the progenitor of today's organisms. It was just chance that it all went one way rather than any other. Life has no ultimate meaning and history shows this. Those who think otherwise, Darwinians particularly, are just plain wrong. Gould spoke of the idea as "a noxious, culturally embedded, untestable, nonoperational, intractable idea that must be replaced if we wish to understand the patterns of history" (Gould 1988, 319). It is a delusion engendered by our refusal to accept our insignificance when faced with the immensity of time (Gould 1996).

Undoubtedly, it was the decline in enthusiasm in the twentieth century for all ideologies of progress that led to a decline in enthusiasm for traditional evolutionary ethics. After world wars, depressions, fascism, bombs, and more, many agreed with the Anglican poet T. S. Eliot: "We can assert with some confidence that our own period is one of decline; that the standards of culture are lower than they were fifty years ago; and that the evidences of this decline are visible in every department of human activity" (quoted in Wagar 1972, 225). This, combined with the undoubted fact that many social Darwinian prescriptions are morally repellent, led to a decline in enthusiasm for any evolutionary approach to ethics, and renewed appreciation of the philosophers who argued that the whole approach is simply invalid because one is illicitly moving from fact to obligation. As the philosopher C. D. Broad put things against Julian Huxley, raising the key question of "whether knowledge of the facts of evolution has any bearing on the question of what is intrinsically good or bad," there is simply no way in which you can get a value claim (like "support major government projects") out of a purely factual claim (like "humans have evolved with certain mental capacities not possessed by other animals"). "For the premiss required asserts a connection between certain of those facts and laws and something else, viz., intrinsic value or disvalue, which forms no part of their subject-matter" (1949).

New Life

Why then have things changed in the past three or four decades, and in what direction? A major reason has been the growth in evolutionary biology of much more sophisticated ways of handling social behavior, together with the realization that now we can properly explain ethics without simply reading in the ideology that we want later to extract. There is a feeling that, even though Edward O. Wilson may not himself have got it quite right, his sentiments are on target.

> The biologist, who is concerned with questions of physiology and evolutionary history, realizes that self-knowledge is constrained and shaped by the emotional control centers in the hypothalamus and limbic systems of the brain. These centers flood our consciousness with all the emotions — hate, love, guilt, fear, and others — that are consulted by ethical philoso-

39

phers who wish to intuit the standards of good and evil. What, we are then compelled to ask, made the hypothalamus and limbic system? They evolved by natural selection. That simple biological statement must be pursued to explain ethics and ethical philosophers, if not epistemology and epistemologists, at all depths. (Wilson 1975, 3)

How then are we to set about relating ethics and biology? We go back to Darwin, who noted in the *Descent* that, apart from our speech, one of the most distinctive aspects of humankind is that we are ethical beings. We have a sense of right and wrong, and thus are led to act morally or ethically. We do things for others because we think them right rather than simply because they are in our self-interest. In fact, sometimes we do things that are very much not in our self-interest, like attempting to save a drowning child from a rapid river. If you take a hard-line Darwinian position, arguing that adaptations are produced by selection to aid their possessors — I have eyes and hands because they help me — then the existence of the ethical sense is somewhat of a puzzle (Alexander 1987; Ruse 1989; Ruse 1994). Why do something for others when it puts you at risk? In the family situation, where, for instance, the mother aids her child, this is readily understandable; if the child does not survive then the mother does not reproduce. But what about the cases where there is no relationship? One does not jump into the river only to save one's own children.

It has been stressed by students of animal behavior, especially by students of the behavior of higher organisms like the great apes, that there is no necessity to the appearance of an ethical sense and consequent behavior (Goodall 1986). It is not going to come into existence as a matter of course, even if the brain is growing in size and power. There has to be a reason, and this reason most obviously is that this is an adaptation for social beings. There are great advantages to being social. Two or three can often do that which is impossible for one animal on its own — especially when the animals are foraging or hunting, practices that provide the high-protein supplies needed by organisms with high-maintenance adaptations like brains. At the same time, there are costs to being social, like the potential for spread of disease. Hence, social animals tend to have (and need) special adaptations to exploit their sociality and to prevent the costs. Often, for instance, social animals have much better degrees of immunity against disease than do solitary animals.

Social animals — and humans are, beyond all others, social animals — need abilities to help each other and at the same time to reduce intragroup strife. (It is for this reason that researchers often find that a better model for humans than close relatives like the orangutans — which are asocial — is a less close relative like the wolf — which is very social.) On the negative side, as one might say, humans are notable for not having very good physical methods of attack — our teeth, for instance, are puny beside those of chimpanzees. If we turn on a fellow human, we are not likely to rip them apart physically. Another important negative aspect of humans is the way in which the females do not come into heat or advertise their ovulation. There has been much discussion about the reason for this; sociobiologist Sarah Hrdy argues that a major reason is that it keeps males guessing and hence in doubt about paternity, if they do not stay around and help with the family (1981). Another reason obviously is that it keeps the group quieter and more stable — imagine trying to run our complex social lives if women were often in heat. On the positive side, our sense of morality is surely (in the opinion of Darwinian biologists) an adaptation for sociality. Organisms that take seriously their obligations to others are more stable and work together better than those that do not. Expectedly, we find what one might at least call proto-morality — with senior group members enforcing behavior — in other social animals, especially (as emphasized by ethnologist Frans de Waal [1982]) the chimpanzees.

What sort of morality might one expect an evolutionary process to produce? Will it decide, for instance, between utilitarians and Kantians? Probably not, for it will be too coarse-grained for that, giving just basic directions that will then be fleshed out by culture. Significant is that both utilitarians (like Peter Singer) and Kantians (like John Rawls) have welcomed an evolutionary approach. Rawls in particular points out that it solves the big lacuna in any social contract approach to morality, namely, how did the contract get put in place in the first place. It was not a group of old men around a fire but the genes. "The theory of evolution would suggest it is the outcome of natural selection; the capacity for a sense of justice and the moral feelings is an adaptation of mankind to its place in nature." Rawls continues: "It seems clear that for members of a species which lives in stable social groups, the ability to comply with fair cooperative arrangements and to develop the sentiments necessary to support them is highly advantageous, especially when individuals have a long life and are dependent on one another. These conditions guarantee innumerable occasions when mutual justice consistently adhered to is beneficial to all parties" (Rawls 1971, 502-3).

Altruism

The technical biological term for organisms giving to others, at cost to themselves, is "altruism." It is important to note that this term does not necessarily mean the altruism to which one refers when speaking of a good person, as in "Mother Teresa showed great altruism toward the poor of India." Ants helping others in the nest would be called "altruistic," even though (as against the literal sense) there is clearly no implication that the ants consciously set out to do the right thing. Human altruism — or goodness, as one might say — is therefore a subclass of the general biological notion of "altruism." But why have we developed so elaborate a method of interacting as a moral sense? Why, unlike the ants, are we not simply hardwired? There is a simple reason. Being hardwired has virtues — for example, there is no need for learning — but the cost is high. You cannot regroup and do something else if the situation changes. An ant will behave instinctively even though (because of changed circumstances) it may be doing itself or its nest harm. Generally this does not matter, because ants are produced cheaply — a queen can afford the loss of a few thousand. Humans, on the other hand, are beings that require a great deal of care and only a few can be produced. (Technically, we humans are K-selected as opposed to ants that are r-selected.) We need the ability to respond to change, especially to change brought on by our fellow species members. A moral sense allows us to do this. We can assess different or changing situations and act in our best interests or the interests of our families. As philosopher Daniel Dennett has pointed out, this fact diffuses the oft-brought charge that any evolutionary approach to ethics must fail because it presupposes that we have no real choices; we are "genetically determined" (1984). It is true that we are part of the causal chain, but we have a dimension of freedom not possessed by the ants. (In a sense, humans are like the sophisticated rockets that can adjust to moving targets, whereas ants are like cheaper rockets that cannot change direction once fired.)

How does selection bring on altruism (using this term now in the biological sense)? There is much debate. After Darwin, most biologists assumed that selection could work for the group and that morality would emerge automatically — a species member that helped another was thereby helping the species. Reference has already been made to the notion of "mutual aid," promoted by the Russian-born anarchist Prince Petr Kropotkin. In the 1960s there was a sea change in opinion (going back in fact to the insights of Darwin himself). It was pointed out that group selection (selection for the benefit of the group over the individual) was too open to cheating (Williams 1966). A selfish individual could take advantage of others. Hence came what Richard Dawkins (1976) has labeled the "selfish gene" view of the evolutionary process, according to which all adaptations (including social and behavioral adaptations) must be related back to self-interest. If they do not help the individual first and foremost, they will be wiped out.

Selfish Genes, Unselfish People

The selfish-gene way of thinking was applied very fruitfully to the problem of altruism. William Hamilton introduced the idea of "kin selection" (1964a, 1964b), arguing that altruistic behavior could be a very good strategy if one is helping others who share the same copies of genes as oneself — one is thereby reproducing by proxy, as it were. Most dramatically Hamilton solved the question of why sterile workers (always female) in the hymenoptera (ants, bees, and wasps) devote their lives to their nest-mates. In the hymenoptera only females have two parents; hence females are more closely related to sisters than to offspring and so it pays to raise fertile sisters rather than fertile daughters. More generally, Hamilton showed that in any animal, if the conditions are right, altruism will come into being. Following this, Robert Trivers (1971) introduced a more general mechanism that can function between nonrelated organisms (even organisms of different species). "Reciprocal altruism" suggests that if one gets a benefit by helping others, especially if others will thereby be more likely to help you, then altruistic adaptations should come into play. Essentially, as Darwin himself realized, this is a case of "If you scratch my back, then I will scratch your back."

In complex, thinking animals like humans, one could expect this to be a powerful mechanism. There will be times — when we are young, old, or sick — when even the most powerful of us will appreciate aid. In conjunction with this will be memory, so that we are able to enforce reciprocation and learn quickly to exclude those who do not play the game. Those who receive and do not give will soon be excluded. More generally, the ideas and techniques of game theory have been applied profitably to questions of sociability generally and morality particularly. Sophisticated models can now be built showing how and when particularly moral traits might be expected to emerge (Skyrms 1996). At the same time, experimentation can show whether or not specific hypotheses are well taken. There have, for instance, been serious studies on questions about when commitments are kept and when broken, as well as on how people respond to fairness or the lack thereof.

Criticisms

As you might expect, there have been many criticisms of this whole selfish-gene approach to human behavior. Mary Midgley (1979) objects that the whole point about morality is that it is not selfish, nor is it simply enlightened self-interest. Morality means giving without hope or expectation of reward.

Defenders of the approach reply that this objection misunderstands both the theory and the metaphor. Selfish genes do not necessarily cash out as selfish people. In fact, we might operate more efficiently (in our own biological interests) if what we do is done precisely because we do not think it self-centered. One must make a distinction between what Dawkins (1982) labels the "replicators" (the genes) and the "vehicles" (the whole organism). To speak of selfish genes is to say that selection makes characteristics that rebound ultimately on the actor. Genes themselves are neither selfish nor unselfish. They just are. Individuals (vehicles) might be selfish at times and (genuinely) altruistic at times. It just depends on the situation.

On the other hand, there are objections of a more biological nature. Every biologist recognizes that sometimes a group selective force might overcome the individual selective force. For instance, in a constantly fragmenting and reuniting population (that is, with many sub-populations forming and disappearing) and with strong pressure toward altruistic behavior, group attributes might emerge before they can be eliminated by individual forces — these attributes might persist by being merged into the whole group. It has been suggested that the maintenance of sexuality might result from such a group force (Maynard Smith 1978). (Others however, including Hamilton [Hamilton, Axelrod, and Tanese 1990], think that sexuality can be explained at the individual level.) In particular, in the case of humans, some think that a group selective force might be the key factor in altruism (human, literal altruism, that is).

Biologist David Sloan Wilson and philosopher Elliot Sober argue this way (Sober and Wilson 1998): Illustrating their position with a short story by Stephen Crane, in which a group of people are caught in a lifeboat and can survive if and only if they all work together, Wilson and Sober conclude that only a group analysis will explain the successful outcome. Because of our ability to think and plan, we humans can and do overcome the forces of individual selection and are shaped by group forces. "Behaving as part of a coordinated group is sometimes a life-or-death matter in which the slightest error — or the slightest reluctance to participate — can result in disaster for all. Situations of this sort — in which the members of a group are bound together by the prospect of a common fate — have been encountered throughout human evolution, with the important fitness consequences, so it is reasonable to expect that we are psychologically adapted to cope with them" (335-36).

This is still very contentious. English sociobiologist John Maynard Smith argues that nothing here makes even probable the group selection hypothesis. He argues that even humans are unable to overcome the strong tug of the selfish gene. In the lifeboat case, there is no need to suppose other than that each individual saw that it was in his own interests to cooperate. As Ben Franklin said on signing the Declaration of Independence, "Gentlemen, we must all hang together or assuredly we shall all hang separately." The point for us to note here is not that there is disagreement — there is always disagreement when people are moving into new fields with new ideas — but that today vigorous attention is being paid to the putative biological foundations of human morality.

Metaethics

Finally, what about the other side to the ethical questions? Thus far we have been looking at the ways in which evolution might produce morality and the kind of morality that it might be. In other words, we have been looking more at the normative or substantive side to ethics. What should I do? But what of the other side, the side of justification, the metaethical side? Why should I do what I should do? Some still adopt the old approaches, feeling that in this one case it ought to be possible to bridge the gap between fact and obligation. Recent Templeton Prize winner Holmes Rolston III argues in this fashion. Although he is a practicing Christian and no keen Darwinian, he is virtually at one with the Darwinian nonbeliever Edward O. Wilson in seeing values — their nature and their foundation — come out of the evolutionary process:

> Morality is not intrinsic to natural systems. In fact, there are no moral agents in wild nature. Nature is amoral, but that is not to disparage it. That is to set aside irrelevant categories for its interpretation. Amoral nature is fundamentally and radically the ground, the root out of which arise all of the particular values manifest in organisms and ecosystems. This includes all human values, even though, when they come, human values rise higher than their precedents in spontaneous nature. (Rolston 1999, 286)

And as with Wilson, it is nature and its care that is the highest value of them all.

> Environmental ethics . . . is the most altruistic, global, generous, comprehensive ethic of all, demanding the most expansive capacity to see others, and this now especially distinguishes humans. This is not naturalized ethics in the reductionist sense; it is naturalized ethics in the comprehensive sense, humans acting out of moral conviction for the benefit of nonhuman others. There is a widening sense of shared values, including values produced in the evolutionary genesis. (288)

Generally, however, there is not much enthusiasm for this kind of approach, and recourse is made to more traditional ways of solving the problem. The neo-Kantian John Rawls, for instance, argued that morality gets its necessity from its being the only way in which rational being could exist socially (1980). This is all of the justification that one can have or need. Others take a more Humean approach. This goes back at least to Thomas Henry Huxley, who wrote enthusiastically on the eighteenth-century philosopher. It is all a question of feelings or sentiment.

> In whichever way we look at the matter, morality is based on feeling, not on reason; though reason alone is competent to trace out the effects of our actions and thereby dictate conduct. Justice is founded on the love of one's neighbour; and goodness is a kind of beauty. The moral law, like the laws of physical nature, rests in the long run upon instinctive intuitions, and is neither more nor less "innate" and "necessary" than they are. Some people cannot by any means be got to understand the first book of Euclid; but the truths of mathematics are no less necessary and binding on the great mass of mankind. (Huxley 1879, 239-40)

Is there any justification? Hume would deny that there is. We just behave in the way that we are and that is an end to it. Similar sentiments are to be found in today's literature. Thus the American student of legal philosophy, Jeffrie Murphy:

> The [evolutionist] may well agree . . . that value judgments are properly defended in terms of other value judgments until we reach some that are fundamental. All of this, in a sense, is the giving of *reasons*. However, suppose we seriously raise the question of why these fundamental judgments are regarded as fundamental. There may be only a *causal* explanation for this! We reject simplistic utilitarianism because it entails consequences that are morally *counterintuitive*, or we embrace a Rawlsian theory of justice because it systematizes (places in "reflective equilibrium") our *pretheoretical convictions*. But what is the status of those intuitions or convictions? Perhaps there is nothing more to be said for them than that they involve deep *preferences* (or patterns of preference) built into our biological nature. If this is so, then at a very fundamental point the reasons/causes (and the belief we ought/really ought) distinction breaks down, or the one transforms into the other. (Murphy 1982, 112, n. 21)

It is usually added by people who argue this way that ethics works because we are part of the system. People think that there is an objective morality, even though there is not. As Edward O. Wilson and I once put it: Ethics is a collective illusion of the genes, put in place to make us good cooperators. Nothing more, but also nothing less (Ruse and Wilson 1986). Given a shared evolution, we humans have a shared insight — or rather, sense of insight — into the norms of right and wrong. Some people may disagree with these norms, but as children make mistakes in arithmetic, the disagreement is a function of inadequate training and does not point to an irresolvable subjectivity. Ethics works and that is no small thing.

Conclusion

I offer this as an end to my discussion but also as a beginning to the discussions of others. Evolutionary ethics has had a long and (as we now realize thanks to modern scholarship) a far-from-discreditable history. May it pick up strength and go on to new triumphs!

REFERENCES

Alexander, Richard D. 1987. *The Biology of Moral Systems.* Hawthorne, N.Y.: A. de Gruyter.

Allan, J. M. 1869. On the real differences in the minds of men and women. *Journal of Anthropology* 7.

Bannister, Robert C. 1979. *Social Darwinism: Science and Myth in Anglo-American Social Thought.* Philadelphia: Temple University Press.

Broad, C. D. 1949. Review of Julian S. Huxley's *Evolutionary Ethics.* In *Readings in Philosophical Analysis,* ed. H. Feigel and W. Sellars. New York: Apple-Century-Crofts.

Bullock, Alan. 1991. *Hitler and Stalin: Parallel Lives.* London: HarperCollins.

Crook, D. P. 1994. *Darwinism: War and History.* Cambridge: Cambridge University Press.

Darwin, Charles. 1859. *On the Origin of Species.* London: John Murray.

———. 1871. *The Descent of Man and Selection in Relation to Sex.* London: John Murray.

Darwin, Erasmus. 1794-1796. *Zoonomia; or, The Laws of Organic Life.* London: J. Johnson.

———. 1803. *The Temple of Nature.* London: J. Johnson.

Dawkins, Richard. 1976. *The Selfish Gene.* Oxford: Oxford University Press.

———. 1982. *The Extended Phenotype: The Gene as the Unit of Selection.* Oxford: W. H. Freeman.

De Waal, F. B. M. 1982. *Chimpanzee Politics: Power and Sex among Apes.* London: Cape.

Dennett, Daniel C. 1984. *Elbow Room.* Cambridge, Mass.: MIT Press.

Fisher, Ronald A. 1947. The renaissance of Darwinism. *Listener* 37:1001.

———. 1950. *Creative Aspects of Natural Law. The Eddington Memorial Lecture.* Cambridge: Cambridge University Press.

Goodall, Jane. 1986. *The Chimpanzees of Gombe: Patterns of Behavior.* Cambridge, Mass.: Belknap.

Gould, Stephen Jay. 1981. *The Mismeasure of Man.* New York: Norton.

———. 1988. On replacing the idea of progress with an operational notion of directionality. In *Evolutionary Progress,* ed. M. H. Nitecki, 319-38. Chicago: University of Chicago Press.

———. 1989. *Wonderful Life: The Burgess Shale and the Nature of History.* New York: W. W. Norton.

———. 1996. *Full House: The Spread of Excellence from Plato to Darwin.* New York: Paragon.

Haeckel, Ernst. 1866. *Generelle Morphologie der Organismen.* Berlin: Georg Reimer.

Hamilton, William D. 1964a. The genetical evolution of social behavior I. *Journal of Theoretical Biology* 7:1-16.

———. 1964b. The genetical evolution of social behavior II. *Journal of Theoretical Biology* 7:17-52.

Hamilton, W. D., R. Axelrod, and R. Tanese. 1990. Sexual reproduction as an adaptation to resist parasites. *Proceedings of the National Academy of Science, USA* 87, no. 9:3566-73.

Hrdy, Sarah Blaffer. 1981. *The Woman That Never Evolved.* Cambridge, Mass.: Harvard University Press.

Hume, David. 1978. *A Treatise of Human Nature.* Oxford: Oxford University Press.

Huxley, Thomas Henry. 1879. *Hume.* London: Macmillan.

———. 1893. *Evolution and Ethics and Other Essays.* London: Macmillan.

Huxley, Thomas Henry, and Julian Huxley. 1947. *Evolution and Ethics, 1893-1943.* London: Pilot.

Jones, Greta. 1980. *Social Darwinism and English Thought.* Brighton: Harvester.

Kellogg, Vernon Lyman. 1912. *Beyond War: A Chapter in the Natural History of Man.* New York: Henry Holt.

Kropotkin, Petr. [1902] 1955. *Mutual Aid.* Boston: Extending Horizons Books.

Marchant, James. 1916. *Alfred Russel Wallace: Letters and Reminiscences.* London: Cassell and Company.

Maynard Smith, John. 1978. *The Evolution of Sex.* Cambridge: Cambridge University Press.

Midgley, Mary. 1979. Gene-juggling. *Philosophy* 54:439-58.

Moore, G. E. 1903. *Principia Ethica.* Cambridge: Cambridge University Press.

Murphy, Jeffrie G. 1982. *Evolution, Morality, and the Meaning of Life.* Totowa, N.J.: Rowman and Littlefield.

Rawls, John. 1971. *A Theory of Justice.* Cambridge, Mass.: Harvard University Press.

———. 1980. Kantian constructivism in moral theory. *Journal of Philosophy* 77:515-72.

Richards, Robert J. 1987. *Darwin and the Emergence of Evolutionary Theories of Mind and Behavior*. Chicago: University of Chicago Press.

Rolston, Holmes, III. 1999. *Genes, Genesis, and God: Values and Their Origins in Natural and Human History*. Cambridge: Cambridge University Press.

Ruse, Michael. 1986. *Taking Darwin Seriously: A Naturalistic Approach to Philosophy*. Oxford: Blackwell.

———. 1989. *The Darwinian Paradigm: Essays on Its History, Philosophy, and Religious Implications*. London: Routledge.

———. 1994. *Evolutionary Naturalism: Selected Essays*. London: Routledge.

———. 1996. *Monad to Man: The Concept of Progress in Evolutionary Biology*. Cambridge, Mass.: Harvard University Press.

———. 2000. *The Evolution Wars: A Guide to the Controversies*. Santa Barbara, Calif.: ABC-CLIO.

Ruse, Michael, and Edward O. Wilson. 1986. Moral philosophy as applied science. *Philosophy* 61:173-92.

Simpson, George Gaylord. 1949. *The Meaning of Evolution*. New Haven, Conn.: Yale University Press.

Singer, Peter. 1981. *The Expanding Circle: Ethics and Sociobiology*. New York: Farrar, Straus, and Giroux.

Skyrms, Brian. 1996. *Evolution of the Social Contract*. Cambridge: Cambridge University Press.

Sober, Elliot, and David Sloan Wilson. 1998. *Unto Others: The Evolution and Psychology of Unselfish Behavior*. Cambridge, Mass.: Harvard University Press.

Spencer, Herbert. 1851. *Social Statics; Or the Conditions Essential to Human Happiness Specified and the First of Them Developed*. London: J. Chapman.

———. 1857. Progress: Its law and cause. *Westminster Review* 67:244-67.

Sumner, William Graham. 1914. *The Challenge of Facts, and Other Essays*. New Haven: Yale University Press.

Trivers, R. L. 1971. The evolution of reciprocal altruism. *Quarterly Review of Biology* 46:35-57.

Wagar, W. Warren. 1972. *Good Tidings: The Belief in Progress from Darwin to Marcuse*. Bloomington, Ind.: Indiana University Press.

Wallace, A. R. 1900. *Studies: Scientific and Social*. London: Macmillan.

———. 1905. *My Life: A Record of Events and Opinions*. London: Chapman and Hall.

Wells, H. G. 1895. *The Time Machine*. London: W. Heinemann.

Williams, George C. 1966. *Adaptation and Natural Selection*. Princeton, N.J.: Princeton University Press.

Wilson, Edward O. 1975. *Sociobiology: The New Synthesis*. Cambridge, Mass.: Harvard University Press.

———. 1978. *On Human Nature*. Cambridge, Mass.: Harvard University Press.

———. 1992. *The Diversity of Life*. Cambridge, Mass.: Harvard University Press.

———. 2002. *The Future of Life*. New York: Alfred A. Knopf.

2. Darwinian Evolutionary Ethics:
Between Patriotism and Sympathy

Peter J. Richerson and Robert Boyd

Introduction

Darwin believed that his theory of evolution by natural and sexual selection would stand or fall on its ability to account for human behavior. No species could be an exception to his theory without imperiling the whole edifice (Gruber 1974, chap. 10). He thus eventually devoted the *Descent of Man* to developing an evolutionary account of human origins based on selection, but also on the inheritance of acquired variation.

What Darwin called the "moral faculties" were a major part of his account of humans. One of the most striking features of human behavior is our very elaborate social life involving cooperation with large numbers of other people. As the philosopher-historian Robert Richards shows in elegant detail (1987), the *Descent* was a sophisticated piece of work that even today repays close study, not least for its theory of the evolution of morality. Darwin made four main arguments regarding human morality: (1) that it is a product of group selection; (2) that an immense difference exists between human moral systems and those of other animals; (3) that human social instincts are "primeval" and essentially the same in all modern humans; and (4) that moral progress is possible through using the instinct of sympathy as the basis for inventing and favoring the spread of improved social institutions. Modern studies of cultural evolution suggest that Darwin's arguments about the evolution of morality are largely correct in their essentials.

Darwin's Ethical System

Humans from the Beginning

Darwin's early M and N notebooks on man, mind, and materialism make clear the important place that the human species played in the formation of

50

his ideas on evolution (Gruber 1974). In August 1838, a few weeks *before* his first clear statement of the principle of natural selection was recorded in his notebook on *The Transmutation of Species,* Darwin wrote in his M notebook thus:

> Origin of man now proved. — Metaphysics must flourish. — He who understands baboon would do more toward metaphysics than Locke. (Darwin, in Gruber 1974, 281)

In October 1938, just after he formulated his first clear idea of natural selection, he confided to his N notebook that

> To study Metaphysics as they have always been studied appears to me to be like puzzling at astronomy without mechanics. — Experience shows that the problem of the mind cannot be solved without attacking the citadel itself. — the mind a function of the body. — we must bring some stable foundation to argue from. (Barrett, in Gruber 1974, 331)

These words were written in the heat of Darwin's most creative period and are an expression of hopeful enthusiasm rather than triumph. He was actively pursuing a purely materialistic theory of organic evolution and was already committed to the idea that humans would belong under the theory. Given the scope of the theory, it could hardly be otherwise: If humans were not understandable in evolutionary terms, then critics would suspect deep, general problems with the theory. On the other hand, if evolutionary theory was correct, it should provide powerful tools to understand human behavior.

When Darwin published *Origin of Species,* he included the famous teaser, "light would be thrown on the origin of man and his history." When none of his allies rose to the occasion, he eventually took on the task of writing the *Descent of Man and Selection in Relation to Sex* ([1871] 1874). In the introduction, he wrote of his fear that publication of his views on the subject would inflame prejudices against his theory. This fear was not unfounded. As the *Quarterly Review*'s commentator, probably the long hostile and devoutly Catholic St. George Mivart, gloated, the *Descent* "offers a good opportunity for reviewing his whole position" (and rejecting it) (cited in Dawkins 1871).

Darwin differed from many of his contemporaries in not believing that progress, including moral progress of humans, is a necessary or intrinsic part of evolution. Natural selection's subtractive rather than creative property makes it an implausible force for progress. As Darwin expressed the matter in his N notebook in November 1838,

Man's intellect is not become superior to that of the Greeks (which seems opposed to progressive development) on account of the dark ages. — Look at Spain now. — Man's intellect might well deteriorate.-((effects of *external* circumstances)) ((In my theory there is no absolute tendency to progression, excepting from favorable circumstances!)) (Darwin, in Gruber 1974, 339)

Why were Darwin's contemporaries so keen on progressive theories of evolution? The original nub of the matter was that almost all Victorians understood and feared the impact that a thoroughly Darwinian theory of human origins would have upon morals. As the *Edinburgh Review*'s anonymous commentator on the *Descent* remarked (1871),

If our humanity be merely the natural product of the modified faculties of brutes, most earnest-minded men will be compelled to give up those motives by which they have attempted to live noble and virtuous lives, as founded on a mistake. . . .

According to J. W. Burrow (1966), a significant segment of Victorian opinion was skeptical about conventional religion and was often enthusiastic about evolution. They did believe, however, that human morality required the support of natural laws. If God's Law was dismissed by the scientific-minded as superstition, then it was all that much more important to find a substitute in the natural laws that scientists were elucidating. Darwin's evolutionary theory of morality does have a progressive element, despite his general suspicions about evolutionary progress. Human moral progress is by no means guaranteed by a natural law, however; his theory is much more contingent than that.

Darwin's Four-Part Argument

Group Selection   Darwin's theory of the origins of human morality is sketched in chapter 5 of the *Descent*, "On the Development of the Intellectual and Moral Faculties during Primeval and Civilized Times." He proposed that natural selection *on groups* operated in primeval times to produce human moral capacities (172-80):

It must not be forgotten that although a high standard of morality gives but a slight or no advantage to each individual man and his children over other men of the same tribe, yet that an increase in the number of well-

endowed men and an advancement in the standard of morality will certainly give an immense advantage to one tribe over another. A tribe including many members who, from possessing in a high degree the spirit of patriotism, fidelity, obedience, courage, and sympathy, were always ready to
aid one another, and to sacrifice themselves for the common good, would
be victorious over most other tribes; and this would be natural selection.
(178-79)

Note especially the terms *patriotism* and *sympathy* for future reference.

An Immense Gap   In the chapters of the *Descent* on the "Comparison of the
Mental Powers of Man and the Lower Animals," Darwin summarizes the
issue:

> We have seen in the last two chapters that man bears in his bodily structure
> clear traces of his descent from some lower form; but it may be urged that,
> as man differs so greatly in his mental power from all other animals, there
> must be some error in this conclusion. No doubt the difference in this re-
> spect is enormous. . . . The difference would, no doubt, still remain im-
> mense, even if one of the higher apes had been improved and civilized as
> much as a dog has been in comparison with its parent form, the wolf or
> jackal. . . . The moral sense perhaps affords the best and highest distinction
> between man and the lower animals. (94, 171)

In these chapters he struggles with the challenge that the great gap between humans and other animals poses for his theory of the gradual, step-by-
small-step emergence of humans from their ape ancestors. How much easier
his task would have been if he had seen fit to people the gap with the living
human races, as so many of his contemporaries did! Gaps are an embarrass-
ment to his theory of evolution by gradual changes. As it is, to minimize the
extent of the immense gap he tends to raise nonhuman animals up rather
than cast the lower races down:

> there is no fundamental difference between man and the higher mammals
> in their mental faculties. . . . With respect to animals very low in the scale, I
> shall give some additional facts under Sexual Selection, showing that their
> mental powers are much higher than might have been expected. (95)

Considering the case as a whole, the evidence was clear enough in Darwin's
time. Even the simplest human societies are larger than any other primate so-

ciety. No human society is without ethical rules that make peaceful interactions between nonrelatives routine. These attributes, along with our technological prowess, made us, even as "savages," a widespread and successful species, while the other apes remain confined to the tropical forests of our common ancestor.

Social Instincts Primeval   Darwin pointedly credits "savages" with a loyalty to their tribes sufficient to motivate self-sacrifice to the point of death and with the "instinct" of sympathy, with the objective of making sure that the reader understands that these moral sentiments are of primeval age, shared by the living savage and the civilized alike. Darwin's theory of moral evolution in the *Descent* is in many respects one more typical of the last half of the twentieth century than of the Victorian nineteenth. Just as he did not make progress the centerpiece of his story, he did not rank humans, as regards their minds or their moral intuitions, on a primitive-advanced progressive scale.

Darwin's first published views on humans in the *Journal of Researches (Voyage of the Beagle)* were made several years after he formulated his early ideas on natural selection, but more than a decade before their publication and twenty-five years before the *Descent*. His descriptions of the Fuegans in the *Journal* are often quoted to demonstrate that his views of the hierarchy of races were stereotypically Victorian. He did use the most purple Victorian prose to describe the wretched and lowly state of the Fuegans, whom he had observed firsthand on the *Beagle* voyage (Darwin 1845, 242-47):

> These poor wretches were stunted in their growth, their hideous faces bedaubed with white paint, their skins filthy and greasy, their hair entangled, their voices discordant, and their gestures violent. Viewing such men, one can hardly make one's self believe that they are fellow-creatures, and inhabitants of the same world. (243)

> They cannot know the feeling of having a home, and still less that of domestic affection; for the husband is to the wife a brutal master to a laborious slave. Was a more horrible deed ever perpetrated than that witnessed on the west coast by Byron, who saw a wretched mother pick up her bleeding dying infant-boy, whom her husband had mercilessly dashed on the stones for dropping a basket of sea-eggs! (246)

He goes on at some length in this fashion, but this is the bait rather than the hook of the argument. The passage on the Fuegans begins with a description of the rigors of the environment of Tierra del Fuego and ends by attributing the low nature of the people to the poor quality of the environment rather than to their being inherently primitive people:

> We were detained here for several days by the bad weather. The climate is certainly wretched: the summer solstice was now past [passage is dated December 25] yet every day snow fell on the hills, and in the valleys there was rain. The thermometer generally stood at 45° but in the nights fell to 38° or 40°. (242)

> While beholding these savages, one asks, whence could they have come? What could have tempted, or what change compelled a tribe of men, to leave the fine regions of the North, to travel down the Cordillera or backbone of America . . . and then to enter on one of the most inhospitable countries within the limits of the globe? . . . [W]e must suppose that they enjoy a sufficient share of happiness, of whatever kind it may be, to render life worth living. Nature by making habit omnipotent, and its effects hereditary, has fitted the Fuegans to the climate and the productions of this miserable country. (246-47)

The argument is quite in keeping with his idea that progress under his theory could come only from favorable circumstances. In effect he is saying that any humans — Englishmen, say — forced to live under such conditions with such limited technology would rapidly come to behave similarly. Note the reference to hereditary habits; this concept figures large in his mature ideas on human evolution.

Darwin was also well aware of the evidence that the pioneering ethnographers and archaeologists of his time were producing on the history and prehistory of our species. He reviews this in the *Descent* under the heading *On the Evidence that all Civilized Nations were once Barbarous* (193-95):

> The evidence that all civilized nations are the descendants of barbarians consists, on the one side, of clear traces of their former low condition in still-existing customs, beliefs, language, etc.; and, on the other side, of proofs that savages are independently able to raise themselves a few steps on the scale of civilization, and have actually thus risen. (193)

In Darwin's day no absolute time scale could be put on the rise of civilization, and he makes no attempt to even guess about the matter. The evidence he adduces for the "few steps" comes from ethnographic observations, however, so the time scale for the rise of civilizations must be relatively short.

The climax of Darwin's argument in the *Descent* is chapter 7, "On the Races of Man." He considers two hypotheses: that the races are sufficiently distinct to count as different species, and that they are alike in all important organic respects. He first spends several pages outlining all the evidence in favor of the different species hypothesis (Darwin [1871] 1874, 224-31). Darwin's dispassionate tone in these pages makes it easy for careless readers to believe that this is the alternative Darwin favors. He goes immediately on, however, to demolish the separate species argument in favor of the trivial differences alternative (231-40):

> Although the existing races differ in many respects, as in color, hair, shape of the skull, proportions of the body, etc., yet, if their whole structure be taken into consideration, they are found to resemble each other closely on a multitude of points. Many of these are so unimportant or of so singular a nature that it is extremely improbable that they should have been independently acquired by aboriginally distinct species or races. The same remark holds good with equal or greater force with respect to the numerous points of mental similarity between the most distinct races of man. The American aborigines, Negroes, and Europeans are as different from each other in mind as any three races that can be named; yet I was constantly struck, while living with the Fuegians on board the "Beagle," with the many little traits of character showing how similar their minds were to ours; and so it was with a full-blooded Negro with whom I happened once to be intimate. (237)

The contrast between Darwin and others like Ernst Haeckel who really did think that "natural men (e.g., Indian Vedas or Australian Negroes) are closer to the higher vertebrates (e.g., apes and dogs) than to highly civilized Europeans" could hardly be more stark (Richards 1987, 596).

The extent to which Darwin subscribed to what we now call the doctrine of psychic unity is widely misunderstood. Even otherwise knowledgeable scholars believe that Darwin shared the widespread Victorian belief that the living races could be ranked on a primitive-advanced scale (e.g., Ingold 1986, 53). Bowler (1993, 70) remarks, "The *Descent of Man* takes racial hierarchy for granted and cites the conventional view that whites have a larger cranial capacity than other races." Alexander Alland approvingly quotes Stephen Jay Gould to the effect that Darwin shared the typical Victorian idea that the dark races are lower in the progressive evolutionary sense (1985, 4-5). As Geoffrey Hodgson and earlier Robert Bannister (1979) have shown, Social "Darwinists" of the type imagined by Hofstadter (1945) hardly existed at all

56

and Darwin and his closest followers were not among them! We find it quite odd that contemporary social scientists, operating in a liberal to radical political milieu, fail to recognize that Darwin's general political views, while not often worn on his sleeve to the extent that his views on slavery were, were far to the left for his day, and not so different from those of the modern non-doctrinaire academic Left (Sulloway 1996, chap. 10; Desmond 1989, afterword; Richards 1987, 597).

Moral Progress via Sympathy and Other Prosocial Dispositions   For further advances, Darwin puts great weight on customs acquired by imitation (Darwin 1874, 174). He spends several pages of the *Descent* reviewing the tendency of advancing civilization to, if anything, weaken natural selection (180-93). He summarizes the argument:

> I have already said enough, while treating of the lower races, on the causes which lead to the advance of morality, namely the approbations of our fellow-men — the strengthening of our sympathies by habit — example and imitation — reason — experience, and even self-interest — instruction during youth, and religious feelings. (185-86)

And, in current circumstances,

> With highly civilized nations, continued progress depends in a subordinate degree on natural selection. . . . The more efficient causes of progress seem to consist of a good education during youth while the brain is impressible, and of a high standard of excellence, inculcated by the ablest and best men, embodied in the laws, customs, and traditions of the nation, and enforced by public opinion. (192)

Note that the means of moral progress that apply in his mind to the lower races are virtually identical to those that apply to the highest. *Primeval* evolution endowed savages with the same social instincts as civilized people, and hence they are susceptible to the same improvement from "good education" and the rest. The lower races have the same moral instincts as the higher; the higher have just had the advantage of a favorable environment to push moral progress a little further.

Since people from different places do differ substantially in behavior, Darwin, of course, needed an account of human diversity. In chapter 7 of the *Descent* he makes something like the modern distinction between organic differences and customs. "He who will read Mr. Tylor's and Sir J. Lubbock's interesting works can hardly fail to be deeply impressed with the close similarity between the men of all races in tastes, dispositions and habits," he begins (238). Darwin's favorable citations of Edward Tylor, the founder of cultural anthropology and one of the important nineteenth-century defenders of the Enlightenment doctrine of the psychic unity of all humans, is surely significant and quite in keeping with his sympathy for savages and slaves. Tylor's postulate of organic similarity but customary difference is clear: "For the present purpose it appears both possible and desirable to treat mankind as homogeneous in nature, though placed in different grades of civilization" (1871, 7). Darwin sometimes uses exactly the same distinction: "As it is improbable that the numerous and unimportant points of resemblance between the several races of man in bodily structure and mental faculties (I do not here refer to similar customs) should all have been independently acquired. . . " (239). For Darwin the explanation for differences between races has to do with customs, not organic differences. The story is complicated for us to understand because of Darwin's frequent use of the concept of inherited habits, as in the quote about the Fuegians above. In the preface to the second edition of the *Descent*, Darwin reiterated his commitment to the inheritance of acquired variation:

> I may take this opportunity of remarking that my critics frequently assume that I attribute all changes of corporeal structure and mental power exclusively to natural selection of such variation as are often called spontaneous; whereas, even in the first edition of the "Origin of Species," I distinctly stated that great weight must be attributed to the inherited effects of use and disuse, with respect both to the body and the mind. (3-4)

One of the most important forms of the inherited effects of use and disuse in Darwin's mind is "inherited habits." Custom, good education, imitation, and other manifestations of culture would tend to become hereditary in Darwin's scheme. Lacking the twentieth-century concept of a gene isolated from direct environmental modification, a rigid distinction between inheritance by imitation and inheritance by organic structures was foreign to his thinking. He does seem to divide traits into more and less conservative poles. On the conservative side are basic anatomy and basic features of the mind, little influenced by the inheritance of acquired variation but mainly by selection over long spans of time. More labile traits are much more sensitive to environmental and cultural influences, though they also come to be inherited. Inheritance notwithstanding, the more labile traits are susceptible to being rapidly remodeled again by inherited habit if the environment changes. This feature of his theory was erroneous and archaic; still, the conservative-labile distinction does the same work for Darwin that the genetic-cultural one does for us.

Moral progress in Darwin's theory is clearly not automatic. He is quite alive to the moral deficiencies of the advanced civilizations. In the *Journal* (Darwin 1845, 36-37, 121-25, 561-63) he forthrightly condemns Argentinean General Rosa's war against the natives of Patagonia and expresses sympathy and admiration for the Indian resistance. For example, he recounts the story of an Indian's daring escape with his small son from a genocidal attack on the Argentineans, and ends thus: "What a fine picture one can form in one's mind — the naked, bronze-like figure of the old man with his little boy, riding like a Mazeppa on a white horse, thus leaving far behind him the host of his pursuers!" (124). His anguished paean against slavery (561-63) begins,

> On the 19th of August, we finally left the shores of Brazil. I thank God I shall never again visit a slave country. To this day, if I hear a distant scream, it recalls with vivid painfulness my feelings when, passing a house near Pernambuco, I heard the most pitiable moans, and could not but suspect that some poor slave was being tortured, yet knew that I was as powerless as a child even to remonstrate.

And it ends,

> It makes one's blood boil, yet heart tremble, to think that Englishmen and our American descendants with their boastful cry of liberty, have been and are so guilty: but it is a consolation to reflect that we have made a greater sacrifice than ever made by any nation to expiate our sin. [Britain freed the slaves in all her colonies in 1838.]

Gruber notes that Darwin's deep antipathy to slavery was shared with his extended family circle, though not nearly so widely shared by his contemporaries — a fact which led, for example, to a furious argument with Captain Fitzroy on the *Beagle* voyage (1974, 65-68).

Darwin does not develop a detailed account of what makes for moral progress and regression. He certainly thought that moral progress was possible, and clearly thought that Europeans had achieved some notable advances relative to savages. Things like the rule of law and enacting just laws supported by enlightened public opinion, such as had ended slavery in the British Empire, he counted as progress. Most of us would agree. What about regressions like slavery and colonial genocide? He seems to suggest that patriotism will tend to conflict with and limit the scope of sympathy. Sympathy on its own easily extends to everyone, but patriotism demands allegiance to country, caste, class, or tribe and limits sympathy toward groups outside our own. Slaveowners, through solidarity with others of the slave-owning caste, could develop racist theories and institutions of ruthless subordination that limited the effects of empathy toward slaves. Darwin seems to be arguing that moral progress beyond what natural selection can achieve is accomplished by increasing the scope of empathy at the expense of narrow patriotism.

A Spiritual Foundation?

Darwin's own religious apostasy is well known. In his student years, he had much enjoyed Paley's *Natural Theology.* During the time of the voyage of the *Beagle* (1831-1836) and immediately afterward he read Charles Lyell on geology and adopted a turn of mind that mandated, as the proper scientific approach, a highly mechanistic account of natural processes. His theory of natural selection was an explicitly materialistic explanation for the origins of organic form in which no influence of natural theology remained (Gruber 1974, 125-27). Nevertheless, Darwin sometimes writes so lyrically about the natural world that one is tempted to take him as a sort of nature mystic. The most famous passage of this sort is the last paragraph of the *Origin of Species:*

> It is interesting to contemplate an entangled bank, clothed with many plants of many kinds, with birds singing on the bushes, with various insects flitting about, and with worms crawling through the damp earth, and to reflect that these elaborately constructed forms, so different from each other in so complex a manner, have all been produced by laws acting around us. . . . There is grandeur in this view of life, with its several powers, having originally breathed into a few forms or into one; and that, whilst this planet has gone on cycling on according to the fixed law of gravity, from so simple a beginning endless forms most beautiful and most wonderful have been, and are being, evolved.

Many a scientific naturalist seems to derive a religious experience from the close study of nature. In the modern case, field biologists' devotion to the preservation of nature suggests that such appreciations lead to a powerful ethical impulse as well. By some accounts, Saint Francis was a nature mystic (Armstrong 1973). One wonders if scientists don't often experience the awe of nature but simply not use a theistic vocabulary to describe the experience (Kiester 1996/1997).

A Modernization of Darwin's Argument

In the light of modern evolutionary theory, Darwin's theory for the evolution of morality and moral progress has two main weaknesses. First, Darwin was quite confused about the nature of inheritance, as we have seen. In his mind, inherited habits connected customs — culture, in our terms — directly to the process of organic inheritance. Geneticists long ago showed that the genetic system generally lacks the inheritance of acquired variation. Second, Darwin's theory is heavily reliant on group selection. Most evolutionary biologists believe that individually costly group-beneficial behavior can arise only as a side effect of individual fitness maximization. Many, but by no means all, students of evolution and human behavior have followed the argument against group selection forcefully articulated by George Williams (1966). Several prominent modern Darwinians — W. D. Hamilton (1975), E. O. Wilson (1975, 561-62), R. D. Alexander (1987, 169), and I. Eibl-Eibesfeld (1982) — have given serious consideration to group selection as a force *in the special case* of human ultra-sociality. Most theorists, however, do not believe that genetic systems will maintain enough variation between groups for group selection to be a strong force, except in small groups of close genetic relatives (see Sober and Wilson, 1998, for a contrary view). We believe that *cultural* variation is more plausibly susceptible to group selection than is genetic variation.

This argument is developed below using the idea that Darwinian tools are as useful for understanding cultural evolution as they are for understanding genetic evolution. The basic idea is this: Learning from someone else by imitation or teaching is similar to acquiring genes from parents. A potentially important determinant of behavior is transmitted from one individual to another in both cases. As individuals acquire genes or culture, they draw their genetic parents and cultural models from a large population of potential parents and cultural models. Evolutionary processes then operate on individuals, discriminating in favor of some cultural and genetic variants and against others. The population that exists for the next generation to sample typically differs subtly from the previous one. As many generations pass, changes accumulate and evolution occurs. This analogy between genetic and cultural evolution is undoubtedly what led Darwin to so thoroughly confuse the two. Both are population-level, historical processes that frequently result in the adaptive diversification of behavior. Luigi Cavalli-Sforza and Marcus Feldman (1981) and their followers have developed a considerable body of theory about cultural evolution by modifying standard evolutionary theory to fit the case of culture.

The Evolution of Human Morality

A good deal of our own work and that of our students has been devoted to understanding the evolution of human sociality. Step by step, we have been led to what amounts to a modernization of Darwin's theory of the evolution of human morality. We outline this modernization under the same headings that we used to describe Darwin's original theory: (1) that group selection is the basic mechanism explaining human moral impulses; (2) that an immense gap exists between the moral faculties of humans and other animals; (3) that the moral faculties evolved in the common ancestors of all living humans; and (4) that moral progress arises when humans create social institutions that enlarge sympathy and control patriotism.

What is the phenomenon to be explained? In most animal societies, the animals that cooperate are close kin, as in the colonies of social insects based upon a single reproducing queen. Cooperation in such systems is well explained by W. D. Hamilton's famous inclusive fitness theory, which proposed that individuals can be altruistic toward others to the degree that they share genes "identical by common descent" (1964). While human familial altruism fits neatly into this pattern, human societies always include supra-familial institutions. Some complex of innate predispositions and culturally transmitted dispositions leads human societies to have customary systems of tacit and formal rules that mold family units into a larger social system. Even at their simplest, these social systems differ from those of our close ape relatives in having larger amounts of cooperation between un- or distantly related individuals and in linking together people who do not reside in the same group (Rodseth et al. 1991). To judge from contemporary simple societies, three more or less hierarchical levels of social organization characterized our ancestral Upper Paleolithic societies: the family, the co-residential band, and a collection of bands that routinely intermarried, spoke a common language, and had a common set of myths and rituals. Families were similar to modern families and bands were rather fluid units. Members of the largest unit, often called a tribe, generally maintained relatively peaceable relations with each other, and routinely cooperated in subsistence, defense, and other activities. The tribe often spoke a distinctive language or dialect and consisted of a few hundred to a few thousand people.

Compared to many agriculturally based societies of the last ten thousand years, the sophistication of political organization of hunting and gathering societies is slight. Often such units had no formal political leadership at all — and yet they were able to maintain long-term alliances with other tribes. Often highly egalitarian (although often quite sexist, as Darwin observed), these societies functioned as if every male adult were a member of an informal parliament informally led by the able and respected. Sometimes band headmen were formally recognized and sometimes their consultations were formal enough to warrant calling them a tribal council. Inter-tribal institutions were not uncommon. In addition to alliances, inter-tribal religious organizations were not rare. Inter-band affairs were probably regulated by ad hoc negotiations dominated but not controlled by the headmen.

The important point is that even such simple societies are a moral community, governed by a common set of widely respected rules that vary from tribe to tribe. For example, in many such societies a rich and delicately balanced set of institutions exist that both quietly honor successful hunters (skill in this regard is quite variable) and prevent them from becoming petty tyrants.

The role of religion in simple human societies has been much debated. Suffice it to say here that supernatural beliefs, legends and stories, and collective ritual must have been common if not universal features of our ancestors' societies.

Cultural Group Selection   What if we imagine that cultural rather than genetic variation is the subject of group selection? Several common properties of cultural inheritance make it a much more plausible candidate for group selection than genes.

First, if only a few influential teachers exist in each group, much variation between them is likely to be created (Cavalli-Sforza and Feldman 1981, 204, 338-39). In the case of moral systems, the instant establishment of a major cultural variant by the charismatic founders of new religions and political ideologies is well known (Stark 1997; Abanes 2002). The formation of micro-cults and micro-parties is a rather common phenomenon, and only a handful of these become even modest successes. Clearly a selection process winnows the variants on offer, and we have some idea of how the process works (Stark and Bainbridge 1996). Very rarely, great ethical teachers like Moses, Christ, Confucius, and Mohammed are able to put their stamp on a whole series of civilizations.

Second, the conformist "When in Rome" imitation rule has a strong tendency to minimize the effects of migration on the variation between groups (Boyd and Richerson 1985, chap. 7; Henrich and Boyd 1998). Even if migrants are fairly common, so long as they do not approach half the population of a group, resident culture will have an advantage over that of minority migrants; it will be over-represented due to the conformity of old-stock individuals and second-generation migrants. The very considerable assimilation to British-

American culture of many immigrants to the United States is testimony to the power of this effect.

Third, the symbolic aspects of culture are a potent source of variation between groups (Boyd and Richerson 1985, chap. 8). Symbolic differences can also arise in isolated groups through a kind of runaway process that perhaps explains the extreme exaggeration we observe in fads and fashions, and in the colorful excesses with regard to ordinary utility in many ritual systems. Ritual, religious belief, and language isolate groups, potentiating group selection. Symbolic systems act to protect groups from the effects of migration, much as in the case of conformity, because people ordinarily tend to admire, respect, and imitate individuals displaying familiar symbolic traits. Cultural chauvinism is distressingly common and contributes to sharp, and too-often violent, competition between groups. Directly important aspects of culture, such as the ethical norms that are the basis for patterns of altruism and for the basic form of social organization, are often embedded in richly symbolic belief systems.

The effects of selection on cultural groups can often be fairly rapid because cultural death and reproduction do not necessarily depend upon the physical death and reproduction of people. After a war or dispute, defeated groups often are incorporated into the victorious society, or into friendly groups not involved in the conflict. In simpler societies, defeat in war typically results in more captives and refugees than dead. Thus, war generates migration, which is much more hostile to genetic than cultural group selection. We have attempted to measure the rate of cultural group selection in simple societies, using data on local group extinctions in Highland New Guinea in pre-contact time (Soltis, Boyd, and Richerson 1995). These rates are fairly substantial; they might result in the replacement of less favorable with more group-favorable traits in a large population of societies in something like one thousand years. This seems about right to account for the relatively slow, halting evolution of more complex and more powerful polities over the ten thousand years since crop cultivation made complex societies ecologically feasible.

Other modes of cultural group selection exist besides the one tested by Soltis. Successful societies also attract imitators, so that a culture could expand without any overt conflict at all (Boyd and Richerson 2002). This form of cultural group selection is potentially very rapid. Much of the spread of European culture in the last five hundred years was due to the displacement and/or replacement of indigenous peoples, as in the case of the Indians and European settlers in North America. Currently, however, Europeanization ("modernization" and "globalization") depends much more upon the voluntary adoption of party systems, parliaments, Christianity, university education, factory organization of work, and so forth than it does on displacement or forced conversion. Most likely, both the slow Soltis mode of group selection and the faster intergroup imitation processes are important. Group imitation can only transfer variation that is relatively easily observed. At least the nuances of social organization are often difficult to appreciate from afar and are often difficult to establish piecemeal in a host society. Douglass North (1973), among others (Karl Marx comes to mind; see Bettinger and Baumhoff [1982] for the case of simple societies), argues that innovations in social institutions have been the rate-limiting step in the evolution of more sophisticated social systems. Social organizations probably have elements that evolve on the Soltis time scale. A parliamentary form of government is easy to adopt, but the dispositions, skills, and ancillary institutions necessary to make such a government work like the Western model are not so easily transferred. In this regard, religious conversion is potentially a potent vehicle for the cross-cultural transfer of social institutions because proselytizing religions like Christianity and Islam have well-developed means of making conversion easy. Still, syncretism with local beliefs and practices is also commonplace. The general role of religious conversion in the diffusion of social institutions would repay study.

Finally, theoretical models suggest that group selection is especially potent on systems of punishment (Boyd et al. 2003; Henrich and Boyd 2001). The reason the models work the way they do is easy to appreciate. Helping acts are costly every time one engages in them. As altruists become common, the number of hands to help increases, but so do those in need of help. Helping remains costly. Also, as altruists become more common, they will tend to run the risk of "moral hazard." Knowing that helpful individuals are common, individuals will be motivated to take risks, be lazy, or be otherwise feckless, knowing that plentiful helpful souls will likely aid them. Worse yet, pure altruists may attract con artists who will victimize them. Cooperative communities of many altruists will tend to produce surpluses that attract predators. On the other hand, the costs of being a punisher of those who break moral rules reliably drops as punishers become more common. When punishers are vanishingly rare, each punisher will have a large load of work to do. In an evolutionary sense, punishment is hard to get started. But if punishers ever become common, they will have many hands to share the work of punishment, and fewer individuals will be in need of punishment. In the limit when everyone is a punisher, punishers have absolutely no work to do! In Boyd and company's models, the evolutionary dynamics tend to become complicated since the strategy of being altruistic but not punishing tends to invade a system that is rich in punishers, because non-punisher altruists are both protected by punishers and evade the cost of punishment. So long as any work remains for punishers to do, altruist non-punishers will increase at their expense. But as the number of non-punisher altruists rises, the opportunity for non-punisher, non-altruist rascals to invade the system increases. Nevertheless, models suggest that relatively weak group selection can keep the frequency of punishers high in such a system.

The empirical literature suggests that punishment institutions are a ubiquitous feature of human societies. For example, Elinor Ostrom (1990), one of the leading students of small-scale commons management, details a number of quite sophisticated punishment and monitoring systems and could find no successful commons management schemes without such institutions. The typical systems are elaborately graded and begin with light warnings and only progress to harsh penalties for repeated substantial transgressors. So too with other sorts of transgressions. The rule of law in modern societies is similarly graded, but eventually has recourse to long prison sentences and even death for sufficiently persistent or egregious misbehavior. The pacifist Amish ultimately rigorously shun those who stubbornly disdain gentler attempts to enforce the congregation's rules (Hostetler 1993).

Thus, human-scale societies may have evolved because the peculiar properties of the cultural inheritance system lend themselves to group selection. Originally, processes like conformity may merely have functioned to reduce the risk of adopting foreign traits that are less likely to be useful than homegrown ones in an environment that varies from place to place. Group selection, and resulting indiscriminate altruism from the genetic point of view, may at first have been merely a by-product of adaptation to spatially varying environments (Henrich and Boyd 1998). A number of ingenious hypotheses besides group selection have been proposed to explain human cooperation in recent years (Hammerstein 2003), but we believe that the best evidence supports a major role for *cultural* group selection.

Why can't selection on genes successfully favor innate changes that compensate for any deviations from inclusive fitness optimizing? As Roy Rappaport puts it in the context of cultural rules that prevent over-exploitation of the environment, "to drape nature in supernatural veils may be to provide her with some protection against human folly and extravagance" (1979, 100). Combined with punishment of malefactors, culture encases individuals in a web of institutions that make deviation difficult and dangerous. *Innate* human nature will have been bent by the late Pleistocene under the impact of being selected to live on a tribal scale in a culturally group-selected world. This is an example of culture playing a leading role in the process of gene-culture coevolution.

Nevertheless, the gene-culture coevolutionary system makes the perfection of human altruistic tendencies exceedingly difficult. The problem is that our genetic reproductive system has no analog of the suppression of reproduction among workers. As Donald Campbell perceptively noted (1983), humans are characterized by reproductive competition between the cooperators, quite unlike the social insects. Those who act *entirely* on behalf of the group are likely to be counter-selected at the individual level. Selection on genes to increase our inclusive fitness no doubt goes on side by side with cultural group selection. Conflicts between narrower loyalties to self-interest and kin and larger loyalties to groups generate considerable psychic pain, as if genetic and cultural rules still struggle for mastery of our behavior (Campbell 1975; Richerson and Boyd 1998; Richerson and Boyd 1999). This phenomenon, we suggest, accounts for many of the moral conflicts that are endemic to human life.

An Immense Gap　As Darwin supposed, apes and other animals can do everything we do to some approximation. Primatologists like Christophe Boesch and Frans de Waal (2000) stress how similar chimpanzees are to humans. Social learning turns out to be quite common in animals, yet not even the most sophisticated animal social learners seem to have a system approaching the human level of complexity (Heyes and Galef 1996). Chimpanzees in the wild seem to have a considerable amount of cultural variation (Whiten et al. 1999); for example, the chimpanzees in some populations use stones to crack nuts on a simple anvil. Nevertheless, when Andrew Whiten and Michael Tomasello compared the skills of human children and adult, lab-reared chimpanzees on the same imitation tasks, they found that children as young as three years were more proficient imitators than the chimpanzees (Tomasello 1996; Whiten and Custance 1996).

The long-term evolutionary consequences of the enlarged capacity of humans to imitate and teach differentiate us very markedly from our ape ancestors and relatives. The critical feature is that human imitation is accurate enough and fast enough that we can progressively improve artifacts and social institutions to generate adaptations that rival the famous chestnuts of organic evolution like the vertebrate eye (Boyd and Richerson 1996). The Inuit kayak, for example, is a marvel of traditional engineering. Light, fast, and seaworthy, it was constructed from the very limited inventory of raw materials available in the High Arctic using stone-age tools. Chimpanzees, by contrast, use unmodified stones to crack nuts, and twigs just stripped of their leaves to fish for termites.

The story is much the same regarding social institutions. The kin-based social organization of chimpanzees is not markedly more complex than that of many other social mammals. Primate troops very often number about the same size as hunting and gathering bands, but no other primate has permanent bonds of affiliation linking many troops into anything like a tribe. Robin Dunbar, noting that a good correlation exists in other primates between brain size and group size, plotted humans on the regression line (1993). The predicted group size of humans by this method is about 150. Joseph Birdsell's well-known estimate of 500 for the average size of Australian tribes is considerably larger than this figure, especially given that many individuals would have lived in a larger tribe than the average (1953).

Human artifacts and institutions are not only sophisticated but highly variable and rapidly evolving. By the end of the last Ice Age humans had spread all over the world, adapting to life from the margins of the glaciers to the equator using mainly cultural means. Other apes, by contrast, remain restricted to the tropical forest environments of our common ancestor.

Social Instincts Primeval   Substantial advances in our understanding of human origins have been made since Victorian times (Klein 1999). While the human lineage has been distinct from that of the other apes for some five million years, the final modernization of humans occurred in the late Pleistocene. Richard Klein believes that fully modern humans emerged in Africa rather suddenly about 70,000 years ago. McBrearty and Brooks (2000) argue that a sequence of gradual changes in Africa, stretching back some 300,000 years, led gradually to the level of technical and stylistic sophistication characteristic of modern people. In any case, about 50,000 years ago modern people spread out of Africa to the rest of the Old World, replacing more archaic humans like the Neanderthals of western Eurasia. Analysis of mitochondrial DNA from Neanderthals suggests a rather deep split between these forms and modern humans, dating to about 600,000 years ago (Rightmire 1997). The human genome has quite low genetic variability compared to that of chimpanzees, and all modern humans seem to have shared a quite recent African ancestor (Kaessmann and Paabo 2002; Rogers and Jorde 1995). One of the important genes involved in language production probably originated in its modern form within the last 100,000 years (Enard et al. 2002). Thus, the paleoanthropological and genetic data concur in suggesting that all modern humans are very closely related.

Although the social instincts leave no direct fossil evidence, we can be fairly certain that our common African ancestors were quite modern in this regard. The best indirect evidence comes from the sophistication of stone tools. The people who left Africa 50,000 years ago left with a toolkit of modern sophistication. We know from an inadvertent natural experiment that humans need to maintain a rather large social network to resist the loss of toolkit sophistication. When the Bass Strait flooded with rising sea levels after the last glacier, it isolated about four thousand Australians on Tasmania. Over the ensuing ten millennia, their toolkit became gradually less sophisticated until by the time of contact with Europeans they had the simplest toolkit ever collected. According to the analysis of Joseph Henrich (forthcoming), most attempts to teach or imitate the making of a complex artifact lead to slight imperfections. In a small group, these imperfections will accumulate. In a larger group, the occasional gifted artisan will correct the accumulated errors and have the effect of maintaining complex cultural adaptations against this erosion. Humans have to maintain a surprisingly large cultural orbit, far larger than the tribe, to maintain a complex toolkit. Modern humans have tribal alliances, trade networks, intermarriage, and other means of connecting themselves culturally on a much larger scale than the tribal social unit. Neanderthals had as large a brain as Moderns, but a much less sophisticated toolkit. Most likely, their social instincts were rather less sophisticated than ours, but all of us late Pleistocene African hunter-gatherers maintained quite complex toolkits wherever we spread, with the exception of the unfortunately long-isolated Tasmanians.

Moral Progress via Sympathy   The last ten millennia, and especially the last five millennia, have witnessed dramatic moral progress in the sense that humans have come to be able to cooperate in ever larger groups. Archaeologists and historians have filled in many of the details of the evolution of civilized moral communities since Darwin's day. Even more than in the Victorian era, we have learned from the horrors of the twentieth century to view the moral claims of the "civilized" societies with a skeptical eye. While larger-scale societies do not solve all old moral problems and often create new ones, the provision of justice, defense, and social welfare services, however crude, solves problems that tribes cannot. The scope of patriotism was enlarged from the tribe of a few thousand to the scale of nations that today have as many as a billion inhabitants living in the same moral community. Such societies can, for example, manage highly productive economies with a much greater division of labor than is possible in simpler societies.

The cultural evolution of large-scale institutions was, we believe, the product of *work-arounds* (Richerson and Boyd 2001, 1999). The tribal social instincts evolved to underpin only relatively small social systems, but these resources are enough to provide real scope for the evolution of moral progress. By various cultural devices, complex societies have worked around the limitations of the tribal instincts in order to evolve much larger scale and more sophisticated social systems. By such means tribal instincts become foundation blocks of contemporary (and future) societies, even though they did not evolve in such societies and are imperfect raw material for the purpose. We shall concentrate on a specific work-around here for illustrative purposes: the enlargement of the symbolic sphere. Tribal social systems, recall, tended to have a common language, common rituals, common beliefs about the supernatural, common stylistic artifacts, and the like. Those who differed in these regards belonged to other tribes. Thus, our innate psychology seems to be adapted to count those with whom we share such symbols as those to whom sympathy is due.

As state-level systems welded formerly independent tribes into an integrated society, they made lavish use of symbolic systems. Monumental architecture is one of the most common markers of emerging state-level systems. The monuments served as an excuse to mobilize masses of laborers in a common project and as the centerpiece of mass rituals afterward. They symbolized a common religion and usually a common political system. The symbolic unity of the early state — as for many later empires — may often have been as much the unity of the elite as the unity of society as a whole. Elites often have little sympathy for the lower classes, and often the sentiment is reciprocated. Complex societies always encapsulate tribal-scale units that maintain varying degrees of autonomy and resistance against the hegemony of elite institutions. Nevertheless, common religion and common nation often count for a lot. The humble are more or less reconciled to their lot, elites are more or less paternalistic, and society lurches along despite having a far less than perfect moral system. Often, independent societies are knitted together by international institutions of some real force. The ancient Greeks fought zealously to maintain the independence of their poleis, but they had enough common institutions to collectively resist a Persian invasion and later to follow Alexander on his conquests. The great world religions likewise support institutions that incorporate people from diverse societies into a related set of moral communities.

At the same time, symbolic systems evolve rather quickly and easily. New dialects grow up on social fault lines (Labov 2001). Religious heresies are often a tool of the oppressed and are never entirely suppressed, even by such institutions as the Catholic Inquisition or modern secret police. The recent rise of many varieties of fundamentalism is a case in point (Marty and Appleby 1991). Rodney Stark, the prominent iconoclastic sociologist of religion, has mounted an impressive empirical defense of both the functionality and dysfunctionality of fundamentalist-style religious communities (Stark 2003, 1997; Finke and Stark 1992; Stark and Bainbridge 1996).

As Darwin understood, moral progress is never guaranteed. Why not? First, human communities are still subject, as we have seen, to multi-level selection. Small-scale subcommunities are often very successful at socializing their offspring and just plain supporting "natural" increase. Anabaptists are a good example. Thus, the evolution of smaller-scale social units is always tending to undermine larger-scale ones. Second, humans appear to have a strong innate need to be part of a functional small-scale community. If the larger-scale community fails to provide such attachments, smaller-scale organizations with narrower definitions of patriotism will evolve to fill such needs. "Nation" and "tribe" are always in competition for our loyalties (Garthwaite 1993). Sympathy tends to cause us to favor more inclusive systems, but patriotism tends to demand a narrower calculus of friend and foe.

The great moral problem of our time is how to grow larger-scale loyalties to fit the fact that the world is now so famously a global village, while at the same time creating tribal-scale units that reassure us that we belong to a social system with a human face. The existence of weapons of mass destruction and the need to manage important aspects of the environment as a global commons threaten catastrophe if we fail in this project. Persuasive humanistic and other universalistic perspectives in the spirit of Darwin are not far to seek (Coon 2000). The problem is that only a relatively small elite is so persuaded. Even in the most enlightened European countries, internationalism risks a nationalistic reaction. Stark and Bainbridge make the case that secularly and religiously liberal communities in the West are marked by a barely latent demand for tribal identities, manifest in relatively high levels of interest in cults even in the most liberal regions (1996).

If our work-around analysis is correct, a liberalism that does not make ample provision for satisfying tribal-scale loyalties will fail. We have evolutionary debts to individual autonomy, family, and tribe that must be paid. Utopian schemes fail by ignoring these debts, and evil empires flourish by exploiting them. The key is somehow a "federal" world system that encourages small-scale loyalties under a system of legitimate rule of law that enforces mutual tolerance of tribes and nations. On the positive side, tribes have brought families into such systems and nations have effectively bound tribes together. Anthropologist Christopher Boehm (1996) and sociologist Jonathan Turner (1995) note that both simple and complex societies have potent collective decision-making systems to apply to large-scale, deliberate cultural change (constitutional conventions are a good example). On the negative side, universalists have clearly understood the basic problem of bringing nations under an international rule of law since the disaster of World War I, yet progress continued to lag throughout the entire twentieth century behind the growth of threats to the global village. The failure so far of the first reigning superpower since Great Britain in the nineteenth century to lead the establishment of a legitimate "New World Order" is a troubling disgrace. Universalists have an epoch-making piece of difficult work cut out for them — American universalists first among them.

The Parable of the Argentine Ant

We have presented a picture of human society as an evolutionary system that seems to have defied an evolutionary law of gravity. W. D. Hamilton's theory of inclusive fitness says, in effect, that love, empathy, and altruism will be drastically undersupplied by evolutionary processes. Natural selection must discount aid to others by the coefficient of genetic relatedness. This vicious constraint on the potential for the evolution of morality exists despite the fact that in principle altruism could be favored any time its fitness benefits exceed its costs. Given that the closest relationship most organisms have to one another is ½, and that we only have this level of relationship with a handful of other individuals, a staggering number of altruistic deals in the world go begging according to this theory. And so, mainly, it seems to be.

As with gravity, Hamilton's rule cannot be defied, only finessed. Flight is possible by counteracting gravity with other principles of physics; so too with the evolution of moral systems. A relative handful of species, such as ourselves and the social insects, have found various means to make extraordinary altruism fly (Genet 1997). The highest-flying case of social evolution by some standards is a curious one, the Argentine ant (Holway, Suarez, and Case 1998). In its homeland, the Argentine ant is an unremarkable species more or less obeying Hamilton's rule. Unrelated colonies fight ant wars in the familiar fashion. Hitchhiking on human commerce, however, Argentine ants made their way to California, the Mediterranean, and Australia. In each case, the number of founding colonies was so small that genetic variation for colony-recognition odors was minimal. Hence, even colonies that are completely unrelated cannot recognize one another as distinct. Every Argentine ant is a perfect saint as far as other Argentine ants are concerned. The dividend for such inadvertent sainthood is about a twofold increase in colony productivity, making Argentine ants the most successful ants in their adopted homelands. Our children have grown up without ever seeing an ant war around our California homes. Argentine ants have driven other species extinct in most urban habitats and are a major household pest.

Humans are not unlike Argentine ants. We are not so perfectly cooperative as they, but our genius at technology and social organization more than makes up for our fractiousness. If God made us, perhaps he has reason to regret it! The explosive growth of our population and our technology has created dire threats to ourselves and the rest of the planet; we are a pest that threatens to put every other in the dark.

The Argentine ants will presumably gradually evolve colony-recognition odors and vanish into the background. No known mechanism can prolong their extraordinary defiance of Hamilton's rule or extend it beyond their own species. Humans are a different story. In the last ten millennia we have stumbled and staggered forward on our uncertain adventure of moral progress. We routinely, if unpredictably, unreliably, and sometimes foolishly, love dogs, cats, foreign friends, "man" as a whole, gods, and nature. Moral progress is merely a matter of repeating the same tricks that we have used in the past to overcome slavery and similar evils. Universalists — Buddha, Christ, Confucius, Jefferson, Darwin, and so many others — light the way. In an age of weapons of mass destruction, global climate change, and the mass extinction of other species, our collective minds should be well concentrated on the problem. Modern evolution tells a coherent scientific story that takes us back to the origins of the universe. Until the evolution of human sympathy and our species' unique potential to extend sympathy without limits by means of political and ethical action, nothing like our moral communities existed on the face of the earth. We are privileged to participate in the world's first true adventure. Awesome dangers lie on our path. We have not and will not escape all of them. But we are not helpless pawns in the evolutionary game as every species before us has been. Individual by individual, tribe by tribe, nation by nation we have the prospect of passing, by the exercise of a steadfast commitment to sympathy, to a better future by our efforts — mother Nature willing!

REFERENCES

Abanes, Richard. 2002. *One Nation under Gods: A History of the Mormon Church.* New York: Four Walls Eight Windows.

Alexander, Richard D. 1987. *The Biology of Moral Systems.* Hawthorne, N.Y.: A. de Gruyter.

Alland, Alexander. 1985. *Human Nature, Darwin's View.* New York: Columbia University Press.

Armstrong, Edward A. 1973. *Saint Francis: Nature Mystic. The Derivation and Significance of the Nature Stories in the Franciscan Legend.* Hermeneutics, studies in the history of religions series, vol. 2. Berkeley: University of California Press.

Bannister, Robert C. 1979. *Social Darwinism: Science and Myth in Anglo-American Social Thought.* Philadelphia: Temple University Press.

Bettinger, R. L., and M. A. Baumhoff. 1982. The numic spread: Great Basin cultures in competition. *American Antiquity* 47, no. 3:485-503.

Birdsell, J. B. 1953. Some environmental and cultural factors influencing the structuring of Australian aboriginal populations. *The American Naturalist* 87:171-207.

Boehm, Christopher. 1996. Emergency decisions, cultural-selection mechanics, and group selection. *Current Anthropology* 37, no. 5:763-93.

———. 1999. *Hierarchy in the Forest: The Evolution of Egalitarian Behavior.* Cambridge, Mass.: Harvard University Press.

Bowler, Peter J. 1993. *Biology and Social Thought, 1850-1914.* Berkeley: Office for History of Science and Technology, University of California at Berkeley.

Boyd, Robert, Herbert Gintis, Samuel Bowles, and Peter J. Richerson. 2003. The evolution of altruistic punishment. *Proceedings of the National Academy of Sciences (USA)* 100:3531-35.

Boyd, Robert, and Peter J. Richerson. 1985. *Culture and the Evolutionary Process.* Chicago: University of Chicago Press.

———. 1996. Why culture is common but cultural evolution is rare. *Proceedings of the British Academy* 88:73-93.

———. 2002. Group beneficial norms can spread rapidly in a structured population. *Journal of Theoretical Biology* 215:287-96.

Burrow, J. W. 1966. *Evolution and Society: A Study in Victorian Social Theory.* Cambridge: Cambridge University Press.

Campbell, Donald T. 1975. On the conflicts between biological and social evolution and between psychology and moral tradition. *American Psychologist* 30, no. 12:1103-26.

———. 1983. The two distinct routes beyond kin selection to ultrasociality: Implications for the humanities and social sciences. In *The Nature of Prosocial Development: Theories and Strategies,* ed. D. L. Bridgeman. New York: Academic Press.

Cavalli-Sforza, Luigi L., and Marcus W. Feldman. 1981. *Cultural Transmission and Evolution: A Quantitative Approach.* Monographs in Population Biology, vol. 16. Princeton, N.J.: Princeton University Press.

Coon, Carleton S. 2000. *Culture Wars and the Global Village: A Diplomat's Perspective.* Amherst, N.Y.: Prometheus.

Darwin, Charles. 1845. Journal of researches into the natural history and geology of the countries visited during the voyage of H.M.S. Beagle round the world, under the command of Capt. Fitz Roy, R.N. London: John Murray.

Darwin, Charles. 1859. *On the Origin of Species by Means of Natural Selection, or, The Preservation of Favoured Races in the Struggle for Life.* London: John Murray.

Darwin, Charles. [1871] 1874. *The Descent of Man and Selection in Relation to Sex.* Second ed. 2 vols. New York: American Home Library.

[Dawkins, W. B.]. 1871. Review of *The Descent of Man and Selection in Relation to Sex* by Charles Darwin, *Contributions to the Theory of Natural Selection* by A. R.

Wallace, and *On the Genesis of Species* by St. George Mivart. *The Edinburgh Review or Critical Journal* (July): 195-235.

de Waal, Frans. 2000. *Chimpanzee Politics: Power and Sex among Apes*. Rev. ed. Baltimore: Johns Hopkins University Press.

Desmond, Adrian J. 1989. *The Politics of Evolution: Morphology, Medicine, and Reform in Radical London, Science and Its Conceptual Foundations*. Chicago: University of Chicago Press.

Dunbar, R. I. M. 1993. Coevolution of neocortical size, group size and language in humans. *Behavioral and Brain Sciences* 16:681-735.

Eibl-Eibesfeld, I. 1982. Warfare, man's indoctrinability, and group selection. *Zeitschrift fur Tierpsychologie* 67:177-98.

Enard, W., M. Przeworski, S. E. Fisher, C. S. L. Lai, V. Wiebe, T. Kitano, A. P. Monaco, and S. Paabo. 2002. Molecular evolution of FOXP2, a gene involved in speech and language. *Nature* 418, no. 6900:869-72.

Finke, Roger, and Rodney Stark. 1992. *The Churching of America, 1776-1990: Winners and Losers in Our Religious Economy*. New Brunswick, N.J.: Rutgers University Press.

Garthwaite, Gene R. 1993. Reimagined internal frontiers: Tribes and nationalism — Bakhtiyari and Kurds. In *Russia's Muslim Frontiers: New Directions in Cross-Cultural Analysis*, ed. D. F. Eickelman. Bloomington: Indiana University Press.

Genet, Russell M. 1997. *The Chimpanzees Who Would Be Ants: A Unified Scientific Story of Humanity*. Commack, N.Y.: Nova Science.

Gruber, Howard E. 1974. *Darwin on Man: A Psychological Study of Scientific Creativity*. New York: E. P. Dutton.

Hamilton, William D. 1964. Genetic evolution of social behavior I, II. *Journal of Theoretical Biology* 7, no. 1:1-52.

———. 1975. Innate social aptitudes of man: An approach from evolutionary genetics. In *Biosocial Anthropology*, ed. Robin Fox. New York: Wiley.

Hammerstein, Peter, ed. 2003. *Genetic and Cultural Evolution of Cooperation*. Cambridge, Mass.: MIT Press.

Henrich, Joseph. Forthcoming. Demography and cultural evolution: Why adaptive cultural processes produced maladaptive losses in Tasmania. *American Antiquity*.

Henrich, Joseph, and Robert Boyd. 1998. The evolution of conformist transmission and the emergence of between-group differences. *Evolution and Human Behavior* 19, no. 4:215-41.

———. 2001. Why people punish defectors — Weak conformist transmission can stabilize costly enforcement of norms in cooperative dilemmas. *Journal of Theoretical Biology* 208, no. 1:79-89.

Heyes, Cecilia M., and Bennett G. Galef Jr. 1996. *Social Learning in Animals: The Roots of Culture*. San Diego: Academic Press.

Hodgson, Geoffrey M. 2004. Social Darwinism in Anglophone Academia. Intended for *Politics, Philosophy and Economics*.

Hofstadter, Richard. 1945. *Social Darwinism in American Thought, 1860-1915.* Philadelphia: University of Pennsylvania Press.

Holway, D. A., A. V. Suarez, and T. J. Case. 1998. Loss of intraspecific aggression in the success of a widespread invasive social insect. *Science* 282 (October 30): 949-52.

Hostetler, John Andrew. 1993. *Amish Society.* Fourth ed. Baltimore: Johns Hopkins University Press.

Ingold, Tim. 1986. *Evolution and Social Life.* Cambridge: Cambridge University Press.

Kaessmann, H., and S. Paabo. 2002. The genetical history of humans and the great apes. *Journal of Internal Medicine* 251:1-18.

Kiester, A. Ross. 1996/1997. Aesthetics of biodiversity. *Human Ecology Review* 3:151-57.

Klein, R. G. 1999. *The Human Career: Human Biological and Cultural Origins.* Second ed. Chicago: University of Chicago.

Labov, William. 2001. *Principles of Linguistic Change: Social Factors.* Malden, Mass.: Blackwell.

Marty, Martin E., and R. Scott Appleby. 1991. *Fundamentalisms Observed.* Chicago: University of Chicago Press.

McBrearty, S., and A. S. Brooks. 2000. The revolution that wasn't: A new interpretation of the origin of modern human behavior. *Journal of Human Evolution* 39, no. 5:453-563.

North, Douglass Cecil, and Robert Paul Thomas. 1973. *The Rise of the Western World: A New Economic History.* Cambridge: Cambridge University Press.

Ostrom, Elinor. 1990. *Governing the Commons: The Evolution of Institutions for Collective Action.* Cambridge: Cambridge University Press.

Rappaport, Roy A. 1979. *Ecology, Meaning, and Religion.* Richmond Calif.: North Atlantic Books.

Richards, Robert J. 1987. *Darwin and the Emergence of Evolutionary Theories of Mind and Behavior.* Chicago: University of Chicago Press.

Richerson, Peter J., and Robert Boyd. 1998. The evolution of human ultrasociality. In *Indoctrinability, Ideology, and Warfare: Evolutionary Perspectives,* ed. I. Eibl-Eibesfeldt and F. K. Salter. New York: Berghahn Books.

————. 1999. Complex societies: The evolutionary origins of a crude superorganism. *Human Nature — An Interdisciplinary Biosocial Perspective* 10, no. 3:253-89.

————. 2001. Institutional evolution in the Holocene: The rise of complex societies. In *The Origin of Human Social Institutions,* ed. W. G. Runciman. Oxford: Oxford University Press.

Richerson, Peter J., Robert Boyd, and Joseph Henrich. 2003. The cultural evolution and cooperation. In *Genetic and Cultural Evolution of Cooperation,* ed. P. Hammerstein. Berlin: MIT Press.

Rightmire, G. P. 1997. Deep roots for the Neanderthals. *Nature* 389 (30 October): 917-18.

Rodseth, Lars, Richard W. Wrangham, A. M. Harrigan, and Barbara B. Smuts. 1991. The human community as a primate society. *Current Anthropology* 32, no. 3:221-54.

Rogers, A. R., and L. B. Jorde. 1995. Genetic evidence on modern human origins. *Human Biology* 67:1-36.

Sober, Elliott, and David Sloan Wilson. 1998. *Unto Others: The Evolution and Psychology of Unselfish Behavior*. Cambridge, Mass.: Harvard University Press.

Soltis, Joseph, Robert Boyd, and Peter J. Richerson. 1995. Can group-functional behaviors evolve by cultural group selection? An empirical test. *Current Anthropology* 36, no. 3:473-94.

Stark, Rodney. 1997. *The Rise of Christianity: How the Obscure, Marginal Jesus Movement Became the Dominant Religious Force in the Western World in a Few Centuries*. San Francisco: HarperCollins.

————. 2003. *For the Glory of God: How Monotheism Led to Reformations, Science, Witch-hunts, and the End of Slavery*. Princeton, N.J.: Princeton University Press.

Stark, Rodney, and William Sims Bainbridge. 1996. *Religion, Deviance, and Social Control*. New York: Routledge.

Sulloway, Frank J. 1996. *Born to Rebel: Birth Order, Family Dynamics, and Creative Lives*. New York: Pantheon Books.

Tomasello, Michael. 1996. Do apes ape? In *Social Learning in Animals: The Roots of Culture*, ed. C. M. Heyes and B. G. Galef Jr. San Diego: Academic Press.

Turner, Jonathan H. 1995. *Macrodynamics: Toward a Theory on the Organization of Human Populations*. New Brunswick, N.J.: Rutgers University Press.

Tylor, Edward B. 1871. *Primitive Culture: Research into the Development of Mythology, Philosophy, Religion, Art, and Custom*. London: Murray.

Whiten, A., J. Goodall, W. C. McGrew, T. Nishida, V. Reynolds, Y. Sugiyama, C. E. G. Tutin, R. W. Wrangham, and C. Boesch. 1999. Cultures in chimpanzees. *Nature* 399 (17 June): 682-85.

Whiten, Andrew, and Deborah Custance. 1996. Studies of imitation in chimpanzees and children. In *Social Learning in Animals: The Roots of Culture*, ed. C. M. Heyes and B. G. Galef Jr. San Diego: Academic Press.

Williams, George C. 1966. *Adaptation and Natural Selection: A Critique of Some Current Evolutionary Thought*. Princeton, N.J.: Princeton University Press.

Wilson, Edward O. 1975. *Sociobiology: The New Synthesis*. Cambridge, Mass.: Harvard University Press.

3. Explaining the Prosocial Side of Moral Communities

Christopher Boehm

Introduction

If one wishes to reduce moral behavior to its naturalistic essentials, the best place to start, anthropologically, is with the *moral community* as this was defined by Émile Durkheim. Durkheim (1933) abandoned not only traditional philosophical approaches that focused on abstract entities like Truth and Virtue, but also religious approaches that placed ultimate moral authority with God. Instead, he tried to describe scientifically what people actually do when they make and act upon moral decisions, doing so as local groups that are trying to cope with deviant behavior.

Durkheim was talking about the moral authority of the group, and a key concept in his work was the *conscience collective*. This adds up to a local community's sense of what is desirable and undesirable in human affairs. Sir Henry Maine ([1861] 1931) had already identified these behavioral codes as "mores" (see also Kluckhohn 1952), and Durkheim referred to the groups that produced them as "moral communities." Durkheim has been criticized for being a "functionalist" and for focusing too heavily on the negative abilities of such groups to punish deviants, but in fact he put his finger on one of the basics of human life. Human beings are in part anti-social (see Aberle et al. 1950), and only the entire collectivity has the power to curb serious deviants whose predatory acts would otherwise destroy group life.

In effect, Durkheim founded the modern study of social control (e.g., Black 1984, 1998; Edgerton 1975). In sociology and anthropology, studies of social control have tended to focus simultaneously on the deviants whose nefarious behaviors give rise to proscriptions in the first place, and on the capability of any human group to punish and control such deviants. In all its negativity, this proscriptive, punitive side of controlling people socially has been well described, and it has been systematically researched (e.g., Selby 1974).

Here, I shall turn over the coin and address the prosocial side of this same moral process, which not only is much less studied but is inadequately taken into account by evolutionists interested in questions of ethics. I shall be arguing that what can be known about the *positive* side of moral communities can be quite useful, as a means of developing working hypotheses about natural selection and the levels at which it operates for humans. Specifically, it is relevant to the issue of group selection.

The question of levels of selection has recently become prominent in evolutionary biology (see Sober and Wilson 1998; D. S. Wilson 2002). Still pertinent to any such discussion is the long-standing insistence by most evolutionary biologists that natural selection takes place only among individuals *within* groups, on the basis of inclusive fitness (see E. O. Wilson 1975). This has been coupled with a concomitant, long-standing *disinterest* by most biologists (e.g., Dawkins 1976) in what has become known as "group selection." Obviously, the positive side of social control would be much easier to explain if group selection were operating to support altruistic traits — including those by which individuals promote group reproductive interests at the expense of their own. Sober and Wilson (1998) have pointed out that group functionality seems to be a conscious concern of nonliterate people, and later in this chapter we will revisit their assumptions and propose further arguments in this direction.

Within-group selection supports selfish and nepotistic behaviors, and, in what sometimes suggests a precarious balancing act, sociobiologists try to explain all apparent human generosity and cooperation as though it were genetically one hundred percent selfish or nepotistic (e.g., E. O. Wilson 1975, 1978; see also Alexander 1971, 1974, 1987; Alexander and Borgia 1978; Ridley 1996; Wright 1994). They cite powerful mathematical models of gene selection process, which in theory make it highly improbable that group selection forces could ever become strong enough to "win" at the level of supporting traits that are genetically "altruistic" (see Williams 1966).

This conclusion applies to any species whose cooperative groups consist of individuals many of whom are unrelated — but not to social insects or naked mole rats, whose apparent "altruism" is nepotistically explained by kin selection theory. In this context, it bears mentioning that the hunting bands that evolved our nature for us were surely composed of both related and unrelated families (see Boehm 2000a), as with bands today (Kelly 1995). This makes much of their sharing genetically altruistic, rather than nepotistic, whenever the sharing is not fully reciprocated over time.

On the face of it, mammalian gene pools should not contain significant levels of altruistic genes. But elsewhere (Boehm 1996, 1997, 2000a, 2000b), I have argued that this may not hold for our species, in particular, because our morally based cultural practices profoundly influence selection mechanics in ways that favor group selection. Here I would like to elaborate a different kind of argument, to make a similar point. Let us begin with a type of question that many have raised.

Why is it that people risk their lives to pull strangers out of icy waters, or even pull a powerful and hysterically floundering chimpanzee out of the moat that surrounds its zoo enclosure? Why do we make anonymous donations to feed hungry children in strange lands? There are many suggestive questions like these, and generally it is possible to contrive a scientific answer that reduces the underlying dispositions and psychological motives to ones that are either selfish or at best nepotistic. For instance, people give money for university buildings not out of altruism, but because their name appears on the donated facility and their community therefore rewards them with respect. What if the donation is anonymous? In that case, they are being generous not to help others, but because giving makes them feel good — which is "selfish." Or is it?

These arguments present a semantic quagmire (see Boehm 1979) that we shall not enter here. I should mention, however, that if being altruistic *feels* good, feeling good could be the reward that natural selection built into our psyche to make us altruistically sacrifice our individual or familial reproductive interests for those of the group as a whole. Thus, an act that ultimately seems to be "selfish," psychologically, could be "altruistic" by evolutionary definition (see Sober and Wilson 1998). What is clear to common sense, though, is that (1) humans are basically quite selfish; (2) they also are strongly programmed to invest in and protect their offspring and other close kin; and (3) sometimes they do, in fact, reduce their personal chances of reproductive success in order to augment those of a genetic stranger who is a group member — and therefore is a genetic competitor in the Darwinian sense.

The third, altruistic type of behavior has remained an ultimate mystery, insofar as only a sizable minority of the biological community are willing to seriously entertain the group-selection hypotheses (e.g., Boehm 1997; Wilson and Sober 1994) that best explain the continuance of such traits in human gene pools. This chapter is an attempt to further the application of group selection theory — or of any other theory that might help to explain such traits — in trying to understand human moral communities and how they work.

Why Mistrust Common Sense?

Often, evolutionary theory accords with common sense. When we see a winged bird, mammal, or insect, we consider the past environments in question, and then we look for selection pressures that would have supported the development of such features — for instance, a need to quickly cover a lot of territory or escape from predators. We then build scientific hypotheses to explain how the trait in question — wings — could have evolved. The constraint upon such hypothesizing is selection mechanics: the workings of natural selection as outlined by Darwin and amended through the New Synthesis (e.g., E. O. Wilson 1975).

Darwin (1859, 1871) used scientific common sense to adduce his selection model from what species actually do. Most behaviors he was able to reconcile quite nicely with selection taking place among individuals, not groups. In *The Descent of Man*, however, he did raise the issue of group selection because he was puzzled about the extreme altruism that is shown by humans when they engage in patriotic self-sacrifice. His common sense led him to seek a model to explain this, and the model was a genetically naïve group-selection one.

In contrast, what contemporary sociobiologists (e.g., Williams 1966) seem to have done basically is to weigh what common sense and their models are telling them, and then go with the models over common sense. If a model tells them that group selection is too feeble to make any difference, this means that genuinely disinterested unselfishness cannot exist in the real world — in spite of the fact that human beings do jump into icy waters and so forth. They take pride in the fact that *science* leads them to conclusions that contradict common sense (e.g., E. O. Wilson 1975), and in general they seem to be right regarding social mammals. But for humans I suspect they may be wrong in the case of altruism.

Biologists are correct in holding that group selection can be ruled out for any social species that exhibits very robust individual variation at the within-group level, and extremely modest variation between groups, along with very low rates of extinction for groups. This is because variation (along with extinction rates) drives natural selection. But as I have shown (Boehm 1997), humans have unique, morally based ways of reducing within-group variation and augmenting it at the between-group level. The problem is that it is quite difficult to actually quantify these differences in the context of selection scenarios that are applied to the socio-demographics of Upper Paleolithic band life (e.g., Boehm 1997), even though progress is being made in this direction (Bowles et al. 2003) through sophisticated use of computer simulations.

The question is, where do we get our working hypotheses? Is it better to start with a modern mathematical model of gene selection, or to start with common sense as Darwin did? In my opinion, we need to look more carefully at what humans actually do in the way of expressing traits involving compassion and generosity, and see where this leads us — without being *unduly* concerned with what particular existing models seem to be telling us. We must see exactly what kind of a circumstantial case can be made for genetic altruism, in a species that obviously inherits a major dose of selfishness and a substantial dose of nepotism through its "nature." The stronger this case, the greater the need will be either to further re-examine contemporary theoretical models (e.g., Sober and Wilson 1998), or, equally important, to carefully scrutinize the assumptions that are made when these models are applied to actual cases.

I must quickly say that old-fashioned group selectionists (e.g., Wynne-Edwards 1962) used common sense without respecting the available models, and they got themselves into serious trouble (see Williams 1966). That explains why the term "group selection" became anathema to biologists for three decades. But times have changed. With respect to examining the models themselves, Sober and Wilson (1998) have already pointed out some problems involved with understandings of George Price's equations, and the evolutionary biology community is still digesting this critique and other criticisms of theirs as I write. As a result, there seems to be an increasing willingness to consider multi-level selection scenarios. We must keep this in mind, as I examine prosocial attitudes and behaviors as evidence that natural selection in fact might support some genetic altruism.

The Moral Community

Every anthropologist who returns from a year or two of living in a small nonliterate community will acknowledge that Durkheim was right, that wherever people live in small, face-to-face groups there does seem to be a group mind at work. I emphasize this because Durkheim has been widely criticized for being a methodological collectivist, that is, for over-emphasizing the psychic unity of moral communities (see Black 1984). Because methodologically individualistic approaches have been dominant when contemporary evolutionists model cooperation (e.g., Axelrod and Hamilton 1981) it is important, up front, to insist that methodological individualism and methodological collectivism are merely *perspectives,* used to make sense of actual behavior. Neither is intrinsically "right" or "wrong."

Durkheim's psychically unified moral community is quite palpable — if you actually live in one. What anthropologists in the field encounter is a group of people who all know one another by name and also by reputation (e.g., Haviland 1977), and who basically share a set of moral values. We are universally struck with the gossiping that takes place in such communities, and with the ability of these groups to put pressure on deviants (see Edgerton 1975). The communities in question are bands, tribes, villages, towns, urban neighborhoods, street gangs, and so on. They are all local communities, in which a serious deviant will be known by everybody. The same was true of Upper Paleolithic hunting bands (Boehm 2000a).

In fact, the moral community is a human universal. Every group has its moral code, and its means of exerting social pressure or taking out serious deviants. And all such communities have a set of values that define characteristics deemed to be desirable or undesirable in human beings. There are also proscriptions, which define specific types of bad behavior. Another universal is that all of these communities engage in gossip, as people's reputations are sifted and the doings of potential culprits are carefully investigated. Another is that they all engage in social sanctioning: this ranges from being a bit cool upon greeting, to directly criticizing or ridiculing deviants, to ostracizing such people, to ejecting them from the group, and even to their execution by the group (e.g., Boehm 1993). These are elements of the small punitive, moral community as Durkheim (1933) conceived it when he founded the study of social control. On a grander scale, our formal legal systems have added written moral codes, specialist means of detection, and formal systems of manipulation or punishment. This has been true since the Law of Hammurabi in ancient Mesopotamia.

It can be assumed that all of these social constants stem from human nature, but one can be more specific than that. To some degree human beings share with the other three African great apes some fundamental behavior traits that underlie social control. These include an ability to communicate socially and an ability to form defensive coalitions — which come into play when disliked "deviants" become intolerable to the rest of the group (Boehm 1999, 2000a). In addition there is *fear*, which works at two different levels. People fear the scary predators in their midst, and this leads them to gang up against and intimidate or eliminate these deviants. Fortunately, the predators, too, are capable of fear: they usually respect the collective powers of the group and — again, usually — they modify their behavior accordingly.

There are other aspects of human nature, shared to a significant degree with other mammalian social species (Boehm 2000a), that come into play insofar as in humans they make certain *deviant* behaviors extremely easy to learn. Social control was invented and is constantly being reinvented because human group members are prone to aggressiveness that leads to bullying and homicide, to greed that leads to theft and deceit, and to lust that results in rape or incest. These highly antisocial behaviors damage the interests of others, and they stimulate fear, and sometimes revulsion. Human moral codes universally disapprove of them, and human groups invariably form alliances of the entire group to prevent too much bullying and cheating.

The Natural Selection of "Moralistic Aggression"

This depiction of misbehavior and its control by sometimes-desperate human groups properly focuses on the "negative" side of human nature, that is, on the needs of local communities to be vigilant, judgmental, and aggressive (hence, "moralistic aggression") in policing or eliminating their more dangerous or disruptive deviants (see Trivers 1971). Is it possible to construct this as simply a matter of nepotistically selfish individuals forming expedient coalitions in order to collectively police selfish predators who could damage them and their families, with nothing but "selfishness" operating on either side? This would fit with the monolithic type of sociobiological paradigm that Robert Trivers is identified with. Alternatively, this same collective behavior can be seen as also requiring *group* selection of altruistic traits (see Sober and Wilson 1998) if it is assumed that certain individuals are taking the lead in defending group interests. If they are making personal sacrifices in order to implement social control for the good of everyone, then they are genetic altruists.

Actually, there are several good reasons to suggest that group selection is at work. One is that human groups will have varying success in controlling deviants, and groups that police the best will cooperate better and thereby out-compete those which don't. This would feed group selection exactly the kind of phenotypic variation it needs. Another reason, mentioned above, is that there may well be net altruistic costs to individuals who take the lead in sanctioning.

There is also the problem of getting others to join in the sanctioning process to make it unanimous, and this poses an obvious free-rider problem. What about an individual who avoids risk by shirking from sanctioning a dangerous deviant, and what about energetic costs to good citizens who go out of their way to influence or punish such defectors? The latter are expending their energy for the good of the group, and such altruism is best explained by group selection.

These roles have emerged strongly in game-theory experiments (see Gintis 2001), which include cross-cultural work (Gintis et al. 2003; Heinrich et al. 2001) and work done in modern cultures (e.g., Fehr and Gächter 2000; Fehr et al. 2002; Fehr and Rockenbach 2003). What Samuel Bowles and Herbert Gintis (1998; see also Gintis 2000) call "strong reciprocity" emerges

clearly from all of this work: people crack down on those who fail to reciprocate, and expend energy in doing so.

In looking at the hunter-gatherer literature, strong reciprocity emerges
most clearly when individuals are punished because they cheat on what,
among nomads, is a universal system of mostly equalized large game sharing
(see Kelly 1995). Let me provide an ethnographic illustration. In one of our
best anthropological descriptions of social control in action, Colin Turnbull
(1961) tells how one Mbuti Pygmy hunter cheats during a collective net hunt.
He gains meat unfairly and shares it with a couple of allied families, but he is
discovered and the rest of the band criticize and ridicule him, and when he
tries to lie they seriously threaten him with exile. After he admits his guilt, the
ill-gotten meat is given over to the rest of the band.

Bands always make important group decisions by consensus, and even
though it is true that there was some individual division of labor in applying
those sanctions, it was clear that the band had agreed about the nature of the
malfeasance and that people understood that they had the culprit at a serious
disadvantage because they were all ganging up on him. Even women and
younger males dared to join in subjecting this major hunter to ridicule, so the
perceived element of personal risk seems to have been minimal in this case.
But in another case, one involving the !Kung Bushmen, people engaging in
social control of a formidable deviant were at risk of serious injury, or worse
(see Lee 1979).

The Pygmy consensus was not absolutely perfect. The culprit's close allies
did not rise to his defense, nor did they join in the sanctioning. Instead, they
remained mute. With these allies "abstaining," however, an essentially con-
sensual act of social control was possible; had they rallied to his side, there
would have been intra-group conflict rather than an instance of morally
based sanctioning by the group, and in fact the group might have split.

It is worth noting that in Turnbull's detailed account no hostility was directed at the "abstainers," who had not participated in the actual act of cheating but who refrained from actively joining in to put on the social pressure.
Keep in mind that bands tend to be equilibrated at just the right size for subsistence (see Kelly 1995), and this perceived benefit frequently influences hunter-
gatherers. The predictable intent was to correct one man's behavior, not to get
rid of him and his family, or worse, to lose him and several allied families. It is
in view of these political dynamics that I infer that by abstaining the culprit's
close allies were, in effect, going along with the sanctioning process.

A general anomaly we are left with is that among the type of hunter-
gatherer bands that forged our genes, the punishment of "nonpunishers"
does not seem to be prominent. In contrast, in the game-theory experiments

85

it crops up frequently. It is possible that the very strong drive to reach a group consensus that operates in bands either obscures this part of the strong-reciprocity process or else actually reduces its expression. But further research is needed in this area.

Of necessity this discussion has become a bit complicated, so let me state my hypothesis clearly. Ultimately, I believe that within-group gene selection goes a long way toward explaining the aggressive (and sometimes very punitive) side of social control, because fearful people are defending their individual and familial interests by banding together to instill fear in social predators and make them behave. There is a tendency to average out their risks and energetic effort because essentially the entire group has to behave as one, à la Durkheim, or else it can neither reach an effective decision to sanction nor safely implement that decision. Some individuals will be doing more for the group than others, however, so a group selection explanation is needed as well.

On the basis of common sense, we may further suggest, strongly, that group selection could be expected to support this punitive component of social control — be it altruistic, selectively neutral, or even sometimes beneficial at the individual level — because social control makes groups adaptive and because its effectiveness will vary from one group to the next. A band that is disrupted by uncontrolled deviance will reproduce poorly compared to a band that cooperates smoothly.

Although this may not amount to an actual smoking gun for Upper Paleolithic group selection, on the basis of common sense, and also on the basis of what can be adduced about the leveling of within-group phenotypic variance and free-rider suppression during the Upper Paleolithic (Boehm 1997), it can be taken as a very suggestive working hypothesis. Group selection could have operated significantly in supporting altruistic traits during a long period when the basic finishing touches were being put on human gene pools, and negative sanctioning would seem to fit with that level of selection because sanctioning acts involve individual altruism, and because some groups control their deviants much better than others.

Moral Ideals

I now describe the *positive* side of moral communities, which deals in rewards rather than in manipulative punishment or "elimination." This universal, unambiguously prosocial component of moral communities is not at all easy to explain "sociobiologically" (i.e., at the level of within-group selection), and for reasons I shall demonstrate it cries out, at the level of common sense, for group selection explanations.

Every human community has its substantive ideals about how a good person should behave (Boehm 2000a), and every human community shares some abstract ideals about positive "social entities" like cooperation and social harmony. But unfortunately anthropological descriptions of these positive features of moral communities tend to be highly generalized, whereas social control in its negative manifestations has captured the descriptive-ethnographic imagination time and time again, as in Robert Edgerton (1975) or in individual monographs such as *Zapotec Deviance* (Selby 1974) or *Gossip, Reputation, and Knowledge in Zinacantan* (Haviland 1977).

This disparity is no accident, for every anthropologist listens to gossip, does so for a living, as it were, and the preponderance of such indigenous "talk" does deal with people's moral deficits. Furthermore, we actually witness groups as they come down hard on serious deviants (e.g., Turnbull 1961; Boehm 1986), so the sheer drama of negative social control captures our imagination. For instance, Haviland's (1977) book on peasants is based on intensive collection of gossiping texts, and the great preponderance of such conversations deal with identification and evaluation of *negative* traits in others. This study is specific to a particular Mayan-speaking culture, so it would be unwise to generalize too quickly, but in fact any anthropologist reading the book will have a sense of *déja vu*. As another example, I spent two years living with a pastoral Serbian "tribe" in Montenegro (see Boehm 1986), and my impression, from hundreds of gossip sessions I listened to or was actively involved in, was that such "talk about people" tended strongly toward the negative. Interestingly, though, the people there had a special term for gossipers who concentrated *exclusively* on negative reports — and took malicious pleasure in doing so. This was an instance of the social control process acting on itself, as it were, for hyper-gossips were themselves the subject of negative "talk."

What I discovered, living in the Upper Moracha Tribe, was that even though the preponderance of "gossip items" were negative, meaning that they identified people who were breaking cultural prohibitions, the moral pillars of the community also received their due in terms of respect and praise. So social malfeasance was roundly condemned, but at the same time social harmony was being upheld and people who promoted it were commended. And because their reputations were good, it was easier for them to find high-quality spouses for their children or cooperation partners in subsistence. Being "good" pays off reproductively.

Sober and Wilson (1998) emphasize the cultural diversity of morals in their discussion of proscriptive norms, so I should mention that at least a few moral prohibitions seem to be universal (Boehm 2000a). For instance, all societies take a stand against cheating in a situation of cooperation, and against over-stepping legitimate political authority (Boehm 1999). Sober and Wilson also look to the positively phrased "prescriptions" that crop up in their randomized survey of twenty-five nonliterate cultures, making the case that people everywhere seem to be common-sense "functionalists." These positive mores included loyalty, conviviality, sharing with all community members, raising children properly, compromising in dispute settlements, and so on. All promote group functioning, and in fact there was a great vogue for functionalism in sociological theory (e.g., Aberle et al. 1950; Parsons and Shils 1952) and also in anthropological theory (e.g., Malinowski 1939; see also Edgerton 1992), which surely was stimulated in part by indigenous statements like these.

As Sober and Wilson (1998) point out, these prosocial mores contribute to human groups serving as positively functioning collectivities — and as units which lend themselves favorably to group selection (Sober and Wilson refer to this, technically, as "between-group selection"). Sober and Wilson are interested in human groups as candidates for group selection, and they nicely define the general problem I have been discussing here:

Evolutionary biologists are often forced to study the *products* of natural selection — adaptations — without having direct access to the actual *process* of natural selection, which occurred in the past. Methods exist to demonstrate that a trait is an adaptation, but the ultimate proof is to watch it evolve. Kettlewell's (1973) research on industrial melanism in moths earned its place in textbooks because it was among the first to document natural selection in action. More recent investigations — on Darwin's finches (Grant 1986) and other species — have monitored the process of natural selection in even more detail (reviewed by Endler 1986). Our survey and Boehm's more extensive research focus on the *products* of group selection — groups that seem to function as adaptive units. We claim that human social groups are so well designed at the group level that they must have evolved by group selection. (Sober and Wilson 1998, 191)

Sober and Wilson (1998, 191) add:

Except for a few hints about between-group replacement processes that we described earlier, we cannot produce the smoking gun of group selection in action. Kelly's analysis of the Nuer conquest is one such smoking gun —

a social system in the process of replacing another that is less adaptive at the level of large-scale groups. It is likely that the historical record contains many other examples that can be documented with equal or even more impressive detail. As Darwin (1871, p. 166) realized long ago, "at all times throughout the world tribes have supplanted other tribes."

I myself have examined the type of human group that evolved our nature for us — the Paleolithic nomadic hunting band — in the light of what is known about Darwinian selection, and my conclusion (no smoking gun!) was that by means of social control, these hunter-gatherers significantly modified the amount of phenotypic variation present, at both within-band and between-band levels (see Boehm 1997). Two very important effects were that individuals were leveled because of an egalitarian ethos, and that selfish cheaters were suppressed and, if necessary, punished or eliminated because fairness in sharing was so highly valued. Both made group selection better able to support altruistic traits because phenotypic variation was drastically reduced within bands (Boehm 1997).

My focus, there, was exclusively on punitive social control that cracked down on alpha-male bullies and cheaters on the meat-distribution system, and in terms of genetic modeling this crackdown was vitally important because it all but eliminated the "free-rider" problem as emphasized by Williams (1966). Here I will augment Sober and Wilson's (1998) survey of normative statements by ethnographers, to further evaluate the evolutionary implications of social control in its *positive* manifestations.

Evidence: Prosocial Norms and Responsiveness to Such Norms

In his presidential address to the American Psychological Association, Donald T. Campbell (1975; see also Campbell 1972, 1979, 1983) suggested that humans everywhere call for altruistic behavior on the part of group members, and he demonstrated (see also Campbell 1991) that the first six early civilizations all had such exhortations in their religious teachings. David Wilson (2002) has carried this work forward with respect to modern religion. I emphasize, however, that the underlying behavior tendencies were evolved in the Upper Paleolithic, by hunter-gatherers who were anatomically and culturally as modern as we are.

Sober and Wilson's (1998) survey of twenty-five randomly selected nonliterate cultures demonstrates that in both secular and religious contexts people everywhere hold up ideals of behavior to their fellows, as an approach that exactly complements the negative side of social control. For instance, all groups condemn noncooperativeness (including cheating), and at the same time they uphold being fair in cooperating for the welfare of all. The latter is a positive, prescriptive norm.

In my own larger but nonrandomized survey of several dozen band-and-tribal-level egalitarian societies (Boehm 1993), a similar division of labor was in evidence with respect to norms about leadership. In a nutshell, a bad leader was selfish, and overly aggressive, while a good leader was generous and unassuming. The ethnographic evidence shows that if the prohibitions against being selfishly aggressive are broken, the offending leader will be criticized, ridiculed, ostracized, expelled from the group, and even executed (see also Boehm 2000a). With regard to positively oriented prescriptions, it is more difficult to measure their effects. But good leaders appear to be responsive in that they are aware of these ideals and try to fulfill them.

Thus, it is all too clear that a cooperating group is aiding not only its own functionality but also the reproductive success of all its members (save one), when it assassinates a bully who acts only for himself. It is less obvious that a similar practical effect results from people constantly citing cooperative norms and socially elevating and trusting people who set aside selfish objectives to cooperate. Ethnographically, this positive reinforcement would seem to be *much* less obvious than the dramatic instance of a serious cheater's being reformed or a deviant group member's being physically eliminated (e.g., Boehm 2000a). There are good reasons to believe, however, that individuals are generally responsive to such messages, and that these messages have the effect of making individuals set aside their selfish interests in favor of the group even in the absence of negative social pressure or active punishment.

This brings up the issue of genetic altruism. As with gossiping, the efforts to positively influence group members would seem to have little or no net cost, so group selection may not be needed to explain prosocial sanctioning efforts by good citizens. Having a human nature that makes you *responsive* to such preaching results, however, in definite costs, because you are innately disposed to respond to social stimuli that steer you toward setting aside your own selfish prerogatives for the good of the group. Common sense calls for a group selection argument here, but what evidence is there that group selection has actually fashioned human nature so that selfish individuals are vulnerable to such messages?

One very good reason to believe this is that prosocial preaching seems to be a human universal. It seems unlikely that all people, everywhere, would be deliberately steering their fellows in the direction of prosocial behavior unless their fellows were responsive to such guidance. Another is that such preaching is aimed specifically at improvement of group social functioning. Such preaching takes place within families and kin groups, and it also takes place at the level of multi-family bands, and at all three levels it spurs cooperation and reduces maladaptive conflict. People obviously know what they are doing when they manipulate others to live up to social norms, so it can be said in this case that human intelligence is working hand in hand with natural selection at the group level. Wilson's (2002) work on institutionalized religion attests to the universality of this argument.

In this context, it is of interest that recently extant hunter-gatherers, and surely their predecessors in the Upper Paleolithic, all lived in *multi*-family groups. This makes group selection theory an excellent candidate for explaining these universal, prosocially oriented efforts to actively influence individuals to be less selfish and thereby promote local-group functionality.

Evidence: Conflict Intervention

Another type of commonsensical evidence that group selection may have acted on past human populations involves a different prosocial behavioral universal: everywhere, people work directly to control or "manage" the conflicts that arise in every human group. In the type of hunting band in which these attitudes and behaviors evolved, today we see solemn pronouncements that conflict is bad for the group, along with praise for social harmony, and we also see active and practical attempts to head off conflicts or control their deleterious effects.

These efforts are not punitive, for getting into a misunderstanding with someone is not necessarily immoral. People in nomadic hunting bands may try to distract those who are quarreling before things become serious, and they may exhort them not to quarrel and help them to reconcile (see Fry 2000). They may even set up nonlethal "duels" to expend negative energies in a contest whose rules include giving up on the conflict afterward; for instance, an Eskimo drum song contest (Balikci 1970) involves the entire band's facilitating a truly nasty verbal duel on the assumption that once spleen has been vented, on both sides, the parties will follow the group's wishes and set aside their grudges.

Another mode of intervention is for a third party to intercede physically. In hunting bands, with their strong aversion to authority, the band leader is in general a mere facilitator who demurely sums up group decisions after a consensus is reached (see Knauft 1991). Once in a while in an emergency, however, he may assume that he has the group's backing and intervene physically to try and separate two males who are getting into a fight. It is an understatement to call such behavior altruistic in the technical, genetic sense of the word, for when a man with so little authority steps into the middle of a fight he himself can be injured or killed (e.g., Lee 1979).

There is little doubt that this strong tendency to "manage conflicts," and to do so in ways that contribute to group functionality, is universal. At the level of immediate, practical motivations, the interventions are intentional. People in bands value having a larger band with more hunters, because the meat supply is steadier that way. They hate to see the size of the band diminished because this impairs subsistence, yet at the same time these people know what the other costs of conflict can be.

When a conflict escalates to a level where homicide is imminent, *usually* the band's headman feels impotent to stop it and the homicide takes place. Immediately, this reduces the band's population by one hunter, but there is further social damage because male relatives of the man who was killed will retaliate and kill the killer. This means the killer is obliged to flee his band (see Knauft 1991). Losing one hunter to homicide and a second to exile reduces the group's subsistence potential significantly, and that specter makes people work hard to stop conflicts preemptively. Preaching in favor of harmony is one way to do this — a generic methodology, as it were. A more immediate means of preemption is to intervene effectively when conflict looms, and head off what could be a social disaster.

Aside from practical coping, there is also an ultimate reason for all this preemption. By "ultimate," I mean that human nature is involved; and more generally, perhaps, the nature of all African great apes is relevant. Seven million years ago, humans had an African ancestor that they share with today's three other African great apes, and any behavior that the four extant species share can be assumed to be present in this Common Ancestor (see Wrangham 1987). Active conflict interventions are to be found in all four species (Boehm 1994, 1999); for instance, silverback gorillas use a hostile "pig grunt" to warn members of their harems not to quarrel, and they will intervene physically if need be (see Fossey 1983); chimpanzee alpha males display at those fighting in order to drive them apart, and sometimes use direct physical force to separate them (Boehm 1994); bonobos are far less studied, but fight interventions are reported anecdotally along similar lines.

Humans do this too. We have seen that hunter-gatherer bands have headmen who, in spite of their weak power positions, sometimes intervene physically. As human societies become larger, and more politically centralized, there are leaders who can wield some real authority in intervening in quarrels or in persuading the parties to compromise. The upshot of all this is that we can make a general assumption about the nature of our distant ancestor, about ourselves, and about all members of the direct evolutionary lineage that led from that ancestor to ourselves, including Upper Paleolithic hunter-gatherers. Throughout our evolutionary history, an aversiveness to conflict has been present, as a fundamental behavioral propensity that surely has been supported by natural selection.

Konrad Lorenz (1966) talks about a "Parliament of Instincts," and he identifies instances in which aggressive instincts have "co-evolved" with simple inhibitions that serve to keep aggression under control. Keep in mind that an individual whose aggressions are poorly controlled may not live too long himself. What has happened, in all four African great apes, is that the inhibition of individual aggressions has become relatively complex. In a stickleback fish, conflict is obviated by simple "releasing mechanisms" which enable a dyad to negotiate their territorial-boundary problems strictly on their own. In contrast, within their groups these four great apes (humans are included) expend their own energy to help others stop fighting — which makes for triadic behavior and, probably, genetic altruism. When the fish dyadically mediate their territorial conflicts, obviously individual reproductive success is the driving mechanism. When, however, an ape in his group stops feeding, takes some small risks, and expends some serious energy in stopping a fight between two other adults who are neither relatives nor political partners, we must seek some other explanation.

A strictly sociobiological theory — one that limits selection in humans to inclusive fitness — will have difficulty in explaining these third-party interventions, which in humans are not only costly to individuals, but are often useful to nonrelatives who in fact are the peacemaker's genetic competitors. Common sense tells us that here a group selection model might work nicely, for a moralistically cooperative group that is less perturbed by conflict can out-reproduce one ridden with dissension.

An Alternative or Co-explanation

If we imagine a single gene that accounts for all conflict interventions, the same group-beneficial behaviors might, in fact, be explained in the absence of group selection — but the explanation would be a bit circuitous (Boehm 1981; see also Simon 1990; J. Q. Wilson 1993). It would go as follows:

In all four of our great ape species, there are very good selfish (i.e., nepotistic) reasons for adults to control the conflicts of their own offspring, so that they do not destroy each other. In behaviorally flexible species that have brains large enough to "generalize," it seems possible that protectiveness toward closely bonded youngsters becomes generalized to *any* adult group member with whom a close social bond is shared — even if there is no tie of kinship (Boehm 2000a; see also J. Q. Wilson 1993). Helping nonkin in this way, though *somewhat* costly to the peacemaker's reproductive success, is by no means costly enough to erase the enormous gains that come from stopping fights among one's own offspring. Thus, the great ape/human approach to generic intervention in adult conflicts might be explained without any reference to group-selection processes: at the individual level it could be a *slightly* costly, "pleiotropic" side effect of nepotistic conflict resolution tendencies that protect offspring — and therefore bring enormous reproductive gains that easily offset the modest losses from assisting nonrelatives.

This simplified "piggybacking" explanation is based on simplified single-gene modeling, and undoubtedly there are a number of polygenes and pleiotropic genes involved. Nonetheless such a scenario could fully explain the adult conflict interventions of the other three African great apes (e.g., Boehm 1981, 2000a), whose general prospects for robust group selection seem to be much more modest than for humans because they lack social control. In humans, however, where a significant degree of group selection could have been operative in the Upper Paleolithic, costly third-party interventions would be still easier to explain because they so obviously benefit group functioning and, ultimately, group reproductive success. I emphasize that group selection and this nepotistic piggybacking mechanism could easily have been working together.

Conclusions

Orthodox sociobiological perspectives (Trivers 1971, 1972; E. O. Wilson 1975) inform a continuing insistence by many that selfish nepotism is the basis of all human behavior, including behaviors characteristic of moral communities. Here I have taken a detailed look at social control and conflict resolution with levels of natural selection in mind, and I have chosen to judiciously trust common sense as a means of arriving at working hypotheses that could lead to new insights about social evolution. As I summarize the findings, please keep in mind that we are focusing on the Upper Paleolithic hunters who evolved our human nature for us (see Boehm 2000b).

First, let us think in terms of individual contributions to the proscriptive, punishing side of moral sanctioning. To a large degree these may be explainable through selection taking place within groups, as sociobiologists say (e.g.,

Alexander 1987; Trivers 1971), because self-interest motivates people in groups to ally against deviants. There are, however, several reasons to suggest that there is a significant altruistic element involved. First, some individuals take greater risks or invest more energy in sanctioning than others. Second, certain group members may be going out of their way to punish defectors. These individual contributions to group welfare call for a group-selection explanation. At the same time, we have seen that negative sanctioning makes groups more adaptive when sanctioning is done well — and this creates phenotypic variation at the group level that could feed nicely into group selection.

Second, we have a universal *prescriptive* phase of moral sanctioning that takes advantage of individual responsiveness to prosocial messages. This process may not be very costly to the prescribers who do the preaching; however, it does strongly suggest a group selection explanation, because we must account for people being so *responsive* to such preaching. I say this because their responsiveness sets them up to go against their own selfish-nepotistic interests in favor of the interests of the group, and *to do so without being threatened by punishment,* which is a different way of getting the same job done (see Boyd and Richerson 1992). This genetically altruistic responsiveness to positive messages, which contributes to group functioning, definitely requires a group-selection explanation. And in turn, this responsiveness, when it is astutely manipulated by groups, makes groups that do this well better-adapted than those that don't.

Piggybacking effects may be helping this process along. Herbert Simon (1990) talks about "innate docility," which strongly rewards individual reproductive success in many contexts because it is beneficial to learn the various important social "messages" of one's culture. He believes, as a slightly maladaptive side effect, that this genetically prepared readiness to go along with the messages of one's culture can make individuals susceptible to occasional calls for altruism and cooperation, which result in their sacrificing their own prerogatives for the group. As in the case of conflict interventions, group selection and such "pleiotropic" side effects of genetically "selfish" behavior can work hand in hand. The result is reproductive generosity toward nonrelatives, or toward "the group" as a whole.

Third, we have individual conflict interventions, which require time, energy, and sometimes some risk-taking. Here, too, a group-selection explanation is needed in terms of common sense, for the interventions can be individually costly, and there can be little doubt that managing its conflicts exceptionally well can make one group grow while another shrinks. This is consistent not only with genetic group selection, but with *cultural* group-selection explanations (see Boehm 1978; Boyd and Richerson 1990; Soltis et al. 1995), which I have set aside during this discussion. The surely intricate interactions of these two very different types of group-selection process will require substantial future attention.

The point of this chapter has been to give the type of scientific common sense that normally enhances the building of working hypotheses a chance it has been denied, until recently, with respect to the explanation of moral behavior. It is to be hoped that these explorations of social control, including social control in its positive manifestations, may lead to further insights about the ultimate nature of human moral communities.

In the future, we must consider other instances of human behavior that are congruent with strong group-selection hypotheses and subject them to as technical an analysis as is feasible. One would be warfare, when this becomes self-sacrificial in an obvious way; another would be the patently altruistic acts, individual-to-individual, which I am currently investigating in hunter-gatherers, in which substantial reproductive interests are sacrificed or risked by helping a genetic and sometimes even a social stranger whose needs are pressing. When this entire array of likely altruistic behaviors is better sorted out, scientific common sense may tell us still more strongly that human beings do not live by inclusive fitness alone.

Acknowledgments

I thank Robert Bellah, Sam Bowles, Herb Gintis, Pete Richerson, and David Sloan Wilson for comments on this paper, most of which I have followed. In addition, I am grateful to the Santa Fe Institute for stimulation through its continuing workshops, to the School of American Research and the Simon J. Guggenheim Foundation for recent fellowships that facilitated research on which this chapter is based, and to the Harry F. Guggenheim and Templeton Foundations for research grants that furthered the same research.

REFERENCES

Aberle, D. F., A. K. Cohen, M. J. Levy, and F. X. Sutton. 1950. The functional prerequisites of a society. *Ethics* 60:100-111.

Alexander, Richard D. 1971. The search for an evolutionary philosophy of man. *Proceedings of the Royal Society of Victoria* 84:99-120.

———. 1974. The evolution of social behavior. *Annual Review of Ecology and Systematics* 5:325-84.

———. 1987. *The Biology of Moral Systems.* New York: Aldine de Gruyter.

Alexander, Richard D., and George Borgia. 1978. Group selection, altruism and the levels of organization of life. *Annual Review of Ecology and Systematics* 9:449-75.

Axelrod, R., and W. D. Hamilton. 1981. The evolution of cooperation. *Science* 211:1390-96.

Bales, R. F. 1950. *Interaction Process Analysis: A Method for the Study of Small Groups.* Cambridge: Addison Wesley.

Balikci, Asen. 1970. *The Netsilik Eskimo.* Prospect Heights, Ill.: Waveland.

Black, Donald. 1984. *Toward a General Theory of Social Control.* Orlando: Academic Press.

————. 1998. *The Social Structure of Right and Wrong.* London: Academic Press.

Boehm, Christopher. 1978. Rational preselection from Hamadryas to Homo Sapiens: The place of decisions in adaptive process. *American Anthropologist* 80:265-96.

————. 1979. Some problems with "altruism" in the search for moral universals. *Behavioral Science* 24:15-24.

————. 1981. Parasitic selection and group selection: A study of conflict interference in Rhesus and Japanese Macaque Monkeys. Pp. 160-82 in *Primate Behavior and Sociobiology,* ed. A. B. Chiarelli and R. S. Corruccini. Berlin: Springer-Verlag.

————. 1986. *Blood Revenge: The Enactment and Management of Conflict in Montenegro and Other Tribal Societies.* Philadelphia: University of Pennsylvania Press.

————. 1993. Egalitarian society and reverse dominance hierarchy. *Current Anthropology* 34:227-54.

————. 1994. Pacifying interventions at Arnhem Zoo and Gombe. Pp. 211-26 in *Chimpanzee Cultures,* ed. Richard W. Wrangham, W. C. McGrew, Frans B. M. de Waal, and Paul G. Heltne. Cambridge: Harvard University Press.

————. 1996. Emergency decisions, cultural selection mechanics, and group selection. *Current Anthropology* 37, no. 5:763-93.

————. 1997. Impact of the human egalitarian syndrome on Darwinian selection mechanics. *American Naturalist* 150:100-121.

————. 1999. *Hierarchy in the Forest: The Evolution of Egalitarian Behavior.* Cambridge: Harvard University Press.

————. 2000a. Conflict and the evolution of social control. In *Journal of Consciousness Studies, Special Issue on Evolutionary Origins of Morality* (guest editor, Leonard Katz) 7:79-183.

————. 2000b. Variance reduction and the evolution of social control. Paper presented at Santa Fe Institute, Fifth Annual Workshop on the Co-evolution of Behaviors and Institutions, Santa Fe.

Bowles, Samuel, Jung-Kyoo Choi, and Astrid Hopfensitz. 2003. The co-evolution of individual behaviors and social institutions. *Journal of Theoretical Biology* 223:135-47.

Bowles, Samuel, and Herbert Gintis. 1998. The evolution of strong reciprocity. Santa Fe Institute Working Paper, SFI 98-08-073E.

Boyd, Robert, and Peter J. Richerson. 1990. Group selection among alternative evolutionarily stable strategies. *Journal of Theoretical Biology* 145:331-42.

———. 1992. Punishment allows the evolution of cooperation (or anything else) in sizable groups. *Ethology and Sociobiology* 13:171-95.

Campbell, Donald T. 1972. On the genetics of altruism and the counter-hedonic component of human culture. *Journal of Social Issues* 28:21-37.

———. 1975. On the conflicts between biological and social evolution and between psychology and moral tradition. *American Psychologist* 30:1103-26.

———. 1979. Comments on the sociobiology of ethics and moralizing. *Behavioral Science* 24:37-45.

———. 1983. The two distinct routes beyond kin selection to Ultrasociality: Implications for the humanities and social sciences. Pp. 11-41 in *The Nature of Prosocial Development: Interdisciplinary Theories and Strategies,* ed. Diane Bridgeman. New York: Academic Press.

———. 1991. A naturalistic theory of archaic moral orders. *Zygon* 26:91-114.

Darwin, Charles. 1859. *On the Origin of Species.* London: John Murray.

———. 1871. *The Descent of Man and Selection in Relation to Sex.* London: John Murray.

Dawkins, Richard. 1976. *The Selfish Gene.* New York: Oxford University Press.

Dunbar, Robin. 1996. *Grooming, Gossip, and the Evolution of Language.* London: Faber and Faber.

Durkheim, Émile. 1933. *The Division of Labor in Society.* New York: Free Press.

Edgerton, Robert B. 1975. *Deviance: A Cross-Cultural Perspective.* Menlo Park: Cummings.

———. 1992. *Sick Societies: Challenging the Myth of Primitive Harmony.* New York: Free Press.

Fehr, Ernst, and Simon Gächter. 2000. Cooperation and punishment in public goods experiments. *The American Economic Review* 90:980-94.

———. 2002. Altruistic punishment in humans. *Nature* 415:137-40.

Fehr, Ernst, Urs Fischbacher, and Simon Gächter. 2002. Strong reciprocity, human cooperation and the enforcement of social norms. *Human Nature* 13:1-25.

Fehr, Ernst, and Bettina Rockenbach. 2003. Detrimental effects of sanctions on human altruism. *Nature* 422:137-40.

Fossey, Dian. 1983. *Gorillas in the Mist.* Boston: Houghton-Mifflin.

Fry, Douglas P. 2000. Conflict management in cross-cultural perspective. Pp. 334-51 in *Natural Conflict Resolution,* ed. Filippo Aureli and Frans B. M. de Waal. Berkeley: University of California Press.

Gardner, Peter. 1991. Foragers' pursuit of individual autonomy. *Current Anthropology* 32:543-58.

Gintis, Herbert. 2000. Strong reciprocity and human sociality. *Journal of Theoretical Biology* 206:169-79.

———. 2001. *Game Theory Evolving: A Problem-Centered Introduction to Modeling Strategic Interaction.* Princeton, N.J.: Princeton University Press.

Gintis, Herbert, Samuel Bowles, Robert Boyd, and Ernst Fehr. 2003. Explaining altruistic behavior in humans. *Evolution and Human Behavior* 24:153-72.

Haviland, John B. 1977. *Gossip, Reputation, and Knowledge in Zinacantan.* Chicago: University of Chicago Press.

Heinrich, Joseph, Robert Boyd, Samuel Bowles, Colin Camerer, Ernst Fehr, Herbert Gintis, and Richard McElreath. 2001. Cooperation, reciprocity and punishment in fifteen small-scale societies. *American Economics Review* 91:73-78.

Kelly, Robert L. 1995. *The Foraging Spectrum: Diversity in Hunter-Gatherer Lifeways.* Washington: Smithsonian Institution Press.

Kluckhohn, Clyde. 1952. Values and value-orientations in the theory of action: An exploration in definition and classification. Pp. 395-418 in *Toward a General Theory of Action,* ed. T. Parsons and E. Shils. Cambridge: Harvard University Press.

Knauft, Bruce M. 1991. Violence and sociality in human evolution. *Current Anthropology* 32:391-428.

Lee, Richard B. 1979. *The !Kung San: Men, Women, and Work in a Foraging Society.* Cambridge: Cambridge University Press.

Lorenz, Konrad. 1966. *On Aggression.* Translated by Marjorie Kerr Wilson. New York: Harcourt, Brace and World.

Maine, Sir Henry. [1861] 1931. *Ancient Law.* London: Oxford University Press.

Malinowski, Bronislaw. 1939. The group and the individual in functional analysis. *American Journal of Sociology* 44:938-64.

Parsons, Talcott, and Edward Shils, eds. 1952. *Toward a General Theory of Action.* Cambridge: Harvard University Press.

Ridley, Matt. 1996. *The Origins of Virtue: Human Instincts and the Evolution of Cooperation.* New York: Penguin.

Selby, Henry. 1974. *Zapotec Deviance: The Convergence of Folk and Modern Sociology.* Austin: University of Texas Press.

Silberbauer, George. 1982. Political process in G/Wi Bands. Pp. 23-35 in *Politics and History in Band Societies,* ed. E. Leacock and R. Lee. Cambridge: Cambridge University Press.

Simon, Herbert. 1990. A mechanism for social selection and successful altruism. *Science* 250:1665-68.

Sober, Elliott, and David Sloan Wilson. 1998. *Unto Others: The Evolution and Psychology of Unselfish Behavior.* Cambridge, Mass.: Harvard University Press.

Soltis, Joseph, Robert Boyd, and Peter J. Richerson. 1995. Can group-functional behaviors evolve by cultural group selection? An empirical test. *Current Anthropology* 36:473-94.

Trivers, Robert L. 1971. The evolution of reciprocal altruism. *Quarterly Review of Biology* 46:35-57.

———. 1972. Parental investment and sexual selection. Pp. 136-79 in *Sexual Selection and the Descent of Man, 1871-1971,* ed. B. G. Campbell. Chicago: Aldine.

Turnbull, Colin M. 1961. *The Forest People: A Study of the Pygmies of the Congo.* New York: Simon and Schuster.

Williams, George C. 1966. *Adaptation and Natural Selection: A Critique of Some Current Evolutionary Thought.* Princeton, N.J.: Princeton University Press.

Wilson, David Sloan. 2002. *Darwin's Cathedral: Evolution, Religion, and the Nature of Society.* Chicago: University of Chicago Press.

Wilson, David Sloan, and Elliott Sober. 1994. Reintroducing group selection to the human behavioral sciences. *Behavior and Brain Sciences* 17:585-654.

Wilson, Edward O. 1975. *Sociobiology: The New Synthesis.* Cambridge: Harvard University Press.

————. 1978. *On Human Nature.* Cambridge: Harvard University Press.

Wilson, James Q. 1993. *The Moral Sense.* New York: Free Press.

Wrangham, Richard. 1987. African apes: The significance of African apes for reconstructing social evolution. Pp. 51-71 in *The Evolution of Human Behavior: Primate Models,* ed. W. G. Kinzey. Albany: State University of New York Press.

Wright, Robert. 1994. *The Moral Animal: Why We Are the Way We Are: The New Science of Evolutionary Psychology.* New York: Vintage.

Wynne-Edwards, V. C. 1962. *Animal Dispersion in Relation to Social Behavior.* Edinburgh: Oliver and Boyd.

4. Hominid Failings: An Evolutionary Basis for Sin in Individuals and Corporations

Michael J. Chapman

Introduction

What is it that really governs our decisions: free will, or evolutionary history? Imagine walking into the self-help section of a local bookstore and reading titles such as "100 Quick Ways to Achieve Bankruptcy," "You Too Can Have a Beer-gut," or "Marital Infidelity for Dummies." Clearly, we need no help in squandering, drinking, or womanizing; on the contrary, thousands of pop-psychology titles and motivational seminars are devoted to self-discipline. Many of us seem fundamentally unable to listen to the "better angels of our natures," to use Lincoln's phrase; instead, we are at the mercy of our animal selves. Perhaps we are caught in evolutionary traps; that is, perhaps evolution drives us toward certain destructive behaviors (Pinker 2002; Schlaepfer et al. 2002; Burnham and Phelan 2000; Ehrlich 2000). Genes that proliferated in ancestral human populations, that were selectively advantageous in a hunter-gatherer society, still influence our behavior in today's consumer culture — with disastrous consequences for many who lack the resources or willpower to change. To make matters worse, genetics seems to offer the ultimate excuse: if genes dictate that we overeat, overspend, or philander, why devote any effort to exercise, thrift, or marriage counseling?

We have evolved to crave certain things over others; our likes and dislikes are different from those of other animals because we evolved under different selective pressures. The Buddhist doctrine that human suffering derives from our cravings dovetails nicely with evolutionary psychology. Like apes and monkeys, for example, humans crave sweets, to the dietary ruin of millions in today's "supersized" world. We yearn for monogamous true love, yet the lion's share of e-commerce derives from online porn. Chimpanzees, our nearest cousins, are also slaves to their passions; rape, murder, and even war are well documented in their society. Behaviors associated with many of the Seven Deadly Sins have been observed among chimpanzees.

It is easy to envision an evolutionary basis for sins of excess, such as greed, lust, and gluttony, because these are behaviors of individuals. Pride, rage, envy, and sloth, by contrast, are sins against the group, sins whose commission depends on a preexisting social structure including a dominance hierarchy. With few exceptions, all primates live in such groups, in which access to mates and resources, and hence evolutionary success, depends chiefly on rank. Group living and dominance hierarchies are not unhealthy per se: indeed, human commensality has promoted behaviors such as teamwork and charity. Groups absolutely require hierarchies, moreover, to manage division of labor and resources, and to enforce the rule of law. Chimpanzee bands, like those of tribal humans, are egalitarian bodies in which coalitions quickly form to prevent any one individual from becoming too dominant; rather, the leader is a "first among equals" whose primary duty is to break up fights — a possible evolutionary precursor to morality (C. Boehm, personal communication). But upbringing within primate society still consists largely of imitative observation of one's betters (witness the verb "to ape"), and privilege comes with rank. Hence by their nature, dominance hierarchies can and do foster vanity and arrogance among rulers, even as they breed envy, sloth, and occasional psychotic rage among commoners. The twentieth-century phenomenon of television has exacerbated these trends to an astounding degree. Heavy television watchers "overestimate the portion of the population who are millionaires, have had cosmetic surgery, and belong to a private gym"; "what we see on TV inflates our sense of what's normal," and sociologists have even documented that "an additional hour of television watched in a week led to an additional $208.00 in annual spending" (Schor 1998, 81-82). Meanwhile, televised self-help gurus such as Oprah and Dr. Phil proffer sound-bite solutions to personal crises of obesity, bankruptcy, and divorce.

Perhaps, instead of TV, we can use the theory of evolutionary traps to better understand our human failings. Richard Alexander, David Sloan Wilson, and others have presented robust models for the evolutionary origins of morality and religion. While much attention has been paid to the foundation of "good" behaviors such as altruism, less work has been published on the origin of evil. It may be no accident that the early Catholic Church defined Seven Deadly Sins of greed, gluttony, lust, sloth, pride, envy, and wrath, because studies now show that our short-term memory can best handle seven bits of information at a time. Catholics (and most Christians in general) view sin as the human legacy of the fall, a distinctly anti-Darwinian stance; some might even be tempted to misread this essay as an evolutionist's excuse for sin. In fact, sin is at present selectively neutral: as self-destructive as the Deadly Sins may be, there is no hard evidence for reduced Darwinian fitness

— that is, fewer offspring surviving to reproductive age — as a direct consequence of such behaviors.

Yet sin can and does lead to personal ruin. If, as countless ethological studies suggest, natural selection is supposed to optimize traits and behaviors in an environment, then how to explain the persistence of our own all-too-common misbehaviors? The answer is ineluctable, and cultural: certain institutions, such as fast food, television, and credit cards, have acquired vast power and influence through exploitation of evolved human cravings and "groupishness." These institutions' very success suggests that as a species we have evolved no effective defense against certain excesses, and that our evolutionary prognosis is grave. Despite that grim outlook, however, we may yet learn to conquer our sins; after all, we are a clever and adaptable species, and hope is also part of our nature.

Individual Selection for Sin: Mean Genes and Evolutionary Traps

Instinct can sometimes drive animals into self-destructive behaviors. Knowledge of the social and physical selective pressures under which an animal species evolved, and of how present conditions differ from those of the species' environment of evolutionary adaptation (or EEA, as I shall designate it from now on), can help conservationists to determine the mechanism of destructive behavior and, in many cases, to remedy its effects (Gavin 1991; Symons 1990; Smith et al. 2001). Evolutionary traps have been described in wild species, such as leatherback turtles *(Dermochelys coriacea)*, whose evolved food preference is for jellyfish, but who now eat floating transparent plastic garbage in the ocean that blocks their digestive tracts. Female wood ducks *(Aix sponsa)* have evolved to follow each other to rare nesting sites, but that behavior now leads female wood ducks to mob nests in wood duck boxes placed by well-meaning conservationists; the resulting intraspecific brood parasitism robs the next generation of a great many eggs (Schlaepfer et al. 2002).

Similar traps in humans are evolved behavioral tendencies that may, in the long run, do us harm. Human failings, such as those that some call the Seven Deadly Sins, may all derive from our evolutionary traps; hence much of redemption may involve coming to terms with our animal nature (Williams 2001). It is important to note that the evolutionary perspective does not necessarily imply genetic determinism: we predict, for humans or any animal under study, what a typical individual might do in a given situation, not what any particular individual will do. Given the complexity of human behavior, the predictive power of evolutionary reasoning decreases with greater distancing of the behavior from our biological functions. That is, behaviors related to our groupishness, mate choice, child rearing, and food or resource acquisition lend themselves best to evolutionary analysis.

Gluttony

Terry Burnham and Jay Phelan (2000) posit the evolution of genes for such behaviors as were advantageous in the EEA — approximately 100,000 years ago in scavenger/hunter-gatherer clans on the African veldt. We often unthinkingly eat things that taste and smell good to us, but evolutionists ask why certain tastes and smells whet our appetite, and why many people continue to eat after they are full. Under feast-or-famine conditions, our ancestors evolved taste buds that crave high-calorie foods full of fat and sugar, stomachs capable of handling much more than one day's caloric requirements, and a pyloric sphincter which slowly parses out stomach contents into the small intestine over many hours. (The African lion, having evolved as a climax predator in the same ecosystem over tens of millions of years, can accommodate forty pounds of meat in its stomach at one sitting, and then may not eat again for three or four days.) Thus many of us do not feel full until after we have ingested two to three days' caloric requirements at a sitting. This fact helps to explain the finding that one in three Americans is clinically obese. The long-term consequences of obesity include diabetes, coronary heart disease, sleep-breathing disorders, and certain forms of cancer (Kopelman 2000).

Greed

Many people find it impossible to balance a household budget. Thrift and moderation, according to Burnham and Phelan (2000), are behaviors that we unfortunately failed to evolve. Labile environmental conditions such as weather, game availability, and predator threats would have allowed little opportunity for long-term planning. Instead, possibly concomitant with toolmaking, or simply as a form of bet-hedging against an unknown future, we have evolved a greed for material objects surpassing that of any other animal. Anthropologist Napoleon Chagnon, the first to study the Brazilian Yanomamo, documented this sad fact in 1964: on arrival at the tribe's village he was immediately robbed of all his possessions. Yet it is getting, not having, that we seem to crave. Corporate awareness of this fact has led to the development of myriad new technological means of consumption such as revolving credit, e-shopping, or the slightly older supermarket (Ritzer 1998). Whatever the need or whim before us, it often supercedes the cognitive knowledge of our growing credit balance. Credit cards, an innovation of American banking after World War II, break down temporal boundaries and allow us to spend money we have not yet earned. In so doing, they exploit our genetic proclivity for greed. As Homer Simpson says of his new car, "It was free! They just made me sign papers."

Lust

Evolutionary accounts of infidelity generally ascribe to men a genetic predisposition to spread their gametes, produced cheaply and copiously throughout their lives. To maximize his reproductive fitness, therefore, a man should attempt to impregnate as many women as possible. For women, whose decision is whether to accept the short-term partner with the best genes or the long-term partner who will likely offer the most care and provisions during pregnancy and early childhood, infidelity can be explained on the basis of choice: an extramarital boyfriend may offer stronger genetic material than a husband, who can still be counted on to provide for the new baby (unless events conspire to raise his suspicions). Like overeating or overspending, cheating is a form of excess; and it can have equally disastrous consequences. Because Bill Clinton was an incumbent president at the time of his much-publicized infidelity, his momentary failure to consider others changed American history.

Greed, gluttony, and lust all originate in a blindness to who and what we are. They express a lack of self-control and an inability to anticipate consequences for others. Evolutionary psychologists construct models to explain what we observe in ourselves. Mainstream psychologists warn of a pandemic "empty self," the disillusioned product of post–WWII American cultural trends: a self that needs to buy new items, adopt new trends, and follow the latest fashions in order to feel "full" (Cushman 1990).

Pride, Envy, Sloth, and Rage

The Machiavellian model for the origin of human intelligence holds that our large cerebral neocortex — that part of the brain devoted to abstract reasoning and ethical decision-making — may have evolved under selective pressure to gain status within a dominance hierarchy. Strong positive correlations have been documented between neocortex ratio (NR) and group size across primate species, and also between NR and the index of tactical deception (a measure of prevalence of "sneaky" behaviors) among the same apes and monkeys (Dunbar 1993, and Byrne 1995, reviewed in Cartwright 2000, 187-88). Estimated average group size among *Homo erectus* was 150 individuals, yet human history since the origin of agriculture (ca. 8500 B.C.) has been marked by a progressive increase from that figure, and by the appearance of bureaucracies and the division of labor for the management of large groups, while our NR has remained unchanged. Cultural group selection (reviewed by Cronk 1994) has driven human groups to increase in size, while economic or military conflict between nations and corporations has replaced ecological competition between hunter-gatherer tribes. One wonders whether our groups have increased in size and complexity beyond our brains' processing and ethical decision-making ability.

Corporations are not individuals. Lacking the unitary sense of self and personal responsibility inherent in each of us as a person, most corporations follow an ethic of enlightened self-interest. Within the corporation, individuals are rewarded with promotion and punished with demotion or firing; yet at all tiers of the dominance hierarchy are people, subject to human failings. Recent news of corporate debacles and golden parachutes for top CEOs at Enron, AOL/Time-Warner, and American Airlines (to name just a few examples) has shown the consequences of overweening pride among top-level management. Meanwhile, lower-level employees who hear such news will understandably fall prey to envy, wrath, and the sloth born of despair.

A Multilevel-Selection Model of Corporate Excess: McDonaldization Theory

David Sloan Wilson has presented a model whereby religious systems might have evolved such that the religious group gained a competitive advantage over others. In fact, this phenomenon could hold true for many human systems, including corporations. Corporate policies — rational protocols for maximizing shareholder value in a competitive economy — are in essence secular value systems. In large multinational corporations such as McDonald's, especially at lower levels of employment, behaviors are often scripted and cheaters punished with all the Darwinian ruthlessness of an ant colony.

In *The McDonaldization Thesis* (1998), Ritzer shows how *hyperrational* systems in many industries have inevitably led to *irrational* consequences.

The adjective "hyperrational" derives from the sociological concept of practical rationality first described by Max Weber. A rational action is one taken solely on grounds of reason, calculation, and enlightened self-interest (Ritzer, 124-25). In a social context, rational actions occur most often in the bureaucratic, economic, or legal spheres. Hyperrational systems, in which *only* rational actions are permitted, are quite common in modern society. Such systems uniformly reinforce rationality, while punishing creativity and original thought, leading to depersonalization and oppressive routine. An evolutionist might also describe a hyperrational system as "hyperteleological"; that is, as a system in which every detail serves some material purpose, and from which feelings, intuition, humor, and other natural human qualities are notably absent. Irrational consequences for such a system would then be anti-teleological consequences: degradation of the environment, of society, and ultimately of the system itself.

Ritzer's observation concerning hyperrational systems — that by their nature, they ultimately give rise to irrationality — is perhaps most true of fast-food chains. In order to serve as many customers as possible per unit time, McDonald's has systematized every aspect of their restaurants. Minimum-wage employees do and say the same things thousands of times per hour; high-calorie, low-cost meals are mass-produced and sold; many tasks are cheerfully performed by the customer (such as beverage service, carrying food, bussing tables, and — at some McDonald's — even preparing sandwiches at so-called "Fixins Bars"). The identical dinner experience can be purchased virtually anywhere in the country. Not only are the actions of McDonald's grill cooks and cashiers scripted, but shift leaders and managers, as well as the instructors at Hamburger University, also have rigorous protocols to follow for the intensive mass-marketing of McDonald's food. Not only has the standardized, mechanized product-delivery system enabled McDonald's to proliferate around the world; it has also been emulated in many other industries such as those dealing with hotels, vacations, office supplies, and housewares.

The proliferation of McDonald's-like corporate policies is at its heart an evolutionary phenomenon. According to Van Valen's Red Queen hypothesis, species' survival in nature is encapsulated by the Red Queen's remark to Alice in Lewis Carroll's *Through the Looking Glass:* "Here, you see, it takes all the running you can do to keep in the same place." An evolutionary arms race exists between species in a community, such that a new adaptation for one becomes the selective force stimulating evolution of competitor species. McDonald's competitors must imitate its policies in order to survive, and thus many businesses become equally specialized for globalization and high-volume output. McDonald's success has produced so many imitators precisely because of its multilevel nature: tightly scripted policies and standardized behaviors by the customers, the line employees, the restaurant managers, and their corporate teachers are all required in order to survive competition with other McDonaldized enterprises. McDonald's itself has succeeded admirably in its economic race with competitors; in fact, its only serious competition comes from chains such as Subway, which imitate its product and marketing strategy but offer a low-fat, supposedly healthier product. The corporate activity of all fast-food restaurants closely resembles that of organisms, which compete for limited resources in natural ecosystems. Like the individual human organism, moreover, McDonald's is prone to gluttony (in its consumption of raw materials), greed (in its treatment of workers and pursuit of the market share), and cheating (in its relationship to the consumer, since McDonald's never delivers the quality or "happiness" promised in its glossy advertisements and on its menus). All of the above, according to Ritzer, are inevitable consequences of McDonald's high-volume competitive strategy.

McDonaldized corporate policies result from the sort of multilevel selection that Wilson has analyzed: selection occurs between corporations on the stock exchange, between departments and individuals within a corporation based on productivity, and between classes of consumers (different age groups, for example) based on demand. Like the multilevel selection that gave rise to hyperrational policy, irrational consequences also occur at many levels: the functional rationality of the McDonald's hamburger line effectively swamps the substantive rationality of the workers, who are deprived of even the most basic autonomy ("Unhappy Meals and Rude Workers Cost McDonald's Millions," *Dow Jones News Service*, July 15, 2001; "Can McDonald's Shape Up?" *Time Magazine*, September 23, 2002). Rainforests are destroyed to provide grazing land for cattle destined to become McDonald's hamburgers. Forests and oilfields are emptied to mass-produce disposable, single-use McDonald's containers, ultimately shunted by customers' unpaid labor into publicly funded landfills.

Corporate mass-consumption of raw materials, dehumanization of the work force, and deceptive advertising, respectively, exemplify the sins of gluttony, greed, and arrogance at the global level. The consequences of these sins are irrational, moreover, in that they ultimately harm the corporation, as major domestic revenues are lost while grass-roots anti-McDonald's movements emerge in many foreign countries whose traditional cultures revolve around cuisine and the dining experience (for example, France or India), or whose people feel marginalized by globalization in general. Even in the United States, to the extent that McDonald's fails to deliver on its advertising promises of serving happiness along with its burgers, its relationship to the consumer suffers. Obese, sugar- and grease-addicted children clamor for McDonald's, drive-through customers are alienated by employee rudeness even at the management level (a canard among store managers and shift leaders is that most customer complaints are scams), and fast-food customers increasingly choose Subway or less obviously scripted chains such as Applebee's or the Olive Garden.

The McDonaldized strategy has proliferated not only in consumer-based industries but also in academia: the much-touted DNA revolution is the product of McDonaldized biology. Molecular biology has become more and more mechanized and scripted, with many tasks which, as recently as 1990, were the exclusive domain of Ph.D.'s and graduate students now performed by robots. A burgeoning biotech industry produces made-to-order enzymes, primers, and disposable supplies for ubiquitous techniques such as the polymerase chain reaction. Since academic supply orders are institutionally funded, there is little personal incentive to be frugal — resulting in mountains of often biohazardous waste. A positive feedback loop between grantees, biotech firms, and ancillary industries such as plastics has become McDonaldized. Perhaps molecular biology is not yet as hyperrational — and irrational — as the fast-food industry; yet Ritzer may be right in describing the process as incremental, and irreversible.

Conclusion: Toward a Multidisciplinary Understanding of Human Nature

I have argued that humans are predisposed to misbehaviors codified as the Seven Deadly Sins — gluttony, greed, lust, vanity, envy, rage, and sloth — because of our evolutionary history. Natural selection, acting on individuals as well as on groups, has imbued the human species with innate drives to acquire food, resources, stature within the group, and access to mates. Like all primates, moreover, we are social beings who live within a dominance hierarchy. Much of our lengthy education consists of observation and imitation of role models. These universal truths about how we live suggest that human behavior has been shaped by continuous and powerful directional selection from our Pleistocene EEA to the present. Many aspects of our sociality and biological drives were essential to our success in the EEA, when we competed against lions, hyenas, and other predators for limited resources on the African plain.

In today's resource-rich environment, however, unhealthy consequences of evolved behaviors (obesity, bankruptcy, and divorce for individuals; robber-baron CEOs and bad public relations for corporations) outweigh their former selective benefits. Chronic overeaters, shopping addicts, and philanderers ignore personal consequences for themselves and their families; arrogant corporate leaders turn a deaf ear to workers and consumers; the disenfranchised succumb to rage and despair. Evolved behaviors echoing the Seven Deadly Sins are well documented in the animal kingdom, and some levels of aggression, greed, and lust were likely instrumental to human survival in the EEA. But different selective forces are at work in modern society. Just as certain animals are threatened with extinction by evolutionary traps, so formerly adaptive human cravings and behaviors lead not simply to personal ruin but also to globally destructive corporate policies. The Seven Deadly Sins may indeed be evolutionary traps: hyperactive expressions of evolved cognitive modules which once helped but now hurt us, both individually and as a species. Documentation of evolutionary traps in other species has been instrumental to conservation efforts. Perhaps evolutionary psychology can likewise help us to understand the roots of our hominid failings and begin to address them.

In the film *Gattaca*, Ethan Hawke plays a social outcast in a dystopian society where everyone's future is predetermined by genetic fingerprinting, administered by robots in practically every sphere of employment. Good jobs and privileges are reserved for the genetically enhanced classes, while the unenhanced "in-valids" labor to clean streets and toilets. Although human genomic mapping may or may not lead in that direction, genes connected to obesity, homosexuality, and alcoholism have already been identified. Only one school of evolutionary theory — the radical reductionists personified by Richard Dawkins — explains these tendencies solely on the basis of genes. Nevertheless, the "gut" reaction of many people with respect to genetics is to resign themselves to the status quo: if I am overweight because of my genes, why diet?

The element missing from radical, gene-machine models of behavior such as those of Alexander, Wilson, and Dawkins is an account of free agency. Morality involves fair exchange between free agents, and evildoing of any sort, at both individual and corporate levels, seems to involve depersonalizing the victim and restricting his or her options. As a consequence of the rapist's or murderer's choices, the victim's free agency is destroyed outright; as a consequence of McDonald's corporate decisions, the free agency of its employees and customers is merely lessened, but on a global scale. In the most radical interpretations of human evolutionary biology, denial of free agency has taken the form of selfish gene theory (Dawkins 1976).

But evolutionary theory does not actually support the reduction to deterministic, gene-based explanations. The notion that organisms are in essence "vehicles" for the transmission of genes ("replicators") ascribes agency where there is none: no gene actually replicates itself or has any activity outside the context of the cell, with all its other genes. A more accurate term might be "replicated object." Nor can we predictably determine what a gene will do when transferred from one organism to another. Many vaunted early successes of genetic engineering, such as the Monsanto Flavr-Savr tomato, have not lived up to expectations. Clonally produced swine are prone to arthritis and have less than half the normal life expectancy. These and other practical failures of industrial biotechnology show that the determinist notion of gene function is at root a fallacy, based on shoddy science (Shiva 1997).

In essence, moreover, the DNA revolution is amoral in that it robs the individual of agency and bestows it instead on genes. Richards (2000) presents a rigorous philosophical proof that our own interests are not the same as our genes' interests. Yet our cravings and our groupishness are products of the evolved human brain, and in our quest for better self-knowledge, we should acknowledge them as such.

Sartre conceived of morality as arising from visual interaction between humans — for example, the gaze; an individual is never more self-conscious than when, caught in some small transgression, she realizes that she is observed (O'Hear 1997). Ayala (1995) considers the ethical sense an epiphenomenon or pleiotropic by-product of the human intellect. Either of these holistic models is a better approximation of human morality than selfish gene theory could ever hope to offer. When people are gluttonous, greedy, envious, or vain, we say that they lack self-control or self-awareness.

Unlike people, however, corporations are not selves; they are incapable of the kind of personal introspection needed for a moral life. While corporate policies are the rational products of decisions made at the group level in the global economic arena, no corporation can ever aspire to true selfhood; like any large group, corporations are subject to attrition, migration, and restructuring. Moreover, the top-heavy dominance hierarchies of many corporations bring out the worst in us, giving rise to pride, envy, sloth, and wrath through the very "executive contract incentives" and "downsizing" policies used by the corporation to maintain its competitive edge. At present there are few internal controls to corporate behaviors, and, until very recently, government controls were much reduced compared to ten or twenty years ago. Perhaps this explains why McDonaldization continues to spread worldwide despite its irrational consequences for individuals, for ecosystems, and for corporations themselves. Corporate policies are secular value systems that have evolved under a mechanism of multilevel selection. Like all value systems, they arise from self-reinforcing peer assemblages, that is, from groups of interrelated selves. Since morality so depends on the self as free agent, a single unifying theory to describe the origin of moral systems will absolutely require multidisciplinary effort. Diverse concepts of the self occur, for example, in biology (immune systems), philosophy and psychology (individuals), sociology and anthropology (groups), and religion (the multivalent nature of divinity).

Providing one instance of such interdisciplinary cross-fertilization, Patricia Williams, a philosopher of both religion and science, suggests that Adam and Eve are mythical figures, and that Jesus came not to atone for their sins but for those of the real human ancestors on the Ethiopian plains. By eschewing power and property, and by exemplifying Christian behaviors such as enemy love, forgiveness, and charity, Jesus showed us the way to atone for our forefathers' sins — the escape from our own all-too-human evolutionary traps (Williams 2001, chap. 11). While it is not surprising that Jesus was a threat to the quintessentially McDonaldized Romans of his day, his death and resurrection showed how atonement can also be a way of transforming politically oppressive institutions: soon enough, Rome had a Christian emperor.

Whether atonement is possible for McDonaldized corporations remains to be seen. Multilevel selection has driven corporations — and each of us, at one time or another — into greed, gluttony, or cheating. Multilevel selection is also the basis for primate groupishness and dominance hierarchies, which by their nature breed vanity, envy, sloth, and wrath. Humility, clear-eyed reflection, and self-discipline are ways for each one of us to address our own human failings. Drastic reformulation of public and corporate policies will be needed to end McDonaldization and to build sustainable corporations. It will take multilevel and multidisciplinary consciousness-raising to release our hyperrational, increasingly global society from these ancient and terrible evolutionary traps.

REFERENCES

Alexander, Richard D. 1993. Biological considerations in the analysis of morality. Pp. 163-96 in *Evolutionary Ethics,* ed. Matthew H. Nitecki and Doris V. Nitecki. Albany: State University of New York Press.

Ayala, Francisco J. 1995. The difference of being human: Ethical behavior as evolutionary byproduct. Pp. 113-35 in *Biology, Ethics, and the Origins of Life,* ed. Holmes Rolston III. Boston: Jones and Bartlett.

Burnham, Terry, and Jay Phelan. 2000. *Mean Genes.* Cambridge, Mass.: Perseus.

Byrne, R. 1995. *The Thinking Ape.* Oxford: Oxford University Press.

Cartwright, John. 2000. *Evolution and Human Behavior.* Cambridge, Mass.: MIT Press.

Cronk, Lee. 1994. Evolutionary theories of morality and the manipulative use of signals. *Zygon* 29:81-101.

Cushman, Philip. 1990. Why the self is empty: Toward a historically situated psychology. *American Psychologist* (May 1990): 599-611.

Dawkins, Richard. 1976. Why are people? Pp. 1-11 in *The Selfish Gene.* Oxford: Oxford University Press.

Dunbar, R.I.M. 1993. Coevolution of neocortical size, group size and language in humans. *Behavioural and Brain Sciences* 16:681-735.

Ehrlich, Paul. 2000. *Human Natures: Genes, Culture, and the Human Prospect.* Washington, D.C.: Island Press/Shearwater.

Gavin, T. A. 1991. Why ask "why"? The importance of evolutionary biology in wildlife science. *Journal of Wildlife Management* 55:760-66.

Kopelman, P. G. 2000. Obesity as a medical problem. *Nature* 404:635-43.

O'Hear, Anthony. 1997. *Beyond Evolution: Human Nature and the Limits of Evolutionary Explanation.* Oxford: Oxford University Press.

Pinker, Steven. 2002. *The Blank Slate: The Modern Denial of Human Nature.* New York: Viking.

Richards, Janet Radcliffe. 2000. *Human Nature after Darwin: A Philosophical Introduction.* London: Routledge.

Ritzer, George. 1998. *The McDonaldization Thesis.* London: Sage.

Schlaepfer, Martin A., Michael C. Runge, and Paul W. Sherman. 2002. Ecological and evolutionary traps. *Trends in Ecology and Evolution* 1, no. 10:474-79.

Schor, Juliet B. 1998. *The Overspent American: Upscaling, Downshifting, and the New Consumer.* New York: Basic Books.

Shiva, Vandana. 1997. *Biopiracy: The Plunder of Nature and Knowledge.* Boston, Mass.: South End.

Smith, E. A., et al. 2001. Controversies in the evolutionary social sciences: A guide for the perplexed. *Trends in Ecoogy and Evolution* 16:128-35.

Symons, D. 1990. Adaptiveness and adaptation. *Ethology and Sociobiology* 11:427-44.

Van Valen, Lee. 1973. A new evolutionary law. *Evolutionary Theory* 1:1-30.

Williams, Patricia. 2001. *Doing without Adam and Eve: Sociobiology and Original Sin.* Minneapolis: Fortress.

5. The Leverage of Language on Altruism and Morality

Joseph Poulshock

Introduction

The existence of altruistic behavior in nature and especially in humans has long posed a fundamental problem for Darwinian accounts of evolution. Among the responses have been some significant breakthroughs in understanding altruism from the perspective of natural selection. The concepts of inclusive fitness (Hamilton 1964) and reciprocal altruism (Trivers 1971), for example, have contributed to the new synthesis, helping to explain how numerous altruistic behaviors cohere with evolutionary processes. Additional explanations, such as sexual selection (Darwin 1871), pleiotropic interactions, genetic lag, and manipulation (see Schloss 2002), have also offered partial explanations for some apparently anomalous altruism that does not cohere with the mainstream doctrine of selfish selection.

Nevertheless, though selfish gene explanations have proven powerful, they are not necessarily complete. For example, some behaviors, such as sacrificial philanthropy across kindred lines or holocaust rescue (Monroe 2002), appear to transcend selfish gene explanations. Moreover, because of this incompleteness and because of the apparent cynicism of these majority explanations, numerous scholars have dissented (de Waal 1996; Sober and Wilson 1998; Bekoff 2002; Preston and de Waal 2002; etc.). Thus researchers have proposed a number of additional explanatory tools to account for altruistic behaviors. The most important are structural-hierarchical approaches, such as multi-level selection theory (Sober and Wilson 1998), and functional-hierarchical approaches (Dawkins 1976; Durham 1991; Blackmore 1998).

This chapter explores a combination of structural and functional approaches, asking in particular how the *function of language* employed in moral codes may aid in promoting both altruism and the *structure of groupishness*. In particular, I defend the concept of *virtual relatedness*. Virtual relatedness promotes forms of altruistic behavior that are detached from genetic relations, and even from reciprocation, and that are leveraged through a linguistically based moral code. Such behaviors can enable individuals and groups to recategorize relatedness in ways that could facilitate altruism, group selection, and even broader forms of extended morality. I shall use the term *altruism* to refer to behavior that incurs a biological, resource, or fitness cost to the actor and a consequent benefit to the recipient. *Morality* refers to what an individual or group considers as good or bad; the term is thus used in a descriptive rather than in a prescriptive sense. Hence, for example, if a group considers a particular kind of altruism good, even though the behavior might actually be detrimental to outsiders, this altruism forms part of the morality for this group (regardless of whether *we* think it good or bad). As a result, the terms *altruism* and *morality* are sometimes used interchangeably in what follows.

Language, Altruism, and Morality in General

Before moving on to the central issues in this discussion on language, altruism, and morality, it is important to delineate the breadth of this topic, since it clearly transcends the scope of a short book chapter. The relationship between language and the development of altruistic and moral behavior is a very complex one. For example, it raises questions about the psychology of caregiving, the ontological development of infants and children, and the role that language plays in the process of their moral development.

Even more generally, if altruism and morality require language, then insights from evolutionary linguistics should also inform our understanding of the foundational elements of altruistic behaviors. For instance, does Dunbar's (1996) work on social cohesion, comparing grooming in primates and language in humans, provide evidence for the thesis that the existence of language facilitates altruism and morality more efficiently than its nonexistence? Likewise, the discussion raises issues in general linguistics — for example, how central design features of language such as naming ability, semantic primitives such as "good" and "bad" (Wierzbicka 1996), recursion, displacement, stimulus freedom, and categorization enable altruism and morality. Additionally, Chomsky's (1965; cf. Jackendoff 2002) universal grammar expresses a number of important parallels and contrasts to human altruistic and moral abilities that shed significant light on this discussion.

Finally, in addition to these issues, there exists an important literature on the human ability to deceive with language, to destroy what is generally considered moral, and to create an alternate morality by employing language, such as in George Orwell's novel *1984,* in which "Newspeak" is used to teach "War is peace. Freedom is slavery. Ignorance is strength" (Orwell 1950, 7). In a word, the topic of language, altruism, and morality is too broad for a short discussion. It has been necessary, therefore, to severely narrow the treatment in what follows and to reserve other major issues for a separate discussion.

Language, Group Identity, and Boundaries

The issue of language and group identity is also large enough for a book-length discussion (see, e.g., McKirnan and Hamayan 1980). For present purposes, however, it is important to reiterate that language can serve to mark the boundaries of groups, insofar as it helps insiders and outsiders to know who is identified with whom (Le Page and Tabouret-Keller 1985). Moreover, as David Crystal (1997) suggests, numerous uses of language exist not to provide information or content, but rather to assist in the expression of group identity. Chants at political rallies ("four more years!"), shouts of "Amen" at church meetings, and phrases cheered at sporting events all employ a language that "unites rather than informs" (Crystal 1997, 13). Additionally, spoken or written language frequently provides the listener or reader with much information about its source, including region, status, education, work, sex, and personality. In other words, "a major function of language is the expression of personal identity — the signaling of who we are and where we 'belong'" (Crystal 1997, 13).

Hence, language pragmatically indicates personal and group identity. At the same time, these expressions of group identification also clearly include implicit moral judgments about what speakers think is good and bad. Chanting "four more years!" at a political rally sends the signal that one shares the values of the group and is most likely willing to act on those values — provided the signal is honest. Although it is possible to deceptively attempt this identification with the group, without commitment to its values, other members will expect a person who identifies with the group to engage in certain actions: to vote in order to back up the chant, to expend money to support the party, or even, depending on how outsiders perceive one's group affiliation, to risk social status. Additionally, in more volatile political contexts, publicly stating one's view can incur the ultimate sacrifice, so that group identification would not be worth lying about.

Whatever sacrifices are incurred by making these identification statements, clear benefits follow from being accepted and protected by the group. Of course, a group that protects its individuals will be stronger than a group that does not. In short, it appears that some of the important functions of language provide groups with a value-laden identity that helps distinguish them from other groups. Moreover, it is essential that language function in this way if there are to be group-level adaptations that depend on higher-level processes and that facilitate altruism or morality.

Code Regulation of Group Behavior

In addition to its function in facilitating identity in groups and individuals, language also plays a crucial role in group *regulation*. Linguistically mediated moral codes *regulate* the behavior of groups, and if the codes did not affect or regulate the behavior of groups, they would be meaningless for structural-hierarchical selection. In a word, the moral code must help selfish individuals to perform altruistic acts, sacrificing their individual fitness for the benefit of the group, and it must stipulate rules and tangible policing systems that catch and stop liars and egoists from cheating the altruists ("taking a free ride") and taking over the group with selfish (i.e., individual fitness-enhancing) behaviors. (For more on the discussion of social controls see Sober and Wilson 2002.) The empirical question, therefore, is whether moral codes exist in real groups which regulate enough altruistic behavior in a sufficient number of individuals to cause the group to out-compete an opposing group of selfish individuals. Moreover — to return to the main point of the argument — what role has language played in regulating this kind of altruism and group selection? Elliot Sober and David Wilson, utilizing a random sample of twenty-five cultures selected from the Human Relation Area Files, reached important results concerning the regulation factor and the importance of social norms:

> The current evolutionary view of human behavior tends to portray individuals as free agents who can employ any strategy they want to maximize their inclusive fitness. This view does not deny the existence of social norms, but it does accord them a minor role in the *regulation* of behavior. In contrast, our survey suggests that human behavior is very tightly *regulated* by social norms in most cultures around the world. (1998, 165, emphasis mine)

This appears to be rather powerful evidence that norms indeed have a regulatory effect on individuals, providing a basis for group selection and for the kind of altruism that transcends selfish gene constraints. Sober and Wilson note that social norms therefore serve as a mechanism "that substitutes for genealogical relatedness, making group selection a strong force in human evolution" (1998, 166). To put it succinctly, *social norms can override selfish selection pressures and produce real altruism.* Ironically, Richard Dawkins himself makes this point by boldly claiming that memes enable us to "rebel against the selfish replicators" (1976, 215). In this assertion, Dawkins cleverly uncouples radical altruism from the influence of genes, something that Sober and Wilson wish to re-couple in their version of group selection.

Interestingly, however, Dawkins does not explicitly acknowledge a logical possibility that could follow from his uncoupling claim. Uncoupling radical altruism from genetic influences could, rather than "biologizing" it, result in a form of group selection in which altruism could occur at a *cultural* level, resulting in differential fitness of groups and consequent differences in group populations. It is a reasonable assumption that norms do affect behavior, of course. The empirical question that then arises is whether one finds evidence that norms strongly regulate behavior to the point of facilitating group selection.

A positive answer is suggested by the evidence from the Human Relation Area Files cited in Sober and Wilson (1998). For example, Sober and Wilson cite the Nuer tribal norms that apparently enabled their conquest of the Dinka as evidence of norms that affect altruism and thereby result in ingroup selection. Though a full treatment of his work goes beyond the scope of this chapter, Donald Brown (1991) also provides important evidence for *regulation.* Based on his research, Brown lists a number of apparent cultural universals: inheritance rules, language employed to manipulate others, laws of rights and obligations, sanctions for crimes against the group, and basic moral sentiments. Likewise, common sense suggests that groups in cultures around the world use language-based norms to regulate individual behavior in ways that benefit the group. Further research is still needed, however, to demonstrate empirically how groups employ the *functions* of language in order to attain the *structural*-level adaptations and fitness that we see in group selection.

Ratcheting Altruism through a Linguistic Mechanism

At this point it is necessary to make explicit a process that has been implicitly presupposed throughout the preceding discussion: the means by which groups inculcate or teach their members their norms. Though transmission of norms may be an obvious element of group-oriented morality, a number of interesting questions regarding moral instruction and group selection are still worth probing. Perhaps the most basic question is, Do groups explicitly instruct their members to be altruistic to those in the group who are nonkin as well as to those who are kin? This leads in turn to another basic, but even more difficult, question: How does this instruction actually affect and regulate the behavior of individuals? Finally, regarding the issue of group-level adaptations, do groups explicitly teach their members overtly group-oriented behavior that might indeed expedite groupishness and a group-level adaptation — that is, one that oversees or moves beyond measures of genetic relatedness?

The answer to the first question is transparent: groups do in fact teach morals to their members through language. For one strong empirical example, Carmen Strungaru and Wulf Schiefenhövel point to the cultural universal of proverbs couched in language, which humans use to teach wisdom, altruism, and morality. Of course, empirically measuring the practical effect of proverbial wisdom is extremely difficult. Still, Warren Brown and Lynn Paul argue that, in order to benefit from the wisdom communicated in proverbs, people need to understand and apply them to specific contexts. Their research shows that diminished wisdom frequently occurs in subjects with agenesis of the corpus callosum, a brain disorder that inhibits the processing of information on both sides of the brain. The dysfunction in these patients — an absence of communication between brain hemispheres — suggests that the *presence* of such connections is required to process and apply the wisdom digested in proverbs. In other words, empirical studies do at least show that and how normally developed humans *can apply* the moral codes we couch in language.

The Dark Side of Group Selection

Regarding the third question mentioned above, the common-sense view is that groups do teach groupishness. For example, Jesus' parable of the Good Samaritan, which deals specifically with the Golden Rule, stands out as a scathing criticism of those who engage in altruistic behaviors only toward the in-group and not toward outsiders. As the parable shows, this kind of in-group-only altruism raises a serious problem, which I call the dark side of group selection. John Hartung (1995) provides one of the most forthright discussions of the topic of in-group versus out-group morality. Interestingly, his data on the subject comes from the written ethical teachings and historical documentation of the Judeo-Christian traditions. Hartung argues, contrary to popular sentiment and the aforementioned story of the Good Samaritan, that the Judeo-Christian normative systems in fact provide no basis for moral behavior and behavior directed toward out-group members, but instead explicitly teach a purely in-group-directed morality. In order to defend the thesis of this chapter — that linguistically mediated moral codes can create a sense of virtual relatedness that fosters out-group altruism — it is important that we pause to reveal the serious flaws in Hartung's argument.

First, it is crucial to note how Hartung sets up the topic of group selection. Although he suggests that the moral principles "love your neighbor as yourself" and "do as you would be done to" were explicitly to be applied *to in-group members only,* he also unequivocally rejects group selection — despite the fact that he interprets these codes as severely groupish. Hartung's claim is problematic not only because standard accounts of Judeo-Christian morality maintain that these moral norms were initially meant to have universal application, but also because there are technical reasons within evolutionary theory to conclude that an in-group morality should tend to promote group selection. Along these lines, Hartung asserts that group selection cannot create a natural harmony between in-group members, that is, a *biologically based* altruistic orientation. Moreover, he suggests that laws compelling cooperation stick out as indicators of kin selection and reciprocal altruism, and he prescriptively categorizes fierce punishments of unlawful behavior as conduct that could not have evolved cooperation through group selection since, he maintains, such punishments are intrinsically bad.

Here we are not concerned with what is good or bad about structural-hierarchal evolution but with what is true or false about it. Note that group selection, as a pluralistic, multi-level selection theory, does not need to start at the biological level in evolving organisms. *Initially group selection may not evolve organisms but groups, and it may select for socially controlled, rather than biologically controlled, behaviors.* Moreover, group selection does not need to be responsible for a natural harmony between members; other mechanisms may impose, facilitate, or create the degree of harmony that is necessary for groups to function, for example through linguistically based moral norms and enforcements. In other words, group selection does not need to facilitate morality, but morality can promote group selection.

Consider the phenomenon of fierce punishments that enforce moral norms. We now see that even severe norms do not need to emerge from some puzzling natural kindness that was first produced by group selection. On the contrary, on the present thesis strict norms might enable a group to coalesce and *after that* to become subject to group selection pressures. In short, group selection does not have to evolve natural or biological niceness; other mechanisms — some severe, some not so severe — can evolve altruism. Perhaps, after many generations, the resulting altruism may be "biologized," that is, genetically coded and transmitted. The present argument neither requires nor denies that possibility. Instead, it emphasizes the role that *a linguistically based moral culture* might play in facilitating altruism, rather than how our biological makeup might act as facilitator. Hence I have focused on how groups structurally coalesce and evolve based on the functioning of linguistic moral mechanisms, subsequently becoming subject to group selection pressures, rather than on how group selection might evolve biologically based altruism in individuals.

Introducing Virtual Relatedness

Hartung also discusses William Hamilton's (1964) idea of relatedness, connecting it with altruism and the Golden Rule, love your neighbor as yourself. Hartung translates this rule into biological terms as "love your conspecific as if $r = 1$." If r, the degree of relatedness, somehow became 100 percent, so that $r = 1$, then there would be no genetic conflict of interest among group members, and they would therefore theoretically sacrifice themselves for others because, in this case, they would share identical genetic interests, as twins do. Hartung concludes, however, that because self-sacrificial altruism is the opposite of individual reproductive fitness, it is obvious that natural selection would eliminate it.

I argue, by contrast, that such altruism could exist *if there were mechanisms to maintain it and to protect the individuals who practice it.* As long as there are mechanisms that support altruism, that police against cheating and intruders — and as long as one insists, with the group selectionists, that comparisons be made between altruistic and selfish groups rather than merely between individuals — the theoretical and empirical possibility of group selection for altruism clearly emerges. Of course, Hamilton's own work does not explicitly extend relatedness in this way. His rule states that altruism pays when *b*, the fitness *benefit* to an organism that receives help, and *r*, the *relatedness* of the receiver to the helper, are greater than *c*, the *cost* of the behavior to the helper, or, in short, as long as $br > c$ (Hamilton 1971). This kind of inclusive fitness does not necessarily entail a group-level structural adaptation. Instead, it simply predicts that genetically related individuals will behave altruistically toward each other. The less-related or nonrelated members of the group will not necessarily benefit from these altruistic acts, since they are driven by kinship relations.

In contrast to Hamilton's rule, I would like to introduce the concept of *virtual relatedness*, which builds on Sober and Wilson's idea (1998, 166) that

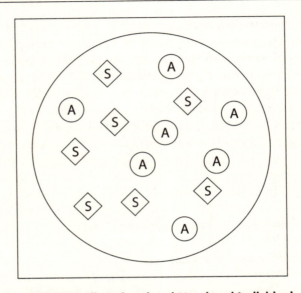

Figure 1: Space of Biologically Related and Unrelated Individuals
In this space, there are two groups of kin, the A group and the S group. S brothers biologically share a relationship of *r = 0.5* and A brothers share a biological relationship of *r = 0.5*, but the biological relation between any S and A nonkin-pair is *r = 0*. A *behavioral* relationship between an S and A non-kin-pair could be virtually similar to a kin pair, however. This would be expressed as a measure of virtual relatedness, e.g., as *vr = 0.5*.

social norms can serve as a mechanism that substitutes for genealogical relatedness. Virtual relatedness, or *vr*, expresses how an individual treats another regardless of biological relatedness; that is, in Darwinian terms, *vr* reflects how *familiarly* one individual treats another individual regardless of actual kinship ties. Thus, from a biological perspective, *vr* quantifies *as-if-behavior*. Behave toward your unrelated neighbor *as if* you were related; treat her *as if* she were your kin, or even *as if* she were you. Take the case of the boating accident in which a teacher sacrifices her life for her student; the teacher's genes are lost, and the unrelated student's genes live on. In this case the teacher gave 100 percent of her fitness to an unrelated individual; she acted *fully as if* the unrelated student were herself, without any interference from genetic conflict of interest. In this particular case, because there was a complete sacrifice of fitness, *vr* would be expressed as 1.

To elucidate *vr*, imagine a selection space with both related and unrelated individuals (see figure 1 above). In this space, assume that all S individuals (shown as diamonds) share a genetic relatedness of $r = 0.5$ and all A individuals (shown as circles) also share a genetic relatedness of $r = 0.5$, but that S and A individuals are completely genetically unrelated. Hence for S and A individuals, $r = 0$. This degree of genetic relatedness will predict altruism among related individuals; moreover, there also exists the possibility of reciprocal altruism between S and A individuals.

The concept of virtual relatedness suggests that behaviors that are completely separate from inclusive fitness and reciprocal altruism might occur in this world. Biologically, an S-A relationship would be expressed as $r = 0$ because they are genetically unrelated. If, however, an A individual were to behave altruistically and sacrificially toward an S individual, a form of virtual relatedness would emerge where, for example, vr could be 0.5. Hence, vr is a measure of behavioral relatedness, not biological relatedness. Moreover, it is not a function of a relationship between replicators; it is an indicator of altruistic behavior that ignores kinship.

Imagine that an A individual has adopted an S individual as a brother and that he behaves toward him as if he were a biologically related brother. In this case the biological relatedness would be $r = 0$ but the virtual relatedness would be $vr = 0.5$. In addition, because vr concerns behavior, an interesting alternative scenario could play itself out. Imagine two A-group individuals who are biologically related brothers, where their biological relatedness is $r = 0.5$, but who have come to hate each other. In actual behavioral terms, their virtual relatedness factor could be $vr = 0$. In this case they are closely related biologically but behave *as if* they are not, since they show no altruism but rather spite toward each other.

The urgent question with regard to virtual relatedness is how it emerges. This is where the moral code comes into play. For the purposes of the discussion, let's imagine that the moral code is some version of the Golden Rule. We express this rule as g, where g represents any specific moral code, idea, or belief couched in language that facilitates altruistic behavior. Now consider the case of the altruistic teacher, which we contemplated above. Presumably the teacher has internalized some g through a very complex process, part of which was linguistic. Note that this fact makes g linguistically detachable from the teacher; hence g is not identical to vr, which expresses the degree of as-if relatedness expressed in her actual behavior. Yet one's linguistically describable moral code, g, clearly *influences* the degree of vr in those conspecifics who have learned and internalized it.

An interesting example of this phenomenon comes to light if we vary the adopted brother scenario above. The adopted brothers' level of biological relatedness is $r = 0$, but their behavioral relatedness could be $vr = 0.5$. Imagine that their behaviors reflect a *vr* of *0.5* because the two brothers falsely believe that they are genuinely biological brothers. Though brothers by adoption alone, they treat each other altruistically *as if* they were biologically related (*vr* represents this altruistic behavior); and their *reason* for being altruistic in their relations to each other is because they believe that they are biological brothers (*g* represents this belief). Their false belief that they are brothers serves as the mechanism that causes them to behave as if they were related.

Of course the belief, or moral code, does not have to be false in order to increase *vr*. A different moral belief could be used, such as "treat your adopted brother as if he were your biological brother." Again, note that *vr* represents the actual level of altruistic behavior, while *g* represents whatever linguistically mediated moral codes, ideas, or beliefs facilitate the altruistic behavior. *In short, the altruistic code,* g, *facilitates* vr, *the altruistic behavior.* In the case of the teacher, *vr* represents her sacrificial behavior on behalf of an unrelated student, and *g* expresses the moral code that she has acquired through a complex process of acculturation in which language serves as an essential ingredient. For example, we might imagine that, when she was still a child, the teacher's parents taught her in word and deed that doing-as-you-would-be-done-to is a good thing.

In short, basic empathy (Preston and de Waal 2002), perception of simple predicates (Hurford 2003), linguistic argument structure, i.e., who does what to whom (Calvin and Bickerton 2000), and the linguistically enabled capacity to categorize and recategorize, that is, to consider X as if it were Y (Chomsky 1965; Monroe 2002), all facilitate the creation, comprehension, and application of altruistic principles *(g)* through language. Such principles (instantiations of the Golden Rule) can be both internalized codes and external codes that are enforced through social controls. Altruistic-moral codes of this type serve as a sort of social calculus, which functions to promote altruistic behavior *(vr)* toward unrelated individuals despite potential genetic conflicts of interest.

Seen from the perspective of group-level adaptation, *g* influences group members toward treating other members of their group as virtual kin. As suggested in this chapter's title, it acts as a lever to ratchet up levels of altruistic behavior. Through *vr* increased and maintained by *g*, individuals engage in fitness-sacrificing behaviors: caring for the sick and less fit; giving food to the needy and weak; providing shelter for the poor; providing medicine, resources, and hygiene for the disabled; and performing the variety of costly behaviors that are necessary to maintain and police the moral order. Although I have used the Golden Rule as a shorthand for such altruistic moral codes, much further work would need to be done to specify the specific behaviors that it entails. The central goal here has been merely to show how linguistic moral mechanisms (which represent a functional hierarchy) might influence group-level adaptations (which are expressed in structural hierarchies). For this purpose it was sufficient to work with the variable g and to use the Golden Rule as a short summary of what is potentially a much larger set of moral codes.

Consider the results we have achieved in terms of two groups of equally distributed biological membership, Group A and Group S, in which altruistic behaviors and selfish behaviors (respectively) dominate. Group A, which is able to increase vr by g, would be more reproductively fit at a group level than Group S, which is not as successful at increasing vr by g. That is, the moral code of Group A enables its members to behaviorally treat nonkin *as if* they were biologically related. Moreover, this selective advantage will remain even though the average *individual* fitness of A-members becomes lower than that of S-members because of their sacrificing individual fitness for the sake of the group. This very simple scenario avoids the averaging fallacy — that is, comparing fitness by means of individual fitness across groups instead of comparing fitness between groups — because it compares groups and not individuals. The key difference between the two groups is the manner in which Group A (the more altruistic group) increases vr, the expression of virtual relatedness. Since both groups will have some kind of linguistically based moral code, the fitter of the two groups is the one that is able to increase and maintain relatedness more efficiently than the less fit group.

The Reciprocity Principle

It is significant that "g plus vr," which in theory can help facilitate individual altruism and group fitness, finds its linguistic formulation in the reciprocity principle, "Do as you would be done to" — or, as George W. Bush has put it, "We must all hear the universal call to like your neighbor just like you like to be liked yourself" (Weisberg 2001, 28). Taking language use as a guide or an empirical pointer, we can track the rule of virtual relatedness as it is articulated in a variety of cultures. Such cross-cultural studies are interesting for at least two reasons: (1) stating the rule requires the use of the argument structure *who does what to whom*, a foundational element of linguistic communication, so that the Golden Rule requires complex human language for its expression; (2) the fact that the Golden Rule finds linguistic expression in cultures and languages all around the world points to the idea that g exists as a cultural universal, a linguistic artifact used by groups to increase and maintain vr. Consider some of the examples collected by Wikipedia (Golden Rule 2003):

900 to 500 BCE — Judaism
"You shall not take vengeance, nor bear any grudge against the sons of your people, but you shall love your neighbor as yourself."

700 BCE — Zoroastrianism
"That nature only is good when it shall not do unto another whatever is not good for its own self."

500 BCE — Buddhism
"Hurt not others in ways that you yourself would find hurtful."

500 BCE — Confucianism
"Do not unto others what you would not have them do unto you."

400 BCE — Socrates
"Do not do to others what would anger you if done to you by others."

150s BCE — Brahmanism and Hinduism
"This is the sum of duty: Do naught unto others which would cause you pain if done to you."

58 CE — Christianity
"And as ye would that men should do to you, do ye also to them likewise."

90 CE — Epictetus
"What you would avoid suffering yourself, seek not to impose on others."

800 CE — Islam
"No one of you is a believer until he desires for his brother that which he desires for himself."

The rule of *vr,* as linguistically articulated in the Golden Rule, is an expression of the effort of human groups to get members to treat nonkin *virtually as* kin, or even as more than kin; it involves the attempt to create a behavioral relatedness where biological relatedness does not actually exist. Incidentally, though we call this rule the ethic of reciprocity, it is different from reciprocal altruism in one significant sense. It is not simply saying to return to others the good (or bad) they have given you. Rather, it says to behave toward others as you would have them behave toward you, or regard others *as if they were you* — or, in Darwinian terms, treat others as if they shared 100 percent of your genes. Treat your neighbor as your twin. Care for conspecifics as clones. Hence, it attempts to push individuals not only to reciprocation, but also to a virtual form of the behavior that facilitates inclusive fitness and kin selection, except that the recipients of the altruistic benefits may be biologically related or unrelated. That is, it calls people to the same kinds of sacrificial behaviors that we associate with kin selection, behaviors that are not conditional on reciprocation. Again: behave as if you were genetically related to this person, even though you are not.

Group Selection, Morality, and Religion

Our focus here has been not so much on how this structural-functional hierarchy would create moral individuals through processes of biological selection, but much more on how a linguistic moral mechanism could at the functional or behavioral level increase the virtual relatedness of individuals. These individuals would in turn coalesce structurally into a group of altruists, especially when compared with another group that is less altruistic. The present thesis thus involves a significantly different claim than that of Sober and Wilson (1998), whose view of group selection holds that genes underlie altruism. By contrast, I have argued that, if a g-code facilitates vr behavior in a group that coalesces and remains more altruistic than another group, the altruistic group will out-compete the selfish group; and group selection will occur because the altruists out-survive the egoists, regardless of what gets biologized. An altruistic cultural influence in g, producing a behavioral element in vr, will help the group attain a higher level of populational or biological fitness than a group with a lower level of vr.

In this scenario, it is important to recognize that the processes, mechanisms, and behaviors affecting altruism can be pluralistic. Some of the altruistic behavior can be produced by inclusive fitness and by reciprocity; not all altruism will be the product of linguistic moral mechanisms or the moral code. From the structural or group selection perspective, a crucial factor is what happens to the group in comparison with other groups.

Moreover, the actual process of group selection may not seem very moral. Thus, for example, Hartung and Pinker (1995 and 2002) decry group selection as involving the morally repugnant kind of evolution co-opted by the Nazis, which is unlikely to produce *good-natured* behavior. Although this is an important concern, the primary focus of my argument is a *descriptive* one: to discover whether group selection actually occurred during human moral evolution. It may well be that we will judge much of the intergroup conflict that accompanies group selection as morally wrong. But whether or not group selection has a dark side is beside the point, at least at first; we simply want to know *whether* it happened. Moreover, there are ways around the dark side of group selection. Moral judgments concerning group selection depend on how the moralizers define the group; since groups manage their moral mechanisms, it should always be possible to expand the circle of the group (Singer 1981; Singer 1997). I return to this issue below.

This brings us to a remarkable feature of Hartung's discourse about intergroup conflict: his dismissal of group selection may actually exemplify a group selection process. Hartung contends that Judeo-Christian teaching has explicitly promoted an in-group morality at the expense of out-groups. At least at one level, this seems to be true: according to the historical data of the Jews, the ancient Israelites in their conquest of Canaan appear to have dispossessed at least seven nations. Moreover, the Hebrew historical records describe the manner in which, in the process of their violent conquest of Canaan, they destroyed out-group members. The data provide other indicators that group-level selection was involved in this process.

Our particular interest lies in the role of the Judaic moral code in relation to the groups involved, and particularly in its role in defining in- and out-groups. Jews verbally prescribed circumcision as a group marker; moreover, and most importantly, they developed numerous strict laws concerning religious ceremonial observance within the group. At the same time, they had a moral law, expressed in the Ten Commandments, that could be significantly summarized in the $r = 1$, "love your neighbor as yourself," command. That is, the logic of the Golden Rule is explicit in each of the commandments that deal with human relations: people do not like being stolen from, so they are told not to steal from others; people do not like being killed, so they are told not to kill; and people do not like having adultery committed against them, so they are told not to commit adultery.

Additionally, many of the punishments for failure to observe the Law were extremely costly to the unlawful, including in many cases the death penalty. It is important to note, however, what emerges when one evaluates the way the Hebrews treated unlawful individuals in their own in-group. *They explicitly treated them as outsiders.* That is, those who defied or broke the code — offspring, parents, siblings, identical twins, cousins, reciprocal neighbors, and any kin or nonkin — were to be treated as outsiders, to various degrees depending on the seriousness of their offenses against the moral mechanism. This is significant because it demonstrates the way in which the moral code defined the group. Egoistic behavior that decreased virtual relatedness was not tolerated at all, and to a significant degree it was *equally* not tolerated in both the in-group and the out-group. Failure to adhere to the moral code, at least in principle, made anyone — regardless of relatedness — an outsider.

If we assume that this severe rule of the moral code actually operated in Hebrew society in the way described in the documents, then these punishments may represent examples of what some call the violent side of group selection. But even if the outsider principle was not actually applied to in-group members in so severe a form, the process described in the texts may still provide a model of the structural-functional process of virtual relatedness. This is because *in either case* the moral rules served to define the group: functioning in this way, they increased the group's fitness by ratcheting up the virtual relatedness of individuals. One may wish to raise moral questions about the fact that this group, with its severe moral code, dispossessed numerous groups with apparently less-strict in-group altruistic codes. But the moral judgments remain secondary to the question of whether linguistically mediated virtual relatedness actually plays the role it appears to play in supporting altruism.

Theoretically speaking, in the process of group selection the group must coalesce to the point of becoming a virtual organism, and organisms build up immunities to viral invaders which block the invaders' selfish attack on the unity of the body. Hence, if the moral code defines the group and blocks or destroys influences that would decrease the virtual relatedness of group members, this is the kind of code that would in fact facilitate group selection — no matter how repugnant we may find it. In summary, then, it appears that there is strong evidence that linguistically based moral mechanisms are able to advance virtual relatedness, to punish offenders (by decreasing their fitness) or to eliminate them (by selecting them out of the environment), regardless of their actual biological relationship or status as insiders or outsiders. The code not only characterizes the group; *the code literally identifies, perpetuates, and regulates the group.*

Conclusion

Studies on altruism stand out as vital today for at least two significant reasons. First, as the Darwinian paradigm continues to find more and more universal application, it still faces serious challenges with regard to explaining altruism, ethics, and morality. Though inclusive fitness and reciprocal altruism have proven to be relatively successful explanations of altruism, serious problems remain unsolved. These unresolved issues represent areas where knowledge is still needed, regardless of what methodology finally provides the answers. This chapter embodies an attempt to demonstrate how insights into human linguistic and categorical abilities shed light on these problems, providing answers that cohere with, but also transcend, mainstream Darwinian explanations of our moral underpinnings.

Second, and most importantly, our moral systems form a compass with which to navigate our individual, communal, national, and global future. It seems undeniable that deepening our understanding of altruism and morality — of what prevents it and what promotes it — represents a beneficial, worthwhile, and intriguing endeavor. The human concern with ultimate issues suggests that we should place a high priority on studies of altruism and morality. It therefore registers a call to scholars across the disciplines — to biologists, philosophers, theologians, sociologists, psychologists, linguists, and others — to continue to enrich our knowledge about what makes humans selfish or spiteful and about how we can develop more altruistic and moral behavior.

REFERENCES

Bekoff, M. 2002. Virtuous nature. *New Scientist* 176:34.

Blackmore, Susan J. 1998. *The Meme Machine.* London: Oxford University Press.

Brown, Donald E. 1991. *Human Universals.* New York: McGraw-Hill.

Brown, Warren S., and Lynn K. Paul. 2002. Broken light: Wisdom and the disconnected brain. http://www.science-spirit.org/articles/articledetail.cfm?article_id=124 (30 September 2003).

Calvin, William H., and Derek Bickerton. 2000. *Lingua ex Machina: Reconciling Darwin and Chomsky with the Human Brain.* Cambridge: MIT Press.

Chomsky, Noam. 1965. *Aspects of the Theory of Syntax.* Cambridge: MIT Press.

Crystal, David. 1997. *The Cambridge Encyclopedia of Language.* New York: Cambridge University Press.

Darwin, Charles. 1871. *The Descent of Man, and Selection in Relation to Sex.* London: John Murray.

Dawkins, Richard. 1976. *The Selfish Gene.* Oxford: Oxford University Press.

de Waal, Frans. 1996. *Good Natured: The Origins of Right and Wrong in Humans and Other Animals.* Cambridge: Harvard University Press.

Dunbar, Robin. 1996. *Grooming, Gossip, and the Evolution of Language.* London: Faber and Faber.

Durham, William H. 1991. *Coevolution: Genes, Culture, and Human Diversity.* Stanford, Calif.: Stanford University Press.

Golden rule, The. 2003. In *Wikipedia: The Free Encyclopedia.* http://www.wikipedia.org/wiki/Golden_rule (25 July 2003).

Hamilton, William D. 1964. The genetical evolution of social behavior, I and II. *Journal of Theoretical Biology* 7:1-52. Also published in *Group Selection,* ed. George C. Williams (New York: Aldine-Atherton, 1971).

Hamilton, W. 1971. The genetical evolution of social behavior, I-II. In G. C. Williams, ed., *Group Selection.* New York: Aldine/Atherton.

Hartung, John. 1995. A light unto the nations: Judeo-Christianity, morality, and group selection. Paper presented at the Human Behavior and Evolution Society Conference (June 28–July 2, 1995) at the University of California, Santa Barbara.

Hurford, J. 2003. The neural basis of predicate-argument structure. *Behavior and Brain Sciences* 23:6.

Jackendoff, Ray. 2002. *Foundations of Language: Brain, Meaning, Grammar, Evolution.* Oxford: Oxford University Press.

Le Page, R. B., and Andrée Tabouret-Keller. 1985. *Acts of Identity: Creole-Based Approaches to Language and Ethnicity.* New York: Cambridge University Press.

McKirnan, D. J., and E. V. Hamayan. 1980. Language norms and perceptions of ethnolinguistic group diversity. Pp. 161-69 in *Language: Social Psychological Perspectives,* ed. H. Giles, W. P. Robinson, and P. M. Smith. Oxford: Pergamon.

Monroe, K. 2002. Explicating altruism. In *Altruism and Altruistic Love: Science, Philosophy, and Religion in Dialogue,* ed. S. G. Post, L. G. Underwood, J. P. Schloss, and W. B. Hurlbut. Oxford: Oxford University Press.

Orwell, George. 1950. *1984.* Harmondsworth, Middlesex: Penguin.

Pinker, Steven. 2002. *The Blank Slate: The Modern Denial of Human Nature.* London: Penguin.

Preston, S., and Frans de Waal. 2002. Empathy: Its ultimate and proximate bases. *Behavioral and Brain Sciences* 25:1.

Schloss, J. P. 2002. Emerging accounts of altruism. In *Altruism and Altruistic Love: Science, Philosophy, and Religion in Dialogue,* ed. S. G. Post, L. G. Underwood, J. P. Schloss, and W. B. Hurlbut. Oxford: Oxford University Press.

Singer, Peter. 1981. *The Expanding Circle: Ethics and Sociobiology.* New York: Farrar, Straus and Giroux.

————. 1997. The drowning child and the expanding circle. http://www.newint.org/issue289/drowning.htm (30 September 2003).

Sober, Elliot, and David Sloan Wilson. 1998. *Unto Others: The Evolution and Psychology of Unselfish Behavior.* Cambridge, Mass.: Harvard University Press.

————. 2002. The fall and rise and fall and rise and fall and rise of altruism in evolutionary biology. In *Altruism and Altruistic Love: Science, Philosophy, and Religion in Dialogue,* ed. S. G. Post, L. G. Underwood, J. P. Schloss, and W. B. Hurlbut. Oxford: Oxford University Press.

Strungaru, Carmen Adriana, and Wulf Schiefenhövel. 2002. The word to the wise: Proverbs and the patterns of the mind. http://www.science-spirit.org/articles/articledetail.cfm?article_id=131 (30 September 2003).

Trivers, Robert L. 1971. The evolution of reciprocal altruism. *Quarterly Review of Biology* 46:35-57.

Weisberg, Jacob, ed. 2001. *George W. Bushisms.* New York: Fireside.

Wierzbicka, Anna. 1996. *Semantics: Primes and Universals.* Oxford: Oxford University Press.

6. "You Have Heard . . . but I Tell You . . .": A Test of the Adaptive Significance of Moral Evolution

David C. Lahti

Darwin suggested that human cultures have tended to progress from a primitive state of morality that only applies to one's own social group to a broader view that accepts all humans, and perhaps even nonhuman organisms, as morally considerable (Darwin 1871, chap. 4). What are the causes of this or other temporal changes in a culture's typical moral attitudes? In this chapter I illustrate how a hypothesis rooted in Darwin's own ideas might contribute to an understanding of such moral evolution.

Morality originated, according to Darwin, as within-group cooperation arising in the context of between-group competition. This cooperation was, and by this theory still is, primarily maintained by the approval and disapproval of other people. This theory is still current, and has been recast and extended by Richard Alexander (1979; 1987; 1989; 1990; 1992). Two of the points emphasized in the newer formulation may provide a way of analyzing the causes of temporal change in a culture's typical moral emphases. First, social selection tends to be the overwhelming determinant that makes human behaviors adaptive. Social selection is that subset of natural selection where the agent or source of selection is other humans. Other people, then, have the greatest effect on individual fitness. Second, social environments (the array of effects that other people are likely to have on an individual's fitness) vary widely from culture to culture, and within a culture over time. These two realizations together imply that certain changes in a society can lead to shifts in what kinds of behaviors, and therefore attitudes, tend to be adaptive (i.e., productive of individual fitness).

I have recently suggested (Lahti 2003) that moral rules can bring older strategies, or patterns of behavior, up to date, thereby facilitating adaptive behavior in a social milieu that changes over time. Certain species-wide fundamental dispositions, such as dedication to kin and honesty in reciprocal interactions, appear to have characterized human sociality for tens of thousands of years or more. These arguably form the bedrock (historically, not necessarily theoretically) of morality's content, and these dispositions still aid us greatly. A rapidly changing social environment may, however, often require alteration or transformation of such basic strategies if behavior is to stay adaptive. Moral norms may provide a valuable mechanism for tracking the social environment. Although they are conservative, typical or average moral emphases and the relative importance of particular rules change over time and differ across human groups. This moral variation might be explainable; much of it might correlate with variation in social environments.

Here I compare the social environments of two periods in the history of a culture (ancient Israel), and explain how a particular moral reform in the latter period (that of Jesus) may have been an adaptive attitude adjustment given the changes in social environment that had been occurring. If changes in moral norms track changes in adaptive behavior, an effective moralist for a given community should emphasize strategies that are adaptive for a typical member of that community in the current social environment, but at variance with older dispositions. Such moral education would encourage deliberation and help adherents to overcome or alter older dispositions in order to act appropriately in a new social context (Lahti 2003). Specifically, the moral teachings of Jesus should realign or modify earlier Jewish moral prescriptions, encouraging attitudes or actions expected to be more adaptive for a typical hearer in Palestine around the turn of the eras than they would have been earlier, say 1500-400 BCE. Moreover, the teachings should emphasize the novel prescriptions relative to ones that were currently conventional. I show that these expectations are met, using Jesus' teachings as set out in the Sermon on the Mount (Matt. 5–7).

Although I treat attributions to Jesus as authentic here, issues of authenticity and authorship are not relevant to my argument; it is sufficient that the statements originated in first-century Judea, which is not disputed by scholars (Neirynck 1993). These teachings exemplify moral emphases that differ from those prevalent in previous centuries in the same culture (see the next section). Moreover, the sociopolitical environment of the region and the time period is well known (Levine 1998), which permits identification of those interpersonal strategies that may have been changing in adaptive value during the period leading up to the teachings. For Christians, a mechanistic understanding of the social background of Jesus' advent and teachings need not be inconsistent with a theological or devotional understanding of the meaning and significance of those events. In fact, a Christian might expect that Jesus did not arrive at a random point in history, but when "the time was ripe" sociologically. This study explores the match between the moral message of Jesus and the social situation into which he brought it.

The social environment of the Jews between roughly 1500 and 400 BCE is an appropriate baseline for comparison with the reforms of Jesus, because distinctive features of their moral system were fixed during this period. This is shown by (1) the content of the Hebrew Bible; (2) the fact that this content is given special authority in religious writings of later Jews (e.g., in the New Testament [Wilson 1989], the Dead Sea Scrolls [Vermes 1997], and the Midrashim [Epstein 1959]); and (3) the influence this period had and still has on the rituals and self-perception of the Jewish people (Ben-Sasson 1976; Dearman 1992).

The Sermon on the Mount is the longest continuous collection of moral teachings attributed to Jesus, and is generally seen as encapsulating them (Richardson 1958; Stott 1978; Guelich 1993; France 1994). "All the articles of our religion, all the canons of our church, all the injunctions of our princes, all the homilies of our fathers, all the body of divinity, is in these three chapters, in this one Sermon on the Mount" (John Donne, cited by Stott 1978). The teachings are also seen as a departure from earlier conceptions of certain moral norms in the culture. This argument will be developed more fully later.

In this chapter I reduce moral statements to evolutionary terms. Such reduction often distorts or destroys the import of statements in the consciousnesses of the hearers and readers for whom the statements were intended; the most essential parts of a theological or devotional exposition of a statement can be lost. My purpose is to bring into relief only those aspects that are potentially relevant to biological function, i.e., human reproductive success. Reducing moral or religious language to biological language is an experimental exercise, performed to facilitate hypothesis generation and testing. This chapter is not intended as a theological revision of the Sermon or an attempt to identify the intentions or knowledge of either Jesus or the Gospel writer. I use "morality" and "morals" in this chapter in the restricted sense of generalized rules for attitudes and behavior, except that I include rules that have been abandoned or considered less relevant in later periods of history. Commonly in writings on morality, the concept is applied preferentially to those rules that rise above, or are robust to, the effects of history or particulars of social environment. This search for a "perennial morality" is worthwhile, but my intention here is precisely to investigate temporal *variability* in moral customs or emphases.

English quotations from the Bible are from the 1971 edition of the Revised Standard Version unless otherwise indicated.

Relations between Social Environment and Morality in Pre-Hellenistic Israel

Two aspects of ancient Hebrew culture are of paramount importance in understanding the relationship between the Hebrews' social environment and their moral code. First, they were monotheistic. Yahweh was the sole God, in full control of the origin and destiny of every individual human and indeed of the whole world (Job; Ps. 104), as well as being the author and enforcer of all laws (Exod. 19–20; Ps. 119). Their monotheism renders plausible an assumption that God's general commands as represented in the Torah approximate the morals generally accepted by the ancient Hebrews. The Hebrew religious system officially permitted no other source of values.

Second, the ancient Hebrews saw themselves as ethnically homogeneous. Jacob, Abraham's grandson, was renamed Israel, and all Hebrews who established the nation of Israel claimed descent from him. (The later term "Jew" originally referred to the southern of the two kingdoms, largely the tribe of Judah, after the civil war [2 Kings 15:6].) The Hebrew people may actually have been a conglomerate of various Semitic peoples (Knight 1993), but in the Torah the Hebrews are distinguished from every other people with whom they come into contact (e.g., Gen. 43:32; Exod. 1:19; 1 Sam. 14:11). The people of Israel are called children of Abraham in several places. Although there are other peoples said to have descended from Abraham, those considered God's people and with whom he made suzerainty or vassalage covenants (Youngblood 1971) are the children of Israel (God chooses Isaac over Ishmael [Gen. 17:20-21] and Jacob over Esau [Gen. 28]). To be a child of Israel was to enjoy a special status with the one true God. Likewise, the moral laws given to the Hebrew people were to be considered in the context of a special covenant with God (Goodman 1998).

Monotheism and ethnic homogeneity were intrinsically complementary. The effect of this combination in the broader polytheistic environment was, however, an unrelenting threat to Hebrew survival as a people throughout their early history. One Judaic scholar writes, "As bearers of the only pre-Christian monotheistic tradition, Jews had often faced extinction by more powerful polytheistic peoples" (Greenspoon 1998, 422). The (at least official) exclusive monotheism of the Hebrew people is thought to have been their most significant point of contention with neighboring peoples, whose polytheistic religious systems were more accommodating to outside deities (Goodman 1998). The Hebrew Bible is filled with accounts of clashes that endanger Hebrew religious identity because of the possibility of idolatry (the worship of gods besides Yahweh). Religious and ethnic considerations were closely linked, such that a threat to either was viewed as a threat to the integrity of the people as a whole. Prospects of their being scattered, mixing with other peoples, or failing to produce offspring were disturbing enough concepts to be the frequently threatened punishments for violating the established covenant with God (e.g., Gen. 11; Lev. 36:33; Deut. 4:27; 1 Kings 14:15; 2 Chron. 18:16; Jer. 9:16; Ezek. 5:10; Zech. 1:21). Ethnic and kin disintegration, together with reproductive failure, was the most widespread curse or ultimate punishment in the Hebrew Bible. Moreover, the threat was real; the Hebrews were subjugated to the Egyptians, Assyrians, Babylonians, Ptolemies, Seleucids, and finally Romans, and for only brief periods of their history were allowed unmolested self-rule, much less expansion (Rajak 1998; Greenspoon 1998).

If moral rules produce adaptive attitude adjustments, one would expect the norms embraced by the Hebrew community to counteract the particular threats they faced. One way in which norms in ancient Israel may have contributed to a preservation of ethnic and religious identity was through moral restrictions on relationships with those outside of the community. Although there are rules even between Hebrew groups (e.g., Gen. 49:7; Lev. 21; Num. 36), the rules governing interaction with non-Hebrews are particularly striking and frequent. The reason given in the Scriptures for the complete removal of the peoples in the Promised Land upon the Hebrews' arrival with Moses is "that you may not be mixed with these nations left here among you, or make mention of the names of their gods, or swear by them, or serve them, or bow down yourselves to them" (Josh. 23:7). In later history ethnic mixing following captivity caused the prophet Ezra to pull out his hair in disgust (Ezra 9:2). Hosea ridiculed the tribe of Ephraim for failing to realize that mixing with foreigners sapped its strength (Hos. 7:8-9). A significant example of this moral emphasis concerns the treatment of foreign women. While Israel was still fighting to conquer a territory for themselves after their return from captivity in Egypt, all women were to be killed in the areas to be assimilated, although women from more distant areas could be taken as wives, presumably to speed the initial process of repopulating the region (Deut. 20–21). After Israel had become established in the Promised Land, intermarriage was strictly forbidden with the remnants of any enemies which still existed around them. God imposed this as a condition for Israel's continued occupation of the land (Josh. 23). Neither women nor men were allowed to marry non-Hebrews (Neh. 13). Soldiers under good leaders would stay chaste during military expeditions to preserve their holiness (1 Sam. 21). The harshest consequences, ranging from execution to widespread plague to the permanent breakup of Israel (1 Kings 11), resulted from Hebrew men taking foreign women, whether as wives or simply as sexual partners.

A broader investigation of the Hebrew social system has yielded results consistent with the biblical emphasis on ethnic homogeneity. In anthropological terms, the Hebrew people were traditionally endogamous, patrilineal, patriarchal, patrilocal, extended, and polygamous. That is to say, they tended to marry close relatives, descent was determined from the father's line, the father was the head of the household, a married woman entered her husband's family, the patriarch's entire family lived with him, and a man could have more than one wife. The central message of the study of Patai (1959) is the strongly kinship-based social system of the Jews, and of other Middle Eastern peoples.

Again, all of this stress on ethnic homogeneity was closely linked to an even greater stress on exclusive monotheism. Idolatry (the worship of gods besides Yahweh) was the first prohibition in the Hebrew Decalogue, and the most mentioned sin in the biblical histories. Often the reason given for the rules against intermarriage was the prevention of idolatry. Thus ethnic homogeneity was considered in the Hebrew Bible to be a means of assuring the proper and exclusive worship of God.

I contend, and hereafter assume, that the moral emphasis among the ancient Hebrews on *one God, one people* was adaptive for an early Hebrew in the face of threats to the integrity of the community, and by extension every individual in it. The *one people* theme ensured that the offspring of a Hebrew individual and relatives would continue to proliferate, that they might (in language redolent of evolutionary meaning) "multiply" their "descendents as the stars of heaven and as the sand which is on the seashore" (Gen. 22:17). The *one God* aspect of their moral code preserved a body of values that kept this ethnic homogeneity and mutual benefit among kin from disintegrating. Without God's laws restricting interaction between the Hebrews and foreigners, the Hebrew people probably would have gone the way of the Hivites, Jebusites, and Amorites, small polytheistic peoples in the region whose group identities disappeared sometime during the tides of empires, if not before. I assume this hypothesis for purposes of this chapter, although more work would be required to carefully present it, and even more to adequately test it.

Changes in Social Environment
Approaching the Time of Jesus

Whatever the reasons for the spread of Greek culture from the third century BCE it was clearly manifested in Palestine, whose integrity as a homeland of the Hebrews (by then largely considered Jews) was already severely disrupted. This disruption was likely due partially to the great might of the empires in comparison to the local enemies of early Hebrew history, and partially to the fact that the Hebrews themselves were becoming less unified against the cultural intrusions. Some of the ruling high-priestly families embraced the Hellenistic movement, causing dissension against them among the people. At one point a pagan cult was even established in the Temple. Only a small portion of the Promised Land was still home to the descendents of Abraham, Isaac, and Jacob, and only a minority of these descendents actually lived in the area any more. During a period of self-rule Israel tried to increase its territory and to convert (and to some extent assimilate) foreigners, Idumaeans, and Itureans. The region was increasingly international and multiethnic. By the time the Roman province of Judea was governed by Herod (himself an Idumaean convert), it contained a mixture of Jews, Greeks, Samaritans, Syrians, and Arabs. In sum, Hebrew cultural integrity was increasingly assaulted in the Hellenistic period, due to both external influence and, partially as a result, internal divergence, in ethnicity and societal values.

After the only partially successful traditionalist revolt led by the Maccabee family, the Jews were "divided over the nature of their privilege and separation." A variety of opinions surfaced as to how best to deal with the apparently inexorable foreign influence. Movements towards stricter isolationism persisted. By the time of Jesus, however, many Jews understood that some degree of reinterpretation of their distinctiveness was necessary. In biological terms, attitudes and behaviors adaptive in an earlier era were becoming less effective in furthering their interests, and they began to explore various prospects for either extending or altering these strategies.

Evolutionary Expectations for Moral Reform

According to the evolutionary account of human morality, what might an updated set of moral norms look like in such a social environment? If the hypothesis is correct that morality tends to adjust the customs of a people adaptively in a changing world, new moral emphases should arise. Moreover, individuals in the population might respond to social trends with different strategies. One possibility is an attempt to reverse the external influence and internal divergence through stricter and more vigorously enforced isolationist policies. Other possibilities would probably involve accommodation to the social changes to some extent.

I propose one key aspect of moral reform in accommodation to a change toward a more socially mobile or multi-ethnic society. Wherever individuals tend to interact with nonrelatives and even members of other ethnic groups on a regular basis, instead of generally dealing closely only with the extended kin group as the Hebrews had in their early history, a *shared values* aspect to social norms should increase in emphasis, relative to the *shared kinship* aspect. Members of such a society will make moral distinctions less often on the basis of relatedness, and more often on the basis of the values people hold and portray. The traditional Hebrew moral perspective emphasized shared kinship, which in a society like theirs would also have been a reliable indicator of shared values. If the above historical account is accurate, by the turn of the eras an individual was increasingly dealing with nonkin and even non-Jews. In certain areas of Palestine, to refuse to interact because others were not closely related or even not Jewish might have carried detrimental social consequences outweighing the benefits accrued through interacting preferentially with kin. Moreover, Jewishness itself was less reliable as a guarantee of shared values due to factions and dissension. From a biological point of view, I propose that the social strategies yielding fitness benefits via nepotism and via indirect reciprocity, though once coincident, were now diverging. Instead of choosing one's interactants solely on the basis of relatedness, social selection in the new environment might have favored those who chose interactants on the basis of their shared value system, thereby gaining greater benefits through indirect reciprocity. Aid given to like-minded members of the community would be returned with interest by them and other like-minded members (regardless of relatedness), producing benefits that would include improvements in one's reputation (Alexander 1987).

Table 1. Socially selected strategies in human societies

Returns to fitness	*Social strategy*
Group stability (benefit accrues to all members)	Foster suppression of competition
	Spread values of group-service (beneficence)
Profitable personal interactions (benefit accrues to self and close kin)	Track the reputations of others; ally with the beneficent; detect and avoid cheats
	Foster a beneficent reputation for oneself; avoid being considered a cheat

Table 1 presents typically adaptive behavioral strategies, according to an evolutionary explanation of human moral systems in large-scale or mixed societies where indirect reciprocity is likely to be of primary importance. If the moral reform of Jesus as portrayed in the Sermon on the Mount reflects an adaptive adjustment to a new social environment, and if the particular mode of adjustment is accommodation rather than isolationism, then the moral statements in the Sermon should emphasize strategies in Table 1, particularly when they are at variance with, or at least not emphasized in, traditional Hebrew morality.

A Test of the Adaptive Significance of Jesus' Moral Reform

I have found 105 statements in the Sermon on the Mount (Matt. 5–7) that I interpret as making moral claims, statements as to what actions or attitudes are to be viewed as good and bad. Statements repeated two or three times I considered separately, to reflect the emphasis given in the text. A veiled style of presentation (parable or metaphor) was employed in twenty-two cases (21 percent). I distilled these statements to thirteen general principles espoused by at least three statements each in the text (Table 2). When statements were specific to an issue (e.g., on divorce, Matt. 5:31-32; on oaths, Matt. 5:34-37) I derived general principles from them consistent with critical commentary (especially Henry [1721] 1991; Vincent 1886; Bruce 1897; Stott 1978; France 1994). These principles were not selected to fit an evolutionary hypothesis, nor were they reduced to evolutionary terms (see Appendix for data by passage). As such, they are intended as a broad survey of the moral emphases of the Sermon. Some statements espouse more than one principle, and some principles overlap in their relevance to particular statements.

Intentionally Introducing Moral Change

One of the central themes or principles of the Sermon on the Mount is the deliberate contrast between the new norms being presented and the norms that would have been familiar to the Jewish people. Among the thirteen principles in Table 2, the theme of changing moral emphases ranks third. Moreover, Jesus indicates with explanation and several examples the intended relation between the new laws and the old (Matt. 5:17-48). The new laws are extensions or modifications of accepted conventions. The repeated phrases "You have heard . . . but I say to you . . . ," and their contexts, make clear that innovations were intended from previous interpretations of the Torah, or Law. Nevertheless, the Law itself was still to be obeyed (Matt. 5:19), and not relaxed or dissolved. Traditionalism and innovation are therefore in tension

Table 2. Thirteen moral principles espoused in the Sermon on the Mount.
Some statements espouse more than one principle.

Principle	Number of statements espousing it	Mentions of reward or consequences
1. Focus on God and perfection	40	19 (48%)
2. Pursue humility	30	15 (50%)
3. New law rises above or extends old law	29	7 (24%)
4. Forgive and reconcile	23	12 (52%)
5. Trust God for needs	14	5 (36%)
6. Be magnanimous	11	3 (27%)
7. Beware of others' wickedness	11	2 (18%)
8. Spread these ideas and lifestyle	9	6 (67%)
9. Do not seek human praise	7	7 (100%)
10. Do not be a hypocrite	7	4 (57%)
11. Thought is as important as deed	6	1 (16%)
12. Seek heavenly, not earthly, goals	6	3 (50%)
13. Suffering can be beneficial	5	5 (100%)

here, which can be appreciated from extra-Sermon statements such as Mark
2:21-22, where the new morality is poetically described as bursting or pulling
away from the old. The remaining sections of the present chapter focus on the
substance of these aspects of contrast.

Redefining Criteria for Membership in the Social Group, and Its Implications

The most important aspect of Table 2 for the purposes of this analysis is what
principle is absent from the list. The greatest contrast in moral emphasis between Jesus' teachings and the lists of prescriptions in the older sections of
the Hebrew Bible is that not a single one of the 105 moral statements in the
Sermon on the Mount encourages moral distinctions based on relatedness,
tribal affiliation, or ethnicity. In fact, consistent with the contempt Jesus
shows for such rules elsewhere (Matt. 8:5-13; Luke 7:1-10; Luke 10:25-37; John
4), he claims them to be inadequate: "If you love those who love you, what reward do you have? . . . And if you greet only your brothers and sisters, what
more are you doing than others?" (Matt. 5:46-47). Jesus recognizes the stereo-

types current under Jewish custom, such as that Jews are more righteous than Gentiles. He uses this stereotype ironically as a mirror to illustrate its falsity, however, and to argue that Jews would need to disintegrate this very division in the service of true righteousness. More often, Jesus' departures from the traditional kinship-based system were implicit, but the differences would not have been missed by audiences in his day. For example, Deuteronomic law prescribed lending freely to those of one's community (Deut. 15:7-8). Jesus, however, taught free lending without qualification (Matt. 5:42). This teaching encourages the very change of attitude that Darwin observed in human cultures: toward moral consideration for all persons regardless of relatedness.

In Jesus' teachings, the concept of kinship is, like all other animal or organic concerns, important only as an analogy for relationships of an entirely different sort, the sort an evolutionary biologist would relate to social selection via indirect reciprocity. Consistent with the hypothesis that the limiting factor on an individual's reproductive success is less often food, wealth, or ethnic group, and more often one's social interactions, especially one's reputation for espousing and acting on group-service values (Alexander 1990), the teachings encourage a transfer of attention from the former considerations to the latter (Table 2, principles 5, 12, 13). In this context, Matthew 6:33 nicely presages the evolutionary expectations from this strategy, assuring that if one attends to what kind of person one is, the meeting of all physical needs will follow. Jesus then redirects kinship language, instructing people to look at the morally perfect Being as their heavenly Father (Matt. 7:11), and to look at each other as kin to the extent that they share values: "Whoever does the will of my Father in heaven is my brother, and sister, and mother" (Matt. 12:50; see also Mark 3:34-35). The prayer he suggests to his audience relates God universally to heaven and earth (Matt. 6:9-10), not just to Israel as did the predominant prayer of the Torah (the *shemah,* Deut. 5:4; 9:1). Instead of ethnic dispersion being the doom of evildoers, Jesus speaks of an eventual ostracism from God and the godly (Matt. 7:2-23). Much of the Sermon on the Mount indicates divisions analogous to kin and nonkin, friend and enemy, Jew and Gentile, but based on *moral* differences rather than kinship, political, or ethnic differences. The concept of "neighbor" is reinterpreted along exactly the same lines, implicitly in the Sermon on the Mount, and explicitly in the Good Samaritan parable. The neighbor is not the person most closely related to you, nor the person who happens to be near you; the neighbor is the person with a certain set of values (Luke 10).

Darwin and Alexander claimed that the division between in-group and out-group formed the social background for the evolution of human morality from its most primitive state. The considerations presented above show that this division is not abolished or ignored by Jesus' teachings in the Sermon on the Mount. Rather, the division is preserved but is placed along different lines. The social world is still binary, with a group to be for and a group to be against. One still must beware and distrust the majority of people, those who enter the broad gate rather than the narrow, the evildoers who are headed for destruction (Matt. 7:13-14; others in Table 2, principle 7). Jesus does not speak against foreigners and the uncircumcised, but he does condemn devious wolves in sheep's clothing, dogs and swine who are dangerous confidants, and foolish men without moral foundation (although these points must be considered alongside the important fact that people can change their group status). In the words of Stott (1978, 19), "There is no single paragraph of the Sermon on the Mount in which this contrast between Christian and non-Christian standards is not drawn. It is the underlying and uniting theme of the Sermon; everything else is a variation of it." Group-sensitive aspects of moral thought and behavior which evolved in a kin-dominated environment are thus redirected in Jesus' teachings, to fit with a more complex social environment. The in-group, delineated primitively on the basis of kinship, is recast in the Sermon on the Mount on the basis of shared values.

Strengthening the Group by Suppressing Aggression

Human propensities that evolved in a nepotistic social environment may lead to problems with aggression and dominance in a society with greater anonymity, mobility, and diversity. Moral norms might accommodate to such a social system via the first adaptive social strategy in Table 1: suppression of competition within the group. Accordingly, nearly every moral prescription in the Sermon fosters suppression of competition either directly or indirectly. Most direct are the exhortations to humility, forgiveness, magnanimity, and the endurance of suffering (Table 2: principles 2, 4, 6, 13).

Enlarging the Group by Fostering Shared Values Universally

The one apparent exception to the Sermon's effect of suppressing competition is the encouragement to spread all of these particular ideas of good and evil to other people (Matt. 5:13-16). This is consistent with the idea of the universal truth of Jesus' claims and the hope that other people, Jew and Gentile, domestic and foreign, will eventually embrace these truths. This value was not emphasized in the Hebrew Scriptures, but is one of Jesus' strongest emphases (e.g., Matt. 25:32-33; Matt. 28:19-20; Mark 13:10; Luke 14:47; John 14:6).

A proselytizing attitude is likely to meet with competitive resistance from other people who hold differing views, as Jesus reminded his disciples, even as he told them to evangelize anyway, and boldly (Matt. 10:13-23; 24:9; Mark 6:10-11; Luke 9:5, 10:10-16). This encouragement to spread the values espoused by the Sermon is precisely the expected strategy according to evolutionary theory (Table 1, second strategy). If, as I have proposed, values and not kinship are the primary basis for moral distinctions among people in the new social environment, then values constitute the primary criterion for membership in one's social group, and the spread of one's values enlarges the group. Thus, moral emphases of Jesus that differ from those in earlier Hebrew tradition are tailored to at least the first two adaptive strategies in Table 1, those that serve group stability.

Assuring Shared Values in Personal Relations

The last two strategies in Table 1 relate to personal benefits from social interactions, where indirect reciprocity is a primary force. As discussed above, the lack of emphasis on kinship as a basis for moral distinctions in the Sermon is accompanied by an increased emphasis on shared values. In earlier periods, kinship would have served as an effective proxy. In a more diverse and mobile social environment such as was developing by Jesus' time, evolutionary theory implies that giving greater priority to critical awareness of the actions and attitudes of others would be adaptive. Eleven (10.5 percent) of the statements in the Sermon are devoted to this issue (Table 2, principle 7). For instance, disciples are warned to watch out for those who may attempt to gain benefits from others' adherence to community norms without abiding by them themselves (Matt. 7:15-23). These people are precisely the "cheats" of evolutionary studies of human sociality (Trivers 1971; Dawkins 1976). Cheats are a dangerous component in society because their strategy will be successful until enough members of society bear grudges against them and refuse to succumb to their parasitism. The fact that cheats will disguise themselves as reciprocating members of the community is central in the Sermon, and also in contemporary evolutionary theory. A cheat must avoid detection, for if detected the society is expected to begrudge the cheat the benefits that accrue to truer social participants. The Sermon's discussion of good and bad trees and their fruit (Matt. 5:16-20) can be understood in evolutionary terms as a lesson in cheat-detection. All nine instances in Jesus' teachings of the two cautionary words translated "beware" (προσεχω, βλεπω) warn against the dangers of others' moral deceit or corruption.

Enhancing Individual Reputation

In line with the final strategy in Table 1, the directive to manage one's own character is the most prominent theme in the Sermon on the Mount (especially Table 2, principle 1). The strategy Jesus preaches (and the one evolutionary theory predicts would be preached, if not followed) is to be "single-minded" in one's commitment to the values one presents (Bruce 1897). The word used (Matt. 6:22) is ἁπλοῦς, which creates an image of "a piece of cloth or other material, neatly folded *once*, and without a variety of complicated folds" (Vincent 1886, 41). The contrast is to a hesitancy or calculation of a double-minded person (e.g., Matt. 6:24). Half of all the Sermon's statements include a mention of consequences, and in all of them adherence to the guidelines produces benefits for the individual so adhering, and failing to adhere produces long-term costs. Appropriately, from the perspective of indirect reciprocity, the word used for the effect a moral violation has on a person (usually translated "offend") is σκανδαλίζει, literally "scandalize" (Matt. 5:29).

The Sermon particularly addressed temptations that would have been prevalent in a society where deception as to one's commitment to group values might increasingly be perceived as a shortcut to benefits (on which see Alexander 1989). Accordingly, there were seven prohibitions against boasting, and seven against hypocrisy (Table 2, principles 9, 10). Regarding boasting, France (1994) points out that "deliberate ostentation for one's own prestige" is warned against (Matt. 6:1), and is distinct from the "natural testimony of a godly life," which is encouraged (Matt. 5:16). Unfairly impugning the reputations of others was harshly condemned (Matt. 7:1-5), which is unsurprising considering the high importance of reputation in the context of indirect reciprocity. As Bruce (1897, 128) writes, the traditional *lex talionis* of "eye for eye" was reformed by Jesus into "character for character." In fact, the text deals with public perception of character, so the reformation is more precisely into "reputation for reputation." If you injure another's maliciously, yours will be harmed in return.

Conclusion

The principles espoused in the Sermon on the Mount (Table 2) can be related to strategies that, according to a Darwinian account of the evolution and biological function of morality, would have been adaptive in the changing social environment of the Hebrews (Table 1). Although a much closer study could be made, and much more data is available in addition to the Sermon on the

Mount, the limited analysis here shows that Jesus' moral reform accords with expectations from evolutionary theory in a multi-ethnic society where shared values do not necessarily follow lines of shared ancestry, and where social costs and benefits require cooperation with nonkin. Moreover, Jesus' moral teachings represented a realignment of traditional Hebrew morality (Rousseau 1998). In the words of another commentator, "preexisting traditions were transformed" (Verhey 1993). What is suggested here is that these changes in emphasis are in line with Darwin's understanding of the evolution of morality, as recently expounded by Alexander and others. A Christian interpretation of this finding is that Jesus' life and teachings existed at a time when they would have maximal societal impact. This is consistent with the conventional theological position that God accommodates himself to human limitations and particular states of development. The fact that evolutionary biology can help address the question of why Jesus came when he did is surprising, and perhaps ironic, considering the animosity toward the science in many Christian circles.

These results lend support to the hypothesis that variation in morality, including moral reforms, can serve a biological function by acting as a cultural surrogate for genetic adaptation, as many other plastic human traits do. Change in moral norms can sometimes update or adjust typical human attitudes and behaviors in ways that are adaptive in new social environments. For the Christian the implication is that Jesus' morality is not a limitation on health and happiness in this life, but is in fact a means to it. This is consistent with the original meaning of "blessed" (μακάριοι), the repeated promise in the Beatitudes (Vincent 1886).

Besides the prospects of a more detailed study of Jesus' moral reform, two other lines of research would further illuminate the relation of social changes in ancient Palestine to changes in morality. First, Hebrew culture before Jesus was not monolithic, nor was its state of morality constant. A closer look at later writings in the Hebrew Bible and afterward would shed light on precisely how Hebrew culture was evolving. Given the diversity of perspectives at the time, some of these later writings are likely to have exhibited isolationist tendencies, but others might have approached Jesus' innovations, particularly among people who could benefit from interaction with foreigners. Second, Jesus and the Christianity he inspired constitute only one of the two major traditions to arise from the social upheaval of late antiquity in Palestine. Religious historians and Jewish scholars, not surprisingly given the hypothesis presented here, generally present Judaism as entering its second major phase (often termed rabbinic or pharisaic-rabbinic) during this time period. A look at the synapomorphies, or shared derived features, among the two traditions would provide further insights. What aspects of Christianity and rabbinic Judaism caused both groups to succeed and others to fail? According to Barbara Geller (1998) they appear to have shared several cultural characteristics. Isolationism or insulation from outside influence may have persisted in areas where they were feasible and beneficial. Among other more cosmopolitan subgroups, rabbinic Judaism might have undergone a moral evolution that bears interesting parallels to that encouraged by Jesus.

Appendix

Categories of moral principles espoused in the Sermon on the Mount by passage. See Table 2 for principles corresponding to codes 1-13.

Passage	Codes	Passage	Codes
Matt. 5:3	2	Matt. 5:30	1, 13
Matt. 5:4	2, 13	Matt. 5:31	3, 4
Matt. 5:5	2	Matt. 5:32	3
Matt. 5:6	1	Matt. 5:34a	2, 3
Matt. 5:7	4	Matt. 5:34b	2, 3
Matt. 5:8	1	Matt. 5:35a	2, 3
Matt. 5:9	4	Matt. 5:35b	2, 3
Matt. 5:10	1, 13	Matt. 5:36	2, 3
Matt. 5:11	1, 13	Matt. 5:37	2, 3
Matt. 5:13	8	Matt. 5:39a	2, 3, 4, 6
Matt. 5:14	8	Matt. 5:39b	2, 3, 4, 6
Matt. 5:15	8	Matt. 5:40	2, 3, 6
Matt. 5:16	8	Matt. 5:41	2, 3, 6
Matt. 5:17a	3	Matt. 5:42	3, 6
Matt. 5:17b	3	Matt. 5:43	3, 6
Matt. 5:19a	3	Matt. 5:44a	2, 3, 4, 6, 8
Matt. 5:19b	3, 8	Matt. 5:44b	3, 4, 6, 8
Matt. 5:20	1, 3	Matt. 5:46	1, 3, 4, 6, 8
Matt. 5:21-22a	3, 4, 11	Matt. 5:47	1, 3, 4, 6, 8
Matt. 5:22b	3, 4, 11	Matt. 5:48	1, 3
Matt. 5:23-24	4	Matt. 6:1	2, 9
Matt. 5:25	4	Matt. 6:2	2, 9
Matt. 5:28	3, 11	Matt. 6:3-4	1, 2, 9
Matt. 5:29	1, 13	Matt. 6:5	2, 9

Passage	Codes	Passage	Codes
Matt. 6:6	1, 2, 9	Matt. 6:34	5, 12
Matt. 6:7	1, 2	Matt. 7:1	2, 4, 10
Matt. 6:8	1, 2	Matt. 7:2a	2, 4, 10
Matt. 6:9	1	Matt. 7:2b	2, 4, 10
Matt. 6:10a	1	Matt. 7:3	2, 4, 10
Matt. 6:10b	1	Matt. 7:4	2, 4, 10
Matt. 6:11	1, 5	Matt. 7:5	2, 4, 10
Matt. 6:12	4	Matt. 7:6a	7
Matt. 6:13a	1	Matt. 7:6b	7
Matt. 6:13b	1	Matt. 7:7a	1, 5
Matt. 6:14	4	Matt. 7:7b	1, 5
Matt. 6:15	4	Matt. 7:7c	1, 5
Matt. 6:16	2, 9	Matt. 7:9-11	1, 5
Matt. 6:17-18	2, 9	Matt. 7:12	3, 4, 6
Matt. 6:19	1, 2, 12	Matt. 7:13a	1
Matt. 6:20	1, 12	Matt. 7:13b	1, 7
Matt. 6:22	1, 11	Matt. 7:14	1, 7
Matt. 6:23a	1, 11	Matt. 7:15	7
Matt. 6:23b	1, 11	Matt. 7:16a	7
Matt. 6:24a	1, 12	Matt. 7:16b	7
Matt. 6:24b	1, 12	Matt. 7:17	7
Matt. 6:25a	5	Matt. 7:18	7
Matt. 6:25b	5	Matt. 7:19	7
Matt. 6:26	1, 5	Matt. 7:20	7
Matt. 6:27	5	Matt. 7:21	1
Matt. 6:28	5	Matt. 7:22-23	10
Matt. 6:28-30	1, 5	Matt. 7:24-25	1
Matt. 6:31	5	Matt. 7:26-27	1
Matt. 6:33	1, 5, 12		

REFERENCES

Alexander, Richard D. 1979. *Darwinism and Human Affairs.* Seattle: University of Washington Press.

———. 1987. *The Biology of Moral Systems.* Hawthorne, N.Y.: Aldine de Gruyter.

———. 1989. Evolution of the human psyche. Pp. 455-513 in *The Human Revolution,* ed. P. Mellars and C. Stringer. Edinburgh: University of Edinburgh Press.

———. 1990. How did humans evolve? Reflections on the uniquely unique species. *University of Michigan Museum of Zoology Special Publication* 1:1-38.

————. 1992. Biological considerations in the analysis of morality. Pp. 163-96 in *Evolutionary Ethics*, ed. M. H. Nitecki and D. V. Nitecki. Albany, N.Y.: State University of New York Press.

Barkow, Jerome H., Leda Cosmides, and John Tooby, eds. 1992. *The Adapted Mind: Evolutionary Psychology and the Generation of Culture*. New York: Oxford University Press.

Ben-Sasson, Haim H., ed. 1976. *A History of the Jewish People*. Cambridge, Mass.: Harvard University Press.

Bruce, Alexander Balmain. 1897. The Synoptic Gospels. Pp. 3-651 in *The Expositor's Greek Testament*, ed. W. R. Nicoll. London: Hodder and Stoughton.

Darwin, Charles. 1871. *The Descent of Man, and Selection in Relation to Race*. London: John Murray.

Dawkins, Richard. 1976. *The Selfish Gene*. Oxford: Oxford University Press.

Dearman, J. Andrew. 1992. *Religion and Culture in Ancient Israel*. Peabody, Mass.: Hendrickson.

Epstein, Isidore. 1959. *Judaism*. Baltimore: Penguin.

France, R. T. 1994. Matthew. Pp. 904-45 in *New Bible Commentary*, ed. D. A. Carson, R. T. France, J. A. Motyer, and G. J. Wenham. Downers Grove, Ill.: InterVarsity.

Geller, Barbara. 1998. Transitions and trajectories: Jews and Christians in the Roman Empire. Pp. 561-96 in *The Oxford History of the Biblical World*, ed. M. D. Coogan. New York: Oxford University Press.

Goodman, Martin David. 1998. Jewish religion. Pp. 592-94 in *The Oxford Companion to Classical Civilization*, ed. S. Hornblower and A. Spawforth. New York: Oxford University Press.

Greenspoon, Leonard J. 1998. Between Alexandria and Antioch: Jews and Judaism in the Hellenistic period. Pp. 421-65 in *The Oxford History of the Biblical World*, ed. M. D. Coogan. New York: Oxford University Press.

Guelich, Robert A. 1993. Sermon on the Mount. Pp. 687-89 in *The Oxford Companion to the Bible*, ed. B. M. Metzger and M. D. Coogan. New York: Oxford University Press.

Henry, Matthew. [1721] 1991. *Commentary on the Whole Bible*. Vol. 6. Peabody, Mass.: Hendrickson.

Kellner, Menachem. 1991. Jewish ethics. Pp. 82-90 in *A Companion to Ethics*, ed. P. Singer. Oxford: Blackwell.

Knight, Douglas A. 1993. Hebrews. Pp. 273-74 in *The Oxford Companion to the Bible*, ed. B. M. Metzger and M. D. Coogan. New York: Oxford University Press.

Lahti, David C. 2003. Parting with illusions in evolutionary ethics. *Biology and Philosophy* 18:639-51.

Levine, Amy-Jill. 1998. Visions of kingdoms: From Pompey to the first Jewish Revolt. Pp. 467-514 in *The Oxford History of the Biblical World*, ed. M. D. Coogan. New York: Oxford University Press.

McConville, Gordon. 1994. Biblical history. Pp. 20-42 in *New Bible Commentary*, ed.

D. A. Carson, R. T. France, J. A. Motyer, and G. J. Wenham. Downers Grove, Ill.: InterVarsity.

Neirynck, Frans. 1993. Genre of Gospel. Pp. 258-59 in *The Oxford Companion to the Bible,* ed. B. M. Metzger and M. D. Coogan. New York: Oxford University Press.

Patai, Raphael. 1959. *Sex and Family in the Bible and the Middle East.* Garden City, N.Y.: Doubleday/Dolphin.

Rajak, Tessa. 1998. Jews. Pp. 380-83 in *The Oxford Companion to Classical Civilization,* ed. S. Hornblower and A. Spawforth. New York: Oxford University Press.

Richardson, Alan. 1958. *An Introduction to the Theology of the New Testament.* London: SCM.

Rousseau, Philip. 1998. Christianity. Pp. 153-58 in *The Oxford Companion to Classical Civilization,* ed. S. Hornblower and A. Spawforth. New York: Oxford University Press.

Stott, John R. W. 1978. *The Message of the Sermon on the Mount.* Downers Grove, Ill.: InterVarsity.

Trivers, Robert. 1971. The evolution of reciprocal altruism. *Quarterly Review of Biology* 46:35-57.

Verhey, Allen D. 1993. Ethical lists. Pp. 201-2 in *The Oxford Companion to the Bible,* ed. B. M. Metzger and M. D. Coogan. New York: Oxford University Press.

Vermes, Geza. 1997. *The Complete Dead Sea Scrolls in English.* New York: Allen Lane, Penguin.

Vincent, Marvin R. 1886. *Word Studies in the New Testament,* reprint. Vol. 1. Peabody, Mass.: Hendrickson.

Wilson, Marvin R. 1989. *Our Father Abraham.* Grand Rapids: Eerdmans.

Youngblood, Ronald. 1971. *The Heart of the Old Testament.* Grand Rapids: Baker.

II. Religious and Evolutionary Ethics — Are They Compatible?

7. Evolution and Divine Revelation: Synergy, Not Conflict, in Understanding Morality

Loren Haarsma

Is Guilt Adaptive? Is Morality Relative?

A cartoon by Sidney Harris pictures two atoms, one captioned "atom in a bird's brain," the other, "atom in a human's brain." The two are identical (Harris 1997). This makes us laugh precisely because it makes us uncomfortable. We have made peace with the idea that human and animal bodies are composed of exactly the same atoms obeying the same physical laws. Discussing the human brain, however, involves human intelligence and behavior. We find unsettling the suggestion that human behaviors — including moral sentiments — were shaped by the same evolutionary processes that shaped animal behaviors. This disturbing claim is at the heart of sociobiology and evolutionary psychology.

Consider feelings of guilt. Lions, we presume, feel no guilt when they kill in order to eat. An evolutionary argument could be made that guilt is maladaptive. Lions who felt guilty about killing gazelles would not hunt as well, and therefore would leave fewer offspring. Humans do feel guilt, at least when harming other humans. We say that it is pathological for humans not to feel guilt. First, we ask a scientific question: Can we construct an evolutionary explanation for why human ancestors who felt guilt tended to produce more offspring than those who did not? Second, we ask a philosophical question: If we can construct an evolutionary explanation for human guilt, would that mean that guilt is nothing but an evolutionary construct imposed by our genes, so that there is no longer any objective reason for one human to feel guilt when harming another?

There is considerable debate regarding the philosophical implications of sociobiology and evolutionary psychology. Much of the debate concerns morality. The term *moral relativism* is used several ways. In this chapter, moral relativism refers to the view that each individual and each culture develops moral standards acceptable to itself, and that there are no universal or objective standards, true for all humans, by which one individual or culture should judge the moral standards of another. By *objective*, I mean standards which have their essential reality grounded in something outside of particular human individuals or cultures. Objective standards are considered by various people to be grounded in God, in fundamental laws of nature, in logic and self-evident principles, or in a "universal" human nature common to all (or at least the vast majority of) humans. Objective moral standards are correct whether or not any particular individual or culture assents to them.

Sociobiology and evolutionary psychology are used by some scholars to support versions of moral relativism (Alexander 1993; Blackmore 2000; Cronin 1991; Cronk 1994; Dawkins 1976; Ruse 1994; Ruse and Wilson 1993; Trivers 1991; Voorzanger 1987; E. O. Wilson 1978), and to support the claim that religion is essentially a cultural delusion which, at best, might help one individual or group compete against another individual or group (Alexander 2001a; Blackmore 2000; Miller 1999; Mithen 1999; D. S. Wilson 2002). These arguments require at least two steps. First is the scientific claim that we can construct accurate evolutionary explanations for the existence of moral and religious sentiments. Second is the philosophical claim that, because these sentiments evolved, moral and religious beliefs have no objective status or truth content.

Problem in Science or Problem in Philosophy?

Many people dispute this philosophical claim. Traditional Christian theology, in particular, holds that moral and religious beliefs do have objective status and truth content. Individuals who believe that Christian theology is correct on this point could choose to attack the scientific claim that human moral and religious sentiments evolved. Many writers have done so (e.g., Colson 1998; Yancey 1998). The scientific fields of sociobiology and evolutionary psychology are young. Because these fields presently have theories running well in advance of empirical data, this might seem an attractive strategy. Nevertheless, I believe it is the wrong strategy. The problem does not lie in the scientific claim. The problem lies in the philosophical claim that *if* our moral and religious sentiments evolved, *then* moral and religious beliefs cannot have objective status or truth content.

When pursued with proper scientific care, the scientific claim is compatible with essential Christian beliefs about morality provided two things are done. First, science must be considered separately from some unnecessary philosophical additions. Second, at some points in human history, the evolutionary development of morality must be augmented with divine personal revelation.

Scientific Baby: Evolutionary Accounts of Altruism and Morality

Others in this book have written about kin selection and reciprocal altruism (see also, respectively, Hamilton 1964 and Trivers 1971). Because of space constraints, I will only briefly summarize four competing scientific hypotheses for why humans display altruism beyond kin and beyond reciprocation. Such "extended" altruism is considered an important element of human morality.

One hypothesis is that altruism beyond kin and beyond reciprocation is a non-adaptive side effect of other adaptive traits (Ayala 1995; Gould and Lewontin 1979; Oyama 2000; Schwartz 1986; Vine 1992). Humans are intelligent. We can predict probable outcomes of our actions. We can make value judgments, that is, select some outcomes as more desirable than others. We are self-aware. We perceive other humans as self-aware individuals with their own knowledge and goals. We have empathy for the mental state of others. All of these abilities might be adaptive. (Individuals who have them in greater degrees are more likely to produce offspring.) In combination, these abilities produce extended altruism and morality as a side effect.

A second hypothesis is that altruism and morality are cultural phenomena (Blackmore 2000; Schwartz 1986; Smith 2000; Williams 1988). Our genes do not predispose us to morality beyond kin or reciprocation, but our culture teaches us to act this way. Groups that have a culture that promotes morality and altruism tend to out-compete groups that have selfish cultures. Cultures that promote morality tend to replace or convert cultures that do not.

A third hypothesis proposes that altruism and morality are adaptive and have a genetic basis. Being altruistic and behaving morally enhances your reputation, increases your social status, and thereby brings you benefits in the long run (Alexander 1993, 2001b; Cronin 1991; Cronk 1994; Miller 1999; Ruse and Wilson 1993). A variation on this hypothesis is that behaving morally is a "price of admission" for group membership. An individual's reproductive success is greatly enhanced when he or she belongs to a successful group. Groups don't tolerate members who are constantly selfish.

A fourth hypothesis is that altruism and morality are adaptive at the group level (D. S. Wilson 2002). Altruistic individuals produce fewer offspring than selfish individuals within the same group; however, the benefits of being in a group composed mostly of altruists outweigh the costs imposed by the small number of selfish individuals within the group. Altruism is group-selected if there is a large amount of group-group competition and if there is occasional mixing of group membership — especially if altruists can cluster when forming groups.

These four types of hypotheses are quite different scientifically but have interesting common features. All presuppose critical roles for human intelligence, memory, rationality, and long-term interpersonal interaction in complex social groups. Under those conditions, all these hypotheses agree that the evolutionary development of altruistic sentiments and moral systems is not only possible, but perhaps inevitable.

Some Philosophical Bathwater

Much of the popular literature — and some of the professional literature — in sociobiology and evolutionary psychology mixes philosophical arguments with scientific hypotheses. It often takes serious effort to understand where science ends and philosophy begins. The philosophical bathwater repels many Christians, and non-Christians, from the scientific baby of evolutionary psychology. It's not necessarily improper to argue philosophical inferences from scientific results, or to mix science and philosophy in popular or professional articles. There is, however, good reason to be cautious when doing so. By critiquing philosophical inferences in some recent literature, we will see how the science of evolutionary psychology and sociobiology is compatible with multiple philosophical views, and in particular is compatible with Christian theological beliefs about morality.

From "How Morality Evolved" to "Why Morality Exists"

Once we have a scientific hypothesis for *how* something exists, it is tempting to make the philosophical inference that this is also *why* it exists. Richard Dawkins (1976), as well as Michael Ruse and Edward O. Wilson (1993), do this in the evolution of human morality. Scientifically, they hypothesize that, once humans started living in large, complex social groups, individuals whose genes made them constantly selfish were punished by the group and therefore produced fewer offspring than individuals whose genes made them believe in an objective moral code. Moving into philosophy, Ruse and Wilson (1993) write, "Morality, or more strictly our belief in morality, is merely an adaptation put in place to further our reproductive end."

To avoid Ruse and Wilson's philosophical conclusion, we need not dispute their scientific hypothesis about how morality evolved. We need only dispute their philosophical extrapolation as to why morality exists. Even if we restrict ourselves to an atheistic worldview, this extrapolation is questionable. Donald MacKay (1965) would call this an example of "the fallacy of nothing but-tery." This is the assertion that a description of something at one level renders other levels of description meaningless. From our everyday experience, we know that a successful description on one level does not invalidate other levels of description. For example, one might assert that a Shakespeare sonnet is "nothing but" ink blots on a page (MacKay 1965). True, one way to describe a sonnet is to precisely specify the page coordinates of every ink blot. This description is valid and complete on its own level; however, one could also analyze the sonnet linguistically, emotionally, socially, historically, and on other levels. If one is programming an inkjet printer, the most important description is in terms of ink blot coordinates. For almost every other purpose in life, however, that is an unimportant level of description. In the same way, a complete evolutionary description of the existence of morality does not necessarily invalidate the truth, utility, or significance of other levels of description of morality.

If we do not restrict ourselves to atheism and instead allow for the existence of a creator, the extrapolation from *how morality evolved* to *why morality exists* fails further. Consider an analogy. Suppose an inventor builds a robot which could do a variety of useful things — mow the lawn, clean the house, grade homework, write book chapters, and so on. One thing this robot can do, given a complete set of spare parts, is build a replica of itself. Whenever the inventor needs another robot, she gives one robot a set of spare parts and has it build a replica of itself. Amongst all the software subroutines within this robot, there is a set of subroutines that govern the robot's self-replication, including the replication of those self-replication subroutines. Would it be correct to say that the purpose of the robot's existence is merely to reproduce those particular self-replication subroutines? Do all of the other software and hardware of the robot — which allow it to mow the law, and so on — merely further the reproductive ends of those self-replication subroutines? At one level, the robot's hardware and software do serve to reproduce those self-replication software routines. At another level of analysis, however, those self-replication software routines serve the robot to produce more copies of itself. At still another level, those self-replication software routines serve the robot's creator. The creator of the robot should get the last word as to which of those levels of description is most important.

In humans, does morality exist to further the reproduction of certain genes, or do those genes exist in order to allow for the production of new human beings who can behave morally? If human beings have a creator, the creator gets the final word on the question of purpose. The mechanism which the creator used to make those genes — whether *de novo* or via evolution — is secondary. The creator's purpose in creating those genes decides the issue.

"Selfish" Language

Some popular literature in sociobiology and evolutionary psychology employs a linguistic maneuver in which every action that improves one's reproductive chances is labeled "selfish" (Alexander 2001b; Cronk 1994; Dawkins 1976; Ruse and Wilson 1993). No matter how altruistic one's motives might be psychologically, if the action has the slightest long-term benefit to one's reproductive chances, the action is labeled "selfish."

Let us for now explore the scientific hypothesis that some human actions which are psychologically altruistic might also be evolutionarily adaptive — if we are nice to other people out of a genuine desire to be nice, we tend on average to have more children. One philosophical spin to put on this hypothesis is to describe such psychologically altruistic acts as "reproductively selfish." A second, equally supportable, philosophical spin is that being nice to others causes individuals and groups to flourish. Evolution operates such that, when intelligent individuals live in complex social groups where individuals interact over long periods of time and where cooperation is frequently rewarded, nice people really do finish first on average. The scientific hypothesis seems compatible with at least two different philosophical interpretations.

Humans display a spectrum of behaviors. Some behaviors have almost purely selfish motives, some have almost purely altruistic motives, most are somewhere in-between. If the goal is to understand the rich spectrum of human behaviors and motivations, then the linguistic trick of giving every action on that spectrum a single label, "selfish," is counter-productive.

Moral Responsibility

Sociobiology and evolutionary psychology make hypotheses about genetic predispositions toward behaviors. This raises philosophical questions about human responsibility for actions. It is tempting to conclude that if someone knows she has genetic predispositions toward a certain behavior, then she is less responsible for that behavior. The opposite conclusion could be argued, however. Knowledge about genetic factors which influence one's behavior should actually increase one's responsibility for one's behavior. Both our everyday experience and the results of modern neuroscience indicate that we cannot separate our biological and psychological aspects. As neuroscientist Malcolm Jeeves (1993) and others point out, the direction of causation in our brains seems to go both bottom-up (levels of neurotransmitters in the brain can affect the conscious state of mind and decisions) and top-down (conscious decisions can, over time, affect neurotransmitter levels).

The more we know about genetic predispositions, the more we can take responsibility for our actions. Note the peculiar phrase, "*taking* responsibility." We acknowledge that biological factors beyond our control were, to a greater or lesser extent, responsible for our current unpleasant situation, whether that is drug addiction, depression, a quick temper, or a hateful attitude. Now that we are aware of those biological factors, however, we can do something about them, which makes us responsible for doing something about them. Armed with knowledge about biological factors, we are better able to design an effective strategy — possibly using a combination of medical, behavioral, social, and spiritual strategies — to improve our behavior. The more we know about our genetic predispositions, the more we can take responsibility for our actions.

Science-or-God Fallacy

Implicit in many popular writings on human evolution is the fallacy that finding successful scientific explanations for human behavior, in terms of natural evolutionary processes, is tantamount to proving that God is uninvolved, even nonexistent. It's not unusual for people to classify events as being due *either* to God *or* to natural processes, as if those were exclusive categories. This may be a commonly held picture of how God interacts (or doesn't interact) with the universe, but it is not the picture presented in the Bible or Christian theology. Scripture proclaims that God is sovereign over all events, ordinary or extraordinary, natural or supernatural.

With this biblical perspective in mind, a successful scientific explanation of the evolution of human moral sentiments does not threaten to remove God from the picture. The biblical response, and the response of traditional Christian theology, is that even if we can describe how human morality evolved through natural laws, God — the creator and sustainer of natural laws — could still be in charge. We have simply learned how God accomplished that particular event (MacKay 1965, 1988).

Theological versus Mechanistic Explanations

Another philosophical question concerns the apparent conflict between the teleological nature of theological explanations and the mechanistic nature of evolutionary explanations. To analyze this, we first consider a simple question for which an evolutionary explanation might seem to conflict with a theological explanation. Question: *Why do polar bears have thick fur?* Theological answer: *Polar bears have thick fur because God created them to live in cold climates.* Evolutionary-answer-A: *Polar bears have thick fur because they evolved through natural processes to live in cold climates, where thick fur provided selective advantage.* The apparent conflict between these two answers is resolved by rewriting the evolutionary explanation without the word "because." Evolutionary-answer-B: *Millions of years ago, ancestors of polar bears had thinner fur. Some individuals had genetic mutations which gave them thicker fur. In their environment (where, presumably, there were readily available food sources to the north in colder climates), individuals with thick-fur mutations tended to produce more offspring. The mutations spread through the population. This continued through several mutations until reaching the current species of thick-furred polar bear.* The apparent conflict is eliminated if one accepts the idea that God might choose to create thick-furred polar bears over time through a process of mutation and natural selection.

This analysis does not imply that science is restricted from answering "why" questions. "Because they evolved to live in cold climates" is a valid, albeit brief, scientific answer to the question, "Why do polar bears have thick fur?" Scientific answers to "why" questions, however, focus on natural mechanisms, and are therefore different in character from theological answers, which typically focus on teleology. Evolutionary answers A and B, above, are interchangeable and convey essentially the same information. Evolutionary-answer-A and the theological answer, above, are not interchangeable but are complementary, each supplying information which the other lacks.

Now consider human religious sentiments. I focus on religious sentiments, rather than moral sentiments, because there would seem to be greater potential for conflict here between theological and evolutionary answers. Question: *Why do humans have religious sentiments and spiritual beliefs?* Theological answer: *Humans have religious sentiments and spiritual beliefs because we were created to live in a relationship with God.* Evolutionary-answer-A: *Religious sentiments and spiritual beliefs evolved in humans because, millions of years ago, individuals and groups who had religious sentiments were better able to compete, and therefore left more offspring, than individuals and groups who lacked them.* Following the previous example, we

restate the evolutionary explanation without the word "because." Evolutionary-answer-B: *Thousands or millions of years ago, hominids lived in social
groups. Some individuals had genetic mutations that predisposed them to religious sentiments and beliefs. Groups that had these individuals developed religious cultures. Groups with religious cultures, and individuals whose genes predisposed them to religious beliefs, were better able to compete and therefore left
more offspring than individuals or groups that lacked religious beliefs.* Evolutionary-answer-B does not conflict with the theological explanation if one
accepts the idea that God might choose to create behavioral dispositions in
humans over time by using the natural evolutionary mechanisms that God
designed in the first place.

Evolutionary explanations do not explain why one particular random
mutation occurred. Rather, they only postulate that such random mutations
do occur, and then consider under what conditions those mutations are
adaptive. Evolutionary explanations are statements about changes in groups
and populations, not about why a particular genetic mutation might have
happened. To illustrate how evolutionary explanations function at the group
level, rather than the individual level, it is worth considering in detail a particular recently published work.

David Sloan Wilson believes that religious sentiments are adaptive, and
he is particularly interested in the group-selection hypothesis. Looking for
evidence in favor of that hypothesis, he studies modern religions to find examples of groups whose religious beliefs caused them to be successful relative
to neighboring groups. In a recent publication, Wilson (2002) studied the city
of Geneva at the time of John Calvin. He gathered historical evidence that
John Calvin's teachings did much to turn the quarrelsome city of Geneva into
a smoothly functioning, successful city. The teachings of Calvinism did this
by instituting an effective system of group control over individual selfish behavior and by motivating Geneva's citizens to subordinate their selfish goals
to the common good. Wilson knows that this example does not prove his hypothesis about the evolution of religion. It does, however, provide an example
of how religion might have operated in the past to help some groups unite,
work together for the common good, and thereby succeed where other
groups failed.

Within Wilson's analysis of Calvinism is an idea that could be trouble-
some to Christian theology. Wilson appears to propose that Calvinism was
successful in Geneva, and spread beyond Geneva, precisely *because* Calvinism
was so good at instituting social controls.

We could frame the issue as follows. Question: *Why did many people in
Geneva and beyond Geneva come to believe in and practice Calvinism?* Theo-

logical answer: *Calvinism spread in Geneva and beyond because, when people heard the gospel preached by Calvinists and saw the gospel lived by Calvinists, the Holy Spirit worked in their hearts and gave many people a living faith.* Evolutionary-answer-A: *Calvinism spread in Geneva and beyond because Calvinism was so good at implementing social controls, which resulted in great benefits both to individuals and to the entire city. Therefore, more individuals and groups adopted Calvinism and it spread beyond Geneva.* Those two explanations appear incompatible; however, as before, we can remove the "because" word from the evolutionary explanation. Evolutionary-answer-B: *In Geneva at the time of Calvin, some individuals happened to start believing and practicing Calvinism. Once enough powerful citizens of Geneva became Calvinists, Calvinism became the basis for Genevan society. Calvinism was good at implementing social controls, which resulted in great benefits both to individuals and to the entire city. The city prospered. Individuals and groups outside Geneva saw this. Calvinism was adopted by individuals and groups outside of Geneva.*

Evolutionary-answer-B does not necessarily conflict with the theological answer. The focus of possible contention seems to be this question: Why did some individuals, and not others, come to believe and practice Calvinism? Traditional Christian theology, while accepting the importance of social factors in the preaching of the gospel, also stresses the work of the Holy Spirit in prompting true faith.

There are at least two ways of interpreting Wilson's analysis. The first interpretation functions purely at the level of groups and populations, as follows. When Calvinism, or any religion, functions well at coordinating group action, we should expect more individuals to come to believe that this religion is true. We expect a correlation between the success of a religion at promoting collective action and the number of individual people who come to believe that religion. This interpretation is compatible with Christian theology. Indeed, St. Paul writes that when Christians love each other, this is a powerful witness, which the Holy Spirit can use to convince people of the truth of the gospel. In Christian theology, love for others is part of the web of causes that brings people to faith. Scripture reinforces the idea that we should expect correlations between the success of a religion at promoting collective action and numbers of individual people coming to believe that religion. In this sense, Wilson's analysis could be both true and compatible with Christian theology.

A second interpretation of Wilson's analysis is to augment the purely group-level explanation with an auxiliary hypothesis at the individual level. This auxiliary hypothesis would propose that, in conjunction with other psychological and social factors, Calvinism's success at coordinating collective action functioned as a purely natural mechanism to *cause* many individuals to believe in Calvinism. Calvinism's ability to promote social order was sufficient, at a neuropsychological level, to cause many individuals to believe that Calvinism is true — irrespective of whether or not Calvinism actually is true.

It could be argued that this auxiliary hypothesis, at the level of neuropsychology and individual belief, conflicts with Christian theological teachings that the work of the Holy Spirit is necessary for individuals to become believing and faithful Christians. It could also be argued that there still isn't a conflict because the Holy Spirit can work through natural mechanisms as well as through miraculous mechanisms. That's an issue for another book.

For now, it is sufficient to note that this second interpretation of Wilson's work requires an auxiliary hypothesis that goes beyond evolutionary explanations, which function only at the group level, into the realm of neuropsychological explanations, which function at the individual level. If we restrict ourselves to purely evolutionary hypotheses, all that is required for Wilson's evolutionary analysis to be correct is that there is a correlation between the success of a religion at promoting collective action and numbers of individual people coming to believe that it is true. This is easily compatible with Christian theology.

Functional Arguments

Some authors argue, perhaps correctly, that human religious sentiments have an adaptive function (promoting individual or group fitness) regardless of whether or not God actually exists (Alexander 2001a; Blackmore 2000; Dawkins 1991; Miller 1999; Mithen 1999). Suppose it is scientifically true that religious sentiments can function as a purely naturalistic mechanism to promote reproductive fitness. Would this undercut belief in God's existence? I believe it does not. A scientific explanation for the existence of religious sentiments should not undercut belief in God any more than would scientific explanations for the existence of stars and planets. Suppose that one of God's goals in creating the universe was the production of intelligent persons with moral and religious sentiments. In order for these persons to exist in this universe, stars and planets must exist. We have already noted that scientific explanations for the existence of stars and planets should not undercut belief in God — at least not the God of the Bible — because this God works through natural processes just as much as through miracles. From a theological perspective, scientific explanations for the existence of anything — stars, planets, or religious sentiments — do not imply a lack of God's activity, but rather give us information about how God created those particular things. Thus, the adaptive status of moral and religious sentiments does not serve as a strong argument either for or against God's existence.

Philosophical Materialism, Moral Relativism, and Objective Morality

Some philosophers and scientists have published articles arguing that if evolutionary accounts of morality are true, then some form of moral relativism (as previously defined) is the inevitable result (Alexander 1993; Blackmore 2000; Cronin 1991; Cronk 1994; Dawkins 1976; Ruse 1994; Trivers 1991; Voorzanger 1987; E. O. Wilson 1978). Others have published articles arguing that moral relativism does not follow (O'Hear 1997; Richards 2000). The central issue in these arguments is not evolutionary theory per se, but philosophical materialism. Does the worldview of philosophical materialism allow for normative, objective moral systems, or does philosophical materialism necessarily imply some form of moral relativism?

When Christians enter this debate, it is tempting to agree that philosophical materialism does, indeed, imply moral relativism. There are at least three reasons why Christians advancing this argument should be cautious. First is the trap of tautology. It is easy to start with an unstated premise that in order to have objective morality, there must be some supernatural basis for those moral standards. Starting from this premise, an author can write many paragraphs and pages "proving" something that was already an unstated premise of the argument.

Second, it is important to distinguish various kinds of philosophical materialism. One version, reductive materialism, states that matter and anything composed of matter is *nothing but* matter-in-motion. Moral relativism seems to follow from this version of materialism. Many philosophical materialists, however, believe some form of emergent materialism, which holds that mind, awareness, and self-consciousness are emergent properties of matter when it has the right sort of organized complexity. It's not immediately obvious that emergent materialism necessarily implies moral relativism. Perhaps it does, but the arguments must be constructed more carefully.

Third, some arguments that philosophical materialism implies moral relativism rely on an unbiblically low view of creation and general revelation. Of course, traditional Christian understanding of morality is informed by God's special historical revelation; however, God's general revelation in nature also contributes something to our understanding of morality. Our biology, our community, our reason, our conscience, our sense of self-evident principles — all part of God's general revelation — teach all humans the importance of doing good rather than evil. St. Paul wrote, "Even when Gentiles, who do not have God's written law [special revelation], instinctively follow what the law says, they show that in their hearts they know right from wrong. They demonstrate that God's law is written within them, for their own consciences either accuse them or tell them they are doing what is right" (Rom. 2:14-15 *NLT*). Our reason, our moral sentiments, and our community, though marred by sin, still can point us toward good and away from evil, albeit imperfectly.

For these reasons, Christians should be cautious in arguing that philosophical materialism implies moral relativism. Christian theology does not stop with general revelation, however. No matter how close humans can come to discovering objective moral standards using the resources of God's general revelation alone, God's special revelation offers something richer.

Divine Special Revelation Augments, Rather Than Replaces, Evolutionary Accounts

The approach I am advocating for Christians is not to try to replace the theories of sociobiology and evolutionary psychology with statements about divine special revelation, any more than we should try to replace astronomy with special revelation. Astronomy tells us true and useful things about the history and present functioning of stars and planets. Evolutionary biology tells us true and useful things about the history and present functioning of our biology and ecology. Sociobiology and evolutionary psychology have the potential to tell us some true and useful things about the history and present functioning of our moral sentiments. As important as those truths are, for Christians, the story does not stop there. By itself, a purely evolutionary account is incapable of achieving the full picture of human morality that traditional Christian theology requires. Christian theology teaches not only that moral and religious sentiments are intrinsic parts of our human nature, but also that God has personally revealed himself to human beings. This second element, divine personal revelation in human history, augments and completes the picture. Personal revelations — personal relationships between human creatures and their Creator — necessarily bring new standards of objectivity and accountability.

In this discussion of what divine special revelation adds to our understanding of morality, I am deliberately avoiding two things that a Christian might choose to add to an evolutionary account of human morality: miracles, and a dualistic conception of the human soul. Many Christians may believe that while evolution might explain many things about human biology and might even explain some things about human psychology, God must nevertheless also have performed some miracles during human biological history in order to give humans our moral sentiments. (Perhaps God miraculously rewrote portions of human DNA at some point in history to give us a genetic basis for moral sentiments.) I chose not to include this type of miracle in this picture. Although I do believe that God can and sometimes does perform miracles, the hypothesis that God *must* have performed some miracles during human biological history *in order to* give us our basic moral sentiments is an unnecessary hypothesis. Evolutionary processes plus divine personal revelation are all that is needed to give an account of morality compatible with Christian theology. Similarly, many Christians may believe that while evolution might explain many things about human biology and the human brain, any account of human morality must nonetheless make explicit reference to the human soul. There is an ongoing debate among Christian scholars today regarding whether human nature is fundamentally dualist (with an immaterial soul animating a material body) or monist (all of one nature). I make my arguments from a monist point of view because dualism is simply unnecessary for these arguments. If these arguments are valid under monism, they will also be valid under dualism.

Suppose that God used evolutionary mechanisms to create human beings with moral and religious sentiments. What would divine, personal revelation in human history add? I suggest nine points.

Content: Our biology underdetermines the content of our moral and religious beliefs. Our culture determines much of the detailed content of our belief systems. Divine revelation can add information at the cultural level about the proper content of moral and religious beliefs.

Clarification: When we rely on our reason, our conscience, and our collective wisdom, we do not all agree on the correct moral code. On some moral questions we nearly all agree, but on other questions we disagree. Divine revelation could clarify moral ambiguities.

Objectivity: Divine special revelation delivers objective, normative standards for morality, which we find difficult, perhaps impossible, to obtain from general revelation alone. God knows, and can communicate, the objective moral standards by which I ought to live, even if I refuse to assent to those standards.

Scope: Without divine revelation, it is tempting for humans to think that morality consists of loving those who love us and hating those who hate us. Divine revelation tells us to increase the scope of our love to include strangers and enemies.

Significance: Through divine revelation, we learn that the consequences of our moral choices are not limited to this world and this lifetime. What we do to help or harm our fellow human beings has consequences, on them and on ourselves, beyond our earthly lives.

Divine context: Through divine revelation, we learn that our relationship with our Creator depends intimately on how we treat our fellow human beings. We cannot love our Creator while hating our fellow human beings.

Accountability: Through divine revelation, we learn that we are morally accountable for our actions not only to our family and tribe but also to our Creator, who can hold us to account more perfectly than family or tribe ever could. The word "sin" becomes an important part of our moral vocabulary because of divine accountability.

Ordering: Of all our moral obligations, which are the most important? Divine revelation offers, "'Love the Lord your God with all you heart and with all your soul and with all your mind.' This is the first and greatest commandment. And the second is like it: 'Love your neighbor as yourself'" (Matt. 22:37-39 *NIV*).

Grace: One of the first things we learn, when we encounter our Creator personally, is that we cannot live up to divine moral standards. God's answer to our failure is divine grace. In response to divine grace, we are instructed to extend grace to others (Edwards 1999; Schloss 2001).

Although this list is incomplete, it already appears that divine personal revelation makes up exactly what was lacking in even the best evolutionary account of morality. Divine revelation enriches the horizontal, interpersonal axis of morality and adds a vertical, divine-human axis to morality.

In summary, sociobiology and evolutionary psychology, when pursued with proper scientific care and humility, are fully compatible with essential Christian beliefs about morality provided two things are done. First, the science of these fields must be separated from some unnecessary philosophical additions. Second, at some points in human history, evolutionary processes must be augmented with divine personal revelation. Christian theology need not shy away from advances in these scientific fields. Christians and non-Christians who want to advance scientific knowledge can work side by side — just as they do in every other branch of science — without needing to constantly defend their worldviews. Christians can draw the scientific knowledge gained from these fields, just as they do with knowledge gained from other fields, into the larger picture afforded by theology.

REFERENCES

Alexander, Richard D. 1993. Biological considerations in the analysis of morality. Pp. 163-96 in *Evolutionary Ethics,* ed. Matthew H. Nitecki and Doris V. Nitecki. Albany: State University of New York Press.

————. 2001a. Group-living, conflicts of interest, and the concept of God. Talk presented at Calvin College on 13 June 2001.

————. 2001b. Evolutionary selection and the nature of humanity. Talk presented at Calvin College on 13 June 2001.

Ayala, Francisco J. 1995. The difference of being human: Ethical behavior as an evolutionary byproduct. Pp. 113-35 in *Biology, Ethics, and the Origins of Life,* ed. Holmes Rolston III. The Jones and Bartlett Series in Philosophy. Boston: Jones and Bartlett.

Blackmore, Susan. 2000. The memes' eye view. Pp. 25-42 in *Darwinizing Culture: The Status of Memetics as a Science,* ed. Robert Aunger. Oxford: Oxford University Press.

Colson, Charles. 1998. The devil in the DNA. *Christianity Today* 42, no. 9:80.

Cronin, Helena. 1991. Pp. 253-65 in *The Ant and the Peacock: Altruism and Sexual Selection from Darwin to Today.* Cambridge: Cambridge University Press.

Cronk, Lee. 1994. Evolutionary theories of morality and the manipulative use of signals. *Zygon: Journal of Religion and Science* 29, no. 1:81-101.

Dawkins, Richard. 1976. Pp. 1-11 in *The Selfish Gene.* Oxford: Oxford University Press.

————. 1991. Darwin triumphant: Darwinism as a universal truth. Pp. 23-39 in *Man and Beast Revised,* ed. Michael Robinson and Lionel Tiger. Washington, D.C.: Smithsonian Institution Press.

Edwards, Denis. 1999. *The God of Evolution: A Trinitarian Theology.* New York: Paulist.

Gilkey, Langdon. 1995. Evolution, culture, and sin: Responding to Philip Hefner's proposal. *Zygon: Journal of Religion and Science* 30, no. 2:293-308.

Gould, S. J., and R. C. Lewontin. 1979. The Spandrels of San Marco and the Panglossian paradigm: A critique of the adaptationist programme. *Proceedings of the Royal Society of London, Series B, Biological Sciences: The Evolution of Adaptation by Natural Selection* 205, no. 1161:581-98.

Hamilton, William D. 1964. The genetical evolution of social behavior I. *The Journal of Theoretical Biology* 7:1-16.

Harris, Sidney. 1997. *Freudian Slips: Cartoons on Psychology.* New Brunswick, N.J.: Rutgers University Press.

Jeeves, Malcolm. 1993. *Mind Fields: Reflections on the Science of Mind and Brain.* Grand Rapids: Baker.

MacKay, Donald. 1965. *Christianity in a Mechanistic Universe.* Chicago: InterVarsity.

————. 1988. *The Open Mind and Other Essays.* Leicester, England: InterVarsity.

Miller, Geoffrey. 1999. Sexual selection for cultural displays. Pp. 71-91 in *The Evolution of Culture: An Interdisciplinary View,* ed. Robin Dunbar, Chris Knight, and Camilla Power. New Brunswick, N.J.: Rutgers University Press.

Mithen, Steven. 1999. Symbolism and the supernatural. Pp. 147-72 in *The Evolution of Culture: An Interdisciplinary View,* ed. Robin Dunbar, Chris Knight, and Camilla Power. New Brunswick, N.J.: Rutgers University Press.

New International Version of the Bible (NIV). 1996. Wheaton, Ill.: Tyndale House.

New Living Translation of the Bible (NLT). 1985. Grand Rapids: Zondervan.

O'Hear, Anthony. 1997. *Beyond Evolution: Human Nature and the Limits of Evolutionary Explanation.* Oxford: Clarendon.

Oyama, Susan. 2000. Pp. 153-66 of *Evolution's Eye: A Systems View of the Biology-Culture Divide.* Durham: Duke University Press.

Richards, J. R. 2000. *Human Nature after Darwin: A Philosophical Introduction.* New York: Routledge.

Ruse, Michael. 1994. Evolutionary theory and Christian ethics: Are they in harmony? *Zygon: Journal of Religion and Science* 29, no. 1:5-24.

Ruse, Michael, and Edward O. Wilson. 1993. The approach of sociobiology: The evolution of ethics. In *Religion and the Natural Sciences,* ed. James E. Huchingson. Fort Worth: Harcourt Brace Javonovich.

Schloss, Jeffrey P. 2001. "Love creation's final law?": Emerging accounts of altruism's evolution. In *Altruism and Altruistic Love: Science, Philosophy, and Religion in Dialogue,* ed. Stephen Post, Lynne Underwood, Jeffrey Schloss, and William Hurlbut. Oxford: Oxford University Press.

Schwartz, Barry. 1986. Pp. 182-215 of *The Battle for Human Nature: Science, Morality, and Modern Life.* New York: W. W. Norton.

Smith, Eric. 2000. Three styles in the evolutionary analysis of human behavior. Pp. 37-46 in *Adaptation and Human Behavior: An Anthropological Perspective,* ed. Lee Cronk, Napoleon Chagnon, and William Irons. New York: Aldine de Gruyter.

Trivers, Robert. 1971. The evolution of reciprocal altruism. *The Quarterly Review of Biology* 46:35-39.

———. 1991. Deceit and self-deception: The relationship between communication and consciousness. Pp. 175-91 in *Man and Beast Revised,* ed. Michael Robinson and Lionel Tiger. Washington, D.C.: Smithsonian Institution Press.

Vine, Ian. 1992. Altruism and human nature: Resolving the evolutionary paradox. Pp. 73-103 in *Embracing the Other: Philosophical, Psychological, and Historical Perspectives on Altruism,* ed. Pearl M. Oliner, Samuel P. Oliner, Lawrence Baron, Lawrence A. Blum, Dennis L. Krebs, and M. Zuzanna Smolenska. Albany: State University of New York Press.

Voorzanger, Bart. 1987. No norms and no nature — The moral relevance of evolutionary biology. *Biology and Philosophy* 2:253-70.

Williams, George C. 1988. Huxley's evolution and ethics in sociobiological perspective. *Zygon: Journal of Religion and Science* 23, no. 4:383-407.

Wilson, David Sloan. 2002. *Darwin's Cathedral: Evolution, Religion, and the Nature of Society.* Chicago: University of Chicago Press.

Wilson, Edward O. 1978. Pp. 149-67 of *On Human Nature*. Boston: Harvard University Press.

Yancey, Philip. 1998. The unmoral prophets. *Christianity Today* 42, no. 11:76-79.

8. Darwinian and Teleological Explanations: Are They Incompatible?

René van Woudenberg

It has often been remarked that the true genius of Darwinism is that it offers nonteleological explanations in a context where teleological explanations had always been presumed essential (Dawkins 1986; Dennett 1995; Cartwright 2000; Richards 2000). Darwinian explanations, it is often claimed, have made teleological explanations obsolete; their very possibility shows that teleological explanations must be false. This chapter is an investigation of this claim. More specifically, it investigates whether or not teleological and nonteleological explanations are indeed incompatible. Still more specifically, it investigates whether or not teleological explanations are incompatible with so-called evolutionary psychological explanations (EP explanations, for short) of certain specific human traits such as moral behavior, i.e., explanations of such behavior in terms of the evolutionary advantage such behavior affords.

This chapter is organized as follows. The first section seeks to give rough and ready characterizations of teleological and nonteleological explanations. The second section argues that the two types of explanation are not necessarily incompatible, although sometimes they are. This clears the ground for an inquiry into the alleged incompatibility between Darwinian (EP) explanations of specific human traits and teleological explanations of those same traits; this third section provides a characterization of EP explanations, whereas the final section investigates the alleged incompatibility of an EP and a teleological explanation of the same phenomenon.

Teleological and Nonteleological Explanations: Clarifications

I will be using the notions involved as follows. Teleological explanations are explanations in which at least one of the following concepts figures essentially: "goal" (or "purpose," or "end"), "intention," "actor" ("designer"), and "reason."[1] These concepts form a fairly tight circle that cannot be broken into from the outside. By this I mean that they are needed in each other's definitions. For example, something cannot be a "goal" unless it is intended; and what is intended is always a certain goal. Furthermore, the only sort of being who can intend something is an actor, in other words, a being with consciousness, beliefs, and certain abilities for acting. Finally, the goal that an actor is aiming at is the, or a, reason for his doing what he does. Given this understanding of these notions, we can say that to give a teleological explanation of what has happened[2] is to indicate that a particular outcome occurred because a certain goal was achieved by this means; it is to indicate that what happened is due to an actor who intended it to happen; it is to indicate that what happened occurred because some actor had a reason for making it happen.[3] A teleological explanation of the event that consists in the breaking of a particular ladder may therefore consist in indicating that John had sawn halfway through the rung for revenge. This explanation refers, either explicitly or by implication, to a goal (the breaking of the ladder when climbed by a particular person), an actor (John), an intention (to make a particular person fall off the ladder), and a reason (the sawing halfway through of the rung for revenge).

Since the concepts I have mentioned are interdefinable, the explanations that involve any of them may be named "teleological explanations" as well as "intentional explanations," "agent explanations," "design explanations," and "reason explanations." In what follows I will use primarily the first two names.

Darwinian explanations, by contrast, are non-intentional in that they do not involve any such concepts as "goal," "intention," "designer," or "reason." Darwinian explanations explain what has happened not as something that was aimed for by an agent for a reason, but as something that is due to "mechanical," organismic, and environmental causes. To give a non-intentional explanation of what has happened is to indicate that what happened is due to

1. It is the *concepts* of "goal" and so on that figure in such explanations, and not necessarily the words "goal," "designer," etc. — for, as the examples to be given in the text indicate, teleological explanations of events can be given in which the words "goal," "designer," and so on do not occur.

2. Teleological explanations may also be given of what is happening currently. In order to avoid cumbersome locutions, however, I will be talking about teleological explanations of what has happened in the past tense.

3. It should be noted that in explanatory contexts "reason" may also indicate a non-intentional cause, as when it is said that the reason why the iron expanded was that it was heated. In this chapter, however, I will be using "reason" exclusively in the sense of something that motivates an actor to pursue a certain goal.

causes that have no intentions. A non-intentional explanation of the warming of a particular stone is that the sun shone on it for many hours. The sun, most of us think, has no intentions; still it is responsible for the warming of the stone. It is responsible for this outcome in the sense that the shining of the sun somehow necessitates the warming of the stone.

To be sure, many evolutionary biologists nowadays are much less shy about using the term "teleological" than their predecessors were some decades ago. They say, for instance, that animals, and even plants, "do things for a purpose." But they don't mean by this that animals (save perhaps the higher primates) have intentions and "do things for a reason" (as I have defined that expression in note 3), and hence they use that expression in a different sense than I do.[4]

When Do Teleological and Nonteleological Explanations Exclude Each Other?

There is, of course, much more to be said about both kinds of explanation.[5] But no more needs to be said in order for us to be able to see that the two kinds don't necessarily exclude one another. For example, the breaking of a particular ladder may not only be (intentionally) explained by indicating that John had sawn halfway through the rung for revenge, but also non-intentionally explained by pointing out that Henry, who climbed the ladder, was very heavy and the rung was weakened. Likewise, Jack's stealing of the car may be (intentionally) explained by pointing out that Jack wanted to impress his friends; but it may also be explained (in a non-intentional manner) by indicating that Jack had a deprived childhood. As a final example, Mary's looking after her elderly mother may be explained (intentionally) by pointing out that she cared about her mother's happiness; but it may also be explained (non-intentionally) by pointing out that Mary was brought up to care for the well-being of others.

Intentional and non-intentional explanations, then, don't always exclude one another. But sometimes they do. Suppose Mary fell to the floor during a reception. An intentional explanation of this behavior might be that she wanted to cause a diversion, and a non-intentional one might be that she

4. For a discussion of various notions of "teleology" used by biologists, see Kass 1985, chap. 10.

5. For instance, note that I have used "teleological explanation" such that it isn't equivalent with "functional explanation" and hence that my handling of these notions differs from Ernest Nagel's; see Nagel 1961, 23.

fainted. These explanations cannot both be true and hence are incompatible. The same holds for the explanations of Richard's failing the examination: an intentional explanation might be that he failed because he didn't want to seem more clever than his friend; and a non-intentional one might be that he simply wasn't clever enough.

Thus sometimes intentional and non-intentional explanations of one and the same event are compatible, and sometimes they are incompatible. This gives rise to the question of what it is about pairs of intentional and non-intentional explanations of one and the same event that makes one pair of explanations compatible and the other pair incompatible?

One possible answer would be that the explanations in one pair are compatible when the non-intentional explanation points to what is sometimes called the *immediate cause* of an event, whereas the intentional explanation points to what is often called the *remote cause* of the event. Let us see whether this answer is correct. In the ladder case, is heavy Henry's stepping on the weakened rung the immediate cause of the breaking of the ladder, whereas John's having sawed the rung halfway through is its remote cause? This is not an easy question to answer, due to familiar problems that beset the notion of a cause. As has been pointed out often enough, what we usually call "the cause" of a certain event is that element of a complex that is, in our eyes, the most salient one in bringing about that event. Of course, it is likely that the ladder would not have broken had John not sawed through the rung. Thus we call John's having sawed the rung "the cause" of the breaking of the ladder, for this feature is salient in our eyes. But the ladder would *also* not have broken had Henry not been that heavy, or had the ladder not been made of such materials that, when the rung was sawed halfway through, it was no longer strong enough to hold heavy Henry. Therefore Henry's weight and the ladder's material also contribute to the ladder's collapse and hence may be called "causes." Since we don't consider these things salient enough, however, we don't call them by that name. Suppose, however, we call everything that contributes to the bringing about of an event "a cause" (and we may call the set of all of these "The Cause," and that part of it that is, in a given context, considered to be salient, "the salient cause"), is there any use for calling some of these causes "immediate" and others "remote"? Although a thing may be "immediate" or "remote" relative to another thing in different senses — spatially, temporally, and perhaps in other senses as well — it is clear that the sense in which John's having sawed the rung is "remote" relative to the collapse of the ladder is a temporal sense. Likewise, the sense in which stepping on the weakened rung is more "immediate" to the collapse of the ladder is a *temporal* sense too.

Ample reflection on the ladder case reveals another problem for how to think about causes — one that has a bearing on the subject matter of this chapter (and one that has also been widely recognized by philosophers). I said that John's sawing the rung halfway through is a cause (or, in the sense just explained, the salient cause) of the ladder's collapse. Formulated this way, the cause of the collapse is an *event,* viz. the event that consisted in John's sawing the rung. But it is also natural for us to say that *John* is the cause of the collapse. Formulated this way, however, the cause is not an *event* but a *person,* or, as is sometimes also said, an *agent.* This reflection has inspired a number of philosophers to distinguish between two kinds of causation, event-causation and actor-causation. The rock's hotness is caused by the event consisting of the shining of the sun, whereas the salient cause of the rung's being sawed halfway through is not an event but an actor, John, who operated the saw. Much more can be said about this distinction, but I won't do that now. I will simply assume that there is an important difference between event causation and actor causation.[6] This distinction is relevant for my purposes in the following way: intentional explanations point to causes that are agents, whereas non-intentional explanations point to causes that are not.

Let me sum up what has been said about the ladder case thus far. The collapse of the ladder may be given a true non-intentional explanation by pointing to a certain event, namely, the event that consists in heavy Henry's stepping on a weakened rung; this is the immediate cause of the collapse. It may also be given a true intentional explanation by pointing out that the collapse is caused by John who sawed the rung and who is the ultimate cause of the event. We noted that these explanations are compatible. And they are compatible, I suggest, because they point to different members of the set that constitute The Cause. The non-intentional explanation points to an immediate event-cause; the intentional explanation to a remote agent-cause. And these causes can co-exist because the remote agent-cause can, so to speak, "use" the immediate event-cause in order to achieve his goals. The relation between an agent-cause and an event-cause is like the relation between an actor and his goals when that actor selects certain means to attain his goals. At least, that is the way it looks in this particular example. It needs to be seen whether we can generalize over this case.

6. One difference is that the conditions that have to be satisfied for X to be the agent-cause of event E include the condition that it was in X's power *not* to bring about E. This condition is absent from the set of conditions that have to be satisfied for X to be the event-cause of E. The shining of the sun caused the warming up of the stone; but it was not in the sun's power *not* to heat the stone. Two powerful expositions of the notion of agent-causation are Chisholm 1976, chap. 20, and O'Connor 1995, 173-200.

Jack's stealing of the car, I said, may be intentionally explained by pointing out that Jack wanted to impress his friends, but also non-intentionally explained by pointing out that he had a deprived childhood. In this case too, it would seem, there is both an immediate and a remote cause. In contrast with the ladder case, however, in this case the immediate cause is an agent-cause, and the remote cause an event-cause. Hence we cannot say that the agent-cause "used," or brought about, the event-cause in order to attain its goals, since no such instrumental relation obtains in this case. Still, the causes to which these explanations refer are serially linked. Somehow Jack's deprived childhood caused Jack to want to impress his friends. Since in the ladder case the causes are serially linked too, we may launch the hypothesis that sets of explanations are compatible, provided the causes to which they point are serially linked.

Let us test this hypothesis by looking into the other two pairs of incompatible explanations. Recall Mary's falling to the floor. That event may be teleologically explained by pointing out that she wanted to cause a diversion, and nonteleologically by pointing out that she fainted. These explanations, I claimed, are incompatible. The reason for this is, as the hypothesis I launched a moment ago suggests, that the putative agent-cause and the putative event-cause cannot be serially linked. And it is not difficult to see why. For it is implausible to think that a person's wish to cause a diversion can cause her to faint, and equally implausible to think that someone's fainting can cause her to wish a diversion. It would seem, then, that the hypothesis survives the Mary case. It survives the Richard case as well, for Richard's not being clever enough cannot cause Richard's not wanting to seem more clever than his friend, nor can his not wanting to seem more clever than his friend cause him to be not clever enough. The event-cause and the agent-cause involved are not, and cannot possibly be, serially linked.

If my hypothesis is true, we have a handle on the claim that Darwinian nonteleological explanations have made teleological explanations of the same phenomena intellectually illegitimate, or obsolete, or redundant. If the causes of the phenomena that Darwinian explanations aim to explain can be serially linked with an agent-cause, a teleological explanation of the same phenomenon is still possible, and hence cannot be rejected as intellectually substandard, or obsolete, or redundant.

Moreover, it is, I think, a fact that where a teleological and a nonteleological explanation of the same phenomenon are compatible, the former provides a genuine intellectual insight into the explanandum. That Jack sawed halfway through the rung so that it would not carry heavy Henry (who is the only user of the ladder) provides a genuine intellectual insight into the ladder's collapse. A nonteleological explanation of the ladder's collapse is blind to Jack as agent-cause, and hence misses something of utmost importance. It misses out on something that is essential for understanding what has happened, thereby cutting off genuine insight. It is tempting to say that the teleological explanation affords "more" insight into, or provides "more" understanding of, the explanandum than does a nonteleological one. But since there is no measure for "insight," or "understanding," we should presumably leave this unsaid and simply state that where a pair of explanations (of the sort I have been dealing with) are compatible, the teleological explanation, if true, provides insight, or understanding, or intellectual illumination that the nonteleological explanation, even if true, cannot possibly give. Of course, one may willingly abstain from teleological explanations. But any such decision comes at the price of not even allowing oneself to seriously consider the possible illumination that teleological explanations may afford. And since, as I should think, one of the aims of the intellectual life is to gain insight, understanding, or illumination, we are ill-advised to ban teleological explanations without a hearing, all the more so when such explanations are not necessarily incompatible with nonteleological ones.

The question now before us is whether the causes that Darwinian explanations point to can be serially linked with an agent.

Darwinian and EP Explanations: Clarifications

In order to be able to deal with this question, I need, of course, a more informed explication of what "a Darwinian explanation" of some phenomenon *is* (it is radically insufficient just to know that such explanations are nonteleological). Since such explanations figure within the framework of evolutionary theory, I will first give a thumb-nail sketch of that theory and on that basis erect a definition of "an EP explanation of a phenomenon."

We can think of evolutionary theory as the conjunction of the following theses, together with what they imply:

1. Organisms tend to produce more offspring than can possibly survive.
2. Some organisms have more offspring than others.
3. Offspring vary among themselves.
4. Some of this variation is passed down by inheritance to future generations.[7]

7. Darwin, of course, did not know the Mendelian mechanism of heredity.

From these theses the following famous principle can be derived:

> *Principle of natural selection [PNS]:* If many offspring must die (for not all can be accommodated in nature's limited ecology), and individuals in all species vary among themselves, then on average survivors will tend to be those individuals with variations that are best suited ("fitted") to their particular local environment. Since genetic heredity exists, the offspring of survivors will tend to resemble their successful parents. The accumulation of these favorable variants through time will produce evolutionary change.

If the four theses plus PNS together constitute the theory of evolution, then we may ask, What is "an evolutionary (or Darwinian) explanation of a phenomenon" and what kinds of phenomena fall within its scope? As to the latter, the phenomena that are the objects of evolutionary explanation may be such phenotypical traits as having a trunk, walking in an upright position, and turning white in the winter. As to the former: If we assume that "an explanation" is a statement, we may say that an evolutionary explanation of a phenomenon is a statement that interprets that phenomenon in the light of the principle of natural selection. More specifically, it is a statement that interprets the coming about of a certain phenotypical trait as the result of years (and sometimes many centuries) of natural selection acting upon ancestral populations. Still more specifically, it is a statement that interprets the trait to be explained as conferring an adaptive advantage on the organism that has it, in the environment it happens to be in. Whether or not a trait may be considered as conferring an adaptive advantage is measured by the relative number of offspring an organism with it produces, or, in terms of Dawkins' gene-machine view, by the relative frequency of genes it is able to get into the subsequent generation.

Many evolutionists, however, don't confine themselves to evolutionary explanations of phenotypical traits of organisms. They also aim to explain what have traditionally been thought of as specifically human "mental" or "psychological" traits. For this reason such explanations are often referred to as "evolutionary psychological explanations." Says Janet Radcliff Richards:

> [The idea of natural selection] raised, more seriously than ever before, the idea that no supernatural life breathed into matter to make it animate, and that no soul was infused to make it conscious. Consciousness and all that goes with it — culture, art, science, philosophy, moral ideas — are just things that appear when matter gets into these arrangements, and the idea of natural selection shows in principle how these arrangements are possi-

ble. . . . [T]he threat of their being taken up into a Darwinian synthesis opens the way for the[ir] scientific explanation. . . . It may mean that [they] . . . are ultimately to be explained as devices that exist only because they have been successful in achieving our evolutionary survival. (Richards 2000, 23)

Richards tells us, I take it, that such phenomena as consciousness, culture, art, science, philosophy, and moral ideas are explained in an evolutionary psychological manner when it has been made clear that they exist only because they have been successful in achieving our evolutionary survival. Presumably we have to think of these phenomena as traits or properties of human organisms. And the idea is that these traits are explained in an evolutionary psychological way only when it has been shown how these traits enhanced the evolutionary success of their bearers, that is to say, conferred adaptive advantages over their competitors. Assuming, again, that an explanation is a statement, the rough and ready idea of evolutionary psychological explanations (or EP explanations, for short) can be put as follows:

Statement S is an EP explanation of trait X of a human organism =df. S makes it clear that the human organism has X only because X has been instrumental to the evolutionary success of the human species (or: only because it is fitness-enhancing in this sense).

And, as I have said before, evolutionary success depends on the measure in which a species is able to maximize its "genetic legacy" in the environment it happens to live in, in other words, on the measure in which the species, within the environment it inhabits, is able to get its genes into the next generation.

The definition just given stands in need of further clarification. First, what exactly is it for a statement "to make it clear" that a species S has X only because X has been instrumental to S's evolutionary success? It is this: it tells us how, given the thesis of natural selection (the thesis that survival is the result of selective pressures), X can be interpreted as the result of years of selection acting upon ancestral populations.

Second, the explication just given doesn't set a very rigorous standard for EP explanations. It says only that the trait to be explained "can be interpreted" as the result of selection working on ancestral populations. I presume that with sufficient imagination and ingenuity it is always possible to concoct a story (an interpretation) in which the environment is such that, given the traits of various organisms, natural selection favors certain (types) of organisms over others. But this concocting of stories is hard to take seriously in the context of science. If they are to be taken seriously, various constraints will have to be placed on the interpretative stories. They should be reasonable, justified, evidence-based, coherent with other things we know, and the like (they should be truth related). Let us call stories that satisfy these constraints "serious interpretations."

I take it that offering an EP explanation that meets these constraints is a daunting affair. Fortunately however, given the goal of this chapter, I need not go into this. All I am presently interested in is whether or not EP and teleological explanations of the same phenomenon can be compatible. The way to answer this question is to see whether the causes these explanations refer to can be serially linked.

Are EP Explanations and Teleological
Explanations of Morality Incompatible?

I now want to investigate whether or not EP explanations are compatible with teleological explanations. I want to focus this investigation on the moral life. More specifically, I want to focus attention on the explanations of the following two facts (I won't argue for it, but I do take [A] and [B] to be facts):

- [A] that human beings have the propensity to form beliefs about what ought and ought not to be done;
- [B] that human beings perform acts that, from a more or less traditional or commonsensical point of view, can be described as "morally right acts."

A teleological explanation of [A] might go something like this: human beings have the propensity referred to because God *intended* them to have that propensity and brought about what he intended. The teleological cause, the agent-cause, of fact [A] would be God. Of course, this explanation doesn't go into any detail as to *how* God brought about human beings with that propensity. But this, I hold, is nothing against its being a teleological or intentional explanation.

Let us now take a look at Michael Ruse and Edward O. Wilson's EP explanation of [A] (Ruse and Wilson 1991). Human beings, they hold, have innate dispositions that incline, but don't determine, them to act in certain ways. Among these dispositions is the propensity to believe certain things. Some of the things they believe concern what *ought* to be done, for instance that one ought to help one's fellows, or that one ought to keep one's promises. Humans believe furthermore, say Ruse and Wilson, that their moral beliefs are "objectively based," by which they presumably mean that moral beliefs are objectively true or false, i.e., that their truth or falsehood in no way depends on what humans believe, or think, or accept. Ruse and Wilson explain this propensity to form such beliefs as follows:

> Our belief in morality is merely an adaptation put in place to further our reproductive ends. (Ruse and Wilson 1991, 310)[8]

This statement, of course, is not yet a "serious EP explanation," in the sense defined above. After all, it merely *asserts* that the human capacity for having moral beliefs is instrumental to their evolutionary success, but it doesn't *make it clear* that it is (as required by my definition of an EP explanation). Ruse and Wilson, however, hold that the well-known theories of kin-selection and reciprocity do just that: they make it clear that the capacity for having moral beliefs has survival value.[9] The first theory suggests in what ways a particular type of morally condoned behavior — namely, altruistic behavior with respect to kin — furthers the cause of reproductive success. The basic supposition of this theory is that the unit of selection is not the individual organism, but the gene.[10] And its basic claim is that it makes clear how the gene may do

---

8. To this they add: "In an important sense, ethics, as we understand it is an illusion fobbed off on us by our genes to get us to cooperate. . . . Ethics [shared moral beliefs] is a shared illusion of the human race. If it were not so, it would not work." I take this to mean that none of our moral beliefs are true — all are false. The argument they give that seems to support this interpretation is this: "Suppose that, instead of evolving from savannah-dwelling primates, we had evolved in a very different way. If, like the termites, we needed to dwell in darkness, eat each other's faeces and cannibalise the dead, our epigenetic rules [i.e., the rules that incline us to certain sorts of behavior] would be very different from what they are now. Our minds would be strongly prone to extol such acts as beautiful and moral. And we would find it morally disgusting to live in the open air, dispose of body waste and bury the dead" (311).

The argument seems to be that since humans could have been a very different sort of creature, their current moral beliefs are false. I don't think this argument is any better than this one: we could have been a very different sort of creature, therefore our current mathematical beliefs are all wrong. In both cases it is very hard to see how the conclusion follows from the premise. I therefore won't pay any attention to the morality-is-an-illusion claim. In short, the way I am constructing "an EP explanation" is such that it doesn't automatically carry with it a strong commitment to moral anti-realism.

9. These theories are due to W. D. Hamilton and Robert Trivers, respectively. Discussions of these theories that I found particularly helpful are Richards 2000, 162-68; Cartwright 2000, 74-89; Cronin 1991, chap. 11; Irons 1996; Vine 1992, chap. 4.

10. This theory's supposition is often referred to as "the gene machine view." See Dawkins 1976.

better if the organism shows some degree of altruism toward other organisms. The way it claims to make this clear goes something like this: a particular human organism HO shares half of its genes with its own offspring as well as with its siblings, and it shares a quarter of its genes with its cousins and grandchildren. In acting upon the moral belief that one should help one's kin, HO in effect helps to get its own genes into the next generation, for part of HO's genes are the same as theirs.

The theory of kin altruism, even if true, does not explain altruism to unrelated others. The second theory, the theory of reciprocal altruism, aims to explain just that. Heavily based on game theory, it suggests in what ways reciprocity with nonkin may further the cause of reproduction of an individual organism. The theory's basic point is that, as the Prisoner's Dilemma makes clear, the pay-off of cooperative behavior is much greater than the pay-off of purely selfish behavior.

Let us assume that these theories do what Ruse and Wilson want them to do: they explain the occurrence of altruistic behavior, and since they think of such behavior as resulting from moral beliefs, these theories also explain our *having* moral beliefs and our having the *propensity* to form moral beliefs as well. So, let us assume that moral beliefs incline us to acts that further the cause of reproduction. These explanations, we may say, indicate *the cause* of humans having moral beliefs as well as having the capacity to form moral beliefs. The cause is natural selection operating on organisms in a certain environment. Organisms in which this capacity is operative have an evolutionary advantage over organisms in which it is not. Of course, this isn't a full description of The Cause as I have defined that earlier. But it singles out the salient cause.

Let me now take the final step in my discussion of [A]: do the teleological and EP explanations of fact [A] exclude one another? This question translates into this: Can the causes that these explanations refer to be serially linked? It seems to me that they can: God, the agent-cause of there being humans with the propensity to form moral beliefs, can make use of the cause that the EP explanation refers to. Natural selection can be the means by which God brings about the occurrence of humans with this propensity.

This last assertion may give rise to some doubts, for it may be asked how something that involves chance or randomness, such as natural selection (which works on random genetic mutations), can be an instrument in someone's hands. As has been argued by various philosophers, however, something's involving randomness doesn't forestall its being a means to attain a certain goal (Ratzsch 1998; van Woudenberg 2002; van Inwagen 2003). One rather quick way to make this point is by drawing an analogy (taken from van

Inwagen 2003, 354). Mathematicians have designed a device for calculating the surface of areas that have irregular boundaries. Those who use the device, then, aim at something: they want to calculate the surface of areas with irregular boundaries. The means by which they do so, however, the device, involves randomness. This is the way it works: after you have drawn the area on the device's screen, the device selects random points on the screen and sees whether or not they fall within the area. As the number of selected points increases, the ratio of the selected points that fall within the area to the total number of selected points tends to the ratio of the area to the total screen.

I probably don't need to stress the fact that this claim to compatibility has no implications whatsoever with respect to the truth of the EP explanation offered. All that is claimed is that the two explanations do not exclude one another, not that both are *true* (although both *may* be true). So, there being an EP explanation of [A] in no way counts against there being a teleological explanation of the same fact, and vice versa.

Let us now turn to [B] and its explanations. To be sure, facts [A] and [B] aren't neatly separated, so neither will be their explanations. But there are important differences between them. [A] is a fact about a certain propensity we have, namely, the propensity to form moral beliefs; [B] is a fact about a certain class of acts, namely, the class that from a traditional point of view can be described as "morally good acts." Another difference comes out when we reflect on possible teleological explanations of [B]. It will, I believe, facilitate the discussion if we focus on cases of "morally good acts" such as the following:

a. Wilberforce's relentless striving for the abolition of slavery;
b. Jack's saving a child that is about to drown;
c. Jane's helping her sister who is suffering from financial problems.

Teleological explanations of these acts involve the intentions, goals, and reasons that Wilberforce, Jack, and Jane have for doing what they do. We may say that Jane helps her sister for the reason that her sister is having financial problems and is in need of help. We may also say that Jane acts on certain beliefs, such as the beliefs that her sister is suffering financial problems, that her sister is in need of help, that she is able to help, and that she ought to help her sister. Similar things may be said about Jack. We may say that he jumped into the water for a reason, namely, the reason that there was a child about to drown. But we may also say that he acted on certain beliefs, such as the beliefs that there is a child in the water that seems to be drowning, that we have the duty to help those who are in danger, that he has the duty to help this child that is in grave danger. There is currently a discussion going on about the question of whether explanations in terms of reasons and beliefs are reducible to one another, and there is still debate about Hume's old assertion that a person's beliefs don't motivate her to act — it is, Humeans assert, exclusively passions and feelings that do.[11] But whatever one's position in these debates, both reason-explanations and belief-explanations of actions are teleological explanations. They refer to an agent-cause, one who performs an act out of a certain intention.

So there is this big difference between teleological explanations of [B] and [A]: our performing acts that can be described as "morally right acts" is due to human agent causes, whereas the *propensity* to form moral judgments and beliefs is not.

EP explanations of [B], however, are closely related to EP explanations of [A]. When it is claimed that natural selection selects for the propensity to form moral beliefs (beliefs that are claimed to motivate us to certain types of behavior), what is in fact claimed is that what is selected for is a propensity not just to form any old belief, but a propensity to form highly specified sorts of belief, namely, beliefs that traditionally have been described as *moral* beliefs. The theories of kin selection and reciprocity are then again invoked to do the explanatory work. What this comes to is that Wilberforce, Jack, and Jane do their deeds because natural selection selects for beings like them, beings who perform acts that can be described as "morally good acts."

The question now before us is whether the teleological and EP explanations of [B] are compatible. This boils down to the question of whether the causes that are referred to in these explanations can be serially linked. And it would seem that they can be, for if natural selection selects for beings that are agents who have certain beliefs and display a certain repertoire of actions (namely, ones that can be described as "morally good") then agent-cause and non-agent–cause (natural selection) seem to be serially linked. The analogue here is with the case of Jack, which I discussed earlier in the second section. Hence both types of explanation are compatible.

My conclusion is therefore that EP explanations of [B] (or of individual acts a, b, and c that have traditionally been described as morally right acts) are compatible with teleological explanations of the same fact.

Thr way I have been arguing may give rise to the following worry. Haven't I, so to speak, been giving much too much away to EP explanations of actions that have traditionally been described as "morally good acts"? After all, don't

11. For this discussion see McNaughton 1988.

EP explanations proceed from the assumption that all actions that have traditionally been described as morally good acts are actions that are fitness enhancing? And isn't this assumption itself already objectionable? Don't explanations that proceed from this assumption necessarily denigrate or debunk moral actions? Doesn't this assumption tell us that "at the bottom" moral actions are "really" actions that are fitness enhancing?

No doubt, some advocates of EP explanations of so-called moral behavior do want to denigrate and debunk the moral quality of those actions that we like to think of as morally right actions. Nothing in EP explanations as such commits one to taking a debunking stance, however. The thing to see is that one and the same act may have both the properties of *being an act that is morally good* and *being an act that tends to be fitness enhancing*. To put the same point differently, one and the same act may fall both in the extension of "morally good act" and at the same in the extension of "act that tends to be fitness enhancing." But this does nothing to show that these properties are "at bottom" really the same property. Here is an analogy. It is a fact that every vertebrate with a heart has a liver, and every vertebrate with a liver a heart. We may therefore say that there are animals that have the property of *being a vertebrate with a heart* as well as the property of *being a vertebrate with a liver*. Clearly, the fact that one and the same animal has both of these properties does nothing to show that these properties are "at bottom" the same property. And so it is, one might think, with the properties of *being an act that is morally good* and *being an act that is fitness enhancing*. It is clearly possible that one and the same act has both of these properties. Whether *every* moral act is such that it is fitness enhancing is, as far as I can see, an open question. But even if it is answered in the affirmative, this need not have any debunking implications.

REFERENCES

Cartwright, John. 2000. *Evolution and Human Behaviour.* London: Macmillan.

Chisholm, Roderick. 1976. *Person and Object: A Metaphysical Study.* LaSalle, Ill.: Open Court.

Cronin, Helena. 1991. *The Ant and the Peacock: Altruism and Sexual Selection from Darwin to Today.* Cambridge: Cambridge University Press.

Dawkins, Richard. 1976. *The Selfish Gene.* Oxford: Oxford University Press.

———. 1986. *The Blind Watchmaker.* London: Longman.

Dennett, Daniel. 1995. *Darwin's Dangerous Idea.* Harmondsworth: Penguin.

Gould, Stephen Jay. 1997. *Life's Grandeur: The Spread of Excellence from Plato to Darwin.* Harmondsworth: Penguin.

Irons, William. 1996. Morality as evolved adaptation. Chap. 1 in *Investigating the Bio-*

logical Foundations of Human Morality, ed. James P. Hurd. Lewiston: Edwin Mellen.

Kass, Leon. 1985. *Toward a More Natural Science: Biology and Human Affairs*. New York: Free Press.

McNaughton, David. 1988. *Moral Vision*. Oxford: Basil Blackwell.

Nagel, Ernest. 1961. *The Structure of Science*. London: Routledge and Kegan Paul.

O'Connor, Timothy. 1995. Agent causation. Pp. 173-200 in *Agents, Causes, and Events*, ed. Timothy O'Connor. Oxford: Oxford University Press.

Ratzsch, Del. 1998. Design, chance, and theistic evolution. In *Mere Creation: Science, Faith, and Intelligent Design*, ed. William B. Dembski. Downers Grove, Ill.: InterVarsity.

Richards, Janet Radcliff. 2000. *Human Nature after Darwin*. London: Routledge.

Ruse, Michael, and Edward O. Wilson. [1991] 1993. The evolution of ethics. In *Religion and the Natural Sciences: The Range of Engagement*, ed. J. E. Huchingson. Orlando: Harcourt Brace.

Van Inwagen, Peter. 2003. The compatibility of Darwinism and design. In *God and Design: The Teleological Argument and Modern Science*, ed. Neil A. Manson. London: Routledge.

Van Woudenberg, René. 2002. *Ontwerp en toeval in de wereld (Design and Chance in the World)*. Amstelveen: De Zaak Haes. (Inaugural address, Free University Amsterdam)

Vine, Ian. 1992. Altruism and human nature. Chap. 4 in *Embracing the Other*, ed. Pearl M. Oliner et al. New York: New York University Press.

9. Is There an Evolutionary Foundation for Human Morality?

John Hare

This chapter is about the question of whether we can find an evolutionary basis for human morality (see Hare 2003). I am not a scientist, but a philosopher, and I am not professionally competent either to pass a positive or negative judgment on the theory of evolution itself, except insofar as there are philosophical commitments embodied in it. But as a philosopher I am interested in the gap between the demands of morality on us and our natural capacities to meet those demands. So I want to ask the conditional question: *if* we assume that the theory of evolution as it applies to human beings is correct, does this help us answer the questions of whether we *can* be morally good and why we *should* be morally good? The first question, whether we *can* be morally good, is the question raised by the moral gap between the demands of morality and our natural capacities. It is only after answering this first question, "yes, we can be morally good," that the second question arises of why we *should* be morally good, for we can only be held accountable or responsible for standards that we are able to reach. The burden of my presentation will be to show that we do *not* get an answer to these two questions from the theory of evolution. I am not arguing here that the theory is false, but that *even if* it is true, it doesn't give us an answer. I will be looking at a number of recent attempts to provide such an answer from the theory, but I will claim that all of them fail.

The Nature of Human Morality

In order to answer my conditional question, I need to describe first what I take the nature of human morality to be. There are many different philosophical accounts here to choose from. The account I am going to give takes its inspiration from John Duns Scotus, a Franciscan theologian and philosopher of the late Middle Ages (Hare 2001, chap. 2). He formulated in more detail what he had already found in Anselm of Canterbury and, before Anselm, in Augustine. He started from the idea that we ought to obey the moral law because God commands it, and that we have a love for God by a special affection of the will, which Scotus calls "the affection for justice." The contrast is "the affection for advantage," which is an inclination or movement in the will toward one's own happiness or perfection. The affection for justice is drawn toward the good in itself and thus to God, without reference to any advantage to the self. Loving an enemy is the paradigm case because it so clearly leaves behind the self and its extensions to others in one's community and tribe. The Good Samaritan in Jesus' parable (Luke 10:30-37) showed the affection for justice in being moved by the plight of the man wounded by the side of the road, even though that man was a traditional enemy of his race.

On this account there is nothing wrong with wanting to be happy, or with being concerned about oneself, but what counts morally is the ranking of the two affections. I might, for example, be giving a lecture, and I might have two different kinds of motivation. I might be giving my attention to the subject matter for its own sake, and to my audience, trying to communicate to them as well as I know how. Or I might be psychologically focused on myself delivering the lecture and trying to make my audience like or admire *me*. This example illustrates that our motivational and affective state is usually a mixture, and this is what Scotus says. I will probably have both affections as I lecture, both the affection for advantage and the affection for justice, and they will operate in me simultaneously. The key moral question, however, is how I *rank* the two. If the affection for advantage is ranked first, it will become an *improper* regard for the self. The proper ranking is that we are to seek *first* the kingdom of God and his righteousness, and then the other things will be added to us. An extreme form of this thought is the expression by Jonathan Edwards in *Religious Affections* (part III, chap. X), "to be even willing to be damned for the glory of God." He was echoing words of Moses and also of Paul (Exod. 32:32; Rom. 9:3; see also Matt. 27:45). He was not saying that God in fact requires such a sacrifice, but that he would choose this ranking if God did require it. Our problem after the fall is not, Scotus says, that we are born with the affection for advantage, but that we are born with a wrongful ranking of the two affections. And we are not able, by ourselves, to reverse this ranking, since the preference for the self already underlies all our choices. Changing this ranking requires God's assistance.

The choice of Scotus as a starting point is not arbitrary. There is a line of development, which I will not try to trace here, from Scotus to Luther and Calvin. From Luther, the German pietists learned the same theory, and we find the same basic framework in the most important philosopher of modern times, Immanuel Kant, who himself was deeply influenced by the pietists (especially Crusius, from whom he learned the idea of a categorical imperative; see Schneewind 1998, chap. 20). Most contemporary moral philosophers in the Western philosophical tradition define themselves in relation to Kant, so Scotus is a reasonable starting point if we are interested in the genealogy of contemporary moral theory.

Scotus says that we only have freedom because we have the affection for justice in addition to the affection for advantage. If we had merely the affection for advantage, like nonhuman animals, we would not be free, because we would pursue our own advantage by necessity. Here Scotus departs from another tradition in Western philosophy, which we can find in its purest form among the ancient Greeks, in Plato and Aristotle, for example. The understanding of happiness in Greek philosophy is complex, but both Plato and Aristotle hold that every motivation that we have is in the end to be understood as a motivation toward our own happiness. Scotus expresses a different thought, though it is not original with him. He finds in the Scriptures the idea of repentance, of a fundamental reorientation of the heart away from the old man and toward the kingdom of God. Unlike Plato and Aristotle, Scotus sees that we have within us the possibility of choosing to rank something else above our own happiness. What gives us this possibility is hearing the call of God, whose goodness so far transcends us that it has the power to reduce our self-love, our affection for advantage, to submission. It is this call, therefore, and our ability to hear it, which lies behind our freedom. In the Greeks, there is no freedom in this sense, and there is no will in the sense of a part of us that does this fundamental ranking.

Here it is natural to make the following objection: "Of course, *if* you build God into your account of morality, then the evolutionary account will fail; but this is simply begging the question." To respond to this I need to say that I am not *defining* morality in terms of God's role in it. Rather, I am proposing that what I will call "the gap picture" is a significant component of "our" Western morality, whether we are theists or not. The gap picture describes a gap between the moral demand and the capacities we are born with and naturally develop. Theism gives one coherent (though conceptually ambitious) background for this picture, and the question is whether a non-theist evolutionary account provides another. If it does not, and no alternative non-theist picture is found, we still have the option of rejecting the gap picture. But it is important to consider the consequences for our ethical lives of such a rejection.

The Problem of the Gaps

If the gap picture of human morality is right, there are two kinds of gaps. First, there is what I will call the "affection gap" between those animals who have only the affection for advantage and humans who have also the affection for justice. Second, there is the "performance gap" within our own lives between the demand to be moral and our actual performance. Being moral demands a revolution of the will. Before the revolution we have a set of priorities: we will only do what we see to be good if we can see that it will cause or constitute our happiness. But morality demands a kind of revolution or reversal of those priorities: that we only do what we think will make us happy if we can see that it is in itself good. In other words, the moral demand is to rank the affection for justice over the affection for advantage. A consequence of this is that we are not allowed morally to give ourselves any greater moral weight or importance than we give any other human being, for my goodness or worth is not in itself any greater than anyone else's. We *do* have, as human beings ourselves, the same moral weight as any other, so that we are also not allowed morally to make ourselves doormats for other people to walk on. We also have a greater responsibility for ourselves than we do for others, because we control our own lives directly. But morally we all count the same.

If this is the moral demand, there is a performance gap between it and the natural capacities with which we are born. We are born, Scotus and Kant agree, with the wrongful ranking of the two affections, and we cannot without assistance change this. So, it looks as though there is a kind of incoherence in the moral life, the incoherence of holding ourselves to a standard that we are unable to reach. Christianity gives us a background for this picture. God is seen as both the source of the moral demand on us and the enabler of our compliance. Augustine says, "God commands some things which we cannot do, in order that we may know what we ought to ask of Him. For this is faith itself, which obtains by prayer what the law commands" (*Grace and Free Will*, 759). Upon first hearing, this idea sounds odd, as though God is holding us accountable to a standard we are unable to reach. But Augustine is not saying we cannot reach the standard; he is saying we cannot reach it on our own, or by our own devices. Luther uses the illustration of a parent who tells his young child to walk to him. The child takes a few steps and totters, and then reaches out for the help of the parent's hand, which is offered to bring him the rest of the way (*The Bondage of the Will*, 152). On this view God intervenes in our lives to change us so that we can live by the demand. God does this in part by revealing something of the divine nature to us, as Paul says in the first few chapters of Romans, and this revelation has the power to subordinate our love of the self and our affection for advantage, and so to change the ranking of the two affections in us. Then the apparent incoherence I mentioned of holding us to an impossible standard disappears.

Contemporary moral philosophy uses at least three strategies to get over the problem of the performance gap without invoking God's assistance (I have described these strategies at greater length in Hare 1996 and 2002). I mention these strategies here because we will see examples of all three of them in the literature on evolutionary ethics. The first strategy is to hold our natural capacities where they are on the picture I have just drawn and then to reduce the moral demand in order to fit them. The second strategy is to keep the moral demand where it is on the picture I have drawn and then exaggerate or puff up our natural capacity to meet this demand. The third strategy is to hold both the demand and our capacities constant, and then find some naturalistic substitute to do God's work in bridging the resultant gap. The picture of the moral gap is a very familiar picture of how we tend to think about morality in the Western world; it is familiar even among those who no longer believe in God. But there are problems internal to this picture if God is omitted, concerning *how* we can live morally and *why* we should live morally, and my claim is that the theory of evolution has not solved these problems.

The Affection Gap

With this brief account of human morality, we can now return to sociobiology and evolutionary ethics. I want to deal separately with the two gaps I mentioned. First, the affection gap. Nowhere in the literature about nonhuman animals have I found an example of what Scotus calls the affection for justice, but only complicated forms of the affection for advantage. This means that the animals do not have freedom of the Scotist kind either, since, if Scotus is right, it is only beings who have the affection for justice that have this kind of freedom.

In dealing with these two gaps separately, I am responding to two different arguments that can be found in evolutionary ethics. The first argument is that we can understand how humans can be morally good by looking at the source of this goodness in capacities that nonhuman animals already have. This makes human goodness nonmysterious and forestalls the need to appeal to anything spooky, like the assistance of God. By claiming that there is an affection gap, I am saying that there is something crucial about human morality that is not found in nonhuman animals. Evolutionary ethicists also make a second argument, which concerns the performance gap. Even if they cannot appeal to common origin to explain human moral capacity, they can appeal to evolutionary pressure during early periods of human history. On this view, human morality is just like every other part of human life, or the life of any species, for that matter: the fundamental explanation is in terms of natural selection or adaptation, and hence reproductive advantage. I am going to claim that there is something crucial about human morality that cannot be explained by locating its source in natural selection.

What do I mean by saying that nonhuman animals have only complicated forms of the affection for advantage and do not have the affection for justice? I will give three examples, from the social insects, from vampire bats, and from chimpanzees. The first example is of kin selection, the second of so-called reciprocal altruism, and the third of social control. These are all forms of self-benefit. Darwin says, in one of his moods, "Natural selection will never produce in a being anything injurious to itself, for natural selection acts solely by and for the good of each" (Darwin [1859] 1999, 167). But according to the picture of morality I have been drawing, the affection for justice leads to a radical willingness to sacrifice the self.

Kin selection is a solution to the problem of the sterile castes among social insects. Its discovery is what gave the impetus to the first great wave of sociobiology in the early 1970s, culminating in the publication of E. O. Wilson's *Sociobiology* in 1975. In 1977 I went to a six-week conference called "Biological and Sociological Perspectives on Human Nature," and the furious reaction to Wilson was in full swing, with the main speakers being Stephen Jay Gould and Dick Levin, an ant specialist from Harvard. I remember a whole afternoon on hands and knees in the Garden of the Gods in Colorado in the middle of July looking at ant battles in the sand. My point for the present chapter is just that we have nothing here that takes us beyond the affection for advantage into the affection for justice. Compare kin selection with the parable of the Good Samaritan, who was not related by blood or tribe and was, in fact, a traditional enemy of the man who was wounded by the side of the road. The affection for justice requires my action on behalf of someone without regard to that person's relation to myself, merely because I see he or she is in need.

My second example is so-called "reciprocal altruism" among vampire bats (Cartwright 2000, 87-88). It is not altogether clear whether this kind of reciprocity can be detached from kin selection because the association into bat-clusters may be a marker for kinship. In any case, suppose here we do have something like reciprocity between unrelated members of the same species. It may be true that cooperation can be a fitness-maximizing strategy under certain conditions. For example, one such strategy that has been modeled is what is called "tit-for-tat," where benefits and harms are both reciprocated. My point is just that we are still within the range of the affection for advantage. One way to illustrate this is to compare tit-for-tat with the reply Socrates first gets in the *Republic* (334b) when he asks what justice is. The reply is: Justice is to do good to your friends and harm to your enemies, and most Greeks of Socrates' time would have said the same thing. I suspect that common sense still holds much the same opinion. For Socrates, by contrast, it is always wrong to do harm, even in retaliation against your enemies (*Crito* 49, *Gorgias* 508-9). In the same way, Jesus says in the Sermon on the Mount, "You have heard that it was said, 'You shall love your neighbor and hate your enemy.' But I say to you, Love your enemies and pray for those who persecute you" (Matt. 5:43-44).

My third example is social control among chimpanzees (de Waal 1996, 91-92). There is something almost moral here, what de Waal calls a "precursor" to morality. But in terms of the distinction from Scotus, there is not yet the affection for justice. What seems to be going on here is a form of social control in which rules that are beneficial to the group are enforced by a kind of communal sanction. But this is a precursor in the sense in which, for example, John the Baptist was a precursor, or forerunner; he was not already the Christ, but pointed toward him. Social control is not already morality in the sense I have been describing because it is directed by its nature toward the benefit of one group as opposed to others. To be sure, if morality were given a different account than the one I have given, we could find here a precursor in a stronger sense, where morality would be already present in outline, and characteristically human morality would require merely changing some of the details.

We do not get, in any of these three cases, any example that requires us to bring in the affection for justice. We do not know, to be sure, that there is no affection for justice, since we could not see into these animals' hearts even if they did have hearts in the relevant sense. Perhaps the bees or the vampire bats or the chimpanzees do have the same two affections we do, and merely have a performance gap just like us. But it is more economical to suppose that what we get here are various complex forms of the affection for advantage. Having said that, the analyses of kin selection, reciprocal altruism, and social control are still important for the moral philosopher. According to the moral theory I started with, we are born with a mixture of two affections. By describing in other species one part of this mixture, the affection for advantage, these analyses give us fresh detail about the moral gap. The kind of evolutionary psychology I have been describing could give us an understanding of just how close the affection gap comes to being bridged naturally, and yet what differences between humans and nonhuman animals still remain.

The Performance Gap

In the rest of this chapter I will reply to three kinds of attempts in the recent literature on evolutionary ethics to provide an answer to the problem of the *performance* gap. These are attempts to bridge the gap without bringing in God's assistance, and I will discuss them in terms of the framework of the three strategies I mentioned earlier for dealing with the problem of the moral gap, namely, the strategies of reducing the moral demand, puffing up the human capacity, and finding a substitute for God's assistance. These three strategies are used in the contemporary world outside evolutionary ethics, but for the purposes of the following argument I want to focus on the examples inside evolutionary ethics, and especially examples of the first strategy. I will mention the other two briefly at the end.

The First Strategy

The first of these strategies starts by conceding that we naturally rank the self first and motivate all action by our own happiness; and then the strategy reconceptualizes our situation by reducing the moral demand to fit our natural capacities so described. In that way, there is no longer any moral gap. I am going to discuss two ways of carrying out this strategy, one way in the work of Larry Arnhart, a political theorist, and one way in the work of two very different biologists, Richard Alexander and David Sloan Wilson.

I am discussing here Arnhart's book, *Darwinism Natural Right*, some parts of which he has recanted in his essay in the present volume, which I have not had a chance to read. One way to assess the strength of the arguments in my paper is to compare Arnhart's original views with his new version. In his book, Arnhart starts from two identifications. He says that the good is the desirable, and the desirable is the generally desired. By "generally desired" he means what humans have desired throughout their evolutionary history. This gives special weight to the great length of the Pleistocene period, when humans were hunter-gatherers and when natural selection presumably exercised most of its effects on variation within human populations. Arnhart accordingly draws up a list of twenty desires that are "generally desired" in this sense. The list includes such items as high social status, political rule (though this is, he says, a natural male desire, not a natural female desire), and the desires for war (again a male desire), for wealth (that is, enough property to equip one for a good life and to display social status), and for justice as reciprocity (Arnhart 1998, 17, 29-36). There is not an affection for justice in the Scotistic sense anywhere on the list, and there is no general desire to be recognized as a human with the same infinite value as any other human being. Darwin's occasional appeal to universal humanitarianism can be explained only, Arnhart thinks, as a utopian yearning for an ideal moral realm that transcends nature, which contradicts Darwin's own general claim that human beings are fully contained within the natural order. Arnhart concludes that since humans are *not* "bound together by a universal sentiment of disinterested humanitarianism, then deep conflicts of interest between individuals or between groups can create moral tragedies in which there is no universal moral principle or sentiment to resolve the conflict." He says, "When individuals or groups compete with one another, we must either find some common ground of shared interests, or we must allow for an appeal to force or fraud to settle the dispute. The only alternative, which I do not regard as a realistic alternative, is to invoke some transcendental norm of impartial justice (such as Christian charity) that is beyond the order of nature" (146-49).

To see the effect of Arnhart's view, consider the case of slavery. Arnhart is not entitled to condemn it morally, since it results from the satisfaction of natural desires for dominance, and he thinks the satisfaction of natural desires is good. The most he is entitled to say is that slavery is *tragic,* since it results from the conflict of natural desires between the masters and the slaves. Since he thinks there is no universal principle or norm to appeal to, unless there is a common interest, we have to appeal to force or fraud to settle the dispute. Arnhart thinks he can appeal here to reciprocal justice. But reciprocal justice as he defines it requires an expectation of benefit on both sides, or tit-for-tat. Suppose we lived in a society in which those whom we exploited could not harm us because of their relative weakness. Suppose we knew that. We would not be moved by justice as reciprocity to end the exploitation even in the face of our victims' suffering and hatred of us. The restraints of this kind of reciprocal justice would be totally useless. But alas, this has been the situation with slavery for most of its history. The effect of ruling out impartial justice as "utopian" is to lower the moral demand to fit our "natural" capacities, or to fit the affection for advantage. We will say, for example, that we do not have obligations to starving children in Africa because they are not part of our group; we do not even know who they are (Noddings 1984, 86). If that is the way our society in fact goes, we will be regressing to tribalism.

The second way to carry out the strategy of reducing the demand does not start out, as Arnhart does, by putting normative limits on the moral demand, but it changes the source of the demand, and this has the same effect as reducing its normative force. It locates the origin or source of the moral demand not in God (as Scotus does) but in natural selection or adaptation, and thus in a version of the affection for advantage, either at the level of the genes or at the level of the group. Evolutionary biologists differ in terms of which of these two levels they stress. I will talk about one of each. Twenty-five years after I went to the conference in Colorado, I participated in a seminar at Calvin College called "Biology and Purpose: Altruism, Morality and Human Nature in Evolutionary Theory." Sociobiology has been reborn with the new label "evolutionary psychology," and I wanted to study the similarities and differences between the two movements. Two of the main speakers, both of them biologists, were especially relevant to this project. Richard Alexander was one of the founding figures of sociobiology, especially with his book *Sociobiology: The New Synthesis,* in 1975. He emphasizes the level of the gene. David Sloan Wilson is one of the new leaders in the field and emphasizes the level of the group (Wilson and Sober 1998). But both biologists locate the source of the affection for justice in the affection for advantage, and I will claim that this ends by reducing or undercutting the moral demand.

Alexander finds in the theory of evolution the fundamental explanation of everything about life, including human life. If there were some part of life that the theory could not explain, the theory would be, he said, a "piddling" theory. The fundamental explanation of all the behaviors of all the various life forms is the final bottom-line pay-off of differential gene replication. Thus religion is to be explained in terms of "one group besting another" and so promoting the survival and reproduction of its members, and moral behavior is to be explained in terms "of enlightened genetic self-interest" (Alexander and Richards forthcoming, 5, 12, 15). Alexander thinks we should base models of the concept of God and of right and wrong on the "reproductive interests of individuals, either as such or as achieved via success of their group," and then we could test those models by measuring differential reproductive rates.

But why should the theory of evolution be seen this way? If we find a part of human life like mathematics that cannot as far as we know be itself explained by evolutionary theory, why should that be construed as a failure in the theory of evolution? Why should we think that because evolution explains some important features of life, it therefore has to explain all of them? Half-humorously, in the spirit of evolutionary ethics, let me suggest that perhaps there is a discrete cognitive module in our brains, which leads us to expand theories globally when they are only locally appropriate.

Alexander's view is that humans invented mathematics, and therefore mathematics has to be understood fundamentally in terms of genetic self-promotion, just like religion or any other feature of life. But then this claim is no longer a part of the theory of evolution, but rather a metaphysical view added onto it: that every domain above the physical and the chemical which human life encounters is to be explained ultimately by natural selection at the genetic level. It is important to see that this metaphysical view cannot itself be justified biologically; it is, I believe, an article of faith for Alexander, though it is not recognized as such. If we deny this metaphysical view, we can say that human life brings us into contact with all sorts of domains, like mathematics or ethics or religion, which are not themselves subject to evolutionary explanation, although evolution may have illuminating things to say about how it is that we have the equipment to access those domains. In saying this, we might still be after a single explanatory theory, but it will be a single theory in a quite different sense. It will be the coherent conjunction of all the different theories that make sense of all our experience, without any expectation that one of these theories has to be the ultimate cash value or bottom line for all the others. Or perhaps "theory" is the wrong word for what we would be after; some less rigorous word like "understanding" is more adequate, since some parts of our experience do not seem to be amenable to theory at all in any rigorous sense.

In contrast to Alexander, David Sloan Wilson emphasizes (like Darwin in one of his moods) the role of morality and religion in group-selection. Altruistic groups can prosper compared to non-altruistic groups. At the same time selfish individuals within an altruistic group can prosper compared to the altruistic individuals within that same group. This means that the two levels of selection (individual and group) can be in tension, and an adequate explanatory theory has to take account of both. Wilson is more inclined to take seriously the mechanisms of social cohesion within altruistic groups, including their religious and ethical codes, as having themselves selective advantage. He also allows that cultural systems that have adaptive advantage can produce as by-products elements that are themselves adaptively neutral, or even to a limited degree counter-adaptive. But Wilson is no more inclined than Alexander to suppose that the claims internal to the domains of religion and ethics as divine command are *true*. Take, for example, his case study of Calvin's Geneva. Wilson sees Calvin's claims about God's adoption of the elect and the unworthiness of, for example, unduly quarrelsome elders to receive Communion as mechanisms of social control, as useful *fictions*. Wilson's analysis is that Geneva was on the verge of dissolution as a viable community before Calvin arrived, and was enabled by Calvinism to prosper in the face of severe external and internal pressure; so its citizens were assisted in their evolutionary role of surviving and reproducing (Wilson 2002). Although Wilson allows more autonomy to the level of group selection than does Alexander, there is still a reductive explanation of the affection for justice in terms of adaptation.

"Barring theological explanations" (Wilson allows no such explanations) "all designing agents must ultimately be traced back to a process of blind variation and selective retention" (Wilson 2002, chap. 3, p. 37). Wilson's account is less reductionist than Alexander's, but both biologists have the same metaphysical commitment to a naturalistic explanation for all the phenomena of human life in terms of the theory of evolution.

The Publicity Standard

We can now face both biologists with the problem of what I will call, in Kant's term, the publicity standard. The publicity standard is that a normative theory should be able to make public what it claims as the source or origin of the normative demand, without thereby undercutting the demand. Here is where we get back to the problem of reducing the moral demand. Let me give an example. Suppose we thought that ethical demands and religious authority were both invented by the powerful political elite in order to maintain their own power. Some of the sophists suggested this in ancient Greece. The idea was that the powerful wanted to control the weak even in their thoughts, and so they invented the idea of gods who could look at the heart and who would punish disobedience and disloyalty. Suppose we discovered that this was the origin of our ethical striving and our religious belief: we had been programmed that way by a culture that was basically under the control of a powerful elite. This discovery would tend to undercut our ethical commitment, which is hard enough to sustain even without such discoveries. If I found that my efforts to be impartially benevolent were programmed into me by Big Brother, I would start to think of myself as Macbeth, a poor player who struts and frets his hour upon the stage, my life full of sound and fury but signifying nothing. Why would these discoveries be undercutting? Because Big Brother is concerned not with right but with his own power.

The discovery that adaptation through group selection was the source or origin of the normative demand would have much the same effect. I would regard myself as programmed by something that was itself at odds with morality, for adaptation is aligned with the affection for advantage. The proposed evolutionary explanation is that it is good for my group in competition with other groups that I feel the demand of the affection for justice. But the affection for justice is required by its nature to be blind to my relationship to one group rather than another, like the Good Samaritan. The proposed explanation therefore undercuts the demand, and therefore fails the publicity standard.

This point is valid also against the views of Michael Ruse. Ruse holds that the objectivity of the normative demand is an illusion, produced in us by our genes, for our own (and their) benefit (Ruse 2001). But this view fails to meet the publicity standard just as Alexander's and Wilson's views fail. If the source of the moral demand is an illusion produced by selective advantage, like an optical illusion produced in our visual apparatus, then this undercuts the force of the demand for advantage-blind choices or for justice in the Scotistic sense.

There is some evidence of this effect in the psychological literature. When people believe that psychological egoism is true, they are less inclined to be helpful to others. A before-and-after study was done on students enrolled in two introductory economics courses and an introductory astronomy course. The students were asked at the beginning and at the end of each course what they would do if they found an addressed envelope with $100 in it. I do not at all mean to insult my distinguished colleagues in economics, but while the students scored the same in the economics and astronomy courses at the beginning of the semester, the economics students were more willing to keep the money at the end. The difference probably resulted from exposure to the theory found pervasively in economics that motivation is fundamentally egoistic (Frank, Gilovich, and Regan 1993, 168-70).

The Second and Third Strategies

I will mention the second and third strategies for dealing with the problem of the performance gap because I want to give an idea of the scope of the analysis, but I will not try to discuss the details of these views. The second strategy is to keep the demand where it is, including the affection for justice, and then pretend that we are able by our own natural capacities to meet this demand. There are examples of this outside evolutionary ethics. For example, there is the view that only ignorance and lack of education hold us back from being morally good, not some fundamental failure of the will. The Humanist Manifesto, published in 1933, stated that "Man is at last becoming aware that he alone is responsible for the realization of the world of his dreams, that he has within himself the power for its achievement." This was just before the Second World War, in which the people who carried out the massacres and Holocaust were the most educated people in the world's history to that point. There are also examples of this strategy, which I call "puffing up our capacities," within evolutionary ethics. Both Anthony O'Hear and Janet Richards propose that the affection for advantage is enough to take us to morality when it is added to our natural capacities for language and reason. Their idea is that reflection in itself carries with it a kind of distancing from our desires, and since we are by nature reflective beings, expressing our thoughts in universal concepts through language, we are led despite ourselves into an impartial moral perspective, adopting the aspiration to look at the world from the viewpoint of an ideal observer (O'Hear 1997; Richards 2000). The trouble with this view is that reason and language are *not* sufficient, when added to the affection for advantage, to get us to the right ranking of the two affections for advantage and for justice. It is quite possible to be reflectively and rationally self-interested. The meticulous lists of Holocaust victims kept by the Nazis suggest an exaggeration of reason, not a defect in it. The question here turns on what is meant by "reason." If we build the notion of morality into the notion of reason, then indeed reason will take us to morality. But this is a hollow victory, produced merely by re-definition; for then living by reason, or rationally, will no longer be merely a natural capacity in the sense I have been using the term, and there will be the same gap I have been describing all along but now labeled differently as the gap between our natural capacities and reason in this exalted sense.

The third strategy for dealing with the problem of the moral gap without bringing in God is to find a naturalistic substitute for God's assistance. An example outside evolutionary ethics is the Marxist view that our capacities for a good life will be changed if the proletariat takes ownership of the means of production. Here is a substitute for God's assistance, something that will change our capacities so that they become adequate to the moral demand. Within evolutionary ethics, there are thinkers who want to make evolution itself the substitute for God's assistance. Some of the thinkers I have in mind would resist this description of what they are doing, because they are themselves theologians. They do not think of themselves as making evolution a *substitute* for God, but that is because they have made evolution God. They talk, like Philip Hefner, of God as the way things really are, and since they think the way things really are evolves, they talk about the evolution of God (Hefner 1993). They translate God's transcendence into omnipresence, which means that God transcends any *part* of the universe and any *particular* time in the universe. Within this universe, they say, there is a direction of emergence, what the Romantics in the nineteenth century called a life force, which is making possible first life itself, then higher forms of life, then finally culture and freedom. With this strategy we retain the traditional view of both the moral demand, which Hefner says is self-emptying love, and also of our natural biological tendency to prefer the self, which Hefner says is our sin of origin. So a moral gap remains, but defined now as a gap between morality and biology. This view gives us a gradual synchronized rise of the moral demand

and our cultural capacities linked together, against the background of a bio-logical lag. My problem with this view is that it does not take seriously enough the distinction between creature and creator. Scotus puts this in terms of God's existence being necessary and the universe being dependent, and so, possibly, non-existent. I think the resources for our salvation are lo-cated not within our freedom and culture, and not within some internal force of evolution, even if it is called "the evolution of God," but in the goodness of a transcendent God whose existence is independent of the universe. But I am just stating my opinion at this point and not attempting an argument, which would be beyond the scope of this chapter.

Conclusion

Let me try to tie some of the thoughts of this chapter together. The theory of evolution, I am claiming, does not solve for us the problem of the moral gap. There are two gaps here: the affection gap between us and other animals, and the performance gap between our aspirations and the actual living of our lives. Human responsibility is located in this performance gap. We are re-sponsible to live by the moral demand, but we do not seem to be able to do so by our own resources. Because of the affection gap between us and other ani-mals, there is one answer to the problem of the moral gap we cannot give. We cannot explain our moral capacities by finding them already in nonhuman animals from which, according to the theory of evolution, we evolved. But would we learn anything useful about human morality *if* the theory of evolu-tion were true in its application to human beings? We would learn something about the raw material, so to speak, on which God's assistance works. We would learn more detail about what our natural capacities are, or, in Scotistic terms, we would learn more about the affection for advantage.

But if evolution were proposed as a substitute source of the moral de-mand, we would be in danger of losing both morality and responsibility. Why is this? Because we would end up reducing the demand in one of the ways I have described. If I have been right so far, we need an account of how the moral gap might be bridged that does not either lower the demand or exag-gerate our natural capacities, and we need a theory of the source of the moral demand that passes the publicity standard. Christianity has some resources here and this is not surprising, for Western morality has its roots deep in Christian doctrine, though not only there. If we try to detach or unmoor or uproot ourselves from this doctrine, we should expect certain kinds of inco-herence to result. For example, we will lose the traditional answers to the two questions, "Can we be morally good?" and "Why should we be morally good?" and it will be hard to find a substitute. Christian moral philosophy has as one of its tasks to uncover this kind of incoherence, and point us to a retrieval of the resources for overcoming it.

REFERENCES

Alexander, Richard D. 1979. *Darwinian and Human Affairs*. Seattle: University of Washington Press.

Alexander, Richard D., and Andrew F. Richards. Forthcoming. Group-living, conflicts of interest, and the concept of God.

Arnhart, Larry. 1998. *Darwinian Natural Right: The Biological Ethics of Human Nature*. Albany, N.Y.: State University of New York Press.

Auer, J. A. C. Fagginer, et al. 1973. *Humanist Manifesto I*. Buffalo, N.Y.: Prometheus. First published in *The New Humanist* 6, no. 3 (1933).

Augustine. 1948. *Grace and Free Will*. In *Basic Writings of Saint Augustine*, ed. Whitney J. Oates. Vol. 1 of *A Select Library of the Nicene and Post-Nicene Fathers of the Christian Church*, ed. Philip Schaff. New York: Random House.

Cartwright, John. 2000. *Evolution and Human Behavior: Darwinian Perspectives on Human Nature*. Cambridge, Mass.: MIT Press.

Darwin, Charles. [1859] 1999. *The Origin of Species By Means of Natural Selection or The Preservation of Favored Races in the Struggle for Life*. New York: Bantam.

De Waal, Frans. 1996. *Good Natured: The Origins of Right and Wrong in Humans and Other Animals*. Cambridge, Mass.: Harvard University Press.

Frank, Robert H., Thomas Gilovich, and Dennis T. Regan. 1993. Does studying economics inhibit cooperation? *Journal of Economic Perspectives* 7, no. 2.

Hare, John E. 1996. *The Moral Gap*. Oxford: Clarendon.

———. 2001. *God's Call*. Grand Rapids: Eerdmans.

———. 2002. *Why Bother Being Good?* Downers Grove, Ill.: InterVarsity.

———. 2003. Christian scholarship and human responsibility. In *Christian Scholarship — for What?* ed. Susan M. Felch. Grand Rapids: Calvin College.

Hefner, Philip. 1993. *The Human Factor: Evolution, Culture, and Religion*. Minneapolis: Fortress.

Luther, Martin. 1957. *The Bondage of the Will*. Trans. J. I. Packer and O. R. Johnston. London: James Clarke.

Noddings, Nel. 1984. *Caring: A Feminine Approach to Ethics and Moral Education*. Berkeley: University of California Press.

O'Hear, Anthony. 1997. *Beyond Evolution: Human Nature and the Limits of Evolutionary Explanation*. Oxford: Clarendon.

Richards, Janet Radcliffe. 2000. *Human Nature after Darwin: A Philosophical Introduction*. London: Routledge.

Ruse, Michael. 2001. *Can a Darwinian Be a Christian? The Relationship between Science and Religion.* Cambridge: Cambridge University Press.

Schneewind, J. B. 1998. *The Invention of Autonomy.* Cambridge: Cambridge University Press.

Wilson, David Sloan. 2002. *Darwin's Cathedral: Evolution, Religion, and the Nature of Society.* Chicago: University of Chicago Press.

Wilson, David Sloan, and Elliott Sober. 1999. *Unto Others: The Evolution and Psychology of Unselfish Behavior.* Harvard: Harvard University Press.

Wilson, Edward O. 1975. *Sociobiology: The New Synthesis.* Cambridge, Mass.: Belknap Press of Harvard University Press.

10. The Darwinian Moral Sense and Biblical Religion

Larry Arnhart

For a number of years now, some Christians have put Jesus fish medallions on the back of their cars. Some people have responded to this by putting Darwin fish medallions on their cars. And just the other day, I saw a car with a bumper sticker that showed a giant Jesus fish eating a tiny Darwin fish. Under the picture it said "Survival of the Fittest."

I don't have either a Jesus fish or a Darwin fish on my car, because I don't accept the idea that these fish are predatory competitors. I think the Jesus fish and the Darwin fish can swim together without one eating the other.

To be more exact, I believe that Charles Darwin's biological view of the moral sense is compatible with biblical religion. Darwin's idea of a moral sense rooted in human nature belongs to a tradition of moral naturalism that includes the idea of natural law as elaborated by Thomas Aquinas and other Scholastics. And that idea of natural law is the moral expression of the biblical doctrine of creation.

The opposing tradition is that of moral transcendentalism, which is based on the thought that human nature is not moral, and therefore morality requires a transcendence of nature through human reason and will. That tradition of moral transcendentalism includes Thomas Hobbes and Immanuel Kant. In its most extreme form, moral transcendentalism denies the biblical doctrine of creation and expresses a Gnostic dualism that scorns nature and regards true morality as a denial of natural inclinations by human reason or will. The Hobbesian-Kantian transcendentalist insists on a radical separation between the realm of natural causes and the realm of moral freedom. By contrast, the Darwinian-Thomistic naturalist insists that human morality expresses the natural inclinations of the human animal as belonging to a natural world created by God, who saw his creation as entirely good.

I am grateful to the Earhart Foundation for a research grant that supported the writing of this chapter.

To lay out my argument for these claims, I will begin with a brief sketch of the tradition of moral naturalism that connects the Bible, Thomas Aquinas, the Scottish moral sense philosophers, and Charles Darwin. I will then respond to five criticisms of my position offered by biblical believers who think that Darwinian science must contradict biblical morality.

Biblical Morality, Natural Law, and the Moral Sense

"In the beginning God created the heaven and the earth." After that opening sentence of the Bible, the first chapter of Genesis gives the account of God's six days of creation. The chapter ends by declaring, "And God saw every thing that he had made, and, behold, it was very good" (Gen. 1:1; 1:31).

This teaching that God created the world and saw that it was all good is the first, and perhaps most fundamental, doctrine of the Bible. Any orthodox biblical believer must affirm the goodness of nature as the product of the Creator. It follows from this doctrine of creation that biblical morality should overlap with natural morality. To insist on the radical uniqueness of biblical morality as completely transcending natural moral experience would be to deny that God created the natural world and saw that it was good. To assert that biblical morality has no roots in natural morality would move toward the heresy of Gnostic dualism, which teaches that nature is evil and that moral freedom requires a transcendental escape from the natural world (Jonas 1958).

Prior to the revelation of the Mosaic law, the Bible speaks of many moral laws as part of the natural human condition. So, for example, after human beings are created as male and female, God blesses them and says, "Be fruitful, and multiply, and replenish the earth" (Gen. 1:28). When God blesses Noah, he repeats this injunction (9:1). Sexuality and sexual reproduction are thus acknowledged as part of human nature. The bonding of male and female and parental care of offspring are presented as essential human traits. To restrain the human propensity to violence, God declares to Noah: "Whoso sheddeth man's blood, by man shall his blood be shed: for in the image of God made he man" (9:6-7). The moral law against murder is thereby enforced by the natural inclination of human beings to take vengeance on murderers. These and other moral laws given to Noah were interpreted in the Jewish rabbinical tradition as a natural moral law that was comprehensible by all human beings (Novak 1998).

Later in the Bible, when God's commandments are revealed to Moses, the moral laws are presented as natural conditions for a flourishing human life on earth. To justify the commandments, Moses repeatedly declares to the people of Israel that they must obey these commandments so that they and their children will live and prosper in the land God has given them (Deut. 4:40; 30:15-20; 32:45-47). In the New Testament, Jesus specifies the Second Table of the Ten Commandments — which includes the commandments that one should honor one's parents and that one should refrain from murder, adultery, stealing, and false witness — as the laws that must be obeyed for a good life on earth (Matt. 19:16-26).

In the first chapters of Paul's Letter to the Romans, Paul declares that God's moral law is evident in his creation and is therefore knowable to all human beings, Gentiles as well as Jews. Here Paul uses the Greek word for "nature" — *physis*. He declares: "For when the Gentiles, which have not the law, do by nature the things contained in the law, these, having not the law, are a law unto themselves: Which shew the work of the law written in their hearts, their conscience also bearing witness" (Rom. 2:14-15). This Pauline teaching that all human beings by nature know that moral law that is "written in their hearts" is the primary scriptural authority for Thomas Aquinas's idea of natural law.

Aquinas and other Scholastics saw the moral laws of the Decalogue as natural laws rooted in human nature that should be comprehensible to all human beings. One motivation for this Scholastic emphasis on natural law was to answer the Cathars, a Gnostic movement that gained strength in the twelfth century in southern France and Italy (Porter 1999, 73-75, 171-72). The Cathars were radical dualists who believed that the natural world was so evil that it could not be the creation of a good God, and so they argued that salvation required a denial of all natural human inclinations. Against such Gnostic transcendentalism, Aquinas and the Scholastics argued that nature and natural inclinations were inherently good as products of the Creator.

In explaining the natural law, Aquinas insists that "all those things to which man has a natural inclination are naturally apprehended by reason as being good and, consequently, as objects of pursuit, and their contraries as evil and objects of avoidance." Consequently, "the order of the precepts of the natural law is according to the order of natural inclinations." Many of these natural inclinations are shared with other animals, and therefore Aquinas agrees with Ulpian's declaration that natural law is "that which nature has taught all animals." Human beings share with all animals a natural inclination to self-preservation. Human beings share with some animals natural inclinations to sexual mating and parental care of offspring. And, as uniquely rational beings, human beings have natural inclinations to organize themselves into social institutions and to search for the divine causes of nature (*Summa Theologica*, I-II, q. 94, a. 2).

In explaining the animal nature of natural law, Aquinas repeatedly employs the biological psychology that he learned from the biological works of Aristotle and Albert the Great (Albertus Magnus 1999). So, for example, he explains that human marriage is natural because it satisfies natural desires for mating, parenting, and conjugal bonding, desires that human beings share with other animals. The disposition to marriage, he says, is "a natural instinct of the human species" (*Summa Contra Gentiles,* bk. 3, chaps. 122-23).

This biological psychology allows him to distinguish between natural and unnatural systems of marriage. Monogamy is fully natural because it satisfies the sexual and parental instincts. Polygyny (one husband with multiple wives) is partly natural and partly unnatural, because while one husband can impregnate many wives, the natural tendency to sexual jealousy among the co-wives disrupts the household. Polyandry (one wife with multiple husbands) is totally unnatural, because the uncertainty of paternity and the intense jealousy of the husbands would make it impossible for them to share a wife (*Summa Theologica,* suppl., q. 65, a. 1; *Summa Contra Gentiles,* bk. 3, chap. 123).

Aquinas did not interpret the doctrine of original sin as denying natural law, because he believed that although the fall had obscured the human understanding of moral law, fallen human beings still had some natural sense of right and wrong (*Summa Theologica,* I-II, q. 63, a. 2, ad 2; q. 65, a. 2; q. 93, a. 6, ad 2; q. 109, a. 2; II-II, q. 122, a. 1). Even John Calvin agreed with Aquinas on this. Calvin affirmed natural law as "that apprehension of the conscience which distinguishes sufficiently between just and unjust, and which deprives men of the excuse of ignorance" (*Institutes of the Christian Religion* IV.2.22). Aquinas and Calvin could agree on the existence of a natural moral law because they agreed on the doctrine of creation and thus they both rejected any Gnostic dualism that would deny the goodness of natural human inclinations.

The modern break with this Aristotelian and Thomistic tradition of natural law began in the seventeenth century with Thomas Hobbes. Aristotle and Aquinas had claimed that human beings are by nature social and political animals. Hobbes denied this claim and asserted that social and political order is an utterly artificial human construction. For Aristotle and Aquinas, moral and political order was rooted in biological nature. For Hobbes, such order required that human beings conquer and transcend their vicious animal nature. What Hobbes identified as the "laws of nature" that should govern human conduct were actually "laws of reason" by which human beings contrive by rational artifice to escape the disorder that ensues from following their natural selfish inclinations (*Leviathan,* chaps. 14-15).

Hobbes assumed a radical separation between animal societies as founded on natural instinct and human societies as founded on social learning. Human beings cannot be political animals by nature, Hobbes says, because "man is made fit for society not by nature but by education" (*De Cive*, chap. 1). Hobbes argued that this dependence of human social order on artifice and learning meant that human beings were not at all like the naturally social animals (such as bees and ants) (*Leviathan*, chap. 17; *De Cive*, chap. 5, par. 5; *De Homine*, chap. 10). Despite the monism of Hobbes's materialism, his moral and political teaching presupposes a dualistic opposition between animal nature and human will: in creating political order, human beings transcend and conquer nature (Strauss 1952, 7-9, 168-70).

This Hobbesian dualism was developed by Immanuel Kant in the eighteenth century. Kant agreed with Hobbes that the natural state for human beings is a war of all against all, and therefore moral law arises as a contrivance of human reason in transcending human nature. This led Kant into formulating the modern concept of culture. Culture becomes that uniquely human realm of artifice in which human beings escape their natural animality to express their rational humanity as the only beings who have a moral will. Through culture, human beings free themselves from the laws of nature (Kant 1983; Kant 1987, secs. 83-84).

In opposition to the Hobbesian claim that human beings are naturally asocial and amoral, Anthony Ashley Cooper, the Third Earl of Shaftesbury, argued early in the eighteenth century that human beings were endowed with the natural instincts of social animals. He maintained that this natural sociality supported what he called a "natural moral sense," which was a "natural sense of right and wrong" (Cooper 1999, 177-82). This idea of a natural moral sense was elaborated by Francis Hutcheson, Adam Smith, David Hume, and others in the Scottish Enlightenment.

These Scottish philosophers saw nature as instilling those moral sentiments that would promote the survival and propagation of human beings as social animals. But they could not explain exactly how it was that nature could shape the human animal in this way. Such an explanation was later provided by Charles Darwin in the nineteenth century.

Darwin's early notebooks show that he was much influenced by his reading of the Scottish moral sense philosophers, and that he was striving to find a biological explanation for the human moral sense (Darwin 1987, 487-89, 537-38, 558, 563-64, 618-29). In 1871, in his book *The Descent of Man*, Darwin elaborated his biological theory of the moral sense (Darwin 1871, 1:70-106, 2:390-94).

Darwin says that he agrees with those like Kant who "maintain that of all the differences between man and the lower animals, the moral sense or conscience is by far the most important" (1871, 1:70). But Darwin rejects Kant's dualistic separation between the empirical world of natural causes and the transcendental world of moral freedom. Darwin shows how human morality could have developed through a natural evolutionary history.

Like Aquinas and the Scottish philosophers, Darwin observes that one of the central features of the human species is the duration and intensity of child-care. For that reason alone, human beings must be social animals by nature. The reproductive fitness of human beings requires strong attachments between infants and parents and within kin groups (Darwin 1871, 1:80-86).

Natural selection favors not only kinship but also mutuality and reciprocity as grounds for cooperation and morality. Animals with the sociality and intelligence of human beings recognize that social cooperation can be mutually beneficial for all participants. They also recognize that being benevolent to others can benefit oneself in the long run if one's benevolence is likely to be reciprocated. Moreover, they care about how they appear to others. Those with the reputation for fairness are rewarded. Those with the reputation for cheating are punished. Moral emotions such as gratitude and resentment enforce standards of mutuality and reciprocity. The natural inclinations to feel such emotions were favored by natural selection because they contributed to survival and reproductive success in human evolutionary history (Darwin 1871, 1:82, 1:92, 1:106, 1:161-66). As social animals, human beings feel concern for the good of others, and they feel regret when they allow their selfish desires to impede the satisfaction of their social desires.

Darwin concludes, "Ultimately our moral sense or conscience becomes a highly complex sentiment — originating in the social instincts, largely guided by the approbation of our fellow-men, ruled by reason, self-interest, and in later times by deep religious feelings, and confirmed by instruction and habit" (1871, 1:72, 1:165-66).

Thus does Darwin provide a biological explanation for how the moral sense could be rooted in human nature. In doing so, he confirms a tradition of moral naturalism that stretches back through the Scottish moral sense philosophers to Aquinas and the natural law philosophers and finally back to the biblical doctrine that there is a natural sense of right and wrong that is implanted in the human heart by the Creator. And in doing so, he denies the tradition of moral transcendentalism that stretches back through Kant and Hobbes to the Gnostic dualists who rejected the biblical doctrine of creation by denying the goodness of the natural world.

Five Objections

Darwinian Naturalism

But what about those Christians who worry that the Jesus fish can't survive unless he eats the Darwin fish before the Darwin fish eats him? They might offer at least five objections to my argument that the Darwinian moral sense is compatible with biblical religion. The first objection would be that Darwinian naturalism denies any religious belief in a supernatural Creator. The second would be that Darwinian reductionism denies human dignity. The third would be that Darwinian determinism denies moral freedom. The fourth would be that Darwinian emotivism denies the rule of reason in morality. And the final objection would be that Darwinian tribalism denies the morality of universal love. Such Christians believe, then, that Darwinism corrupts our moral life by promoting five "isms" — naturalism, reductionism, determinism, emotivism, and tribalism. I will respond to each of these five objections.

The first objection is that Darwinian naturalism promotes atheism, because in assuming that everything must be explained through natural causes, it denies the possibility of supernatural causes. Philip Johnson and other proponents of "intelligent design theory" often make this claim (Johnson 1991).

In taking this position, however, the proponents of intelligent design assume that God was unable or unwilling to execute his design through the laws of nature. I see no support for this position in the Bible. Christian evolutionists such as Howard Van Till (formerly of Calvin College) have argued that the Bible presents the Divine Designer as having fully gifted his creation from the beginning with all of the formational powers necessary for evolving into the world we see today (Van Till 1999).

Of course, any orthodox biblical believer must believe that God has intervened into nature in miraculous ways. The Christian must believe, for example, that the dead body of Jesus was resurrected back to life in a way that could not be explained by natural causes. But notice that in the Bible, once God has created the universe in the first chapters of Genesis, God's later interventions into nature are all part of salvation history. God intervenes in history to communicate his redemptive message to human beings, but he does not need to intervene to form irreducibly complex mechanisms that could not be formed by natural means. The Bible suggests that God created the world at the beginning so that everything we see in nature today could emerge by natural law without any need for later miracles of creation.

Moreover, the miracles of salvation history — such as the resurrection of Jesus — add nothing to the natural morality required for earthly life. Rather, these salvation miracles confirm the supernatural morality required for eternal life.

To be sure, there are militant Darwinian atheists such as Richard Dawkins. But I see no reason to accept the claim of people like Dawkins that Darwinian science dictates atheism (Dawkins 1986). In fact, it is remarkable that proponents of intelligent design theory such as Philip Johnson actually agree with Dawkins on this point.

Charles Darwin himself was often evasive about his personal religious beliefs. His clearest and fullest statement is in his *Autobiography* (Darwin 1958, 85-96). When he sailed out of England on board the *Beagle* in 1831, he was an orthodox Christian. When *The Origin of Species* was published in 1859, he had moved away from orthodox Christianity and toward a simple theism. By the end of his life, he was an "agnostic," a term he adopted from Thomas Huxley to denote someone who is in such a state of uncertainty about the existence and character of God that he can be neither a dogmatic atheist nor a dogmatic theist (Phipps 2002). Throughout his life, he insisted that ultimate questions of First Cause — questions about the origin of the universe and the origin of the laws of nature — left a big opening for God as Creator. As he said, "the mystery of the beginning of all things is insoluble by us" (Darwin 1958, 94).

Darwin began his book *The Origin of Species* with an epigram from Francis Bacon about the importance of studying both the Bible as "the book of God's word" and nature as "the book of God's work" (Darwin 1936, 2; Bacon 2002, 126). This idea that Scripture and nature complement one another as expressions of God's wisdom follows from the doctrine of creation. It's an old idea that goes back to Calvin, to Aquinas, and to other natural law theologians. This idea of the two books of God is commonly invoked today by people who argue for the fundamental compatibility of biblical religion and modern science (Peacocke 1979).

Darwin's last sentence in *The Origin of Species* conveys a vivid image of God as Creator. Darwin writes, "There is grandeur in this view of life, with its several powers, having been originally breathed by the Creator into a few forms or into one; and that, whilst this planet has gone cycling on according to the fixed law of gravity, from so simple a beginning endless forms most beautiful and most wonderful have been, and are being, evolved" (1936, 374). There is indeed "grandeur in this view of life," and this grandeur can evoke a natural sense of piety, a reverence for nature that might lead some of us beyond nature to nature's God.

As a natural science, Darwinian biology cannot confirm the supernatural truth of biblical religion in its theological doctrines. But Darwinian biology can confirm the natural truth of biblical religion in its practical morality. Similarly, sociologist Emile Durkheim explained religion through its social function of uniting human beings into social groups. David Sloan Wilson, in his recent book *Darwin's Cathedral*, provides a Darwinian argument to support Durkheim's view (Wilson 2002). Wilson's book shows how a Darwinian theory of human social evolution can support the moral utility of religion in bringing individuals into well-organized groups. From Wilson's Darwinian point of view, religion causes human groups to function as adaptive units by coordinating behavior and preventing or punishing cheating. In other words, religion teaches believers to act for the benefit of their group.

One of Wilson's best case studies to support his view is a study of John Calvin's plan for reforming Geneva. The city of Geneva was divided by factional conflicts. When Calvin first proposed his plan for the social organization of the city, the plan was rejected by the city council, and Calvin was expelled. But three years later, a desperate city council invited him back, and eventually the extraordinary success of Calvin's reforms in bringing order to the city made Geneva internationally famous as a model of republican governance. A Darwinian scientist like Wilson cannot judge the theological truth of Calvin's religious doctrines. But he can see the moral truth of Calvin's reforms in promoting a shared sense of morality that turned a badly divided city into a single adaptive social unit.

This concern for the natural moral truth of biblical religion is evident in the Bible itself. Moses promised the people of Israel that if they obeyed God's commandments, they would survive and prosper as a social unit, and other peoples would admire them for the wisdom and prudence of their laws and social institutions (Deut. 4:6-8, 39-40; 30:15-20). That's just what one should expect if one accepts the doctrine of creation. If God is the Creator of nature, then his eternal laws should conform to the natural laws of life on earth.

Darwinian Reductionism

And yet, a crucial part of the biblical creation story is the teaching that human beings were created in the image of God. Many biblical believers worry that Darwinism rejects this teaching by promoting a reductionistic view of human origins that denies human dignity in claiming that human beings are just animals. This criticism might seem to be confirmed by an often-quoted remark by Darwin in one of his early notebooks. Darwin writes, "Man in his arrogance thinks himself a great work, worthy of the interposition of a deity. More humble, and I believe more true, to consider him created from animals" (Darwin 1987, 300).

According to Darwin's account of human evolution, the appearance of human beings in the evolutionary history of life on earth did not require a special miraculous intervention by God to create the human soul. Rather, Darwin believes, the human species arose by natural causes from ancestral species of animals.

But I see no reason why the biblical doctrine of creation could not be compatible with this Darwinian understanding of human evolution. If God originally created the universe with all of the formative powers necessary to develop into the world we see today, then God could have designed those original formative powers such that human beings would eventually emerge as evolutionary descendents of some ancestral species.

The biblical doctrine that human beings were created in God's image suggests that human beings differ in kind and not just in degree from other animals. Darwin, on the other hand, insists that human beings differ only in degree and not in kind from other animals (Darwin 1871, 1:185-86, 2:390). Yet Darwin is unclear on this point, because he also says that human beings are unique in their capacities for morality, language, and other intellectual traits, which implies a difference in kind from other animals (Darwin 1871, 1:54, 1:70, 1:88-89, 2:391-92).

The best way to resolve this confusion is to employ the modern biological idea of "emergence." Biologists recognize that as one moves through the levels of complexity in the natural world, novel traits arise at higher levels of organization that cannot be found at lower levels. They speak of these as "emergent" traits (Blitz 1992; Morowitz 2002). While biological phenomena are constrained by the laws of physics and chemistry, biological phenomena are not fully reducible to those laws. This general principle applies particularly to the evolution of the brain and nervous system among animal species. As the brain becomes larger and more complex in the evolution of animals, we expect that the more intelligent species will have cognitive capacities that cannot be found among species with smaller and less complex brains. We might expect, then, that as the primate brain grew larger and more complex in evolutionary history, it passed a critical threshold among the hominid species; the human species came to be endowed with a brain having all of the uniquely human capacities for speech and thought that make them the extraordinary creatures that they are. Differences in degree that pass over a critical threshold of complexity can produce emergent differences in kind.

I see no reason why an omnipotent and omniscient God could not have originally designed the universe so that it would develop toward this outcome. We could say, then, that God created human beings in his image by designing a world in which they would be "created from animals."

Darwinian Determinism

One expression of the special status that human beings have as created in God's image is that they have a moral freedom that other animals do not have. Some religious believers warn that a Darwinian view of human nature promotes a determinism that denies this moral freedom, because a Darwinian science assumes that everything human beings do must have a natural cause. The argument here is that if human behavior were as completely determined by the laws of nature as animal behavior is, then human beings would not have "free will" and could not be held morally responsible for their actions. A biological science of human nature cannot explain human morality if morality presupposes a human freedom from nature that sets human beings apart from the animal world.

In response to this argument, I would agree that if moral freedom required a "free will" understood as an uncaused cause — that is to say, a will acting outside the causal laws of nature — then Darwinian science would deny moral freedom. But this notion of "free will" understood as an uncaused cause is contrary both to our common experience and to biblical religion.

This idea of "free will" as uncaused cause is a Gnostic idea that treats the human will as an unconditioned, self-determining, transcendental power beyond the natural world. This Gnostic idea came into modern moral philosophy through the influence of Kant.

Such a notion contradicts biblical religion, because the only uncaused cause in the Bible is God. I agree with Jonathan Edwards, who argued that whatever comes into existence must have a cause. Only what is self-existent from eternity — God — could be uncaused or self-determined. By contrast to the nonsensical notion of "free will," the common-sense notion of human freedom is the power to act as one chooses, regardless of the cause of the choice (Edwards 1995). Edwards was arguing against the Arminian notion of moral freedom as the absolute self-determination of will. That same Arminian notion of "free will" as separated from natural causality was adopted by Kant (1965, 464-79).

A Darwinian science of the moral sense would support this commonsensical notion of moral freedom as described by Edwards. A biological explanation of human nature does not deny human freedom if we define that freedom as the capacity for deliberation and choice based on one's own desires. As Aristotle explained, we hold people responsible for their actions when they act voluntarily and deliberately (*Nicomachean Ethics,* 1109b30-1115a3; *Rhetoric,* 1368b27-1369a7). They act voluntarily when they act knowingly and without external force to satisfy their desires. They act with deliberate choice when, having weighed one desire against another in the light of past experience and future expectations, they choose that course of action likely to satisfy their desires harmoniously over a complete life.

This is Darwin's understanding of moral responsibility. Since he believes that "every action whatever is the effect of a motive," he doubts the existence of "free will" understood as uncaused cause (Darwin 1987, 526-27, 536-37, 606-8). But he believes that we are still morally responsible for our actions because of our uniquely human capacity for reflecting on our motives and circumstances and acting in the light of those reflections. He writes, "A moral being is one who is capable of reflecting on his past actions and their motives — of approving of some and disapproving of others; and the fact that man is the one being who certainly deserves this designation is the greatest of all distinctions between him and the lower animals" (1871, 2:391-92).

Darwinian Emotivism

But what is the ultimate standard for moral judgment or conscience? Kant would say that the standard comes from the rational apprehension of a categorical imperative that gives us the sense of moral obligation that is conveyed in the word *ought.* Yet while Kant speaks of this moral *ought* as a purely rational act, Darwin speaks of it as an instinct, or emotion, or feeling. In explaining the uniquely human experience of conscience, Darwin writes, "Any instinct which is permanently stronger or more enduring than another, gives rise to a feeling which we express by saying that it ought to be obeyed. A pointer dog, if able to reflect on his past conduct, would say to himself, I ought (as indeed we say of him) to have pointed at that hare and not have yielded to the passing temptation of hunting it" (1871, 2:392).

So for Darwin when we use the word *ought* in a moral sense, we are expressing a strong feeling or emotion. If we think parents *ought* to care for their children, it is because we have a strong feeling of approval for parental care and a strong feeling of disapproval for parental neglect. If we think soldiers *ought* to be courageous, it is because we have a strong feeling of approval for courage and a strong feeling of disapproval for cowardice. This emphasis on the role of emotion in moral experience is evident among the Scottish moral sense philosophers, who stressed the importance of moral sentiments or feelings in motivating moral conduct. But one could easily trace this idea through the whole tradition of moral naturalism. Aquinas spoke of the natural law as rooted in the emotional desires or inclinations of the human animal. And Aristotle argued that "thought by itself moves nothing," and consequently moral deliberation requires a union of reason and desire (*Nicomachean Ethics*, 1139a36-b7). Our emotional desires depend upon beliefs about the world, and reason can guide our conduct by judging the truth or falsity of those beliefs. But the motivation to action comes not from reason but from emotion.

Some Christian critics of Darwinian morality have complained that this reliance on the moral emotions denies the moral primacy of reason in ruling over the emotions. But to assume a radical opposition between reason and emotion manifests a Gnostic dualism that is contrary to the biblical doctrine of creation.

It is surely true that the emotions often need to be guided by reason. But this rational guidance works by leading the emotions to their fullest, most harmonious, satisfaction. After all, the Bible teaches us that obedience to the moral law comes from the emotion of love — love of one's neighbor and love of God.

Moreover, those who show no respect for moral law suffer not from some intellectual deficiency but from some emotional poverty. Psychopaths are often very intelligent people; but they have no moral sense because they are not moved by moral emotions such as guilt, shame, and love (Arnhart 1998, 211-30). Pure psychopaths show this early in their childhood. They are completely unresponsive to parental discipline since they lack the social emotions that would make them care about parental love and social approval. Moses prescribes that such a child must be brought before the elders of the community for judgment, and then the citizens must stone him to death (Deut. 21:18-21).

Darwinian Tribalism

This leaves me with the last of the five criticisms of Darwinian morality — the charge of tribalism. Darwin stresses the role of tribal warfare in the development of morality. In the violent competition between neighboring tribal communities, a tribe whose members cooperated for the good of the tribe would have defeated those tribes whose members were less cooperative with one another. Thus, moral dispositions to loyalty, courage, and patriotism would tend to be favored by natural selection working on tribal groups. Human beings were naturally inclined to cooperate within groups so as to compete successfully with other groups (Darwin 1871, 1:84-85, 97-96, 158-67, 173). As a result, Darwin explains, savage human beings don't extend their moral community beyond the membership of their own tribe. And they certainly have no sense of universal humanitarian concern.

Many Christians object to this tribal xenophobia as violating the morality of universal love taught by Jesus. And yet the Hebrew Bible shows the tribalism of the people of Israel, who were brutal in their attacks on those outside their group (Num. 31; Deut. 20:10-20). Even in the New Testament, we are taught by Paul that "if any provide not for his own, and specially for those of his own house, he hath denied the faith, and is worse than an infidel" (I Tim. 5:8).

Most Christians would agree that we have stronger moral obligations to our families, our friends, and our fellow citizens than to strangers, which reflects the natural order of our moral emotions in which we tend to feel more concern for those close to us than to those far away. An utterly indiscriminate love of all humanity would require the abolition of family life, and few Christians would accept that, although Jesus is sometimes brutal in dismissing familial attachments as an impediment to his redemptive mission (Matt. 10:35-36). Christian theologians such as Thomas Aquinas have affirmed the natural order of love, which corresponds to the kind of natural order in the social affections that a Darwinian biologist would expect of the human animal (Pope 1994).

Like Aquinas and the Scottish moral sense philosophers, Darwin thinks a universal sympathy for humanity is possible, but only as an extension of social emotions cultivated first in small groups. He assumes that as we expand our social sympathies to embrace all of humanity, and perhaps even all sentient beings, these sympathies become weaker as we move farther away from our inner circle of family, friends, and fellow citizens. And yet this extension of sympathy to embrace all of humanity is strong enough to support the Golden Rule as the foundation of morality — "As ye would that men should do to you, do ye to them likewise" (Darwin 1871, 1:85, 1:100-101, 1:105-6, 1:165).

In my book *Darwinian Natural Right,* I criticized Darwin's idea of universal sympathy as "moral utopianism" (Arnhart 1998, 143-49). I now think I was wrong, because I would now say that Darwin sees universal humanitarianism as compatible with the natural inclination to feel more sympathy for those nearest to us than for strangers. Darwin does not suggest that humanitarianism will ever completely eliminate tribalism. Darwin would not agree with Peter Singer's implausible claim that morality requires an utterly indiscriminate concern for the interests of all sentient beings, such that the natural love of one's own must be denied (Singer 2000).

Sometimes humanitarian sympathy is strong enough to move people to make heroic sacrifices for others. One dramatic illustration of this would be those people who rescued Jews in Nazi Europe during World War II. Kristen Monroe interviewed some of these rescuers, and she found that they were not moved by the rule of reason over selfish passions, as Kant might have thought. Rather, they were moved by an emotional sense of shared humanity with those they helped. "But what else could I do?" they told her. "They were human beings like you and me." Monroe found that while some of these rescuers were motivated by religious beliefs, many were not. She concluded that this perception of a shared humanity that inclines some people to heroic altruism expresses an innate moral sense that is somehow part of human nature, just as the Scottish moral sense philosophers argued (Monroe 2002). It seems that while religious belief can reinforce humanitarian sympathy, religion is not required, because such sympathy is a natural human capacity. But if both humanitarianism and tribalism are natural for human beings, then we must wonder about how we can best resolve the tragic conflicts between those natural motives.

One regrettable manifestation of tribalism is the assumption that those who love the Jesus fish must hate the Darwin fish. I have argued that this should not be the case. It is true that the Darwin fish cannot offer us a supernatural redemption from earthly life and entrance into eternal life, which is the promise of the Jesus fish. But when it comes to purely earthly morality, the Darwin fish and the Jesus fish are swimming in the same school.

REFERENCES

Albertus Magnus. 1999. *On Animals: A Medieval Summa Zoologica.* Translated by Kenneth F. Kitchell Jr. and Irven Michael Resnick. Baltimore, Md.: Johns Hopkins University Press.

Aquinas, Thomas. 1956. *Summa Contra Gentiles.* Translated by Vernon J. Bourke. South Bend, Ind.: University of Notre Dame Press.

———. 1981. *Summa Theologica.* Translated by the Dominican Fathers. Westminster, Md.: Christian Classics.

Aristotle. 1984. *The Complete Works of Aristotle.* Edited by Jonathan Barnes. Princeton, N.J.: Princeton University Press.

Arnhart, Larry. 1998. *Darwinian Natural Right: The Biological Ethics of Human Nature.* Albany: State University of New York Press.

Bacon, Francis. 2002. *Francis Bacon: The Major Works.* Edited by Brian Vickers. New York: Oxford University Press.

Blitz, David. 1992. *Emergent Evolution.* Boston: Kluwer Academic Publishers.

Calvin, John. 1960. *Institutes of the Christian Religion.* 2 vols. Translated by Ford Lewis Battles. Philadelphia: Westminster.

Cooper, Anthony Ashley, Third Earl of Shaftesbury. 1999. *Characteristics of Men, Manners, Opinions, Times.* Edited by Lawrence Klein. Cambridge: Cambridge University Press.

Darwin, Charles. 1871. *The Descent of Man.* 2 vols. London: John Murray.

———. 1936. *The Origin of Species.* Sixth ed. In *The Origin of Species and The Descent of Man.* New York: Random House, Modern Library.

———. 1958. *The Autobiography of Charles Darwin.* Edited by Nora Barlow. New York: Norton.

———. 1987. *Charles Darwin's Notebooks, 1836-1844.* Edited by Paul H. Barrett et al. Ithaca, N.Y.: Cornell University Press.

Dawkins, Richard. 1986. *The Blind Watchmaker.* New York: Norton.

Edwards, Jonathan. 1995. Freedom of the will. Pp. 192-222 in *A Jonathan Edwards Reader,* ed. John E. Smith, Harry S. Stout, and Kenneth Minkema. New Haven: Yale University Press.

Hobbes, Thomas. 1957. *Leviathan.* Edited by Michael Oakeshott. Oxford: Basil Blackwell.

———. 1991. *Man and Citizen: De Homine and De Cive.* Edited by Bernard Gert. Indianapolis: Hackett.

Johnson, Philip. 1991. *Darwin on Trial.* Downers Grove, Ill.: InterVarsity.

Jonas, Hans. 1958. *The Gnostic Religion.* Boston: Beacon.

Kant, Immanuel. 1965. *Critique of Pure Reason.* Translated by Norman Kemp Smith. New York: St. Martin's.

———. 1983. *Perpetual Peace and Other Essays.* Translated by Ted Humphrey. Indianapolis: Hackett.

———. 1987. *Critique of Judgment.* Translated by Werner S. Pluhar. Indianapolis: Hackett.

Monroe, Kristen Renwick. 2002. Explicating altruism. Pp. 106-22 in *Altruism and Altruistic Love: Science, Philosophy, and Religion in Dialogue,* ed. Stephen G. Post, Lynn G. Underwood, Jeffrey Schloss, and William Hurlbutt. Oxford: Oxford University Press.

Morowitz, Harold. 2002. *The Emergence of Everything: How the World Became Complex.* Oxford: Oxford University Press.

Novak, David. 1998. *Natural Law in Judaism.* Cambridge: Cambridge University Press.

Peacocke, Arthur R. 1979. *Creation and the World of Science.* New York: Oxford University Press.

Phipps, William E. 2002. *Darwin's Religious Odyssey.* Harrisburg, Pa.: Trinity Press International.

Pope, Stephen J. 1994. *The Evolution of Altruism and the Ordering of Love.* Washington, D.C.: Georgetown University Press.

Porter, Jean. 1999. *Natural and Divine Law: Reclaiming the Tradition for Christian Ethics.* Grand Rapids: Eerdmans.

Singer, Peter. 2000. *Writings on the Ethical Life*. New York: Harper Collins.

Strauss, Leo. 1952. *The Political Philosophy of Hobbes*. Translated by Elsa Sinclair. Chicago: University of Chicago Press.

Van Till, Howard. 1999. The fully gifted creation. Pp. 159-218 in *Three Views on Creation and Evolution*, ed. J. P. Moreland and John Mark Reynolds. Grand Rapids: Zondervan.

Wilson, David Sloan. 2002. *Darwin's Cathedral: Evolution, Religion, and the Nature of Society*. Chicago: University of Chicago Press.

11. Thomistic Natural Law and the Limits of Evolutionary Psychology

Craig A. Boyd

Introduction

In his recent book *Consilience,* E. O. Wilson develops his most sustained treatment of ethics from a sociobiological perspective (1998). Central to Wilson's view is a distinction between ethical theories that he calls "transcendentalist" and those that are "empiricist." As Wilson sees it, the transcendentalists "think that moral guidelines exist outside the human mind," while the empiricists "believe that moral values come from humans alone; God is a separate issue" (1998, 260-61). Accordingly, Kant and theists who subscribe to natural law morality are transcendentalists while Hume, Darwin, and Wilson himself are empiricists.

The transcendentalist typically appeals to God as the basis for moral objectivism. God appears to provide a stable and unassailable ground for morality that is somehow "independent" of human experience. Wilson says, "Christian theologians, following St. Thomas Aquinas' reasoning in *Summa Theologiae,* by and large consider natural law to be the expression of God's will" (1998, 261). On this view, any appeal to God, or to transcendent moral principles apart from human nature (e.g., the categorical imperative or the will of God), must be rejected as lacking consilience with natural science's hegemony over all academic disciplines. Ethics must be firmly grounded in an account of human nature, one that is informed primarily by sociobiology. That human nature, according to Wilson, is merely a synthesis of genetic predispositions that have been altered by cultural norms, both of which are the products of an evolutionary process.

Not all sociobiologists and evolutionary psychologists, however, are so blithely dismissive of long-standing traditions of ethics that appeal to the "transcendental." Michael Ruse has recently argued (2001) that one may see in the Christian tradition of natural law morality a philosophical articulation of some of the moral principles sociobiology holds to be necessary for human evolution and survival. On Ruse's view, since morality must be universally shared by all, a natural law position seems to be, at the very least, a plausible approach. Ruse concludes his chapter on morality by observing,

> What God has produced through evolution is good — better than what was before — and it is our obligation . . . to cherish and enjoy and respect it. Sexuality in itself is a good thing, and inasmuch as we use it properly we are "participating" in the eternal law. The Darwinian who is a Christian justifies his or her own position here by reference to the way in which God has made things of positive value through the natural progressive system. Doing things which are natural is not right simply because these things are natural, but because the natural is good as intended by God. (2001, 203)

Larry Arnhart has taken this view one step further and argued that neo-Darwinism can be seen as supporting a Thomistic theory of natural law morality (2001). Arnhart's approach is to consider the almost universal cultural ban on incest as a product of culture and nature. In almost all species of non-human primates, incest is practiced only in highly unusual circumstances. Since these nonhuman primates do not seem to have rules for the behavior, it would appear that there is some source for the behavior in the evolutionary development of the species. In humans, however, we see the ban as a cultural condemnation on the practice. On Arnhart's view natural law morality functions as the normative cultural practice that regulates the biological impulses. In appealing to natural law morality Arnhart continues a long-standing tradition of turning to nature for guidance in understanding the roots of human morality.

Unlike other philosophical theories, especially those that appeal to divine commands or linguistic analysis, natural law morality stresses that any account of morality must recognize the importance of the biological. In this chapter I argue that a natural law morality might plausibly use the findings from research in sociobiology as the basis for much of human morality. From the perspective of natural law morality, however, sociobiology does not, and cannot, provide a sufficient explanation for all of human behavior. I argue that an important distinction between the animal goods and the human goods helps us see that while humans are indeed animals, the existence of reason is necessary if they are to transcend the purely biological.

In the first part of the chapter I briefly present Aquinas's theory of natural law morality and demonstrate precisely how Aquinas grounds the precepts of natural law morality in human nature. In the following section I explore the findings of sociobiology and evolutionary psychology that seem to correlate with Aquinas's natural law morality. Finally, I contend that the merely biological approach to ethics that sociobiology represents fails to account for the development of virtue and the practice of behaviors that do not enhance fitness, such as martyrdom and celibacy.

Aquinas on Natural Law

Before considering Aquinas's views on natural law, we would do well to consider precisely what he means by the term "nature." For Aquinas, there is a clear distinction between the "material" and the natural (*Summa Theologiae* IaIIae.10.1).

A material nature is concerned with the physical constitution and powers of any being in the natural world. Rocks, trees, and squirrels all have a material nature. Yet while rocks possess only a material form, and trees an organic form, squirrels also possess an animal form, which provides them with a principle of locomotion.

For a human, her nature consists of her material form, which includes her matter as well as the various principles of locomotion. Yet humans, on Aquinas's view, are more than merely material beings. Humans possess reason in addition to their biological and material nature.

Accordingly, the term "nature" has a second, more inclusive, meaning than the first. It refers to the specific nature of any being. While the first sense of the term emphasizes the physical nature of a being, the second sense emphasizes the essential characteristics of any being, physical or immaterial. Aquinas makes a careful distinction between the two uses.

> The term nature is used in a manifold sense. For sometimes it stands for the intrinsic principle in movable things. In this sense, nature is either matter or the material form, as is stated in the Physics. In another sense, nature stands for any substance, or even for any being. And in this sense, that is said to be natural to a thing which befits it according to its substance; and this is what is in a thing essentially. (IaIIae.10.1)

A human is essentially a rational creature. Aquinas accepts Aristotle's definition of a human as a "rational animal," which conveys the essential meaning. This point is critical since natural law includes but is not confined to biological impulses and desires. It will, of necessity, also include those specifically human desires for truth, virtue, and God.

In a famous passage from the *Summa,* Aquinas says that natural law is the rational creature's capacity to act freely and to direct herself to various activities (IaIIae.91.2). Unlike the rest of creation, which is governed by physical laws and instincts, humans are self-directed to their proper ends.

Among the precepts of natural law, the most important is that "the good is to be done and pursued while evil is to be avoided" (IaIIae.94.2). This precept serves as Aquinas's initial statement of natural law and it functions as the foundation for all the other precepts of natural law.

All precepts of natural law morality are based upon human nature. This human nature simultaneously shares many features in common with all other forms of life and has unique capacities of its own. Aquinas says that we share the good of self-preservation with all life. We share with sentient animals the "sensitive" goods of procreation, the raising of the young, and so on. Yet Aquinas also says that humans are unique among all animals in that humans alone possess reason. In a crucial passage he argues that

> The order of the precepts of the natural law is according to the order of natural inclinations. For there is in humans, first, an inclination to the good in accordance with the nature which they share in common with all substances, inasmuch as every substance seeks the preservation of its own being . . . and by reason of this inclination, whatever is a means of preserving human life, and of warding off its obstacles, belongs to the natural law. Second, there is in humans an inclination to things that pertain to them . . . according to that nature which they share in common with other animals; and in virtue of this inclination, those things are said to belong to the natural law which nature has taught all animals, such as sexual intercourse, the education of the offspring, and so forth. Third, there is in humans an inclination to the good according to the nature of their reason, which is proper to humans. Thus, humans have a natural inclination to know the truth about God, and to live in society; and in this respect, whatever pertains to this inclination belongs to the natural law: e.g., to shun ignorance, to avoid offending those among whom one has to live, and so on. (IaIIae.94.2)

The organic and biological basis for our inclinations thus plays an important role in natural law morality. The parallels to evolutionary psychology become obvious at this point. The sociobiologist's contention that the genes guide our activities on a subconscious level parallels Aquinas's discussion of the "vegetative" powers of the soul. The evolutionary psychologist's appeal to kin selection theory corresponds to Aquinas's explanation of the "sensitive" powers of the soul.

The specific function of the vegetative power is to preserve the human agent's own being. That is, it looks to the organism's continued survival. The oxidation of blood and the capacity for white blood cells to attack alien matter in the blood stream can be seen as examples of the vegetative powers at work. From this power, Aquinas determines that it is a principle of natural law to avoid suicide, since the good of the vegetative power is the preservation of the agent's own being. Suicide obviously contravenes that basic natural principle and thus it must be avoided.

In addition to the vegetative powers of the soul, the human agent also shares the sensitive powers of the soul with other sentient animals. The sensitive soul has two primary appetites: the irascible and concupiscible (Ia.81.2). These two appetites direct the agent to sensory goods and away from sensory evils. The concupiscible appetite inclines the agent to pursue easily attainable goods and avoid pains. In particular it seeks the sensory goods of food, drink, and sex and thus has for its proper object the pleasurable or the painful.

From the desires of the concupiscible appetite, Aquinas derives various precepts of the natural law. One such precept is that humans should engage in monogamous, heterosexual activities within the confines of marriage. Another natural obligation is that parents must care for their children.

The irascible appetite operates when we struggle to a good. It seeks the difficult goods of resisting attack and fighting on behalf of a sensory good. Aquinas sees that the care and defense of one's children is a precept of natural law morality as based upon the irascible appetite's desire to protect the young. The irascible and concupiscible appetites are shared with other animals and appear to be instinctive behaviors; on account of this Aquinas quotes Justinian in saying that the natural law is "that which nature has taught all animals." Yet for humans it is possible for these appetites to come under the sway of reason.

The goods of reason transcend the biological not merely because reason is able to adjudicate among competing biological desires, but also because there are goods appropriate to humans *qua* rational. In order to make the distinction absolutely clear, Aquinas says, "By the intellectual appetite we may desire the immaterial good, which is not apprehended by sense, such as knowledge, virtue, and the like" (Ia.80.2.ad 2).

According to Aquinas, the rational soul has for its proper object universal being. And since the vegetative and sensitive powers can only apprehend the sensible as such, it follows that they are incapable of the understanding that is proper to humans. There must therefore be a "rational" soul that enables us not only to understand concepts but also to think in a way that transcends all merely sensual activity.

The rational soul not only enables humans to understand the concept of universal being, it also enables us to "reason." Unlike other animals, humans practice deliberation in their daily activities. While nonhuman animals have instincts, and on occasion benefit from nurturing, humans must also deliberate concerning how they go about pursuing the good.

Aquinas argues that knowledge of the truth, the pursuit of the good, and contemplation of God are all part of what it means to be a rational being. The human agent pursues both truth and goodness as rational goods. In contrast to nonrational animals, humans have the capacity to think conceptually and pursue those things that fall under the categories of truth and goodness.

Since humans always pursue their specific desires *sub ratio boni,* that is, under the formality of the good, we see that all actions are undertaken with a view to the good; yet no individual object is to be mistaken for the good itself. Accordingly, Aquinas maintains that we pursue the goods of the sensual appetite not as the good *qua* good but as fulfilling some aspect of our sensual nature. As a result, the attainment of our sensual desires can never satisfy us as rational beings. The rational desire for truth, especially truth about God, propels us beyond the merely biological. A closely related point is that although the sensual inclinations are part of our nature, they themselves are not moral. It is the existence of reason that enables humans to make moral judgments that differentiate them from nonhuman animals who share the same sensual appetites.

For Aquinas, the natural law includes all the characteristics of human nature that apply to humans as human. This means that human biology is the source for many of the precepts of natural law morality. Aquinas also holds, however, that whatever pertains to reason also falls under the domain of the natural law. Included in the goods of reason are the peaceful coexistence with others, the pursuit of truth, the desire for the good, the acquisition of virtue, and the knowledge of God.

Evolutionary Psychology and Natural Law

The upshot of our discussion so far is that the various kinds of activities humans engage in are rooted in both the animal and rational aspects of human nature. Instead of positing the existence of Aristotelian "souls," however, we might say that there are principles of organic life, principles of animal life, and principles of rational life. What we have then is a philosophical account of human nature that attempts to see the continuity, as well as the differences, between human and nonhuman life. In this section we explore how the findings of sociobiology and evolutionary psychology might be seen as consistent with a natural law morality.

Dawkins and Selfish Genes

In his approach to natural law morality, Aquinas believes that there is a principle of life that directs each organism to its own preservation. Following Aristotle, Aquinas sees the function of each nonhuman organism as the perpetuation of the species. While these organisms do not consciously direct themselves to their own self-preservation and perpetuation of the species, there is some principle at work that governs this behavior. There is, thus, a teleological principle that functions in all living beings. Since humans are also animals, it follows that there must be principles at work in us that do not rise to the level of consciousness but yet still operate in such a way as to preserve the individual as well as the species.

In his provocative work *The Selfish Gene,* Richard Dawkins contends that all human behavior is based upon genetic foundations (1989). These foundations, Dawkins argues, have a long evolutionary history of survival, and they determined to a large extent just how humans behave. According to Dawkins' theory, after eons of time proteins evolved from the primordial soup. These molecules copied themselves repeatedly and eventually various strands of DNA developed. The role of DNA is to copy itself and inform the organism, so that it can perform those tasks necessary for survival. The fundamental rule is that the DNA directs all organisms, from amoebas to apes, for the purposes of adaptation, survival, and reproduction.

Dawkins advanced the thesis that the genes function as "replicators"; these replicators' primary task is survival by whatever means necessary. So for Dawkins, individual humans simply function as "vehicles" for the replicators' survival.

For Dawkins, the genotype determines not only the phenotype but also to a great extent the organism's behavior. Just as nonhuman animals act according to the evolutionary development of their own genes, so humans are also subject to the same kind of genotypical tyranny. Yet, on Dawkins' view, humans do possess a means of resisting the genetic urgings of the replicators.

As genes desire their own survival, so memes (units of culturally developed ideas) also have a drive to survive (1989, 180). Ideas such as the soul, God, and beauty are all memes. These memes are transferred from human brain to brain and their survival is predicated upon their ability to function in culturally significant ways (for example, threats of hell can serve as a means to gain compliance). In this way Dawkins argues that it is possible for memes to enable humans to resist the power of the genes. A specific instance of the meme's ability to resist biology is the issue of celibacy. Since a gene for celibacy cannot survive (since it cannot be inherited) the sociobiologist must give some account of its persistence. According to Dawkins, it must be transferred mimetically. Some religious groups expend vast amounts of energy praising the value of celibacy and extolling its eternal value; in this way the meme survives from one generation to the next, not genetically, but mimetically.

In Dawkins' work a structure — that is to say, the genotype — functions in a profoundly similar way to the manner Aquinas sees the vegetative powers of the soul. It is a principle of organic life that humans share with all other forms of life. Dawkins contends that the only "telos" operating in the genotype is self-replication. One may say that this certainly plays a part in all biological organisms, but it is not the only possible teleology, at least from a philosophical perspective. Dawkins' arguments clearly move from the empirical to the philosophical without the slightest hesitation.

Westermarck on Incest Avoidance

As we have seen, Aquinas saw the basis for much of human behavior in the natural instincts that humans shared with other animals. Specifically, these instincts were found in the irascible and concupiscible appetites. The basis for reproductive behavior and care for the young is something that humans obviously share with other animals. But it is the moral sanctioning and forbidding of various activities, among other things, that make humans unique.

Larry Arnhart is one scholar who has understood that it is indeed possible to find a link between sociobiology and natural law ethics (1998, 2001). Arnhart's focus is on those behaviors that have their origin in what Aquinas calls the concupiscible appetite: marriage customs and the prohibition on incest, among others.

Arnhart sees a foundation for Aquinas's natural law account of the rules for marriage and family life as compatible with Darwinian sociobiology. According to Aquinas marriage functions for three purposes: procreation, raising the young, and companionship. As a result, promiscuity is forbidden since it undermines the paternity of the child (which would result in males failing to provide for the children) and violates the bond between husband and wife. Humans are unique in their capacity to formulate rules for marriage. The moral rules humans employ are those that forbid promiscuity and encourage fidelity. Arnhart notes, "rules for marriage provide formal structure to natural desires that are ultimately rooted in the animal nature of human beings" (2001, 5).

Drawing on the work of Westermarck, the noted anthropologist, Arnhart attempts to find a basis in sociobiology for the almost universal incest taboo.

Westermarck's study demonstrated that all cultures (with rare exceptions) have taboos on marrying one's close relatives.

There are three critical issues here. First, incest runs contrary to the evolutionary tendency toward fitness. This is so because the offspring of incestuous relationships typically suffer from mental and physical deficiencies (Wilson 1998, 188). Second, since there is a fitness problem associated with incest, humans, by means of natural selection, tend to feel a sexual aversion toward those to whom they are closely related (Wilson 1998, 190). Third, the natural avoidance of incest results in a moral prohibition on the practice within all cultures.

Various studies on incest seem to confirm Westermarck's views. Arthur Wolf has shown that in China boys and girls raised from childhood together for the purposes of marriage tend to have less sexual satisfaction in their marriages than those who are not raised together (1970). Likewise, Israeli children on the kibbutzim, raised like siblings, do not marry, since they view their companions as brothers or sisters but not as potential spouses (Parker 1976).

From the natural law morality perspective, the incest avoidance taboo can be seen as an instinct generated by the concupiscible appetite. This natural instinct has two purposes. First, it inclines all humans to avoid genetic damage to future generations, and second, it regulates familial life in a way that prevents serious intrafamilial conflict.

The Evolutionary Basis for the Murder Prohibition

Societies of all kinds and all cultures prohibit murder. Indeed, it would be impossible for any form of human society to exist without prohibitions on the taking of innocent life. Aquinas sees the prohibition on murder as one of the primary precepts of natural law morality (IIaIIae.64). It is based on the rational good of living together peacefully and not "offending those with whom we must live." It is, so to speak, a most fundamental way of pursuing good and avoiding evil in the widest possible social context.

From the perspective of sociobiology, it can be seen that the prohibition on murder may have evolved in at least two ways: by way of kin selection theory and by means of reciprocal altruism.

Kin selection theory holds that those biological organisms that are most closely related will practice benevolent behavior to each other and more hostile behavior to "outsiders." Indeed, some organisms may even forego reproduction in order to raise the offspring of a close relative. William Hamilton first developed this approach to explain the behavior of *hymenoptera,* in other words, bees, ants, and wasps (1964). For example, a worker bee acts in ways that do not favor its own reproduction but favor the reproduction of a close "relative," that is, the queen. Female bees, since they have both mothers and fathers, are distinguished from male bees, who have only mothers. Females therefore have a full set of chromosomes while males have only half a set. Females who reproduce thus have a 75 percent genetic relatedness to their sisters but only a 50 percent relatedness to their own daughters. Hamilton held that sisters would have a greater evolutionary interest in practicing cooperation with their sisters than with their own daughters and this prediction was empirically confirmed. Thus, it is possible to see how a "co-efficient of relatedness" can anticipate the potential benefit to an organism relative to the cost.

Yet kin selection is not the only explanation for apparently benevolent behavior in animals. Not only will some animals behave "altruistically" toward their biological relations, many will practice a quid pro quo relationship with others. Two well-known examples in nonhumans demonstrate how reciprocal altruism works.

G. S. Wilkinson has shown that vampire bats will share blood meals with other roost-mates (1984, 1990). Since vampire bats can live only three days without a blood meal, frequent access to blood is critical to their well-being. On any given night, however, up to 33 percent of juveniles and 7 percent of adults will not be successful in locating a blood meal on their own. Successful bats, however, will share their blood meals by regurgitating blood for their roost-mates. One interesting point to note is that this practice is found not only among bats who are related (which is not surprising) but also among those that do not have a significant co-efficient of relatedness.

Another example of reciprocal altruism is Frans de Waal's studies of captive chimpanzees (1997, 1998). According to de Waal's research, chimpanzees "exchange" grooming behavior for food. Thus, if one chimpanzee grooms another up to two hours before feeding time, the second chimpanzee is much more likely to share his food with the "groomer" than if no grooming had taken place. This quid pro quo relationship seems to facilitate group cooperation to the point that one might even say, as Robert Wright has, that these animals develop a kind of "friendship" (1994). Although the human type of friendship may have its origin in evolutionary history, the rules we develop governing our relationships with others are cultural products that reflect the synthesis of both culture and nature. In humans one sees a convergence of biological factors (kin selection and reciprocal altruism) and cultural influences (moral sanctions) on the evolution of cooperation.

The application to the issue of murder becomes obvious. In early hominid societies, the community consisted largely of those to whom one was related. The good of the society was critical to the good of the individual member. Thus, prohibitions on arbitrarily taking the life of a valuable member of the community would naturally evolve.

Recent research seems to corroborate these ideas concerning the evolutionary basis for prohibitions on harming one's close relatives. Martin Daly and Margo Wilson, in their study on homicides in the city of Detroit from the late 1970s to the early 1980s, collected data on murder rates and focused upon the relatedness of the murderer to the victim (1988). Their research showed that a homicide victim was much more likely to be unrelated to the murderer than to be one's own kin. Indeed, they determined that a stepchild was 100 times likelier to be murdered by a stepparent than by a natural parent. This may suggest that, as the sociobiologists would contend, there is a natural disposition to protect and nurture one's offspring whereas investing in the offspring that are not one's own is foolish from an evolutionary perspective.

One could also see the prohibition on murder develop on the basis of reciprocal altruism, however. One needs to practice benevolence to others in the community in order for others to act benevolently to oneself. Just as vampire bats share blood meals with other bats and later receive the same assistance, and as primates may exchange grooming for food, human practices of benevolence may have developed in an evolutionary process influenced by reciprocal altruism. This explains why murder could never have evolved as a culturally sanctioned activity.

It could be argued that in many early human societies murder of those in one's society was prohibited on the basis of inclusive fitness and reciprocal altruism. By contrast, the prohibition on killing nongroup members might have been lifted because there would be little chance of relatedness and little chance of repeated encounters with the nongroup members. In any case, it appears that the prohibition of murder encourages "in-group niceness," while war may be encouraged as a means of "out-group nastiness."

The natural law prohibition on murder can therefore be understood as reason's ability to see the necessary relationship between the principle of nonmaleficence and social cohesion. Normative judgments follow from the synthesis of biological impulses and reason's insight into the complexities of human relationships and the various contingencies affecting social order.

The Limits of Biological Explanations

Critics have raised at least two serious problems for sociobiology and evolutionary psychology. First, if all behavior is fitness enhancing, then how is it that humans practice behaviors that are genuinely altruistic (i.e., benefiting others without any return either to oneself or to one's kin)? Second, how is it possible to adjudicate among a variety of natural impulses?

Sociobiological accounts of morality as presented by Dawkins and Wilson attempt to be explanations of all human behavior. Wilson's approach is to reduce all moral principles to biological explanations. While Dawkins agrees that human nature is simply the result of millions of years of surviving "replicators," he suggests that humans should sometimes resist the power of the genes by appealing to the power of moral inculturation. For both Wilson and Dawkins, the human agent's ability to resist the power of the biological is a problem yet to be solved.

Behaviors like celibacy and martyrdom are enduring practices that have not been weeded out by selection. As we saw earlier, Dawkins introduces his highly controversial meme theory in order to explain the persistence of these "aberrant" behaviors.

Appealing to memes, however, is a metaphysical position that seems subject to a number of criticisms. First, it begs the question concerning the existence of such elusive entities as God and the soul. Dawkins begins by assuming that they are merely fictions and in the end he implies that they really don't exist; indeed, given his own materialist metaphysic they *can't* exist. Dawkins' mimetic theory is subject to the same criticisms as any other naively reductionistic materialism.

A second problem for meme theory is what we might call sociobiology's "anthropological dualism." That is, there seem to be two kinds of inheritance, genes and memes. But they are two entirely different kinds of entities. Moreover, it is difficult to understand just how they correspond. Jeffrey Schloss raises a critical problem with this dualistic approach when he writes, "[I]t is not clear how biology gives rise to something that resists or contravenes biology" (2002, 231). That is, how could evolution operate in such a way as to promote nonfitness enhancing characteristics? It is contradictory to suggest that biology evolves in ways in order to resist itself. A house divided cannot stand.

The second major criticism of sociobiology is, "How is it that any human creature is able to adjudicate among competing natural impulses?" Is it merely the stronger impulse that wins in the end? If Mary Midgley is correct in suggesting that contemporary sociobiologists follow Hume, believing that reason really is the slave of the passions, then, one wonders, "how is it supposed to know which of them to obey?" (1995, 184). If an early Christian had to decide whether to recant her faith or go into the coliseum and face the lions, what natural impulse urged her to choose martyrdom? Unless humans have the capacity to adjudicate among competing desires (both animal and rational), then the stronger passion always wins. But this is plainly false, as the persistence of martyrdom and celibacy proves.

Natural Law and the Virtues

We have seen that it is possible to offer an account of natural law morality that incorporates recent biological research into its own account of human nature. While sociobiology and evolutionary psychology provide important elements for a natural law morality, it seems that these explanations cannot account for all human behaviors, especially those that contravene basic biological impulses. Natural law morality, however, has adequate means to resolve these problems.

In the passage from IaIIae.94 of his *Summa,* Aquinas states that what pertains to the natural law as proper to humans is knowing the truth about God and living peacefully in society. Although Aquinas rarely spends much time developing elaborate lists of the primary precepts of natural law, we see that any operation of the intellect toward the good is properly related to the natural law. So it is that the intellectual appetite pursues the truly human goods: "By the intellectual appetite we may desire the immaterial good, which is not apprehended by sense, such as knowledge, virtue, and the like" (Ia.80.2.ad 2).

This reference to the acquisition of virtue is especially important to our discussion. Natural law serves as the basis for our moral drives, yet it does not spell out the details of moral behavior. Indeed, this is the reason Aquinas's theory of natural law requires a theory of the virtues. I postulate that anything that pertains to reason is a matter of natural law morality. And since the acquisition of virtue is a function of reason, it follows that the human agent's pursuit of virtue would be prescribed by the natural law. Aquinas directly addresses this important aspect of natural law morality:

> Since the rational soul is the proper form of the human, there is thus in every human a natural inclination to act according to reason; and this is to act according to virtue. Thus, all the acts of the virtues are prescribed by natural law, since each person's reason naturally dictates to that one to act according to virtue. (IaIIae.94.3)

The key point here is that all the acts of the virtues fall under the sphere of the natural law since they are prescribed by reason. The natural law does not dictate precisely how one is to act according to reason, however. It simply determines what specific kinds of actions are good and what kinds are evil. Aquinas does not indicate in his natural law morality just how one goes about determining what kind of behavior is required, since the natural law simply indicates what Aquinas calls the "object of the act" (IaIIae.18.1). One must not only know what kind of act is required in any given moral situation, however; one must also act for the right purposes and in the right circumstances. So it is that natural law does not simply prescribe certain kinds of actions; it also requires the development of virtue, which enables a person to act consistently for the right reasons and in the right circumstances. Aquinas discusses an instance of how one deliberates well and acts virtuously in the question "On Martyrdom."

According to Aquinas, the practice of martyrdom is an act of virtue (IIaIIae.124.1). Since virtue's purpose is to "preserve a person in the good as proposed by reason," it follows that martyrdom is a "rational good" that apparently conflicts with the animal good of self-preservation and the flight from danger. Aquinas is aware of the conflict:

> A person's love for a thing is demonstrated by the degree to which, for its sake, one puts aside the more cherished object and chooses to suffer the more odious. It is manifest that among all the goods of this present life a person loves life itself the most, and on the contrary, hates death the most, and especially when accompanied by the pains of physical torture — from fear of these even brute animals are deterred from the greatest pleasures, as Augustine says. (IIaIIae.124.3)

Since there is this conflict, how is it that one would willingly sacrifice his life for his faith?

Aquinas thinks that martyrdom is not simply enduring suffering and death for the sake of some vaguely defined religious principle. Rather, martyrs endure death for the sake of the truth (a rational good). But it is not merely any truth; it is "the truth involved in our duty to God" (IIaIIae.124.5).

This appeal to God demonstrates the hierarchy of impulses in action. Even though we have duties to preserve our own lives and to flee harm, we also have a greater duty to God. Since God is the Good itself, we recognize that no human good, even life itself, can compete with the possession of everlasting goodness. The agent's highest end consists in loving God above all created goods and therefore has the character of an ultimate obligation (Hayden 1990). The natural hierarchy of goods that natural law morality proposes and human virtue enacts enables the individual to judge among the many goods that vie for her attention.

Conclusion

In this essay, I have argued that a natural law morality may use the findings of sociobiology with reference to various "animal goods." Sociobiology seems to provide ample evidence for drives for self-preservation, marital practices, and prohibitions on murder that fit well with the principles of Thomistic natural law morality. We may say that sociobiology is compatible with some version of natural law morality. There seem, however, to be areas of natural law morality that transcend purely sociobiological explanations (Midgley 1980). Sociobiology encounters two significant problems as it attempts to explain behaviors that are not fitness-enhancing, that is, behaviors that cannot be accounted for by appeals to inclusive fitness or reciprocal altruism.

As I see it, explanations of rational and moral behavior necessarily move beyond merely scientific explanation and must invoke philosophical explanations. Dawkins' appeal to mimetic theory is the most obvious example of the move from the empirical to the philosophical. Sociobiology's explanations now become simply one of a number of competing philosophical theories. And their value as philosophy is suspect. As evolutionary psychologist Henry Plotkin has argued,

> Underlying all the biological and social sciences, the reason for it all, is the "need" (how else to express it, perhaps "drive" would be better) for genes to perpetuate themselves. This is a metaphysical claim, and the reductionism that it entails is . . . best labeled as metaphysical reductionism. Because it is metaphysical it is neither right nor wrong nor empirically testable. It is simply a statement of belief that genes count above all else. (1998, 94)

Plotkin's analysis of sociobiology's metaphysical reductionism is surely on target. One need not endorse Plotkin's skepticism regarding all metaphysics, however. Simply because metaphysical views are not "empirically testable," it does not mean that some are not closer to the truth than others.

An alternative philosophical theory to the one offered by sociobiology is that of natural law morality. On this view, biology plays a central role in explaining any account of human behavior, yet the analysis of human morality is not limited entirely to the realm of biology. Natural law morality includes "human goods," or rational goods, in addition to the goods of our biological nature.

While I have attempted to explain how a natural law morality might constructively make use of sociobiology, I have not attempted to delineate precisely how the rational soul evolves or whether, as Pope John Paul II has maintained, God simply creates it by divine action. These questions I leave for another essay.

REFERENCES

Aquinas, Thomas. 1892. *Summa Theologiae.* All references are from the Leonine edition, Rome. All translations are mine.

Arnhart, Larry. 1998. *Darwinian Natural Right: The Biological Ethics of Human Nature.* Albany, N.Y.: State University of New York Press.

—————. 2001. Thomistic natural law as Darwinian natural right. *Social Philosophy and Policy* 18 (Winter): 1-33.

Boyd, Craig A. 1998. Is Thomas Aquinas a divine command theorist? *The Modern Schoolman* 75:209-26.

Daly, Martin, and Margo Wilson. 1988. *Homicide.* New York: Aldine de Gruyter.

Dawkins, Richard. 1989. *The Selfish Gene.* New edition. Oxford: Oxford University Press.

de Waal, F. B. M. 1997. The chimpanzee's service economy: Food for grooming. *Evolution and Human Behavior* 18:375-86.

—————. 1998. Food transfers through mesh in brown capuchins. *Journal of Comparative Psychology* 111:370-78.

Hamilton, William. 1964. The genetic evolution of social behavior, I and II. *Journal of Theoretical Biology* 7:1-52.

Hayden, R. Mary. 1990. Natural inclinations and moral absolutes. *Proceedings of the American Catholic Philosophical Association* 64:130-50.

Midgley, Mary. 1980. Rival fatalisms: The hollowness of the sociobiology debate. Pp. 15-38 in *Sociobiology Examined,* ed. Ashley Montagu. New York: Oxford University Press.

—————. 1995. *Beast and Man: The Roots of Human Nature.* New York: Routledge.

Parker, S. 1976. The precultural basis of the incest taboo: Towards a biosocial theory. *American Anthropologist* 78: 285-305.

Plotkin, Henry. 1998. *Evolution in Mind: An Introduction to Evolutionary Psychology.* Cambridge, Mass.: Harvard University Press.

Porter, Jean. 2000. *Natural and Divine Law: Reclaiming the Tradition for Christian Ethics.* Notre Dame, Ind.: University of Notre Dame Press.

—————. 1986. Natural desire for God: Ground of the moral life in Aquinas. *Theological Studies* 47:48-68.

Ruse, Michael. 2001. *Can a Darwinian Be a Christian? The Relationship between Science and Religion.* Cambridge: Cambridge University Press.

Schloss, Jeffrey. 2002. Emerging evolutionary accounts of altruism: "Love creation's final law." Pp. 212-42 in *Altruism and Altruistic Love: Science, Philosophy, and Religion in Dialogue,* ed. Stephen G. Post, Lynn G. Underwood, Jeffrey P. Schloss, and William B. Hurlbut. Oxford: Oxford University Press.

Westermarck, E. A. 1891. *The History of Human Marriage.* New York: Macmillan.

Wilkinson, G. S. 1984. Reciprocal food sharing in vampire bats. *Nature* 308:181-84.
————. 1990. Food sharing in vampire bats. *Scientific American* 262:76-82.
Wilson, E. O. 1998. *Consilience: The Unity of Knowledge*. New York: Vintage.
Wolf, Arthur. 1970. Childhood association and sexual attraction: A further test of the Westermarck hypothesis. *American Anthropologist* 72:503-15.
Wright, Robert. 1994. *The Moral Animal: Evolutionary Psychology and Everyday Life*. New York: Vintage.

12. The Good Samaritan and His Genes

Holmes Rolston III

The Good Samaritan, with his expansive vision of who counts as a neighbor, has been a role model for millennia. Although there are secular Samaritans, in the Good Samaritan himself Jesus is illustrating the second of the two great commandments to love God and neighbor, a religiously motivated ethic (Luke 10:29-37). Turning a millennium, we find ourselves in the century of genes; we decoded our genome in 2001. The search now is for how these genes shape behavior, and so we need to fit both the Samaritan's ethics and his underlying religion into a genetic account. But then again, there have been surprises; we have fewer genes than we thought, with more plasticity, especially for cultural achievements.

Since people have to eat daily, reproduce each generation, and care for children throughout much of their adult lives, it is unsurprising that fertility — success in staying alive from one generation to the next — is pervasive in religions that have succeeded. Any religion persisting over the centuries will have accompanied reproductive success. We know that before we look. The most plausible theory is likely to be that such religion contributed to this reproductive success — though it is logically possible that the religion was irrelevant or even detrimental but was hitchhiking on some other skills and practices that were the deeper cause of the success.

Mixed in with this raising of families is this Samaritan behavior — helping non–genetically related others. We need to figure out how we reproduce Good Samaritans, generation after generation. Unless biologists can set this too in a Darwinian framework, perhaps this sort of altruism will be revealing counterevidence to current biological theory. Religion would be generating a social phenomenon that biology is incompetent to handle, either to explain or to evaluate. If so, then such naturalistic accounts of the genesis of religion will be partial, at best. Religious accounts of the genesis of this socially beneficial altruism might be complementary or corrective to the biological accounts.

The Good Samaritan "Biologicized" with Adaptive Genes

The Samaritan — and this is important for our case — is not genetically related to the Jewish victim whom he aids. "Jews do not share things in common with Samaritans" (John 4:9). The Jericho road is out of Samaritan territory. The Samaritan spent time, energy, and money helping an alien (nonkindred) genetic line, a victim that his ethics valued as a neighbor. The straightforward account is that the Samaritan is defending an unrelated other altruistically. Parallel models can be found in other traditions, as widespread variants of the Golden Rule illustrate.

From a genetic viewpoint, this victim, so assisted, will be more likely to have offspring. A tribe of such Samaritans would be likely to do well in competition with societies from which such behavior is absent. But this is not a tribal affair; here we have cross-cultural ethics. The determinant here is an "idea" (helping a neighbor, with sympathetic compassion) that is not just subservient to but superposed on the genetics. Such an "idea" can be transmitted nongenetically, as has indeed happened in this case, since the story has been widely retold and praised as a model by persons in other cultures who are neither Jews nor Samaritans. Persons regularly persuade others and are themselves persuaded to adopt ethical creeds.

There is present both an ideal and the real. Persons fail to form creeds, fail to act on the creeds they do form. There is moral selfishness. There are thieves as well as Samaritans, exploiters as well as missionaries, assassins as well as prophets. But such failure is proof, not disproof, of the norm — an ethics that holds that one ought to help others individually, which will also maximize the general sense of "neighborliness" pervading within and across cultures. Neighbors are whomever one encounters that one is in a position to help. The Samaritan respects life not his own; he values life outside his own self-sector, outside his cultural sector.

But perhaps this straightforward account is also superficial. We need to go deeper and find a naturalized ethics, a Darwinized morality.

E. O. Wilson begins and ends his *Sociobiology* with a "biologicized" ethics:

> What . . . made the hypothalamus and the limbic system? They evolved by natural selection. That simple biological statement must be pursued to explain ethics and ethical philosophers, if not epistemology and epistemologists, at all depths. . . . The time has come for ethics to be removed temporarily from the hands of philosophers and biologicized. (1975, 3, 562)

239

> Human behavior . . . is the circuitous technique by which human genetic material has been and will be kept intact. Morality has no other demonstrable ultimate function. (1978, 167)

Michael Ruse, a philosopher, joins Wilson:

> Morality, or more strictly, our belief in morality, is merely an adaptation put in place to further our reproductive ends. Hence the basis of ethics does not lie in God's will . . . or any other part of the framework of the Universe. In an important sense, ethics . . . is an illusion fobbed off on us by our genes to get us to cooperate. (Ruse and Wilson 1985, 51-52)

> Morality is a biological adaptation no less than are hands and feet and teeth. (Ruse 1994, 15; 1986, 222)

Bluntly put, ethics results in fertility; that is its deepest explanation.

A morality that conserves human genetic material is welcome enough. But this also brings deeper trouble. More bluntly put, evolution produces this fertility through a radical selfishness incompatible with any genuine altruism in ethics. George Williams claims, "Natural selection . . . can honestly be described as a process for maximizing short-sighted selfishness" (1988, 385). Richard Dawkins summarizes: "The logic . . . is this: Humans and baboons have evolved by natural selection. . . . Anything that has evolved by natural selection should be selfish. Therefore we must expect that when we go and look at the behaviour of baboons, humans, and all other living creatures, we will find it to be selfish" (1989, 4).

Michael Ghiselin concludes his scientific analysis with memorable rhetoric:

> No hint of genuine charity ameliorates our vision of society, once sentimentalism has been laid aside. What passes for co-operation turns out to be a mixture of opportunism and exploitation. . . . Given a full chance to act in his own interest, nothing but expediency will restrain [a person] from brutalizing, from maiming, from murdering — his brother, his mate, his parent, or his child. Scratch an "altruist" and watch a "hypocrite" bleed. (1974, 247)

All that natural selection permits are forms of quasi-altruism that are actually self-interest, more or less enlightened or disguised forms of selfishness. Richard Alexander concludes:

I suspect that nearly all humans believe it is a normal part of the functioning of every human individual now and then to assist someone else in the realization of that person's own interests to the actual net expense of the altruist. What this "greatest intellectual revolution of the century" tells us is that, despite our intuitions, there is not a shred of evidence to support this view of beneficence, and a great deal of convincing theory suggests that any such view will eventually be judged false. This implies that we will have to start all over again to describe and understand ourselves, in terms alien to our intuitions, and in one way or another different from every discussion of this topic across the whole of human history. (1987, 3; 1993)

Dawkins claims that with the Darwinian revolution begun in *The Origin of Species* (1859), all the old answers to the question about how humans ought to live and act are discredited. "The point I want to make now is that all attempts to answer that question before 1859 are worthless and that we will be better off if we ignore them completely" (1989, 1). Challenged about this, Dawkins insists: "There is such a thing as being just plain wrong, and that is what, before 1859, all answers to those questions were" (1989, 267). These are not modest claims. Robert L. Trivers claims that these are "models designed to take the altruism out of altruism" (1971, 35).

So we need to biologicize this Good Samaritan. Let us see if we can take the altruism out, and find Jesus' answer worthless and plain wrong. Let us start all over and describe his behavior in terms alien to our intuitions. Let us scratch this altruist and see if a hypocrite bleeds. Let us see if we can find what David Barash calls "the ugly underside of altruism" (2001).

The Good Samaritan — so the biologicizing theory holds — is constitutionally (= genetically) unable to act for the victim's sake. And so, there must be a self-interested account. Alexander concludes, "This means that whether or not we know it when we speak favorably to our children about Good Samaritanism, we are telling them about a behavior that has a strong likelihood of being reproductively profitable." Conscience is a "still small voice that tells us how far we can go in serving our own interests without incurring intolerable risks" (1987, 102). "The main reward is reputation, and all the benefits that high moral reputation may yield. Reputation as an altruist pays" (1993, 188). Even the Bible enjoins, "Cast your bread upon the waters, for you will find it after many days" (Eccl. 11:1).

The Deceived Good Samaritan

Of course the Good Samaritan did not think of himself as increasing the likely number of his offspring. He did not even know he had any genes. He knew the difference between crass self-interest and concern for others; thieves had robbed this hapless fellow, and he by contrast was trying to help him. But this concern for others, apparent to him, was only apparent. What the Samaritan intends is not what is resulting. Despite the intended altruism, the Samaritan's act promotes his own genetic interest.

The fact that this appears even to him to be altruism is explained this way: the whole transaction works better if persons are self-deceived. Not only do they not know about their genes; they do not know they are really acting in their self-interest. The Samaritan gets these results by indirection. He has to want what he doesn't really want to get what he really wants. Alexander explains, "I mean that such information is not a part of their conscious knowledge, and that if you ask people what they *think* their interests are they would usually give wrong answers" (1987, 36).

The apparent sincerity guarantees the reciprocity. If the victim knew the Samaritan's real motives (putting genes in the next generation), he would be disinclined later to reciprocate, had he such opportunity. If even the Samaritan knew his real motives, he would be a bad actor and his insincerity would leak out. So the Samaritan has to be blind to his own deepest motives, blind to the genetic impulses that fundamentally frame his behavior; he has to appear convincingly concerned, if the reciprocity is to go through. "If the theory is correct humans could not have *evolved* to know it, and to act directly and consciously in respect to it (1987, 38).

Ruse and Wilson put it this way:

> Human beings function better if they are deceived by their genes into thinking that there is a disinterested objective morality binding upon them, which all should obey. We help others because it is "right" to help them and because we know that they are inwardly compelled to reciprocate in equal measure. What Darwinian evolutionary theory shows is that this sense of "right" and the corresponding sense of "wrong," feelings we take to be above individual desire and in some fashion outside biology, are in fact brought about by ultimately biological processes. (1986, 179)

The Samaritan is operating with an "ideal" of aiding neighbors, but this is his delusion, his hidden reputation-seeking. The Good Samaritan (a half-breed himself, part Jew, part Gentile) really assisted the luckless victim in order to leave more genes in the next generation. What a hypocrite! That selfish bastard!

He doesn't know this, but we can allow no disconfirming or confirming evidence from people's verbal reports. Their conscious motivations are superstructural, epiphenomenal; their deep genetic determinants are not available to them. Genes are microscopic and humans historically knew no more about their genes than do monkeys today. "Genes remained outside the range of our senses in all respects until the twentieth century" (Alexander 1987, 38-39). Humans, however, have long known what it means to be self-interested, and they have had to create an illusion of altruistic morality for the reciprocity to work.

This means that scientists can expect this theory of ethics to be rejected by critics, who continue to deceive themselves. "Natural selection . . . appears to have designed human motivation in social matters as to cause its understanding to be resisted powerfully." This is why "evolutionary biologists who attempt to explicate human behavior are ignored or maligned" (Alexander 1993, 192, 189). Here genes make such hypocrites that it becomes difficult for good science to reveal what is going on.

But then it could be the other way around, that this demanding scientific paradigm is governing the way all evidence is interpreted, and skillfully reinterpreting all apparent anomalies, such as this Samaritan, making it difficult for such science to take seriously what is actually going on. We may be headed toward a puzzle about who has an interpretive framework that is preventing seeing the truth.

There is a presumption here that takes the biological level to be final. If x can be shown to be biological, then no further explanation is permitted or required. There is also a presumed discovery that takes the biological processes to be deceptive. We are programmed to believe what is not so. Explanatory schemes are difficult to deal with when they make an end run around our capacity to reason. There is, of course, a great deal of rationalizing (unconsciously pretended reasons, hypocrisy) in human behavior, as well as much selfishness; and both do undermine our capacity to think. Psychologists and biologists were not the first to discover either tendency; ethicists and theologians had been lamenting it for centuries — if we can trust those verbal reports.

Even if we can get ourselves freed from this selfish rationalizing enough to examine the scientific claims here, matters are going to be tricky to disentangle. The fundamental claim is that selfish persons out-reproduce unselfish ones; that is where the biology starts. But a further claim to be tested is that cooperative persons out-compete combative ones. Good Samaritans out-reproduce thieves. Is there any evidence that thieves are declining over generations, that Good Samaritans are increasing? If so, is the cause of this genetic?

We also have to take care when we switch from within populations (tribes) to interactions between populations (tribe encountering tribe). Generally these biologists seem to think that inside tribes the thieves (the selfish, the cheaters) will out-reproduce the Samaritans (the altruists). But recently group selection has been returning to vogue (Sober and D. S. Wilson 1998; D. S. Wilson 2002), and now the claim is that, if within the tribe we can find ways of policing the would-be cheaters, tribes of Good Samaritans will out-reproduce tribes of thieves. Of course we must not forget that the whole point of the Good Samaritan model is out-group compassion.

Meanwhile to get the altruism established, whether within the tribe or without it, we have superimposed the further claim that (really) selfish persons who are self-deceived into thinking they are unselfish out-reproduce selfish persons who know their own selfishness. Really, those damned thieves will leave fewer offspring in the next generation. Neither the priest nor the Levite will do well either. These compassionate Samaritans, though blind to what is really going on, will out-reproduce all the rest.

Halfway to the biologicized ethic, the claim to be tested is that pseudo-altruism (altruism, really self-interest) out-reproduces unenlightened selfishness. Self-deceived Good Samaritans out-reproduce thieves. But to get the ethic fully in place, the claim is also that tacit pseudo-altruism (altruism, really self-interest, but unawares) out-reproduces even enlightened selfishness (persons made explicitly aware of their self-interest in reciprocal altruism). Deluded Good Samaritans out-reproduce nondeceived, wised-up Good Samaritans.

Testing these claims against facts, although we observe some evident altruism along with much selfishness, we find no evidence that altruistic persons are increasing in the genetic pool over selfish ones, or vice versa. Meanwhile, one hardly needs evidence that cooperators frequently do well in society. If there were some evidence of the increasing genetic frequency of altruists, it might be difficult to say whether it was supporting cooperation over combativeness, or genuine altruism over unenlightened selfishness, or pseudo-altruism over enlightened selfishness. Nor is there any evidence that altruists who are deceived about their motives are, over the centuries, out-reproducing altruists who are introspective enough to realize the benefits of mutual cooperation.

The difficulty of interpreting whatever behavioral patterns we find is going to be compounded by the fact that all verbal reports of motives have to be dismissed as unreliable. Since such psychological and experiential evidence is inadmissible, we could find it difficult to reach any conclusions as to whether biological factors are subliminal and determining the outcome, or incomplete and under-determining the outcome.

More complications follow.

Deceiving the Deceiving Good Samaritan

Past this beneficial self-deception — so continue these ingenious accounts — there is risk of harmful deception when a Samaritan moral agent gets tricked into edging past diminishing returns and moves over into what is in fact real altruism. Here the actor not only thinks he or she is an altruist, the actor is indeed an altruist, and the advantage passes over to the person aided. Truly altruistic acts cannot be favored by selection, but here is selection for "the ability to induce others to behave altruistically" (Williams 1988, 400).

In such "induced altruism" an individual is favored who can trick others into believing that altruism is the right thing to do, thus coupling up with the moralist's own native, naive self-deceptions about his or her duties. "We, therefore, would expect the evolution of abilities and tendencies to deceive potential altruists into serving inadvertently the interests of others" (Alexander 1987, 114; 1993). The hoodwinked altruist's kind will be reduced, and the trickster's tribe increase. So trick prevails over truth.

An ethicist who takes philanthropy as authentic "misses the role of manipulation in philanthropy" (Williams 1988, 400). Such donors are really losers. The only philanthropy that wins, though unawares to itself, is really self-seeking and results in actual gain to the donor. Meanwhile philanthropy that knowingly realizes that it seeks its own interest is not convincing enough to succeed.

Super-Good Samaritans are suckers, out-competed by self-deceived but successful Good Samaritans, who in turn out-compete wised-up Samaritans. Always look for the subtler self-interested motive. If you do not find it, look again. It must be there because the theory demands it. If you cannot find it, there must be a mistake, either yours in not finding the genetic self-interest, or a mistake on the part of the actor. "I do not doubt that occasional individuals lead lives that are truly altruistic and self-sacrificing. However admirable and desirable such behavior may be from others' points of view, it represents an evolutionary mistake for the individual showing it" (Alexander 1987, 191). The Good Samaritan must not edge past the point of his own self-interests, not allow the groans of the wounded man to con him into too much risk, not promise to pay at the inn any more money than he is likely to gain as benefits in return. He should not offer a blood donation. He must resist induced altruism.

But further, a super smart Good Samaritan can himself become a trickster. In the struggle between trick and countertrick, he can con the victim into thinking that his rescuer is more of a Good Samaritan than he really is. "Individuals are expected to parade the idea of much beneficence, and even of indiscriminate altruism as beneficial, so as to encourage people in general to engage in increasing amounts of social investment whether or not it is beneficial to their interests" (Alexander 1987, 103; 1993). This is "inflated altruism."

Though the Good Samaritan must not actually let himself be induced into *being* a super-Good Samaritan, if he can manage to appear this way, then the victim (or other admirers) will be all the more disposed to reciprocate with benefits to the Good Samaritan that now exceed the advantage conveyed by the Samaritan to the victim. Alexander is forthright, claiming a "general theory of behavior":

> Society is based on lies. . . . "Thou shalt love thy neighbor as thyself." But this admirable goal is clearly contrary to a tendency to behave in a reproductively selfish manner. "Thou shalt give the impression that thou lovest thy neighbor as thyself" might be closer to the truth. (1975, 96)

The Good Samaritan, first found to be only apparently a loser in favor of the victim, is, at this second level of deception, found out to be inflating this appearance even more, so that he can win bigger still. That is why he told the innkeeper he would pay more, if needs be, on his return trip. He wasn't being tricked into extra altruism; he was parading his beneficence for future gains. He was image-building. The victim is twice victimized, once by the thieves and a second time by the Samaritan, who inflates his already only apparent altruism and thus will sucker the victim, once he has recovered, into over-reciprocating later on. That selfish bastard is at it again!

Alexander concludes, summarizing both induced and inflated altruism:

> The long-term existence of complex patterns of indirect reciprocity, then, seems to favor the evolution of keen abilities to (1) make one's self seem more beneficent than is the case; and (2) influence others to be beneficent in such fashions as to be deleterious to themselves and beneficial to the moralizer, e.g., to lead others to (a) invest too much, (b) invest wrongly in the moralizer or his relatives and friends, or (c) invest indiscriminately on a larger scale than would otherwise be the case. (1987, 103)

Now biologists realize that the conflicts of interests that exist because of histories of genetic difference imply . . . that nearly all communicative signals, human or otherwise, should be expected to involve significant deceit. (1987, 73; 1993)

Mind initially evolves to know enough truth about the world to be able to cope, to find a way through the world. But later mind further evolves to cope by deceiving others into thinking that they are being altruistically helped, and in such way that the benefactor is self-deceived while doing so. Later still, mind further evolves to deceive by producing virtual altruism, though the weaker minds in these contests are harmed when they are sucked into real altruism by still more clever deceivers.

Perhaps. But first one ought to make sure there is no mistake in the logical structure or empirical adequacy of the core evolutionary theory. We may only be dealing with a blik, that is, a paradigm grown arrogant, resolute about self-interest as the nonnegotiable first axiom of biology, interpreting and reinterpreting all evidence in its favor. The empirical facts, which seem to be frequently examined, may in fact make little difference. The theory absorbs the evidence into its interpretive framework. Perhaps we hardly need bother to bring any further moral behavior into the court of evidence. Alexander knows before he looks that all human behavior, however apparently moral, is selfish (apart from anomalous misfits), just as he knows before he looks that the fittest survive (the misfits soon go extinct).

There *must* be deception here somewhere. The theory demands it, and phenomena cannot gainsay the theory. But the deception could be in the theory, not the phenomena, which is disposing us to interpret as an illusion the altruism that is in fact taking place before our very eyes. So far from understanding what is going on, one will miss a critical new turning point: the emergence of these "ideas" become "ideals" — altruistic love, justice, and freedom.

At this point, one begins to wonder just who is being deceived: the moralist who acts with these altruistic intentions? Or the reductionist scientist whose theory forces a double negation of a positive emergent? The induced blindness as to what is really going on could be either place. Certainly, self-interest is a core principle in biology; but it does not follow that nothing in culture can operate with superimposing principles. There is no particular cause to see ethical advocacy as so much fluff over unconscious genetic determinants. Remember those surprises; we have fewer genes than we thought, with more cultural plasticity. We are still wondering how we reproduce Good Samaritans, generation after generation.

Good Samaritans Converting Others

Samaritans do not just give these victims their time and money, they give them their religion. They convert those thieves too, if they can. Such disciples need not have the genes of the prophets, seers, and saviors who launched these teachings. In a successful world religion, they seldom do. People do better with genes flexible enough to track the best religion, whether their blood kin launched it or not. One does not need Semitic genes to be a Christian, any more than Plato's genes to be a Platonist, or Einstein's genes to adopt the theory of relativity. Religious beliefs overleap genes.

E. O. Wilson claims that the function of religious myths and rituals is indoctrination to produce group loyalty. Such concerted group action conveys survival value on all, on average, so that it is in any individual's probable advantage to cooperate, even though he has some risk of losing (being killed in battle, for instance). Persons act with this pseudo-altruism because it is in their genetic self-interest to bond to others of their kind in this way. "The essential characteristic of a tribe is that it should follow a double standard of morality — one kind of behavior for in-group relations, another for out-group" (E. O. Wilson 1975, 565). Humans are genetically inclined to xenophobia (E. O. Wilson 1975, 249). Possibly natural selection favored those genes that caused the early humans to be altruistic toward members of their own tribe but intolerant of outsiders. Possibly, humans today still have that innate tendency. Plausibly, primitive religions are of this xenophobic kind. Perhaps this explains certain contemporary phenomena, such as the kamikaze pilots of World War II, dying for the Emperor. Group selection, we were saying, has been returning to the biological scene.

But these groups still need to be competing with other groups, so that the benefits gained in out-group competition outweigh the costs of in-group cooperation. David Sloan Wilson finds that group selection builds what he calls "Darwin's Cathedral," an English Westminster Abbey, or a Calvinist Geneva, not (in the universalist sense) a catholic church. "But, alas, group selection merely takes us out of the frying pan of within-group interactions and into the fire of between-group interactions." "Group selection creates a moral world within groups but doesn't touch the world of between-group interactions. . . . Among-group interactions may exhibit the rudiments of moral conduct but are dominated by exploitation on all sides" (D. S. Wilson 2002, 38, 141-43).

David Sloan Wilson, joining with Elliott Sober, finds both self-interest and altruism as we do "unto others." Within the community, we find the patriots in battle, the Rotarians building their public spirit, even the Presbyterians loving both self and neighbors (as with those Genevan Calvinists, studied by Wilson). But equally, Wilson and Sober insist, there is no "universal benevolence."

> Group selection does provide a setting in which helping behavior directed at members of one's own group can evolve; however, it equally provides a context in which hurting individuals in other groups can be selectively advantageous. Group selection favors within-group niceness *and* between-group nastiness. Group selection does not abandon the idea of competition that forms the core of the theory of natural selection. (Sober and Wilson 1998, 9)

But the Samaritan story is not about between-group nastiness. Nor is its retelling over two millennia an expression of ever-continuing group competition. No doubt people who embody this role model do well in their groups and take care of their children (as with the English or the Calvinists), but there can be too much focus on biological fertility, whether individual or tribal. Michael Ruse asks, "Can Selection Explain the Presbyterians?" and he thinks not if this is group selection with within-tribal charity, out-competing other tribes, as David Sloan Wilson proposes. Rather, biologists can explain the Presbyterians with individualist selection and increased fertility (Ruse 2002).

But religion has also to be understood as reproduction cognitively, believers making more converts, as well as biologically, believers having babies. Religions have fertile ideas, illustrated by this Samaritan parable, and people (such as the English or the Calvinists) adopt them the better to cope. You can say if you like that these ideas out-compete other ideas; you could just as well say that these ideas become widely shared. The transmission process is neural, not genetic. One has to be indoctrinated into a religion.

Biologically speaking, the problem now is that the new adherents soon cease to have any genetic relationship to the proselytizers. There are more Christians in Europe or North America than in the Middle East, and more Christians in Asia, or Latin America, or Africa than in Europe. That does not sound like Semitic genetic tribalism. What good are all these English or Calvinist Christians to the Semitic, Greek, or Roman launchers of Christianity, or their present-day descendants? My problem with natural selection explaining the Calvinist Presbyterians is at the other end of the spectrum from Ruse's individualist fertility in Geneva. There are more Presbyterians in Korea than in any other nation in the world; and those Korean Presbyterians have themselves sent out forty thousand missionaries to over one hundred countries. Similarly, Buddhism spread from India to China and from Japan to California.

When disciples convert to these better religions that these Samaritans bring, people are moved to act not just by their genetic programming. Good Samaritans teach kindness by word and example, and preach about the God of love. Indeed, even Alexander and Dawkins, though they have not been converted to the religious view, seem to have been converted to this ethic. When asked what these Samaritans ought to do, "what people *ought* to be doing," Alexander's answer is that biology has "nothing whatsoever" to say (1979, 276). He somehow agrees that "Thou shalt love thy neighbor as thyself" is "an admirable goal" (1979, 96), even if it is an evolutionary mistake. Dawkins concludes, "Let us try to *teach* generosity and altruism because we are born selfish" (1989, 3).

This Samaritan missionary activity brings cultural prosperity to these converts too. This good religion has to be universally shared; it generates concern for other humans near and far, leading its followers to relate to them with justice, love, and respect. The commitment that one has to make transcends one's genetics. Any account of in-group altruism to achieve out-group competitive success is powerless to explain the universalism in the major world faiths.

If the function of a religion is to provide fervent loyalty for a tribal group, urging one's religion on aliens is exactly the wrong behavior. Missionary activity is helping to ensure the replication of genes unlike one's own. If one has a religion that serves his genes, holds his society together well, and produces numerous offspring, then the last thing he wants to do is share this religion with others. One would be giving the secret away. That would be altruism of the most self-defeating kind! This preaching to the unconverted is not predicted by the theory, nor explained retrodictively. The Great Commission is, "Go therefore and make disciples of all nations" (Matt. 28:19). But the "catholicism" is counterproductive to leaving more Semitic genes in the next generation. Proselytizing those with foreign genes is the worst religious mistake you can make from a genetic viewpoint; and yet it has been the secret of success of all the world's great religions: evangelism in Christianity, or the bodhisattvas' vow in Buddhism. The question ceases to be what tribe or clan a person is from, whether he or she is ally or enemy. The question is, Can he or she be saved?

The one thing impossible is a xenophobic universal altruism. But the major world faiths have escaped tribalism, not only in ideal but also in the real proportionately to their success. It is impossible to explain this ecumenical "xenophilia" on the basis of genetics. The widely shared faith no longer provides any selectable advantage. Somehow, somewhere, these missionary Samaritans reached insight into a better standard of what is right. "You have heard that it was said, 'You shall love your neighbor and hate your enemy.' But I say to you, Love your enemies" (Matt. 5:43).

From evolutionary theory one can get some reciprocity with the competing out-groups. The latter form the basis of world trade, both cooperative and competitive. Religion is not adverse to being good neighbors, or to being fair and reciprocating in international business. Maybe the church catholic is a mutually supportive society. But, in the end, when the question is asked, "Who is my neighbor?" the answer comes in terms of who has needs that I can help meet, with my time, or money, or religion, not who is likely to reciprocate with net gain to my genetic line.

The pseudo-altruist will have to say that such missionaries were just setting up a world moral climate in which they themselves were most likely to prosper genetically. One can adamantly hang on to the selfishness paradigm, but this is a topsy-turvy kind of selfishness that has to act on universal altruism, and evangelize this faith to the world, that is, share it with everybody else, before it works most efficiently to one's own benefit. It is odd that to serve their genetic interests people have to go to elaborate efforts to do just the opposite, to believe universal creeds, share them with others, act on universal altruism, and build characters that are caring, fair, sympathetic, forgiving, magnanimous.

One can say, if one insists, that all this is just reputation-building, pretense that creates a climate in which the pretender and his kin prosper owing to the reciprocity generated. But it is difficult to see how they prosper to the detriment of the others who are the beneficiaries of this allegedly pretended altruism. There is no longer any differential survival benefit, because all these out-group converts are also winners. There is no longer that competitive edge that Sober and Wilson required at the core of natural selection. None of this is really very plausible anymore, since it becomes impossible to keep the benefits local and in-group.

These religions crisscross races, nations, and centuries, and involve some logic of the mind that is tracking what is transgenetically right. Genetic success is necessary but not sufficient to explain this universalism. It makes more sense to say that such religions were discovering what is trans-tribally, trans-culturally valuable. Something has emerged for which biology is not giving us a convincing account.

And if some of these Samaritan missionaries say that "God commands this altruism," that this kind of suffering love is divine, there seems no reason yet forthcoming from the biologists to think otherwise. To the contrary, this appearance of universalist religion with its capacity to generate this generous altruism still needs adequate explanation. "Do to others as you would have them do to you" helps us to cope because here is insight not just for the tribe, but for the world; indeed, if there are moral agents with values at stake in other worlds, this could be universal truth.

REFERENCES

Alexander, Richard D. 1975. The search for a general theory of behavior. *Behavioral Sciences* 20:77-100.
————. 1979. *Darwinism and Human Affairs*. Seattle: University of Washington Press.
————. 1987. *The Biology of Moral Systems*. New York: Aldine de Gruyter.
————. 1993. Biological considerations in the analysis of morality. Pp. 163-96 in *Evolutionary Ethics*, ed. Matthew H. Nitecki and Doris V. Nitecki. Albany: State University of New York Press.
Barash, David P. 2001. The ugly underside of altruism. *The Chronicle of Higher Education* 47, no. 42 (June 29): B7-B9.
Dawkins, Richard. 1989. *The Selfish Gene*. New edition. New York: Oxford University Press.
Ghiselin, Michael T. 1974. *The Economy of Nature and the Evolution of Sex*. Berkeley: University of California Press.
Ruse, Michael. 1986. *Taking Darwin Seriously*. Oxford: Basil Blackwell.
————. 1994. Evolutionary theory and Christian ethics: Are they in harmony? *Zygon* 29:5-24.
————. 2002. Can selection explain the Presbyterians? *Science* 297:1479.
Ruse, Michael, and Edward O. Wilson. 1985. The evolution of ethics. *New Scientist* 108, no. 1478 (17 October): 50-52.
————. 1986. Moral philosophy as applied science. *Philosophy* 61:173-92.
Sober, Elliott, and David Sloan Wilson. 1998. *Unto Others: The Evolution and Psychology of Unselfish Behavior*. Cambridge, Mass.: Harvard University Press.
Trivers, Robert L. 1971. The evolution of reciprocal altruism. *Quarterly Review of Biology* 46:35-57.
Williams, George C. 1988. Huxley's evolution and ethics in sociobiological perspective. *Zygon* 23:383-407, and reply to critics, 437-38.
Wilson, David Sloan. 2002. *Darwin's Cathedral: Evolution, Religion, and the Nature of Society*. Chicago: University of Chicago Press.
Wilson, Edward O. 1975. *Sociobiology: The New Synthesis*. Cambridge, Mass.: Harvard University Press.
————. 1978. *On Human Nature*. Cambridge, Mass.: Harvard University Press.

III. The Ethics of Evolution:
Theological Evaluation and Critique

13 A Cross-Section of Sin:
The Mimetic Character of Human Nature
in Biological and Theological Perspective

S. Mark Heim

Christ's teaching, example, death, and resurrection are supposed by Christians to resolve a fundamental estrangement in human life, to overcome sin and bring reconciliation or atonement. This belief presupposes assumptions about human nature that appear to conflict with scientific ones (Williams 2001). An evolutionary biophysical view of humanity identifies no problem for which the Christian revelation might be a solution. Many take the evolutionary view to imply that human moral and religious life consists without remainder in two things. The first is rationalization of rules of simple genetic self-interest, and the second is beguiling mental constructs that outwardly contradict these actual rules yet actually serve them, as the means by which we may deceive ourselves (and so better deceive others) into believing we are altruistic, and so gain genetic advantage from such a reputation. Religious faith does not reduce solely to morality. But if morality itself may be so reduced, then both the context and the content of religious faith are severely constrained. Conversely, if religion must prove that it is inimical to human flourishing and survival in order to prove it is "real" (and not reducible to genetic interest), the inquiry is meaningless. The better question is whether religion brings a new dimension into human life and morality, meeting a need or fulfilling a function that cannot be duplicated without its intrinsic complexity.

The Christian understanding of salvation traditionally has three dimensions: reconciliation between humans and God, reconciliation between humanity and the rest of the created world, and reconciliation among humans. In this chapter I focus only on the last dimension. I argue that it is possible to see a "mimetic transition" in the emergence of human nature. In light of that transition there are at least two ways we can give meaningful content to religious reconciliation, and hence two ways in which religion retains a distinctive integrity. The first is religion's role in curbing and overcoming mimetic conflict and violence. The second is a specifically Christian approach to the sacrificial dynamic of religion. This is a recursive picture. The emergent mimetic quality in humans, I will argue, is an adaptive process for social life. Religion is itself an adaptive process that grows out of this emergent quality, to overcome its inherent generative dynamic for conflict. Christianity shares in this dimension of religion, yet it adds its own further distinctive adaptive process to respond to the sacrificial scapegoating characteristic of religion generally. My approach is stimulated by René Girard's work. Girard assumes the mimetic character of humanity and on this basis develops a distinctive understanding of religion, early human culture, and Christianity. My contention is that research in cognitive studies converges with some of Girard's main points.

From Genetic to Cultural Evolution:
The "Mimetic Transition"

Research is revealing a genetically selected neurological and cognitive structure for imitation, an in-built program that introduces a truly open-ended interaction with the social environment. This research in the cognitive sciences addresses the leap from genetic to cultural evolution, a leap fueled by a dramatic mechanism for transmission of information, social learning, and, finally, shared inner worlds. Though present in some form in organisms as simple as guppies (Dugatkin 2000), imitation may be at the heart of the emergence of key elements of what we take to be human nature itself: consciousness, theory of mind, empathy.

Recent work in the cognitive sciences suggests imitation is a rare, perhaps even uniquely human ability, which may be fundamental to what is distinctive about human learning, intelligence, rationality, and culture. I cannot improve on the brief summary given for a recent conference:

> Developmental psychologists have claimed that newborns imitate in a way that cannot be explained in terms of conditioning or the triggering of innate behaviors (Meltzoff and Moore 1992; Meltzoff and Moore 1997; Anisfeld 1996). Neuropsychologists have discovered and studied various imitative behavioral syndromes in adults, some associated with brain damage, others found in normal subjects (Kinsbourne 2002, Prinz 2002). Animal psychologists have intensively studied the behavior of primates, dolphins and parrots in order to determine whether any creatures other than human beings are capable of "genuine" imitation (Byrne 1995; Byrne 2001; Tomasello 1996; Heyes 1998; Heyes and Ray 2000; Pepperberg 2000). The latter is a question of considerable ongoing controversy, in which the relationship of genuine imitation to related phenomena is at issue. Neuro-

physiologists have found evidence that observing a particular action weakly primes the muscles that would be needed to perform the same action. Moreover, they have discovered an intriguing class of neuron, so-called "mirror neurons," with matching sensory and motor fields: they fire when an action is either performed or observed (Rizzolatti et al. 2001; Rizzolatti et al. 2002; Gallese and Goldman 1998; Decety and Blackmore 2001). Mirror neurons appear to be concentrated in one of the language areas of the brain (or the homologue thereof in other primates), which is activated when imitative tasks are performed. The function of mirror neurons, and their relation to imitation, is a matter of intense interest. One hypothesis is that mirror neurons subserve the ability to attribute mental states to others. (Gallese and Goldman 1998; Gallese 2001)

These developments offer support to the "simulation theory" of mind reading, which suggests that we grasp what is going on in others' minds by a kind of mental mimicry in our own. We reproduce their mental process in our own neurological field, in the same way that, when we observe an action by another, our mirror neurons reproduce the pattern of neurological activity that makes that same motion. There is evidence that such a "mirror" effect exists also in regions of the brain that process emotional responses (Gallese 2001). All of this suggests a profound neurological basis for imitation.

This mimetic capacity to divine others' intentions and emotions may be a key to the great leap in human learning from tightly gene-programmed behavior to the genetically programmed "open loop" learning that involves language, consciousness, and culture. Paul G. Higgs has argued that some time before 1.5 million years ago, "our ancestors passed through a mimetic transition where imitative spread of culture got under way" (Higgs 2000, 1355). Higgs's computer modeling presumed that culturally transmitted "memes" — cultural units passed on by imitation — have both positive and negative effects on individual fitness (on memes see Blackmore 1999). He hypothesizes that "imitative ability increases gradually under the action of selection until a mimetic transition point is reached where memes have the ability to spread like an epidemic" (Higgs 2000, 1356).

The "mimetic transition" also provides the foundation for a theory of mind, that is, for seeing likeness with others not only in outward terms but in internal mental states. For human beings, facial expressions are the primary form of body language by which we read each other's emotions and intentions. Research indicates that facial expressions are read with surprising consistency across cultures (Izard 1971; Ekman et al. 1972; Ekman 1973). And humans from a very early age engage in imitation of facial expressions as a primary form of play. It is very likely that the extraordinary effectiveness with which facial expressions communicate among humans is based on some variation of the mirror phenomenon, where seeing the facial muscles move in a certain way on another face activates a pattern for the same movement on our faces, a pattern we "recognize" as associated with a certain mental state or emotion.

In evolutionary terms, emotions are often viewed as the mediating executioners of the genes. As the social environment becomes more complex, it is less and less feasible for genes to code specific behavior that would be advantageous. You can have an instinct that tells you "defend your territory," but it quickly becomes impossible to have specific instincts to tell you what to do in the myriad different social interactions that arise. Emotions may be an intermediate tool, a kind of wholesale instinct (LeDoux 1996; Damasio 1999). Loving or hating or distrusting certain people is a motivation that can impel you toward certain *kinds* of action, without having to specify them exactly. That specification is left to responses that depend on a range of social cues.

In a recent work, psychiatrists Thomas Lewis, Fari Amini, and Richard Lannon argue that humans are biologically primed to be emotionally programmed by each other (Lewis, Amini, and Lannon 2000). They claim it is our limbic brain that registers emotional resonances with other persons. But they acknowledge, and the research we have been reviewing suggests, that our limbic brain has access to such resonance only because of the mimetic processes in our cerebral cortex and the cultural learning that they make possible. One of the effects of reading minds is that we catch emotions. Lewis and his colleagues point out the well-known fact that human infants, provided with all the necessities of life, wither and die at catastrophic rates when deprived of warmth and interaction, particularly the imitative "child's play" so characteristic of parents. Few impulses could be seen as more basic from an evolutionary biological perspective than that of self-preservation. And yet it seems literally true that we do not even develop a full or robust sense of self-preservation except by "catching" it socially. We learn to effectively love ourselves through the signification of another's perceived desire: their love directed at us. We imitate that love by tuning our affection to its object: us. Once genetic interest has taken this mode, programming our inner lives through the imitative contagion between the subjective contents of one mind, one heart, and other persons, it is ripe not only to drive those forms but to be driven by them.

On the basis of these developments, it is possible to sketch a new story about human emergence and its balance of genetic and cultural components. Humans are genetically programmed to be programmable. What becomes distinctively human is the layering over instinct (a fixed genetic program) of a genetic disposition for social learning (a genetic disposition that does not fix content). The key thing emerging is a grasp of *how* we are so programmed. The central factor in this addition of learning to instinct seems to be mimesis or imitation. This is a supercharged dynamic for learning, plasticity, and innovation. Once engaged, it gives rise to the advances of human culture, where extraordinarily sophisticated practices and recipes for innovation can be handed down by nongenetic routes. We are disposed not only to mimic and internalize the patterns of behavior that are presented to us, but to mimic and internalize the desires and inner life we infer from another's cues, and on the basis of this pattern to produce novel behavior that has never been modeled for us. In fact, the entire existence of our individual inner, subjective, conscious lives is caught from others in this sense. It is this dramatic change that is at the heart of the "big bang" emergence of humanity from its evolutionary background.

Evolutionary accounts of the emergence of consciousness and the theory of mind stress that they appear as adaptations for social life, especially social life in groups larger than the small hunter-gatherer bands of early human history. Consistent with the principle of explaining "higher" human faculties in terms of strictly gene-level selection pressures, a number of uses for human subjectivity have been advanced. One of these sees consciousness as a function of living in larger social groups than earlier primates. In such groups, a larger brain and some system for keeping track of other individuals and past interactions with them would be a selective advantage. Reciprocal altruism is recognized as an important feature of group life, and these capacities allow one to police nonreciprocators and identify reliable cooperators. A related but separate hypothesis is that emotions and thoughts serve to allow us to internalize complex rules for self-interest in a social environment. Richard Alexander, for instance, argues that conscience is a faculty that lets an individual know (by feelings of guilt or anxiety) when she or he is breaking the rules of reciprocal altruism in ways that are likely to be found out. This is what morality is — guidelines that tell us points past which pursuit of our pure genetic interest can become counterproductive, because of the resistance and punishment elicited from others in the group (Alexander 1987). Yet another explanation sees the adaptive value of consciousness in giving us a cost-effective means for trying out alternative behaviors imaginatively. Through consciousness one can compare possible courses of action and anticipate possible results, without the costs of actually acting on these different or incompatible options. Conscious awareness allows us to run our own internal "war games" so that we can anticipate what others are planning to do to us, and counter with what we plan to do to them. The selective pressure toward consciousness lies in the advantages of being able to detect others' deception and to improve one's own deception of others (Trivers 1985).

There is a good deal of truth in these hypotheses. The distinctive complexity of human consciousness has an ambiguous root (as the creation/fall narrative would suggest). And we can also note that the evidence for the mimetic transition, rather than contradicting such hypotheses, in many concrete ways enhances them. But the evidence suggests that those hypotheses are unlikely to tell the whole story. Inner mental and emotional states are not just shorthand to organize behavior in the one who experiences them, and they are not just internal mail that one does not want competitors to read. They are also models on which others form their own inner lives. The accounts just mentioned downplay the positive as opposed to the defensive advantage the mimetic transition offers in individual selection (for accounts that stress the positive see Deacon 1997; Donald 2001). It is not only about outfoxing others through Machiavellian intelligence. Mimetic capacities foster social learning that binds people together in positive ways, including persons who are not closely related genetically. They give a quantum boost to cultural evolution, heightening the importance of multilevel selection theory for understanding humanity. We are profoundly genetically disposed to an openness to each other, a connection we require to even become human. This mimetic character is the key to much of human creativity and to the incredible spectrum of qualities and capacities that are possible, especially to the young.

In evolutionary terms, the image of God would have to be either a genetic endowment or an emergent feature in human nature. Our discussion of the mimetic transition has outlined an emergent dynamic in humanity that seems to fit well into this theological discussion. In fact, this ability to "read each other's hearts" looks like exactly what we would hope to find in humanity reflecting the image of God: the capacity to participate in each other, to indwell each other. Imitative capacities in humans seem to be a matrix involving cognitive skills, freedom, and empathetic relation. These are the same key elements that the image of God traditionally encompasses. Our individual selves are quite literally made, constituted in the image of others, in ways that can now be specified even neurologically. As persons, we are made for communion and constituted by it. We must stress that the biological "fitness" of this genetic disposition is precisely its openness, its *lack* of specific predetermination about which models will be formative or what content will be learned from them. Ours is an emergent freedom.

Girard's Mimetic Theory

The theories of religion so far produced in evolutionary thought do not take adequate account of the mimetic transition we have described. This is a fatal failing if, as I suggest, religion is largely oriented to the mimetic dynamics of human emergence. Some theories view religion in pleiotropic terms, as a kind of "spandrel" (Gould and Lewontin 1999). Others try to understand religion entirely as an individual-level adaptation. Still others see it as in some measure a group-level adaptation (Wilson 2002).

Religion, David Sloan Wilson has proposed, is a "Darwin machine" for groups, as the immune system is for an organism: an adaptive process that continually interacts with the social environment, both inner-group and inter-group (the phrase "Darwin machine" is from Plotkin 1994). This means that religions may have many parts, and several levels, including the dimensions that current evolutionary theories describe. In Wilson's evolutionary account of early Christianity, he notes that Christians extended the emotions, concepts, and intentionality of family to the members of church. In doing so, they increased group fitness (of the church in comparison with outsiders) to the point that truly altruistic behavior within the group became fit enough to be genetically sustainable (Wilson 2002). Certain religious adaptations made the group environment such that it affected what behaviors influence reproduction and survival. Genes, as always, have to adapt to their environment. But the environment they have to adapt to can be the social environment defined in significant part by a religious system. Wilson's work is a significant advance. But there are further distinctive aspects of religion, dimensions that arise in response to the new order of freedom that comes in the mimetic transition, and most particularly in response to a new problem that emerges with this freedom.

Best known for his account of the origin of religion and of human society (Girard 1977; Girard 1989), René Girard regards mimetic theory as the ground of his thinking (Girard 1996). In brief, mimetic theory has to do with the source of human desires. In comparison with our close primate relatives, humans are born with a relatively thin instinctual repertoire and a long period of plastic development. We fix on certain key models in our environment and "update our software" by imitating them, by building an internal life that is an inference drawn from our construal of the inner life of certain others. We do have certain biological instincts that we don't learn — hunger and thirst, sexual desire — but even these are heavily shaped by this process. It is entirely possible to have a whole range of specific, powerful desires that are wildly overdetermined in any biological sense. A sex drive may be a given, but the passion for one specific and perhaps unattainable person over all others is not explicable in the same way. A motive that seeks social status and abundant resources may be understandable in selfish genetic terms, but the resolute longing to succeed at this particular calling, and to pass by other plausible or more lucrative rewards, is something of a mystery.

Our legion desires, and even the "tuning" of biological desires, are specified by contagion or imitation. They are caught from persons who designate by their desires what is to be desired. This is a distinctly human and social characteristic. We are neither autonomous selves nor are we empty vessels filled by society or our genes with some imposed appetites. We are "interviduals" who can have desires of our own only through models who mediate such desire. Mimetic desire and mimetic rivalry are already present among animals in a rudimentary sense. In this respect, mimesis is a quality well suited to express both continuity with other primates and unique emergence in human nature. Mimesis is a simple program that generates extraordinary complexity, particularly when it bears not directly on actions (or secondarily so), nor even ultimately on objects, but on desires. Mimesis is a positive and creative feature of human nature. But it also readily generates conflict and rivalry. The very fact that one or others have singled out something by their desire for it may lead others to desire it as well, and hence lead to conflict. Girard puts special stress on the way in which models easily become (or incite) rivals. Persons who take another as a model grow isomorphic desires and seek the same ends. At some point, they thus can become competitors with their model and conflict ensues. This mimetic dynamic is headlined in the romantic or sexual triangles at the heart of so much human literature.

The mimetic process is part and parcel of human emergence into sociality, but it also threatens to derail human society because of its potential for explosive backlash. Mimesis creatively multiplies complex human skills and capacities by reproducing them within a group and across generations. Yet it also can become a runaway train through this same process of magnification. Sometimes the runaway is localized, as in a romantic triangle where one person's desire confirms and escalates another's, until they reach levels of irrational idealization of the person they seek and of extreme rivalry with each other. By sharing the same desire, they each become obstacles to the other's fulfillment of the desire.

But the runaway can also be social, where the loop includes not just two or three, but large numbers in a group. Mimetic programming that supercharges human learning and links us intimately with each other also has a uniquely conflictive potential. Moving away from a more rote instinctual programming to the more flexible guidance of behavior by emotions can lead to spirals of counterproductive behavior that no self-respecting rodent would adopt. A paradigm example is revenge. Animals fight with their own kind for resources and to establish dominance, but rarely to the death. They do not seem prone to cycles of violence simply based on the prior fact of violence. But this is a very real human possibility and, to Girard's mind, the prime crisis of early human society. The very mimetic facility of human beings that fosters social life and learning and that grounds empathy also threatens to run humans into vicious feedback loops of vendetta, "eye for an eye" reciprocity. An enemy can be a powerful model who generates by his or her desire a form of my own, hate being returned to hate. A revenge feud within a kin group is an example of such behavior. It is precisely the human ability to read others' minds (and also to misread) that creates this problem. When one person or group harms another, the response may not be proportionate to the specific harm, but to the perceived intent. This is a recipe for escalation.

Without finding a way to overcome cycles of retaliation, human society can hardly begin. Girard believes the means to break this vicious cycle appear as if miraculously. At some point when feud threatens to dissolve a community, spontaneous and irrational mob violence erupts against some distinctive person or minority in the group. They are accused of the worst crimes the group can imagine, crimes that by their very enormity might have caused the terrible plight the community now experiences. They are lynched.

The sad good in this evil is that it actually works. In the wake of the murder, communities find that this sudden war of all against one has delivered them from the war of each against all. The sacrifice of one or a few as scapegoats discharges the pending acts of retribution. It "clears the air." This benefit seems a startling, even magical result from a simple execution. The sudden peace confirms the desperate charges that the victim had been behind the crisis to begin with. If the scapegoat's death is the solution, the scapegoat must have been the cause. The death has such reconciling effect that it seems the victim must possess supernatural power. So the victim becomes a god, memorialized in myth.

Rituals of sacrifice originated in this way, as tools to fend off social crisis. And in varied forms they are with us still. The prescription is that divisions in the community must be reduced to but one division, the division of all against one common victim or one minority group. Prime candidates are the marginal and the weak, or those isolated by their very prominence. The process does not just accept innocent victims, it prefers them — "outsiders" not closely linked to established groups in the society. This, in a nutshell, is Girard's account of the origin of religion, which is identical with the beginning of culture itself. Scapegoating sacrifice is the founding good/bad thing, reconciliation in the blood of the innocent. To describe the scapegoat effect another way, the desire feedback loop that had set people within a community against each other is now positively transformed. In reinforcing, by example, each other's rejection of the scapegoat they come to a harmonious unity of desire around an object that unites them.

Girard points to the contradiction anthropologists often note between prohibitions (taboos) and rituals in traditional societies. That is, the very things that are prohibited by the group's elaborate rules are often the things that are explicitly done in ritual contexts, especially sacrificial ones. In his view, this is consistent. Both are organized to avoid or overcome mimetic conflict. The prohibitions are structured to avoid the beginning or escalation of mimetic conflict (do not commit adultery, but also, don't wear the face painting of another clan). Ritual sacrifice, on the other hand, is an antidote when, despite prohibitions, mimetic conflict escalates and a crisis threatens. Instead of damping down the conflict, the community reverses tactics and fans conflict to a climax, a climax that is cathartic and "redemptive" because in the unanimity of all against one (or a few) it restores peace to the social group. It is a hyper-mimetic solution to a hyper-mimetic crisis, driving out violence with violence, albeit of a carefully modulated type.

There are two main points of interest in Girard's hypothesis. The first is that religion itself is an adaptation to the mimetic transition, one that enhances its positive effects for individuals and groups and, most particularly, defends against its dangers. The second point is that in addition to these general features, religion is rooted in a very specific additional feature, sacrifice, which is a ritualized, fallback mechanism to deal with mimetic crises that arise despite religious protections.

Sin and Atonement

Recent developments in the cognitive sciences provide a scientific framework for Girard's hypothesis. The interaction of evolutionary thought and Girard's mimetic theory provides the background for a renewed formulation of the Christian understanding of Christ's reconciling work. In this reading Christ's life and passion illuminate but do not sanctify the reciprocal conflict our mimetic nature fosters, calling us from the scapegoating and substitutionary violence that have been standard religious antidotes for that conflict. Girard has outlined this vision, and the biological context we have reviewed gives it additional power (Girard 1987). Christianity shares with other traditions a spectrum of religious methods to enhance and maintain social learning, as well as features that attempt to preempt mimetic conflict. In continuity with Jewish tradition, it shares an awareness of the religious roots of sacrifice and scapegoating. And in the Gospel accounts of Jesus' life, death, and resurrection, Christianity offers its distinctive religious response to the dangers of religion's own mimetic violence.

For all its powerful new possibilities, the mimetic transition carries a label: "handle with care." It sets up conflicts between humans that would never arise between animals: violence driven by envy, projection, and mirrored retaliation. This human capacity to act apart from strict genetic self-interest (a capacity that itself has been genetically selected because of the adaptive value of a disposition for imitation and supercharged learning) creates a new problem. Nonadaptive, destructive memes can spread like an epidemic through communities so well tuned for such contagion.

Religion may have been the primary adaptation to deal with this problem. Religion is permeated with elements that tend to combat the emergent dangers of hyper-mimesis in humans. The so-called "axial religions" have varied ways of addressing this threat. Some religions (for example, Buddhism) attack hyper-mimetic danger at its roots in consciousness, an internal approach that tries to purge consciousness itself of the mental attachments mimetic relations create. It does this by a highly sophisticated analysis and practice of awareness of our mental processes, "peeling back" and reversing, as it were, the process by which the self is constituted by desires modeled by others. The normative setting for this process is a monastic community, where the volatility of mental life is defused and purified.

Other religions, like Christianity, try to defuse hyper-mimetic conflict through mimetic means themselves. The church puts special emphasis on the role of Christ as sole savior and Lord for the Christian, a unique model. Christ is a model who defuses the conflictual dimensions of imitation in two ways. First, relation with Christ is not an exclusive or zero sum game. No one has less of it because another has more. And Christ is risen and "above" us, on a level beyond rivalry. We are no threat to Christ for the divine position and Christ is no rival to us for the benefits we may seek. Second, Christ is a paradoxical model. The desires that we catch from Jesus are wishes to be a servant, to love the lost. This is a judo-like anti-rivalry dynamic: "whoever would be the greatest among you, let them be the least."

Religion may be other things as well, but it is crucially a response to the destructive potential of our mimetic nature. Humans have introduced a kind of behavior otherwise quite unknown in the natural world, one that gives "sin" a distinctive social meaning. Interestingly, the same capacities for symbolic thought that make possible this new dimension of sin also make possible an awareness and representation of a personal God with a moral will, one toward whom humans can acknowledge responsibility.

One very early layer of human morality may be a warning to members of a group about how far they can pursue their genetic self-interest before others will retaliate by damaging the actor's fitness. But distinctively human morality of the sort manifest in religion addresses a second-order problem, that of curbing the dangerous by-products of the hyper-mimetic human sensitivity to each other, the empathy and contagion of desires that can sweep humans into destructive cycles against individual and even group self-interest.

In this context we can identify three dimensions of sin. At the individual level, there is a dimension of disproportionate desires (what the tradition has called concupiscence). Our mimetic qualities make it possible for individuals to develop drives and desires out of all proportion to their true genetic interest and even counter to it. The sinful dimension lies not in pre-cultural biological inclinations but in the inflammation of mimetically constituted desires to destructive dimensions. A life blighted by a consuming desire for personal revenge, darkened by acts of gratuitous cruelty born of envy, or frustrated by obstinate pursuit of a type of success and eminence for which one is unsuited — any of these reflects this dimension of sin.

The damage done to others and to self in such cases is not biologically necessary. It is reasonable to see such damage as a violation of a moral order for which we can be held accountable. We inevitably form and are formed by others, and we are responsible for our role on both ends. Our inclination toward simple genetic self-interest (for instance, our preferential love for our own offspring) is not itself immoral or sinful. Our mimetic openness to each other introduces an element of freedom and variation, and it is in this sphere that sin enters. It is this same capacity that offers us the opportunity for a new relation with God. Consciousness and theory of mind make it possible to attribute intention and an inner life to God. We can thus perceive God as a model from whom our desires and lives may be formed. Thus we may say that sin emerges as a possibility in two new ways: as a destructive use of our mimetic potential and as a failed relation with God (as when we turn away or willfully misconstrue God's intentions). With each step of growing capacity we have greater accountability.

The first dimension of sin is observed within the individual intra-psychically, though it is formed in relationship. The second dimension is explicitly interpersonal. It is the mimetic "scandal" or stumbling block that arises between persons and that undermines human community itself. Activities like false witness and covetousness are not only offenses, they spread offense. They turn the positive side of mimesis to negative contagion. Jesus in the Sermon on the Mount focuses particularly on those things which are internal but when "read" by others (as humans are extremely good at doing) lead to escalating conflict. His injunction is not only against murder but against hate, for example. This is not only internally preemptive, intended to preclude an individual from developing the motive for murder, but *socially* preemptive, intended to avoid presenting the model that inflames and escalates others' desires toward conflict.

To put it more succinctly, sin is that activity (and it can be a "spiritual" or internal as well as an external act) that deforms the medium of mimetic communion, that turns this powerful emergent human dynamic to destructive and conflictive results rather than those that build up human community. The "altruism" involved in avoiding such sin is possible on several levels. On the first, it is an advanced form of reciprocal altruism, needed for life in human social groups when our inner lives are formed on each other. On the second level, it is a function of true group selection. And on the third level, it is a function of another level of heritability, that of memes that can "jump" from one set of genetic hosts to another. The mechanism of social contagion can spread virtue, even if it diminishes fitness, since mimetic contagion itself is not genetic in nature. Religious antidotes to destructive social contagion would not be necessary if such destructive waves themselves disappeared because they made those affected by them less fit. Even if all of those affected by this contagion die out or fail to reproduce in a given generation, those in the next generation would be no less susceptible to the same contagion. The emergent threat of mimetic escalation is transmitted socially, not genetically. So too is religion. And even if religious altruism decreases individual or group fitness, it can remain as permanent a feature of human culture as the problem it addresses.

The third dimension of sin is found in religion itself. The foundational religious solution to runaway mimetic crises caused by humans' inflammation of each other's desires is itself an innovative and effective kind of sin: scapegoating sacrifice. It restores peace through the death of innocents and becomes, Girard argues, the cornerstone of social life, a kind of original sin. If base-level evolutionary morality is about policing self-interest parameters in a group, then presumably its value consists in enforcing sanctions on those who violate the rules. But sacrifice uncovers great group utility in holding guilty and executing particular victims with no reference to their actual violation of such rules. They are not chosen because they are guilty but because their death can unite the group.

Atonement has all three dimensions of sin in view: first, our intrapsychic wounds; second, the interpersonal contagion of subjective models that lead to runaway social conflict; and third, the specifically religious form of sin, "redemptive" scapegoating, which itself evolved as a way of defusing the crisis created by the first two types. In a profound sense, these dimensions of sin may be regarded as "inherited" and as shared among humans. Our distinctive individual inner lives are caught and formed from others, even though the result in each person is unique. What it means to be in the image of God is to be programmed and formed as a self by participation in the inner lives of others. If others are sinners, I will necessarily be "conceived in sin," not in terms of a genetic code but through my mimetic nature. As Merlin Donald says, our individual consciousnesses are the result of activities distributed over many different brains (Donald 2001). Sin is a condition and a contagion, shared among us all by means of the very common, creative nature that it twists. In light of the mimetic transition we can see sin as an "intervidual" reality, even while each individual rightly has responsibility for his or her own sins. We all participate in sin by virtue of our active and passive participation in the web of human relationships that constitute and reconstitute our selves. And the specific sin of scapegoating is one in which we all share in that it became a fundamental feature of any human social group. Insofar as we belong to a social community, we are complicit in this sacrificial dynamic.

Finally, we can briefly consider the light that this throws on a central aspect of Christianity: the passion narratives of Christ's death and resurrection. Christian theological understanding of Christ's death starts with a paradox. Jesus' death saves the world, and it ought not to happen. The cross can be understood only in light of what Girard regards as the prototypical good/bad thing in human culture: scapegoating sacrifice. Scapegoating is one of the deepest structures of human sin, built into our religion and our politics. It is demonic because it is endlessly flexible in its choice of victims and because it can truly deliver the good that it advertises.

The resurrection makes Jesus' death a failed sacrifice, but of a new kind. When mythical sacrifice succeeds, peace descends, true memory is erased, and the way is smoothed for the next scapegoat. If it fails (because the community is not unanimous or the victim is not sufficiently demonized), it becomes just another killing, simply stoking the retributive proliferation of violence. But in this case, neither does everyone unanimously close ranks over Jesus' grave (as Jesus' executioners hope) nor is there a spree of violent revenge on behalf of the crucified leader. The resurrection, the vindication of the innocent victim sacrificed for social peace, points to a different possibility. An odd new counter-community arises out of previously conflicting groups, dedicated both to the victim whom God has justified by resurrection and to a new life through him, a life that requires doing without such scapegoating. To Girard, this is the good news, the inexplicable revelation, that is found in the Bible. He claims that in light of the cross, scapegoating is increasingly visible for what it is (Bailie 1995).

Precisely because of its collective and ubiquitous character, we can hardly deny that Jesus bears our sin of scapegoating. Christ died for us. He did so first in the mythic, sacrificial sense that all scapegoated victims do. The fact that we know this is already a sign that he died for us in a second sense, to save us from that very sin. Jesus dies in our place, because it is literally true that any one of us, in the right circumstances, can be the scapegoat. As the letter to the Hebrews says, Christ is a sacrifice to end sacrifice, one who has died once for all (Heb. 9:25-28). Christ's passion is the centerpiece of Christianity's vision for reconciliation of mimetic sin.

Conclusion

Cognitive studies and neuroscience are shedding new light on the mimetic dynamics in human development. René Girard's thought offers a complementary perspective on the mimetic transition in human development, on religion's role in that transition, and on Christianity's understanding of sin and human nature. Together, they allow us to grasp some characteristically religious dimensions of morality. This chapter has only attempted to sketch these dimensions, and many further questions remain. One of the most important goes beyond the scope of this chapter. Even if the perspective I have suggested proves to be sound, it is not clear whether the transformative power of religion remains constrained within the bounds of the "in-group niceness/ out-group nastiness" pattern (by which religion promotes altruism and social peace only in a context of between-group competition) or whether it can support a genuinely universal possibility of human community. This issue remains the horizon for further investigation.

REFERENCES

Alexander, Richard D. 1987. *The Biology of Moral Systems.* Hawthorne, N.Y.: A. de Gruyter.
Anisfeld, M. 1996. Only tongue protrusion modeling is matched by neonates. *Developmental Review* 16:149-61.
Axelrod, Robert M. 1984. *The Evolution of Cooperation.* New York: Basic.
Bailie, Gil. 1995. *Violence Unveiled: Humanity at the Crossroads.* New York: Crossroad.

Blackmore, Susan J. 1999. *The Meme Machine.* New York: Oxford University Press.

Boerlijst, M. C., M. A. Nowak, et al. 1997. The logic of contrition. *Journal of Theoretical Biology* 136:281-93.

Byrne, Richard W. 1995. *The Thinking Ape: Evolutionary Origins of Intelligence.* New York: Oxford University Press.

———. 2001. Social and technical forms of primate intelligence. Pp. 145-72 in *Tree of Origin: What Primate Behavior Can Tell Us about Human Social Evolution,* ed. F. B. M. de Waal. Cambridge: Harvard University Press.

———. 2002. A mechanistic theory of skill learning by imitation. A paper given at Perspectives on Imitation: From Cognitive Neuroscience to Social Science, a conference held May 24-26, 2002, at Royaumont Abbey, France. Sponsored by Warwick University. Available at http://www.warwick.ac.uk/fac/sci/Psychology/imitation/ (cited November 4, 2002).

Damasio, Antonio R. 1994. *Descartes' Error: Emotion, Reason, and the Human Brain.* New York: G. P. Putnam.

———. 1999. *The Feeling of What Happens: Body and Emotion in the Making of Consciousness.* New York: Harcourt Brace.

Deacon, Terrence W. 1997. *The Symbolic Species: The Co-evolution of Language and the Brain.* New York: W. W. Norton.

Decety, J., and S. Blakemore. 2001. From the perception of action to the understanding of intention. *Nature Reviews Neuroscience* 2:561-67.

Donald, Merlin. 2001. *A Mind So Rare: The Evolution of Human Consciousness.* New York: W. W. Norton.

———. 2002. Imitation viewed in the light of human genesis. A paper given at Perspectives on Imitation: From Cognitive Neuroscience to Social Science, a conference held May 24-26, 2002, at Royaumont Abbey, France. Sponsored by Warwick University. Available from World Wide Web: http://www.warwick.ac.uk/fac/sci/Psychology/imitation/ (cited November 4, 2002).

Dugatkin, L. A. 2000. *The Imitation Factor: Evolution beyond the Gene.* New York: Free Press.

Ekman, P. 1973. Cross-cultural studies of facial expression. In *Darwin and Facial Expression: A Century of Research in Review,* ed. P. Ekman. New York: Academic Press.

Ekman, P., W. V. Friesen, et al. 1972. *Emotion in the Human Face: Guidelines for Research and an Integration of Findings.* New York: Pergamon.

Gallese, V. 2001. The "shared manifold" hypothesis: From mirror neurons to empathy. *Journal of Consciousness Studies* 8, nos. 5-7:33-50.

Gallese, V., and A. Goldman. 1998. Mirror neurons and the simulation theory of mind-reading. *Trends in Cognitive Sciences* 12:493-501.

Gattis, M., H. Bekkering, et al. 2002. Goal-directed imitation. Pp. 183-205 in *The Imitative Mind: Development, Evolution, and Brain Bases,* ed. W. Prinz. Cambridge: Cambridge University Press.

Gil-White, F. 2002. Memes don't replicate: So what? Undoing the tyranny of the genetic metaphor. A paper given at Perspectives on Imitation: From Cognitive Neuroscience to Social Science, a conference held May 24-26, 2002, at Royaumont Abbey, France. Sponsored by Warwick University. Available at http://www.warwick.ac.uk/fac/sci/Psychology/imitation/pro (cited November 4, 2002).

Girard, René. 1977. *Violence and the Sacred*. Baltimore: Johns Hopkins University Press.

―――. 1987. *Things Hidden Since the Foundation of the World*. Stanford: Stanford University Press.

―――. 1989. *The Scapegoat*. Baltimore: Johns Hopkins University Press.

―――. 1996. *The Girard Reader*, ed. James G. Williams. New York: Crossroad.

―――. 2001. *I See Satan Fall Like Lightning*. Maryknoll, N.Y.: Orbis.

Gould, Stephen J., and R. C. Lewontin. 1999. The spandrels of San Marco and the Panglossian paradigm: A critique of the adaptationist program. *Proceedings of the Royal Society of London, Series B, Biological Sciences* 205:581-98.

Heyes, C. M. 1998. Theory of mind in nonhuman primates. *Behavioral and Brain Sciences* 21:101-48.

Heyes, C. M., and E. Ray. 2000. What is the significance of imitation in animals? *Advances in the Study of Behavior* 29:215-45.

Higgs, P. G. 2000. The mimetic transition: A simulation study of the evolution of learning by imitation. *Proceedings of the Royal Society, Series B, Biological Sciences* 267, no. 1450:1355-61.

Hobson, R. P., and A. Lee. 1999. Imitation and identification in autism. *Journal of Child Psychology and Psychiatry* 40, no. 4:649-59.

Iacoboni, M. 2002. Understanding others: Imitation, language, empathy. A paper given at Perspectives on Imitation: From Cognitive Neuroscience to Social Science, a conference held May 24-26, 2002, at Royaumont Abbey, France. Sponsored by Warwick University. Available at http://www.warwick.ac.uk/fac/sci/Psychology/imitation/pro (cited November 4, 2002).

Izard, Carroll E. 1971. *The Face of Emotion*. New York: Appleton-Century-Crofts.

Kinsbourne, M. 2002. The role of imitation in body ownership and mental growth. Pp. 311-30 in *The Imitative Mind: Development, Evolution, and Brain Bases*, ed. A. N. Meltzoff and W. Prinz. Cambridge: Cambridge University Press.

LeDoux, Joseph. 1996. *The Emotional Brain: The Mysterious Underpinnings of Emotional Life*. New York: Simon and Shuster.

Lewis, Thomas, Fari Amini, and Richard Lannon. 2000. *A General Theory of Love*. New York: Random House.

McNamara, P. 2001. The frontal lobes, social intelligence, and religious worship. A prize paper in *Ideas for Creative Research in Neurobiology: Exploring Deeper Realities through Neurobiology*, a project of the John Templeton Foundation. Available at http://www.templeton.org/pdf/CreativeResearchIdeas2002.pdf (cited November 4, 2002).

Meltzoff, A. N., and M. K. Moore. 1992. Imitation, memory, and the representation of persons. *Infant Behavior and Development* 17:83-99.

————. 1997. Explaining facial imitation: A theoretical model. *Early Development and Parenting* 6:179-92.

Pepperberg, I. 2000. *The Alex Studies: Cognitive and Communicative Abilities of Grey Parrots.* Cambridge: Harvard University Press. "Introduction" for Perspectives on Imitation: From Cognitive Neuroscience to Social Science, a conference held May 24-26, 2002, at Royaumont Abbey, France. Sponsored by Warwick University. Available at http://www.warwick.ac.uk/fac/sci/Psychology/imitation/introduction (cited November 4, 2002).

Plotkin, Henry C. 1994. *Darwin Machines and the Nature of Knowledge.* Cambridge: Harvard University Press.

Prinz, W. 2002. Experimental approaches to imitation. Pp. 143-62 in *The Imitative Mind: Development, Evolution, and Brain Bases,* ed. A. N. Meltzoff and W. Prinz. Cambridge: Cambridge University Press.

Rizzolatti, G., L. Fadiga, et al. 2002. From mirror neurons to imitation: Facts and speculations. Pp. 247-66 in *The Imitative Mind: Development, Imitation, and Brain Bases,* ed. A. N. Meltzoff and W. Prinz. Cambridge: Cambridge University Press.

Rizzolatti, G., L. Fogassi, et al. 2001. Neurophysiological mechanisms underlying the understanding and imitation of action. *Nature Reviews Neuroscience* 2:661-70.

Sosis, R. H., and B. J. Ruffle. 2002. Religious ritual and cooperation: Testing for a relationship on Israeli religious kibbutzim. Ben Gurion University Economics Department working paper. Available at http://econ.bgu.ac.il/papers/137.pdf (cited November 4, 2002).

Tomasello, M. 1996. Do apes ape? In *Social Learning in Animals: The Roots of Culture,* ed. B. G. Galef Jr. and C. M. Heyes. San Diego: Academic Press.

Trivers, Robert L. 1985. *Social Evolution.* San Francisco: Benjamin/Cummings.

Williams, Patricia A. 2001. *Doing without Adam and Eve: Sociobiology and Original Sin.* Minneapolis: Fortress.

Wilson, David Sloan. 2002. *Darwin's Cathedral: Evolution, Religion, and the Nature of Society.* Chicago: University of Chicago Press.

14. Falling Up: Evolution and Original Sin

Gregory R. Peterson

Reinhold Niebuhr is reputed to have observed that original sin is the only empirically verifiable doctrine of Christian theology. Certainly, there is more than a grain of truth to the claim. However positively we wish to think of ourselves, the sad reality is that much of human history has been characterized by the grossest of evils, sometimes done in the name of the highest good. One does not need to look so far, however, for while history is full of evil on a grand scale, we also find our lives full of the petty but nevertheless personal forms of suffering that characterize everyday life. Indeed, since we all fall short of perfection, one need only look at oneself to see the depth of the problem.

The doctrine of original sin has been a significant though not universally endorsed element of Christian doctrine. In many ways, original sin captures Christianity's ambiguous evaluation of human nature. On the one hand, we are made in the image of God, thus partaking in the goodness and beauty of the divine. On the other, we are fallen, descendents of the first sinners, Adam and Eve, who violated God's will and were consequently expelled from the Garden of Eden. On a traditional view that is still held in many quarters, the entrance of sin and suffering into the world is a historic event, and it is from this historical event that we draw our understanding of human nature.

In contrast to these theological accounts, there has been in recent decades a return by scientists and philosophers to evolutionary theory to provide a grounding for scientific theories of human nature. Such efforts have been driven by the field of sociobiology. Since the publication of *Sociobiology* by E. O. Wilson in 1975, sociobiologists have made repeated claims that moral behavior can be reduced to biological categories. In sociobiology, original sin becomes naturalized, providing both an origins story and an account of human behavior.

But is it valid? To its credit, sociobiology has shed light on a number of issues that are of biological importance and which have some impact on how we think of our place in the world. Yet, when we turn to the human being, we are once again confronted with how truly complicated we are. This does not mean that the findings of sociobiology, where valid, are irrelevant. Rather, it means that they must ultimately be correlated with a larger story, one that involves minds, persons, and communities. Realizing this, in turn, provides the opportunity for re-evaluating our theological options. In some ways, the scientific story confirms the theological perspective. Created good, we are nevertheless fallen. In other ways, the scientific story calls for some new wrinkles, ones that may in the end require us to choose between competing theological alternatives.

In the Garden

In its most basic form, the doctrine of the fall is a form of theodicy. How could a good God create a world so full of human suffering? From the very beginning, Christian thinkers have turned to the first chapters of Genesis to explain this seeming conundrum. As testified by the beautiful poetry of Genesis 1, God did indeed create the world good, and the continuing beauty and marvelous complexity of the world serves as a continuing reminder of the basic goodness of God's creation. Human beings, while created good, have nevertheless rejected God, and in that rejection is the source of our human suffering. In Genesis 2 and 3, the cause of this suffering is understood in terms of the story of Adam and Eve, who violated God's will by eating from the tree of knowledge of good and evil. Expelled from the Garden, Adam and Eve were sentenced to mortal lives of hard work and suffering. Human suffering is thus not God's fault, but our own, and our mixed nature, made in the image of God yet fallen, stems from that pivotal event.

While still taken literally by many Christians around the world, the vast majority of biblical scholars and theologians recognize the mythical (in the positive sense) and even allegorical character of the story. Translated from the Hebrew, Adam is literally "man"; the name "Eve" likely stems from the root "to live," and the symbolic meaning of the tree of knowledge of good and evil seems clear enough. For this reason, theologians have taken the doctrine of the fall seriously, even though they recognize that the Adam and Eve story cannot be understood historically.

What the fall and original sin is taken to imply, however, is open to interpretation, and the history of theology reflects this. In the Western theological tradition, Augustine has had the most significant influence. On Augustine's understanding, we are all infected with original sin, transmitted by the sex act of our parents, who received it from theirs, and so on back to Adam and Eve themselves. According to Augustine, we are born sinful, and it is for this reason that infant baptism is practiced. More than this, not only are we born sinful, but we are incapable of any good apart from the grace of God.

This emphasis on human depravity was developed by the Reformers John Calvin and Martin Luther. Luther saw all our works as tainted with sin, and thus deserving of damnation. Taken to its logical extreme, morality in the ordinary sense of the word is not connected to religion at all, but is merely a means for human beings to get along in this penultimate world. Needless to say, however, not everyone has followed so pessimistic a line. Anabaptists and Methodists, for example, acknowledge human sinfulness while at the same time holding out hope for the possibility of human perfection.

It is important to note, however, that the Orthodox tradition of the eastern Roman Empire and, later on, Russia and eastern Europe, never accepted Augustine's account of original sin. The Orthodox tradition embraced a position that stems from the second-century bishop Ireneaus, who saw the failings of humankind as a result of our creatureliness and consequent immaturity. Made in the image of God, we are nevertheless incomplete and need therefore the act of Christ to make us whole. On Ireneaus' understanding, then, our nature is not corrupted by sin but free, and the choices that we make are consequently our own responsibility. Yet, the choices we make are also limited by our own immaturity, and so we are still prone to sinfulness in a way that is difficult to escape, even though the resultant view is not as nearly pessimistic as Augustine's view.

This more optimistic tone is also reflected in the idea of the *felix culpa*, or happy fault. This concept has long been a part of Catholic theology; according to it the fall of Adam and Eve has been sometimes regarded (somewhat paradoxically) as a good thing, since it is the fall that leads to the redemptive action of Christ. While versions of this view strike the modern thinker as a bit bizarre, much like picking a fight in order to be able to make up afterward, the general argument nevertheless is of theological interest. One of the merits of the *felix culpa* is that it suggests that our suffering is not pointless but has some more important value. Indeed, although they are usually portrayed as competing claims, it may be that there are insightful elements in all three approaches, elements that will need to be taken up in any modern theological approach to human nature in the face of our scientific knowledge.

Machiavellian Intelligence?

Why do we cooperate? Are we by nature selfish? If we take the evolutionary account seriously, then human physiology and behavior should have been adapted to its original environment and have developed because such physiology and behavior was more successful than its competitors. If Darwin was right about natural selection, then it seems that we should expect competition between species and even individuals to be dominant, with cooperation present only to the extent that it benefits the individual. We should expect our behavior to be limited and dictated to us by our genes, our minds unconsciously controlled by the laws of natural selection. Or should we? How do the forces of evolution produce intelligent, moral, and spiritual beings?

Evolutionary psychologists, in many ways successors to the discipline of sociobiology, claim that an integration of evolutionary theory and cognitive science is the solution. The program for evolutionary psychology was laid down in an article by John Tooby and Leda Cosmides that has since become a sort of manifesto for the discipline (Tooby and Cosmides 1992). Tooby and Cosmides argue against what they call the Standard Social Science Model (SSSM), the main characteristic of which is to claim that all human behavior is rooted in culture and that biology has no important role to play. In contrast, they argue that the mind is best understood by analogy to a Swiss army knife, composed of numerous mental modules, each of which is designed for a specific function. These modules significantly shape behavior, and do so because in our evolutionary past they were highly adaptive. Since such modules were developed in our distant evolutionary past, they are common to everyone and thus form the basis of a universal human nature. While cultural variations do exist, evolutionary psychologists regard these as rather minor and, ultimately, dependent on the genetic structures that allow such variation.

One of the best examples of such research has been conducted by Cosmides and Tooby on the existence of a cheater detection module (Cosmides and Tooby 1992). Cosmides and Tooby used a logic test called the Wason Selection Task as a means of determining whether we are uniquely adept at detecting cheaters, and do so better than when making logical deductions in other contexts. In the abstract form of the task, subjects are shown the four cards below and given the rule, "If a card has a D on one side, then it has 3 on the other." Subjects are then asked to determine which cards they should flip in order to ascertain if the rule is violated.

| D | F | 3 | 7 |

As any good logic student knows, the cards that should be turned over are the "D" card, since anything other than a three would violate the rule, and the "7" card, since a "D" on the reverse side of this card would also violate the rule. Somewhat surprisingly, most people get this wrong on the first try, usually being tempted to pick the "3" rather than the "7" card, even though anything could be on the reverse side of the "3" card and not violate the rule. The situation, however, is much different if subjects are instead asked to play the role of bartender and given the rule, "If a person is drinking beer, then the person must be twenty-one years old." When subjects are presented the four cards below, the majority (about 75 percent) choose the correct cards "drinking beer" and "16 years old."

drinking beer	drinking coke	25 years old	16 years old

After considering a number of alternative scenarios, Cosmides and Tooby conclude that human beings have a cheater's module built into their brains. Such a mental module would be of immense importance to humankind's hunter-gatherer past, when decisions about who to trust were of prime importance.

But if we have such mental modules, how did they evolve in the first place? Why are we as intelligent as we are? A wide number of candidates have been proposed over the years to account for how our own inordinate level of intelligence might be selected for, from tool use to the need to develop complex mental maps in order to find food. Several of the most influential hypotheses, however, link cognitive evolution with the need to live together as a group. One hypothesis, first suggested by Nicholas Humphrey and developed by Richard Byrne, Andrew Whiten, and others, suggests that it was the social pressures of living in increasingly large groups that required ever increasing brainpower in order to stay ahead (Byrne and Whiten 1988). This "Machiavellian intelligence," as Byrne and Whiten called it, required ever more sophisticated methods of keeping track of individuals, forming alliances, and mind-reading. The task of mind reading, or developing a theory of mind, is seen as particularly important, due to the great amount of cognitive sophistication it would require. If I know that you know what I know, I can make predictions on how you would act. Furthermore, you may try to deceive me (requiring that you know what I know). This would require new skills on your part, which in turn would prompt the selection of new skills on my part, the very cheater's module that Cosmides and Tooby describe.

The Machiavellian hypothesis can be taken two ways. On the one hand, social intelligence can occur only when there are large societies to begin with, so it suggests not only that cooperation is important for evolution, but that it is important for the evolution of intelligent beings specifically. Frans de Waal has argued that research on primate cooperation indicates that not only are strong social bonds characteristic of our species, they are found in primates as well and, as such, should be considered as part of our evolutionary heritage (de Waal 1996). For de Waal, we are moral not in spite of our nature but because of it. Thus, some primates are capable of sympathy with one another, demonstrated by comforting behavior given to those who have lost a conflict or by emotional distress sometimes recorded at the death of kin. Primate societies are made possible by a variety of cooperative behavioral strategies, from established social hierarchies to behaviors, such as grooming, which seem to function as a form of social calming. When conflict does erupt, a new hierarchy is established and, often enough, peacemaking behavior follows. Chimpanzees may reconcile with a kiss on the mouth, and bonobos provocatively enough seem to use sex to ease social tension.

On the other hand, the chosen title of the theory suggests that the kind of cooperation engaged in is of a not very pleasant kind. The ability to deceive and manipulate others plays a primary role, and it is no accident that experiments on deception and detection of deception form a major part of the research work. It is the ability to deceive and to detect deception that is, some argue, the driving force of the evolution of intelligence. To deceive requires being able to project intentions other than those you actually have, and (presumably) to recognize how those false intentions will be interpreted by another. To detect deception, on the other hand, requires not only an interpretation of the intentions revealed, but a correlation with other behavior and possible motives to detect whether the intentions expressed are genuine or false. Even when cooperation does occur, however, a negative side is apparent. One form of cooperation that has received significant attention by de Waal is the capacity for alliance formation by chimpanzees (de Waal 2000). Like other primates, chimpanzees establish a dominance hierarchy, headed by an alpha male who typically possesses food and reproductive privileges. While the alpha male in theory holds all the power, his power is dependent on the tacit support of the group. Inevitably, however, challenges arise. Challengers form their own groups, resulting in the formation of competing coalitions that may vie with one another over prolonged periods, until one or the other side is defeated. Conflict, it would seem, is at the very heart of cooperation.

Organized to Self-Organize

The claims of evolutionary psychology and cognitive evolution have a certain kind of surface plausibility. Obviously, it would seem, if humans are a product of evolution, then it should follow that we will see this fact manifested in the specific nature of our being. Once we accept the primacy of competition, not only with our environment but also in the group and between the sexes, as many evolutionary psychologists do, then evolutionary theory provides a solid basis for studying human behavior. Such straightforward reasoning, however, hides a host of hidden premises that make evolutionary accounts of human nature and cognition difficult to establish. For those familiar with the study of human origins, the first major problem is simply identifying what life was like for the earliest members of the species during the Pleistocene. Too often, an outdated view of "man the hunter" and "woman the nurturer/ gatherer" is simply assumed, together with the sexist assumptions that such a scenario originally implied. Among paleontologists, however, this view is currently under assault. It has been suggested, for instance, that the dramatic hunting of large mammals was not characteristic of everyday life of Pleistocene peoples. If so, this would alter our understanding of male and female roles during the Pleistocene and, therefore, the roots of our evolutionary psychology today (Jolly 1999). To put the problem more generally, we are using one tentative scientific construction (lifestyle and culture of Pleistocene hunter-gatherers) to develop another (fitness-enhancing mental modules that influence behavior). If we are uncertain in important ways about one, this prevents us from being unduly confident about the other. This does not mean that no evolutionary connection should be made or hypothesized, only that we must be appropriately cautious, particularly when we start to hone in on issues, such as sexual morality and gender roles, which are of great cultural importance.

Despite these considerations, the core issue remains. How do genes produce brains? One of the greatest mysteries of the biological sciences (not to mention life in general) is how the individual fertilized egg transforms into the beautiful complexity of a whole organism. It is now estimated that there are some thirty thousand to forty thousand genes that, in the context of their cellular and extra-cellular environment, are responsible for the development, organization, and, in many ways, the maintenance of the body. The fact that this includes the development of the human brain is all the more remarkable when we recall that the difference between ourselves and chimpanzees on the genetic level is, on average, less than 2 percent.

Genes are clearly important for proper development and the physical character of the body. Are they important for behavior as well? Evolutionary psychologists such as Cosmides and Tooby have argued that genes program mental modules that form the Swiss army knife that is the brain. Each module is programmed for a specific, adaptive function that enhances our reproductive fitness. Furthermore, many of these modules operate on an unconscious level, manipulating us in ways that we are not aware of. This emphasis on the unconscious manipulation of such modules gives evolutionary psychology a Freudian cast that is quite different from much of the rest of cognitive science.

The notion of mental modules has some plausibility, but how are such modules linked to our genes? Evolutionary psychologists argue that genes directly program specific mental modules, which in turn program our behavior in relatively rigid ways. Evidence from genetics, however, suggests otherwise, although the story is much more complex than it is usually perceived to be. In the popular press but much less so among scientists, the relationship between genes and traits is understood in terms of direct correlation. That is, for every gene, there is a single, specified trait. On this analysis, we should be able to identify specific genes for specific kinds of behavior. With a few exceptions, such efforts have been significantly unsuccessful. While there have been a number of claims for the discovery of genes for such traits as alcoholism, risk-taking, and homosexuality, none have stood up to serious scrutiny. Indeed, it would be surprising if such claims did hold up. The relation between genes and the traits to which they contribute is far more complex than is usually given credit for, and this is especially true for complex behavioral traits. Genes do not code for behaviors directly, but for specific proteins that play important roles in cellular function and development, the organization of which emerges in the behavior of the whole organism. The impact of genes on behavior and development can often occur in tandem with environmental cues and in interaction with other genes as well.

This does not mean, however, that no links can be made. The most successful studies in this regard have been of monozygotic (identical) twins who were separated at birth and adopted by different families. Studies have generally shown that identical twins reared together are more similar to one another on any given trait than those who are raised apart, but identical twins raised apart are more similar than dizygotic (fraternal) twins. Such studies have shown important correlations for relationships of genes to intelligence as well as for more specifically behavioral traits. Thus, a study conducted by Lindon Eaves compared monozygotic and dizygotic twins on such items as church attendance, educational attainment, sexual permissiveness, and attitudes toward issues such as economics, politics, and the Religious Right (Eaves 1997). In all cases, the study found significant correlations with genetic relatedness. For example, the likelihood of female fraternal twins to share political attitudes was about 28 percent; for female identical twins raised apart the percentage jumps to 47 percent. The likelihood of male fraternal twins to have the same attitudes toward the Religious Right was 31 percent; this likelihood jumps to 51 percent for male identical twins, a surely significant difference!

Do gene complexes program for religious and political values? Not at all. It is more likely that genes program for a complex set of physical traits that in turn lead to certain kinds of personality characteristics, which in turn lead to certain propensities for certain kinds of positions and attitudes within a broader cultural context. The cultural context is certainly not insignificant. If it is indeed the case that there is a genetic component to the development of a kind of personality that would (statistically speaking) find political conservatism more appealing, what counts as politically conservative would vary considerably if one lives in the contemporary United States as opposed to post-Soviet Russia or revolutionary France.

The story is likely even much more complicated than this. While there are about thirty thousand to forty thousand genes in the human genome, there are on the order of 100 billion neurons in the human brain. Not only is it impossible for so few genes to program instructions for every neuron, it is unlikely that genes program the brain in the narrowly specific way that is sometimes suggested by evolutionary psychologists. Indeed, it seems increasingly likely that what genes do, in no small way, is to organize the brain to organize itself. We are born with far more neurons than we end up with, the reason being that during the first years of life the brain experiences a massive die-off of neurons. Why? There is good reason to suppose that during this focal period the mind/brain is essentially programming itself on the fly. Gerald Edelman in particular has developed the hypothesis that brain development is itself a very Darwinian process (Edelman 1987). Once exposed to the appropriate stimuli, neurons go through a process of selection and self-organization. Those that self-organize appropriately survive; those that do not are weeded out. The practical import of this fact is that not only is the proper environment important for development, but the actions of the child are as well. It should be emphasized, contrary to the impression that one might get from evolutionary psychology, that a child's learning process is quite dynamic. A child learns not simply by listening and seeing but by doing.

This suggests that any genetic programming that does go on is a complex interaction of genes, body, environment, and self that is difficult to disentangle. In the case of language, for instance, we may argue that there is a strong genetic component for learning language. This is something that all normal humans do but that seems almost completely inaccessible to other species. Moreover, language learning seems to occur at specific developmental stages. Children who suffer significantly delayed language learning because of a deprived environment will have permanent impairments, a situation which has analogues for vision and personality traits as well.

Other abilities, however, may involve not so much a directly inherited trait as what might be called a cognitive forced move. It is notable that Cosmides and Tooby fail to seriously consider that cheater detection might be a learned behavior of the forced-move kind; that is, dealing with cheaters is frequent enough and significant enough in life that we learn to become quite good at it. It would be interesting if Cosmides and Tooby extended their research to children and combined their work with brain scan and brain lesion studies. Would these show a neurological basis to cheater detection, and would they show it developing at certain stages in life? More important, can the failure to detect cheaters be associated with the lack of a certain gene? I would be surprised if we could show this in any straightforward sense. We can safely say that cheater detection must ultimately have *some* genetic basis, inasmuch that cheater detection is limited to humans and perhaps some primates. But the full story of cheater detection likely involves much more: the interaction of genes-body-mind-self-environment in complex historical interaction. Because this part of the story is similar enough for all of us, virtually all of us are good at cheater detection, but the independent pathways by which we arrive at such a development may be quite different.

Because of complexities of this sort, Francisco Ayala has argued that morality is an indirect result of our more general abilities for intelligence and self-consciousness (Ayala 1998). On Ayala's account, we are not moral because of certain genes that program for morality; we are moral because we are intelligent, self-conscious beings who need to develop moral systems in order to survive and get along. While there is much that is right in this view, I would suggest that it is too weak. Rather, our human nature is complex and multifaceted, influenced by a number of important elements. The genes we have are due to our evolutionary history, a history in which natural selection has played an important role. The genes we have encode for basic physical traits, although such encoding may be significantly sensitive to environmental cues. In the case of the brain, genes set the pattern but do not determine development. Acknowledging this, we may say that genes do contribute significantly to behavioral traits, but that the genetic story is not the only story. Self-culture-environment interactions play an important role. Any satisfactory account of human nature must inevitably include all these levels of analysis.

Realizing this, however, quickly leads one to the conclusion that a strictly biological account of human nature must necessarily be incomplete. Human nature is not simply a matter of genes, and human morality is not simply a matter of cooperation and competition. Rather, it would be more accurate to say that evolutionary biology is the context out of which human nature and human morality emerges. Indeed, it is because of the startlingly excessive character of human intelligence and the extreme plasticity of human behavior that the development of moral codes and, more generally, a moral worldview is even necessary. We are likely the only creatures on Earth who can not only foresee our own death but see beyond it as well. Out of such a context come both tragedy and hope.

Falling Up

How, then, are we to think of ourselves? Theologically, we are said to be originally in the image of God, yet in some sense fallen or incomplete. A scientifically informed perspective suggests that our nature is in no small part a legacy of our evolutionary heritage and our own particular biology. It also suggests, however, that evolution and genes are only part of the story, that our very nature as cognitive, thinking beings makes us subtle, complex, and, in a real sense, free in a way that other organisms are not — so much so, in fact, that we appear capable of overriding what would be in other species basic and inviolable biological drives. We can fast, abstain from sex, and even sacrifice ourselves for others. Such freedom from biological constraints and the ability to overcome them is not always for the good. While rare, parents who kill or abuse their own children are as difficult to explain biologically as the saint who sacrifices all.

Does the scientific account of human nature influence the theological one? On a number of levels, what the biological and cognitive sciences tell us coheres strongly with theological perspectives on human nature. At the same time, however, they may also require subtle shifts on how we think about this most basic of questions.

The origins of sinfulness, it would seem, are rooted not in the act of an original, historical couple, but in the complicated evolutionary process itself. At first blush, such a claim may seem to be at odds with a genuinely theological account of human nature. Where, after all, is God amidst all this suffering? Yet, strictly speaking, such a perspective is not in direct conflict with the theological tradition, and further reflection suggests that there is much to commend it. The apostle Paul himself speaks of the "groaning of creation" (Rom. 8:22), and the book of Revelation speaks not simply of human redemption but of a new heaven and earth. The real difficulty lies in expressing such poetry in a way that makes sense. It is only recently that theologians have begun to take up this task.

On the level of theodicy, John Polkinghorne has argued that freedom is not a category limited to human beings but is in some sense characteristic of the universe as a whole (Polkinghorne 1996). Whereas a traditional move has been to explain the existence of evil as being due to human freedom (with natural evil a result of the fall), Polkinghorne has argued that it is the freedom of creation as a whole that is the cause of suffering in the cosmos. On Polkinghorne's account, then, our fallenness stems from the freedom that God gave the cosmos to begin with, a freedom that is, at least in theory, worth the price of suffering and pain. The implication for human nature is that we are indeed, as Augustine and Luther argued, each in his or her own way, bound to suffer and even to sin. This boundedness is not due to the lust of our parents but to the constraints that evolution itself has placed on human nature. To amplify Polkinghorne's position, we are who we are because of our biological heritage. That heritage provides us with the ability to compete and to cooperate but inevitably compels us to do so in a way that often falls short of our true potential.

Yet there is more that needs to be said. Our current state is portrayed in terms of fallenness, and original sin is understood in terms of the biological and social forces that impel us to *hamartia,* to miss the mark. Calling these biological and social forces "sin," however, is objectionable to some. Denis Edwards, for instance, limits sin to our own voluntary acts (Edwards 1999). On his view, original sin is the sum history of such voluntary acts that each of us, as an individual, has inherited. Original sin is not truly sin as such, since one has no choice in one's inherited history. Moreover, original sin does not include our evolutionary and biological heritage, even though it is acknowledged that we are a "fallible symbiosis of genes and culture" (Edwards 1999, 65).

I would suggest, however, that Edwards's limitation of the category of sin to our own volitional actions is too limiting. Creation as a whole also misses the mark, filled as it is with both beauty and tragedy. Nevertheless, the fallenness of creation, however we may want to characterize it, is not of the same kind as our own fallenness. Liberation theologians, in speaking of the economic and political forces that often overwhelm individual choices, refer to sinful structures. Something similar might be said of natural processes that have their own limiting influences.

Ultimately, however, this approach to natural history and human nature is incomplete, for it fails to explain why there needs to be a distinction between the fallenness of creation and the fallenness of human beings. Here, once again, our nature as cognitive beings plays an important role. Rocks neither feel pain nor suffer anguish. Conceivably, the victims of Darwin's digger wasps suffered pain, although we can perhaps never know whether insects possess conscious experience of anything. Certainly, insects do not experience anguish, and one would be surprised to see a praying mantis mourning over the loss of its young. Anguish is something that humans experience, and which we share, at best, with only a select group of other mammals. In recognizing this, we begin to recognize more fully the character of human nature, for our increased complexity and increased freedom implies, it would seem, an increased capacity to suffer. When Augustine spoke of the fall, he spoke of it as a once and for all event that occurred at a historical point in time. Such a static view, however, is at odds with the fecundity and creativity present in the evolutionary process. In an evolutionary framework, it might be more accurate to speak not of "the fall" but of *falling*. Here, Irenaeus may prove to be more insightful than Augustine in emphasizing suffering as the result of our immaturity. In an evolutionary context, immaturity is not simply that of our own species but of all conscious life. As each new species and even individual comes to be, we see the advent of something new, full of potential but also impeded by tragic limitations.

Recognizing this, we might speak not simply of falling but of *falling up*. However we may construe the cause, the history of life on Earth has been characterized by the continuing appearance of increasingly complex organisms. Increased complexity allows for increased freedom, which in turn allows for greater potential for both good and evil. The emergence of our own species, *Homo sapiens*, is testimony to this fact. The great plasticity of our behavior allows us to act selfishly, to cooperate, and even to cooperate selfishly. Yet our freedom is not complete, and all too often we find ourselves constrained by both biology and culture, unwilling and sometimes simply unable to do the good. As such, falling is in a significant sense a psychological event, both for each of us individually and for our species as a whole. The psychological character of fallenness was first given prominent attention by Søren Kierkegaard, who understood fallenness as a necessary concomitant of human freedom and the anxiety it produces (Kierkegaard [1844] 1981). Falling is not simply what happens to us, it is what we do. But it is only because of our considerable sophistication that we do it in the first place, and it is because of our psychological sophistication that such falling seems an inevitable consequence of human freedom.

Falling, however, indicates only the negative side of human nature. That we are falling up better suggests the full complexity of human nature. We are, indeed, capable of truly good and wonderful things. This complexity of human nature is suggested in John Haught's account of original sin in *God after Darwin* (2001). Haught acknowledges the constraints of our evolutionary heritage but also emphasizes the need for eschatological hope. Rather than lamenting the loss of a paradisiacal past that never existed, we should look forward to the future yet to come. Indeed, it is this ability to envision and even in limited ways to implement realities that have never existed that characterizes the kind of freedom, the kind of nature, that we have.

REFERENCES

Ayala, Francisco. 1998. Human nature: One evolutionist's view. In *Whatever Happened to the Soul? Scientific and Theological Portraits of Human Nature*, ed. Warren S. Brown, Nancey Murphy, and H. Newton Malony. Minneapolis: Fortress.

Byrne, Richard W., and Andrew Whiten. 1988. *Machiavellian Intelligence: Social Expertise and the Evolution of Intellect in Monkeys, Apes, and Humans*. Oxford: Clarendon.

Cosmides, Leda, and John Tooby. 1992. Cognitive adaptations for social exchange. In *The Adapted Mind: Evolutionary Psychology and the Generation of Culture*, ed. Jerome H. Barkow, Leda Cosmides, and John Tooby. New York: Oxford University Press.

de Waal, Frans. 1996. *Good Natured: The Origins of Right and Wrong in Humans and Other Animals*. Cambridge, Mass.: Harvard University Press.

————. 2000. *Chimpanzee Politics: Power and Sex among the Apes*. Baltimore: Johns Hopkins University Press.

Eaves, Lindon. 1997. Behavioral genetics, or what's missing from theological anthropology? In *Beginning with the End: God, Science, and Wolfhart Pannenberg*, ed. Carol Rausch Albright and Joel Haugen. Chicago: Open Court.

Edelman, Gerald. 1987. *Neural Darwinism: The Theory of Neuronal Group Selection*. New York: Basic.

Edwards, Denis. 1999. *The God of Evolution: A Trinitarian Theology*. New York: Paulist.

Haught, John. 2001. *God after Darwin: A Theology of Evolution*. Boulder, Colo.: Westview.

Jolly, Alison. 1999. *Lucy's Legacy: Sex and Intelligence in Human Evolution*. Cambridge, Mass.: Harvard University Press.

Kierkegaard, Søren. [1844] 1981. *The Concept of Anxiety*. Translated by Reidar Thomte and Albert B. Anderson. Princeton, N.J.: Princeton University Press.

Polkinghorne, John. 1996. *The Faith of a Physicist: Reflections of a Bottom-Up Thinker*. Minneapolis: Fortress.

Tooby, John, and Leda Cosmides. 1992. The psychological foundations of culture. In *The Adapted Mind: Evolutionary Psychology and the Generation of Culture*, ed. Jerome H. Barkow, Leda Cosmides, and John Tooby. New York: Oxford University Press.

15. Morals, Love, and Relations in Evolutionary Theory

Thomas Jay Oord

The Love-and-Science Symbiosis

For more than a century now, many Christians have been apprehensive about what they believe are implications of evolutionary theories. This worry has little to do with the age of the earth or the fossil record — although these matters are important. Instead, the worry has to do with the apparent continuity between humans and the rest of the animal world. Recent studies in primatology by the likes of Christopher Boehm (1999), Frans de Waal (1996), and Jane Goodall (1986), and research in neurology by Antonio Damasio (1994) and Thomas Lewis (2000), have only strengthened the belief that humans share an enormous amount in common with nonhumans. In addition, the mapping of the human genome by project leaders Francis Collins and Craig Ventor reveals the vast similarities between humans and nonhumans. Ventor recently remarked, in fact, "If we showed you the mouse genome today, you would not be able to tell its difference from the human genome" (Oord 2001, 2). The oft-quoted words of Mary Midgley — "We are not just rather like animals; we *are* animals" — ring true now more than ever ([1978] 1995, xiii).

The continuity between humans and nonhumans is allegedly not limited to physical and social similarities. Recent scientific evidence and theories emphasize moral correlations between humans and nonhumans as well. The moral behaviors of humans apparently reflect or are extensions of nonhuman ways of living (Katz 2000; Drees 2003). If interactions between humans reflect interactions between nonhumans, the questions arise: What laws or habits regulate nonhuman interactions? And how do these laws or forces affect human morality?

In the previous twenty years or so, those engaged in sociobiology have taken the lead in suggesting theories of nonhuman interaction and what these theories imply for morality. Sociobiology pertains, as E. O. Wilson puts it, to "the biological basis of all social behavior" (1978, 579), and numerous scholars currently bring sociobiological theories to bear on questions of human morality. The majority of those in the field of sociobiology accept as empirically justified the claim that organisms must act selfishly if they are to survive, thrive, and be reproductively successful. Selfishness allegedly drives the engine of evolution, and organisms whose genetic structures help them live and reproduce are those whose genes best promote organismic self-interest. Today, it seems that even the "man on the street" is aware of notorious claims about selfish genes (Dawkins 1989).

Scientific research in the past century, however, indicates that some animal behavior appears to be altruistic rather than egoistic. Various theories seeking to account for this altruism have gained prominence in the scientific literature in the past decades. Many theories assume that whenever organisms seem to act altruistically, they are actually motivated by or survive because of selfish reasons. For instance, the tit-for-tat (or reciprocal) altruism explanation suggests that an organism acts self-sacrificially only when expecting a beneficial response (Trivers 1971; Axelrod and Hamilton 1981). Kin-selection theory suggests that organisms act altruistically in ways that undermine their own survival in order to propagate their genetic lineage. In the case of kin-selection, the selfish inclination to ensure the proliferation of one's genes motivates altruistic actions toward those whose genes are most like the altruist's (Hamilton 1963).

Elliott Sober and David Sloan Wilson have recently offered a group-selection explanation for altruism. This theory suggests that altruists thrive as a group when in competition with groups composed of selfish individuals. "To be sufficient," argue Sober and Wilson, "the differential fitness of groups (the force favoring the altruist) must be strong enough to counter the differential fitness of individuals within groups (the force favoring the selfish types)" (1998, 26). Admittedly, the group-selection theory goes a long way in accounting for how altruism might emerge and succeed, and Wilson has recently employed the theory to account for altruism emergent in religious groups (2002). But, as the authors readily admit, group-selection theory also suggests that "niceness" can predominate within a group while "nastiness" prevails between groups (Sober and Wilson 1998, 9). From this perspective, altruism toward the outsider remains unexplained.

If evolutionary theory entails that humans, like all other animals, are inevitably and invariably selfish, it is little wonder that many Christians are apprehensive about evidence suggesting enormous continuity between human and nonhuman animals. Evolutionary theories claiming that all animals, including humans, are inherently selfish undermine the communal nature of religion in general and the Christian emphasis upon self-sacrifice in particular. Perhaps from the beginning Christians have been hoodwinked to think that morality could or should include altruistic behavior. Philosopher J. L. Mackie may be correct after all when he argues that Christianity promotes a morality for "suckers" (1978, 464).

Perhaps the most effective response to the claim that humans, like all other animals, are inevitably selfish comes from human experience itself. Reports of Christian and non-Christian altruism are common. The recent sociological scholarship of Pearl and Samuel Oliner on the rescuers of Jews during the Nazi Holocaust, for instance, provides case studies of individuals who risked their own interest for the sake of others (1988). Samuel Oliner joins others in noting that many acted altruistically when responding to the crisis of 9/11 in the United States (2003). Kristen Renwick Monroe's recent analysis of such altruistic rescuers corresponds with the Oliners' (1996). These examples and countless others, along with our own personal recollections of how we have acted altruistically, provide empirical evidence that humans can and do act self-sacrificially.

Christians often label altruistic behavior with a word that lies at the heart of how they understand God, the world, and their own obligations. That word is "love." Many believe that Jesus, in his life and death, is the archetype of such self-sacrificial giving. And Jesus explained what love should look like by, among other ways, referring to a story about a good Samaritan man who helped his enemy — a beaten and dying Jew. While the Christian tradition has generally encouraged love of God, family, friends, spouse, and oneself, many have suggested that the self-sacrificial love of one's enemy represents a distinctively Christian contribution to ethics (Grant 2001).

How might these apparently contradictory claims — the claim by some scientific theorists that all organisms are inherently selfish or at least not altruistic toward outsiders, and the claim by Christians and others that some people sometimes act unselfishly or self-sacrificially for the sake of enemies — be reconciled? The work to square scientific theory with the empirical and religious evidence related to love and altruism represents an important project for a new realm of scholarship I call the "love-and-science symbiosis." Scholars engaged in this work investigate science and love as each contributes to how we understand ourselves and the world in which we live.

While it is true that many since antiquity have at least implicitly affirmed a relationship between science and love, the contemporary discussion addresses overtly and methodologically various issues arising in this conversation. Many are finding that the association of love and science generates abundant possibilities for creative transformation (see, for instance, Batson

1993; Hefner 1993; Kagan 1998; Lewis et al. 2000; Murphy and Ellis 1996; Oliner et al. 1992; Oord 2002a and 2003; Polkinghorne 2001; Pope 1994; Post et al. 2002 and 2003; Rolston 1999; Walsh 1991). If love resides at the core of humanity's moral and religious concerns and if science continues to sculpt humanity's ways of living and its worldviews, those working on the love-and-science symbiosis will likely find themselves engaged in matters of enormous consequence.

Many Christians working on the love-and-science symbiosis and attempting to build bridges between Christianity and evolutionary accounts of the human have referred to the self-sacrificial love of altruism as *agape*. But an examination of the literature pertaining to *agape* reveals that scholars of ethics, culture, and religion propose widely divergent definitions of this word for love. Some, following theologian Anders Nygren's lead, simply employ *agape* to distinguish it from other love-types, particularly *eros* and *philia* (Nygren 1969; Soble 1989). Ethicist Gene Outka uses *agape* to refer to an ethics of impartiality or equal-regard (1997). Some draw upon *agape* to specify what they call variously "unconditional," "pure," or "unlimited" love, with the latter designation entailing universal acceptance of others (Post et al. 2002). *Agape* has been defined as gift-love (Lewis 1960) and as bestowal (Singer [1966] 1984). Elsewhere, I have classified *agape* love as action that promotes well-being when responding to activity that has generated ill-being, which is another way of saying that *agape* repays evil with good (Oord 2002a). These definitions obviously generate or reflect widely divergent agendas, expectations, religious orientations, and philosophical presuppositions. The words of Robert Adams apply well to this diversity: "'Agape' is a blank canvas on which one can paint whatever ideal of Christian love one favors" (1999, 136).

What the love-and-science symbiosis seems to need is a definition of love that can incorporate what should be said about *agape* and other appropriate forms of love, while also providing a point of reference for comparison and contrast with various scientific theories. With this in mind, I suggest that love ought to be defined in this way: *To love is to act intentionally, in sympathetic response to others (including God), to increase overall well-being.* Love acts are influenced by previous actions and executed in the hope of attaining a high degree of common good.

This love definition implies that love requires various factors before it can be expressed. In the remainder of this chapter, I explore one aspect of love: relatedness. Love, as I have defined it and as generally conceived, requires relations. The work of science also requires that existing things be related. The most helpful theory of relations, which is applicable to both religious love and scientific endeavor, comes from the process-relational philosophical tradition. I suggest that an open and relational view of reality, which draws from process-philosophical and scientific resources, provides both a framework to account for the continuity between humans and nonhumans, and a conception of a God who can inspire all animals to act altruistically.

Science and Organismic Relatedess

The general principles of science and the practices of scientists presuppose that existing things relate to other existing things. Unfortunately, this presupposition is rarely made explicit in contemporary scientific writing. From theories of relativity and interactions in the micro-world explored by physicists to social theories pertaining to global politics and economics proposed by social scientists, the often-unstated assumption is that cause and effect occurs because existing things relate one with another.

Evolutionary theory, however, perhaps *most explicitly* assumes the relatedness of existence. Although a great deal of debate occurs today about which mechanisms drive evolution, the majority of those engaged in evolutionary research and debate agree that biological life emerges through a process of random variations, natural selection, and adaptation to an environment. Evolutionary theory assumes that nature is a network of interacting organisms, and various forms of organismic life arise through interaction and, at least to some degree, chance.

Mendelian-inspired genetic theory points to the variations of genes as a crucial factor in the evolution of life. The thesis that evolution implies relatedness is evident in the Mendelian claim that genetic variations are passed on through reproduction. Although few today would argue that the organism purposefully acts in ways to change its own genetic structure, many do assume that mutations occur among genes because of relations within an environment. Often tragic occurrences, like the effects of radiation on humans after the Chernobyl nuclear disaster, illustrate the profound influence of a gene's environmental relations. Furthermore, because some organisms select — at least to some extent — the environment in which they relate, some individuals indirectly affect the mutation of their own genes. Some people choose to remain in homes in which high levels of radon have been detected, for example, and this choice results in these individuals being exposed to gene-altering radiation.

More and more scientists are suggesting that science needs to understand genes themselves as involved in give-and-take relatedness. For instance, Stuart Kauffman argues that proteins affect genes, and this relationship in turn affects the mutation or recombination of the genetic structure (1985; 1995). Ford Doolittle argues even more strongly for what amounts to inter-genetic acquisition and exchange, and believes that this relational activity "may be the dominant force over the evolutionary long run" (Doolittle in Oord 2002b, 30). A full explanation of the variety of genetic relations, however, has not been successfully advanced. "Causation is not thought about very deeply in genomics," admits biologist Adam Arkin of the University of California at Berkeley. "We have not derived the dynamical laws for the genomes. We are simply hitting the cell and hearing what the ring sounds like" (Arkin in Oord 2002b, 30).

Darwin's classic evolutionary position is that the particular environment in which an individual organism emerges largely shapes whether that organism will survive and/or thrive. In other words, relations in an environment play a large role in influencing how an organism gains an advantage over other organisms competing for the same resources. In fact, those concerned with the practices that destroy the ecosystems in which these individuals live document the negative effects of environmental damage on individual organisms. This individual selection approach remains a powerful explanatory force in contemporary biology, although some suggest that a multi-level selection approach accounts for more of the data.

While for several decades individual selection has played an almost exclusive explanatory role in evolutionary theory, recent years suggest a shift to the explanatory power of group-selection theory. Group-selection theory also illustrates my thesis that evolutionary theory presupposes organismic relatedness. Some survive or thrive and others do not, says the group-selection hypothesis, because of intra-group cooperation and inter-species interaction. As I noted earlier, Sober and Wilson document growing evidence that groups serve as adaptive units. The selection factors involving how one group fares compared to other groups function as key evolutionary operatives (1998, chaps. 1-5). In his research published as *Cooperation among Animals: An Evolutionary Perspective,* biologist Lee Alan Dugatkin chronicles this fitness advantage of intra-group cooperative relatedness. In fact, Dugatkin devotes individual chapters to examining scientific research on cooperation through relations among fish, birds, nonprimate mammals, nonhuman primate mammals, and insects (1997, chaps. 3-7).

Perhaps biologists detect examples of relational interaction more readily among complex nonhuman creatures because the behavior of these creatures more closely corresponds with human behavior than with behavior among entities at the molecular level. In fact, some argue that these examples of rela-

tions and interaction by nonhuman entities are nothing more than anthropo-
morphic projections by scientific observers. This debate hinges on an
epistemological issue concerning how one knows about the experience and
behavior of those beyond oneself.

An essential aspect of an adequate epistemology is the contention that
what we know best — our own experience — should inform our theories of
knowledge. An epistemology based upon introspection and extrapolation
from personal experience is a necessary element in speculating about the experiences and behaviors of those beyond us. This principle also applies to
what might be said about our knowledge of nonhuman relations. If accepted,
this epistemological principle may go a long way toward discrediting the
claims that humans must invariably be egoistic because we "know" that
nonhumans are so. After all, to begin with what we know least — including,
for instance, the activity of genes — and then to impose this meager data
upon what we know best — our own experience — cannot suffice. This practice led to the unlivable scientific philosophies that emerged in the nineteenth
and twentieth centuries through the reflection of Thomas Hobbes, David
Hume, and the logical positivists.

The epistemological work to be done requires formulating the ways and
degrees to which nonhuman experiences, including relatedness, are analogous to our own experience. This involves making inferences about the experiential states of nonhumans. This practice need not be overly worrisome, because such inferences are not different in kind from inferences we make about
human states. In terms of love, this involves analyzing the structures of human experience while also accounting for what we can perceive with regard
to nonhuman experience. The love that humans express is likely not different
in kind from the love of nonhumans, although observers will likely find that
human love differs from nonhuman love in degree and complexity. Jessica
Flack and Frans de Waal's principle of evolutionary parsimony applies here,
in the sense that we should postulate similarities between humans and
nonhumans along a continuum (Flack and de Waal in Katz 2000, 72). Compelling evidence that humans and nonhumans differ would be required before we should reject these postulated similarities.

That humans relate one with another via cause and effect can only be denied at the peril of committing a performative self-contradiction. Our knowledge of this is as definite as almost anything we claim to know. That is, while
someone may verbally deny the notion that humans are influenced through
relations with others, each of us inevitably exhibits in practice cause-and-
effect relations. David Ray Griffin calls these presumptions "hard-core
commonsense notions," by which he means those beliefs that everyone af-

firms in practice although some may deny them verbally. "We can be confident that particular ideas belong to our set of hard-core commonsense beliefs," argues Griffin, "insofar as we see that they are inevitably presupposed by all human beings, regardless of cultural-linguistic shaping" (2001, 362). This means that "any scientific, philosophical, or theological theory is irrational to the extent that it contradicts whatever notions we inevitably presuppose in practice" (2001, 30).

Relatedness through causal influence is one hard-core commonsense notion that everyone assumes in practice. Scientists assume causal influence through relatedness each time they engage in scientific experimentation. The actions of scientists toward and observation of data beyond themselves reveal their implicit acknowledgement that they experience cause-and-effect relations with what they study. Ironically, any scientist who attempts to convince others that cause-and-effect relations do not exist affirms such relations in that very attempt.

If love requires relations, if humans inevitably relate in cause-and-effect interaction, and if nonhuman organisms down to the smallest of entities apparently also express interactive relations, one seems justified in claiming that relatedness is a natural expression of what it means to be. To say it another way, organismic relatedness is not an emergent property requiring unnatural forces. The ability to love — at least as far as relatedness is concerned — is in principle also available to nonhumans. The apprehension Christians feel about the moral continuity between human and nonhuman animals can be greatly alleviated by viewing the nonhuman world as also capable of genuine altruism analogous to that which humans express. Such analogies are possible, in part, because of the relatedness of all animals — both human and nonhuman.

A Theory of Relations Adequate for Love

The previous paragraphs have shown that scientific theory and the actual practice of scientists presuppose that existing things relate to other existing things. Organismic relatedness resides at the heart of how we understand the world and act in it. Not only does general science refrain from creating obstacles to the claim that organisms relate, but the one who constructs a theory of love adequate for the love-and-science symbiosis can turn to science for an ally to establish the fact of relatedness.

To acknowledge that (1) love requires relations and (2) scientific theory and practice presuppose organismic relatedness does not, in itself, supply a conceptual framework for comprehending love relations. For such a framework, I turn to the process and relational philosophy of Alfred North Whitehead. Those in the science-and-religion dialogue have often acknowledged that their conversation actually involves a triad of speakers, with philosophy entering as the third party. Whitehead himself believed this to be the case, arguing that we "cannot shelter theology from science, or science from theology; nor can [we] shelter either one from metaphysics, or metaphysics from either one of them. There is no shortcut to the truth" ([1926] 1996, 79). The love-and-science symbiosis would do well to turn to Whitehead specifically, and process, openness, and relational thought generally, for the philosophical element of its conversational triad.

The ultimacy of relations in Whitehead's metaphysical scheme leads many to consider him a "relational" philosopher, and the theology that has emerged from his influence has been referred to as "relational theology." Because all organisms are influenced through their relations with others, Whitehead speculates that existence consists of the "essential relatedness of all things" ([1933] 1968, 227-28). This emphasis upon relations and its implications for what might be said about organismic relations is one reason Whitehead's thought assists the love-and-science symbiosis.

At the heart of Whitehead's philosophical proposals is his speculation that all existing things are experiential. Moments of experience are, as he puts it, "the final real things of which the world is made up" ([1929] 1978, 18). Although the specific constitutions of each experiential entity differ radically, "in the principles which actuality exemplifies, all are on the same level" ([1929] 1978, 18). Whitehead contrasts existing things as experiential with that which he believed to be fictional: nonexperiencing substances, or "vacuous actualities" ([1929] 1978, 29). Griffin employs the word "panexperientialism" to capture the claim that all existing entities, from complex creatures like humans to less complex organisms, are experiential. The value that the panexperientialist hypothesis might contribute for science, culture, religion, and philosophy is, as Griffin has argued, enormous (2001).

The vast majority of experiential entities that scientists study are what Whitehead called enduring individuals. To be more technical, Whitehead said that such organisms are personally ordered societies of occasions of experience. A "society" is a set of entities whose members share a defining characteristic mainly as a result of the environment provided by the society itself. "Personal order" means that the society inherits the form of the whole from its predecessor and then hands that form on to its successor. A living person is an enduring individual who inherits its basic structure from its personal past but whose immediate self-determination is unique ([1929] 1978, 89-91). This accounts for the continuous self-identity that creatures experience without making self-identity absolute, in the sense of the absence of any personal change. Enduring individuals are experiential organisms that relate to others.

The hypothesis that all existing organisms are fundamentally experiential provides a crucial basis for constructing an adequate and coherent theory of love. With regard to its value for understanding organismic relatedness as a prerequisite for love, it provides a basis for conceptualizing how organisms are both internally and externally related to others. Distinguishing relatedness into these two types of relations allows one to clarify more precisely what it means to say that all organisms relate and that love requires relations.

By "internal relations," I mean that each experiential organism becomes what it is by its partial inclusion of prior experiences. Whitehead calls the activity of past organisms upon an organism presently in the throes of becoming a "prehension" ([1929] 1978, 41). Through an organism's relations with past others, the "production of novel togetherness" occurs ([1929] 1978, 21). This means that "every actual entity is what it is and is with its definite status in the universe," says Whitehead, because "its internal relations to other actual entities" shape it ([1929] 1978, 59). Each experiential organism begins with an openness to the past, and this open window makes possible the organism's internal relations. Once the influence from the past has entered in, the window closes. The organism enjoys a moment of what biologists call "autopoiesis" as it forms itself in response to past influences. To be constituted internally by those who have come before is the very nature of what it means to arise into existence. To say it another way, every actuality has arisen from the multiplicity of its internal relations.

My definition of love includes the phrase "in sympathetic response" to account for the internal relations of organisms. The actions of lovers do not emerge *ex nihilo;* relations with one's community come prior to individual decision and contribution. Love arises out of sympathetic response to preceding actions. To put it another way, love begins by feeling the feelings of others. My notion that love arises in sympathetic response corresponds with the practice of ethicists, philosophers, and religious scholars who speak of love as tendential, compassionate, or affect-centered (Hazo 1967; Pope 1995).

Sympathetic response that is possible due to internal relatedness provides the basis for what biologists call an organism's "plasticity." Given that plasticity refers to the changes that occur through time as an organism adapts to its environment, claims about organismic plasticity may be identical to claims about the internal relatedness organisms experience toward others.

By the phrase "external relations," I mean that once an organism comes to be, it affects other organisms that will arise in the future. Whitehead likes to explain this influence upon future others by saying that "it belongs to the nature of a 'being' that it is a potential for every 'becoming'" ([1929] 1978, 22). Just as each organism, through its internal relations, drew upon its relations with others as it came into existence, each organism subsequently becomes a datum for future organisms as they come into being. Charles Hartshorne refers to the cause-and-effect relationality of existence when he speaks of "the social nature of reality," in which "to be decided in part by others is essential to being as such" (1951, 527). Each organism acts as a cause upon future organisms and, often, as a cause upon its own future life.

My definition of love includes the notion that love entails attaining a high degree of overall well-being. This often, but not always, includes attaining a high degree of well-being for oneself. Here, the interrelatedness of existence is expressed in reciprocity. In a cosmos in which all existing things are interrelated, each one's own fulfillment connects with the fulfillment of others. The loving act done to attain a high degree of overall well-being often results in the lover enjoying the benefits secured for all. In this theory of love, undergirded by the presupposition that organisms are interrelated, altruism and egoism become blurred.

Although, by hypothesis, all creatures are relational organisms, this does not mean that any one creature is affected by or affects absolutely *all* others via cause-and-effect relations. The influence that an organism has through external relations with others is limited. So too, the influence upon the present individual by those who have come before is limited. Localized individuals sympathize positively with only *some* others, and the complexity of an organism's perceptive capacities partially affects the scope of an organism's sympathy. Relatively simple organisms sympathize with relatively few others, and they are likely to sympathize only with those to whom they are most closely associated (e.g., kin). One reason that creatures do not always act to increase overall well-being (i.e., love) is that their finitude necessarily limits their capacity for sympathy.

One requirement for acting in ways that increase overall well-being, then, is the broadening, to the extent possible, of one's sympathies. In other words, effective expressions of love occur when individuals act out of the broadest possible awareness and the interest that accompanies such awareness. Whitehead puts it this way: "Morality of outlook is inseparably conjoined with generality of outlook" ([1929] 1978, 15). However, the fact that creatures sympathize more with those who are nearest and to whom they most often relate (which includes family, friends, and their personal futures) does not mean that acting in the interest of those near and dear precludes acting for the common good. The essential interrelatedness of all existence entails that actions done for the genuine good of family, friends, and self affect the common good. But how one expresses love to those near and dear must involve awareness, to the extent possible, of how this action might impact all organisms.

The essential relatedness of all existing beings implies that no individual is wholly independent or isolated, and this principle has profound implications when applied to God. It means that God is relational in that God also exhibits internal and external relations. To say that God is internally related to the world is to say that creatures affect deity and that this influence partially constitutes the divine experience. God's external relations, which theists have most emphasized, entail divine influence upon creatures.

The possibility for increased overall well-being, which my definition of love entails, derives from this omni-relational deity. God steadfastly expresses love to all animals, partly because God possesses maximal relational extensivity. God sympathizes fully with all others, and God responds to others with creative love. Because God relates to all, creaturely love is possible as creatures respond sympathetically to their loving Creator. Organismic relations with one who possesses an all-inclusive perspective provide grounds for an optimism that creatures can express love in ways necessary to increase the common good.

Because God influences all organisms in each moment through direct relations, we have reason to affirm that nonhumans capable of being aware of this relation also might become aware of moral demands. The deity who interacts with human organisms and calls them to respond in the best way to what is possible in any given situation is also the God who interacts with nonhumans and calls them to respond in the best way possible given their situations. Because this loving God is both internally and externally related to all creatures, Christians need not feel uneasy about the continuity that might exist between the human and nonhuman capacity for moral response. It seems most plausible, of course, that this capacity differs significantly in degree and scope. But the moral link between nonhumans and humans need not trouble Christians who affirm the existence of an omni-relational and omni-loving deity.

The preceding is offered as groundwork for a comprehensive theory of evolutionary organismic relations that might alleviate some Christian apprehensions concerning evolutionary theory. I have argued that Christians need not be troubled that human morality resides on a continuum that includes nonhuman morality. They need not be apprehensive, because the One with perfect morals — the omni-Lover — relates lovingly and inspires love in all animals, both human and nonhuman.

REFERENCES

Adams, Robert Merrihew. 1999. *Finite and Infinite Goods: A Framework for Ethics.* Oxford: Oxford University Press.

Axelrod, R., and W. D. Hamilton. 1981. The evolution of cooperation. *Science* 211:1390-96.

Batson, Daniel C. 1993. *Religion and the Individual: A Social-Psychological Perspective.* Oxford: Oxford University Press.

Birch, Charles, and John B. Cobb Jr. 1990. *Liberation of Life: From the Cell to the Community.* Denton, Tex.: Environmental Ethics Books.

Boehm, Christopher. 1999. *Hierarchy in the Forest: The Evolution of Egalitarian Behavior.* Cambridge: Harvard University Press.

Damasio, Antonio R. 1994. *Descartes' Error: Emotion, Reason, and the Human Brain.* New York: Grosset/Putnam.

Dawkins, Richard. 1989. *The Selfish Gene.* New edition. New York: Oxford University Press.

de Waal, Frans. 1996. *Good Natured: The Origins of Right and Wrong in Humans and Other Animals.* Cambridge, Mass.: Harvard University Press.

Drees, Willem B. 2003. *Is Nature Ever Evil? Religion, Science, and Value.* London: Routledge.

Dugatkin, Lee Alan. 1997. *Cooperation among Animals: An Evolutionary Perspective.* New York: Oxford University Press.

—————. 1999. *Cheating Monkeys and Citizen Bees: The Nature of Cooperation in Animals and Humans.* Cambridge: Harvard University Press.

Goodall, Jane. 1986. *The Chimpanzees of Gombe: Patterns of Behavior.* Cambridge, Mass.: Belknap/Harvard University Press.

Grant, Colin. 2001. *Altruism and Christian Ethics.* Cambridge: University Press.

Griffin, David Ray. 2001. *Reenchantment without Supernaturalism: A Process Philosophy of Religion.* Ithaca, N.Y.: Cornell University Press.

Hamilton, W. D. 1963. The evolution of altruistic behavior. *American Naturalist* 97:354-56.

Hartshorne, Charles. 1951. Whitehead's idea of God. In *The Philosophy of Alfred North Whitehead,* ed. Paul Arthur Schilpp. Second ed. New York: Tudor.

Hazo, Robert G. 1967. *The Idea of Love.* New York: Frederick A. Praeger.

Hefner, Philip. 1993. *The Human Factor: Evolution, Culture, and Religion.* Minneapolis: Fortress.

Kagan, Jerome. 1998. *Three Seductive Ideas.* Cambridge: Harvard University Press.

Katz, Leonard. 2000. *Evolutionary Origins of Morality: Cross-Disciplinary Perspectives.* Ohio: Imprint Academic.

Kauffman, Stuart. 1985. Self-organization, selective adaptationism, and its limits: A new pattern of inference in evolution and development. In *Evolution at the Crossroads,* ed. David Depew and Bruce Weber. Cambridge: MIT Press.

—————. 1995. *At Home in the Universe.* London: Penguin.

Lewis, C. S. 1960. *The Four Loves*. New York: Harcourt Brace.

Lewis, Thomas, Fari Amini, and Richard Lannon. 2000. *A General Theory of Love*. New York: Random House.

Mackie, J. L. 1978. The law of the jungle: Moral alternatives and principles of evolution. *Philosophy* 53:455-64.

Midgley, Mary. [1978] 1995. *Beast and Man: The Roots of Human Nature*. London: Routledge.

———. 1996. *The Ethical Primate: Humans, Freedom, and Morality*. New York: Routledge.

Monroe, Kristen. 1996. *The Heart of Altruism: Perceptions of a Common Humanity*. Princeton, N.J.: Princeton University Press.

Murphy, Nancey, and George F. R. Ellis. 1996. *On the Moral Nature of the Universe: Theology, Cosmology, and Ethics*. Minneapolis: Fortress.

Nygren, Anders. 1969. *Agape and Eros*. Translated by Philip S. Watson. New York: Harper and Row.

Oliner, Pearl M., and Samuel P. Oliner. 1988. *The Altruistic Personality: Rescuers of Jews in Nazi Europe*. New York: Free Press.

Oliner, Pearl M., et al., eds. 1992. *Embracing the Other: Philosophical, Psychological, and Historical Perspectives on Altruism*. New York: New York University Press.

Oliner, Samuel P. 2003. *Do unto Others: Extraordinary Acts of Ordinary People*. Cambridge: Westview.

Oord, Thomas Jay. 2001. The world in a grain of sand: Genome project center stage at AAAS. *Research News and Opportunities in Science and Theology* 1, no. 8:1-2.

———. 2002a. *Agape*, altruism, and well-being: Full-orbed love for the science and religion dialogue. *Contemporary Philosophy: Philosophic Research, Analysis and Resolution* 25.

———. 2002b. Grappling with bioterrorism at AAAS. *Research News and Opportunities in Science and Theology* 2, no. 8:30.

———. 2003. Love is a many splendored thing. A seven-part series. *Research News and Opportunities in Science and Theology* (February-October).

Outka, Gene. 1997. Agapeistic ethics. Pp. 481-88 in *A Companion to Philosophy of Religion*, ed. Philip L. Quinn and Charles Taliaferro. Cambridge, Mass.: Blackwell.

Polkinghorne, John. 2001. *The Work of Love: Creation as Kenosis*. Grand Rapids: Eerdmans.

Pope, Stephen J. 1994. *The Evolution of Altruism and the Ordering of Love*. Washington, D.C.: Georgetown University Press.

———. 1995. Love in contemporary Christian ethics. *Journal of Religious Ethics* 23, no. 1.

Post, Stephen G., et al., eds. 2002. *Altruism and Altruistic Love: Science, Philosophy, and Religion in Dialogue*. Oxford: Oxford University Press.

———. 2003. *Research on Altruism and Love: An Annotated Bibliography of Major Studies in Psychology, Sociology, Evolutionary Biology, and Theology*. Philadelphia: Templeton.

Rolston, Holmes, III. 1999. *Genes, Genesis, and God: Values and Their Origins in Natural and Human History.* Cambridge: Cambridge University Press.

Singer, Irving. [1966] 1984. *The Nature of Love: Plato to Luther.* Vol. 1. Second ed. Chicago: University of Chicago Press.

Sober, Elliott, and David Sloan Wilson. 1998. *Unto Others: The Evolution and Psychology of Unselfish Behavior.* Cambridge, Mass.: Harvard University Press.

Soble, Alan. 1989. *Eros, Agape, and Philia.* New York: Paragon.

Sorokin, Pitirim. [1954] 2002. *The Ways and Power of Love: Types, Factors, and Techniques of Moral Transformation.* Philadelphia: Templeton Foundation.

Trivers, R. L. 1971. The evolution of reciprocal altruism. *Quarterly Review of Biology* 46:35-57.

Walsh, Anthony. 1991. *The Science of Love: Understanding Love and Its Effects on Mind and Body.* Buffalo, N.Y.: Prometheus.

Whitehead, Alfred North. [1926] 1996. *Religion in the Making.* New York: Fordham University Press.

———. [1933] 1968. *Adventures of Ideas.* New York: Free Press.

———. [1929] 1978. *Process and Reality: An Essay in Cosmology,* ed. David Ray Griffin and Donald W. Sherburne. Corrected ed. New York: Free Press.

Wilson, David. 2002. *Darwin's Cathedral: Evolution, Religion, and the Nature of Society.* Chicago: University of Chicago Press.

Wilson, Edward O. 1978. *Sociobiology: On Human Nature* (Cambridge, Mass.: Harvard University Press.

16. Darwin's Problems, Neo-Darwinian Solutions, and Jesus' Love Commands

Philip A. Rolnick

"Natural selection will never produce in a being anything injurious to itself, for natural selection acts solely by and for the good of each."

Charles Darwin 1979, 229

"Models that attempt to explain natural altruistic behavior in terms of natural selection are models designed to take the altruism out of altruism."

Robert Trivers 1971, 35

"You shall love the Lord your God with all your heart, and with all your soul, and with all your mind, and with all your strength. . . . You shall love your neighbor as yourself."

Mark 12:30-31 RSV

Religion within the Limits of Neo-Darwinism Alone?

Charles Darwin recognized two counterexamples that could "annihilate" his theory: human altruism and the self-sacrificial behavior of sterile castes of insects (Darwin [1859] 1979, 229). Hence, once theories of kinship selection and reciprocal altruism come to provide elegant solutions to these problems (see the introduction to this volume by Jeffrey Schloss), the neo-Darwinian synthesis becomes firmly established.

As a theologian with a realist bent, I find the predictive successes of neo-Darwinism impressive. In particular, its focus on the gene has shown great explanatory power. With the kind of enthusiasm that can be likened to the testosterone-directed behavior of youth, however, its advocates have often indulged in metaphysical hyperbole. A case in point is Daniel Dennett's some-what fiendish comparison of Darwinism and "universal acid":

> Did you ever hear of universal acid? This fantasy used to amuse me and some of my schoolboy friends — I have no idea whether we invented or in-herited it, along with Spanish fly and saltpeter, as a part of underground youth culture. Universal acid is a liquid so corrosive that it will eat through *anything!* The problem is: what do you keep it in? It dissolves glass bottles and stainless-steel canisters as readily as paper bags. What would happen if you somehow came upon or created a dollop of universal acid? Would the whole planet eventually be destroyed? What would it leave in its wake? Af-ter everything had been transformed by its encounter with universal acid, what would the world look like? Little did I realize that in a few years I would encounter an idea — Darwin's idea — bearing an unmistakable likeness to universal acid: it eats through just about every traditional con-cept. (Dennett 1995, 63)

Notwithstanding the considerable accomplishments of Darwinism, has it in fact become the universal acid of our world? Does it successfully account for all human relationships, including relations of love? Let us cross-examine some particular neo-Darwinian claims about love and the moral life, claims that would seem to subject human meaning to universal acid.

In *The Selfish Gene,* Richard Dawkins draws upon some neo-Darwinian research that calls altruistic behavior into question. Dawkins tells us that he would like to have a society based upon cooperation and unselfish behavior oriented toward a common good, but he does not think that our biological nature is helpful in that pursuit. To the contrary, he argues that most individ-ual behavior (including human) is overtly selfish; most important, even those behaviors that appear altruistic or moral are not. These apparently altruistic behaviors are mere apparitions which serve the gene's selfish purpose: "We, and all other animals, are machines created by our genes" (Dawkins [1976] 1999, 2). As the units of natural selection, genes have evolved so that they ma-nipulate the individuals in which they dwell, which Dawkins characterizes as "gigantic, lumbering robots" (Dawkins [1976] 1999, 19). In Dawkins's colorful language, we begin to see the import of the reversal in which the gene, and not the individual, is most important, where "genes are the immortals," "genes are forever"[1] (Dawkins [1976] 1999, 34, 35). Because it would explain

---

1. The general neo-Darwinian consensus around the gene as the sole unit of selection has been challenged by Elliott Sober and David Sloan Wilson with their work, *Unto Others: The*

human altruistic behavior in terms of genetic calculation, this move to the gene depersonalizes human agency and corrodes attributions of higher motivations.

Likewise, Michael Ruse and E. O. Wilson put it bluntly:

> Morality, or more strictly, our belief in morality, is merely an adaptation put in place to further our reproductive ends. Hence the basis of ethics does not lie in God's will . . . or any other part of the framework of the Universe. In an important sense, ethics . . . is an *illusion* fobbed off on us by our genes to get us to cooperate. (Ruse and Wilson 1985, 51-52 [cited in Rolston 1999, 250], my emphasis)

If correct in their claims, Ruse, E. O. Wilson, Dawkins, and Dennett would have truly come upon something revolutionary, perhaps even a universal acid. It is significant that, in spite of what our genes would have us do, all of these neo-Darwinians call for some sort of morality. But if the moral behavior that we often observe among humans is fostered by an *illusion*, then we have come upon a decisive moment of evolution: agents, the "robot vehicles" of the "immortal genes," have become conscious of the illusion.

If Ruse and Wilson are right about the illusion, then is it not the case that, to the degree that they publish this theory and persuade others of it, they undermine the future effectiveness of the illusion? Let us say that all high school and university biology courses adopt their position. Once those educated in this regime *believe* Ruse and Wilson instead of the old "illusion" about altruism, their attitude toward altruism and their behavior toward others could only be expected to change significantly.[2] Yet Dawkins, much like Ruse and Wilson, asserts that "we have the power to turn against our creators. We, alone on earth, can rebel against the tyranny of the selfish replicators" (Dawkins 1999, 201). Having first depersonalized human agents ("robot vehicles"), Dawkins now would re-personalize us by a moral rebellion against our selfish nature. Although his call to morality is to be commended, the rebellion is arbitrary, for we could just as easily choose not to rebel against the selfish genes, but to embrace them in selfish collusion. If, as we saw Ruse and Wilson claim, "the basis of ethics does not lie in God's will . . . or any other part of the

---

Evolution and Psychology of Unselfish Behavior (Cambridge, Mass.: Harvard University Press, 1998). Sober and Wilson have re-opened the controversial issue of group selection en route to an argument for multi-level selection.

2. In his critique of Ruse, John Hare suggests a "publicity standard" by which "a normative theory should be able to make public what it claims as the source or origin of the normative demand, without thereby undercutting the demand" (Hare forthcoming).

framework of the Universe," then what is left except Ruse's, Wilson's, Dawkins's, or others' preferences? But can this groundless sort of ethics be sustained? A mere *preference* for justice and universal fairness is a thin defense against skepticism, and one might just as easily prefer war and conquest. Let us recall Friedrich Nietzsche's preferences:

> What is good? Everything that heightens the feeling of power in man, the will to power, power itself.
>
> What is bad? Everything that is born of weakness.
>
> What is happiness? The feeling that power is *growing*, that resistance is overcome.
>
> Not contentedness but more power; not peace but war. (Nietzsche 1976, 570)

Embracing a skeptical theory of altruism makes altruism less likely.

Coming to awareness of our evolutionary roots is a great moment in human history, but origins do not tell the whole story. Furthermore, biological evolution itself is not original, for it rests upon a remarkable and much longer evolution of forces and particles — the story from the putative big bang to the formation of stars and planetary systems. This expanded story contextualizes biological evolution and calls into question the imperialistic claims that some biologists would make — for unless questions of origin are prematurely, arbitrarily foreclosed, they conjure up the more basic issues of the origin of life from nonlife and the origin of anything at all, including the conditions that might give rise to a big bang. What we have so far glimpsed seems a narrow slice of an ongoing history discovered *in media res*. And this history is now marked by the fact that we actually undertake science, have become aware of genetic effects, and have even made some first attempts to combine our knowledge of genetics and science generally with self-critical ethical enquiry. While scientific influence on ethics is not new, since, for example, Aristotelian science exerted great influence on medieval thought, it is certainly reinvigorated by the methods, wealth, and depth of new scientific discovery. The very act of laboratory investigation or theoretical conversation about genes, however, indicates that we have to some degree transcended genes, for genes did not discover genetics. Just as genes do not undertake the study of genetics, neither do they undertake ethics. Accounts of human endeavor in science, ethics, and religion become unsustainable if we do not allow for the meaning of human personhood. When criticized both for being reductionist and for positing a dualism between genes and culture, Dawkins adopts language of "genes influencing" (rather than determining) in order to fight off the charges of reductionism and dualism (Dawkins [1976] 1999, 332). Rather sensibly, Dawkins comes to recognize an inter-level complexity. But still, if Dawkins recognizes different levels, what is it, apart from personhood, that could *unify* these levels? As Holmes Rolston puts it, "We never become free from nature, but we do become free within nature" (Rolston 1999, 283). The human person is the kind of being that exhibits freedom within biological nature.

What must be resisted is the unfounded and unnecessary reduction of everything to genetics, like the following contention of E. O. Wilson: "No species, ours included, possesses a purpose beyond the imperatives created by its genetic history. . . . The species lacks any goal external to its own biological nature" (Wilson 1978, 2-3 [cited in Rolston 1999, 347]). This kind of claim is simply dogmatic. It is no longer a claim limited to biology but has become a metaphysical assertion about the ultimate nature of reality. Rolston presents it as a syllogism:

1. If E (evolved), then not T (transcendent).
2. E.
3. Therefore not T. (Rolston 1999, 347).

Yet why should we accept the premise that evolution rules out transcendence? What is it that prevents an interrelationship between evolution and transcendence? This much is clear: the kind of consciousness that can discuss evolution, even in those who deny transcendence, actually indicates a relationship between evolution and transcendence. In his Gifford Lectures of 1933-34, William Temple remarked that a world that gives rise to mind says much about that world (Temple 1934, 130, 199). It may be anthropocentric to say that humanity is the chief purpose of evolution, but it may also be right. Consciousness remains a glaring counterexample to claims of mechanistic selection alone.

Michael Polanyi dismisses claims of ontological reductionism because he recognizes the existence of multiple levels that are subject to multiple controls. He uses the term "boundary conditions" to describe the open variability of any lower level, such as chemical and physical principles. Let us consider the example of making a speech. The first and lowest level is the mere production of a voice. In the operations of this material level, laws of physics (acoustics) and chemistry are prerequisites for the eventual speech production. The second level involves the utterance of words. In analyzing this second level, it makes no sense to reduce what is going on to physics and chemistry. Even at this level we are not grunting or barking; we are producing words.

A third level joins the words into sentences. This synthetic activity can only be accomplished with the use of the two lower levels, but again the two lower levels cannot of themselves explain the *meaning* of the sentence. Not every string of words produces a meaningful sentence, as those of us who read and write papers can attest. The mathematical possibilities involved in combining words into a single sentence are hyper-astronomical. Similarly, a fourth level works the sentences into paragraphs or other subsections, and a fifth level forms all the components into a cohesive whole (freely adapted from Polanyi 1969, 154).

Polanyi summarizes:

> Each level is subject to dual control; first, by the laws that apply to its elements in themselves and, second, by the laws that control the comprehensive entity formed by them.
>
> Such multiple control is made possible by the fact that the principles governing the isolated particulars of a lower level, leave indeterminate their boundary conditions for the control by a higher principle. (Polanyi 1969, 154)

This account allows for the full gamut of lower-level powers, such as genetics, without arbitrarily reducing the complexity of the full range of interactions.

Definitional and Experimental Rejoinders

Rather commonly, biologists have recently defined altruism solely in terms of sociobiological assumptions regarding reproductive value: "self-sacrificing behavior whereby one individual sacrifices some component of its *reproductive* value for another individual" (Cartwright 2000, 344). Were we to let that definition stand, however, we could never arrive at the ethical level of Jesus' love commands. As a transition between biology and theology, let us first look at a different understanding of altruism by considering the experimental work and reports of psychologist C. Daniel Batson and his associates. Batson's work uses a broader definition of altruism, one that rejects the ethical conclusions of sociobiologists but leaves intact the more narrow scope of their scientific research.

Batson and Laura L. Shaw challenge the fairly common assumption among psychologists (and sociobiologists) that the motivation for all intentional action, including the intention to help others, is egoistic. Against contentions of "universal egoism," Batson and Shaw argue for empathic emotion that evokes genuinely altruistic motivation. They do so in two powerful ways: first, by defining the critical terms with unusual clarity; and second, by citing numerous experiments, many of them led by Batson, that offer strong evidence against the various versions of psychological egoism. Batson and Shaw are untroubled by the presence of egoism; in fact, they note that one of the difficulties is that altruism and egoism share much common ground. Their target is the one-size-fits-all notion of universal egoism, which of course bears great similarity to the more extreme claims of sociobiology and evolutionary psychology. Instead, by employing empirical studies that confirm altruism as they define it, and that disconfirm the egoistic hypothesis, Batson and Shaw offer strong support for their empathy-altruism hypothesis, which allows a more open-ended, pluralistic explanation of human behavior.

Batson and Shaw ask whether helping others is part of human nature or whether it always involves, however subtly, something that benefits the self. Whereas earlier discussions would use such terms as benevolence, charity, compassion, and friendship, Auguste Comte (1798-1857) was the first to use the term *altruism,* in the sense of living for others (Batson and Shaw 1991, 108). Rejoinders to Comte developed the notion of psychological hedonism, which held that even if we do something to help others, because the helper receives the pleasure of attaining the allegedly altruistic goal, the receipt of such pleasure means that the altruism is actually the product of an underlying egoism. The argument for psychological hedonism confuses two different forms of hedonism, however: a strong form in which *personal pleasure* is always the goal of human action, and a weak form in which *goal attainment* always brings pleasure. Note the reversal of pleasure and goal in the two different forms. The strong form, which holds selfish pleasure as the goal of all human action, effectively rules out altruism. Actually, it is merely another way of asserting universal egoism. The weak form of hedonism, however, the one that holds that attaining a goal always delivers pleasure, offers no obstacle to bona fide altruism.

Batson and Shaw clarify the definitions of altruism and egoism as follows:

> Altruism is a motivational state with the ultimate goal of increasing another's welfare.
>
> Egoism is a motivational state with the ultimate goal of increasing one's own welfare. (Batson and Shaw 1991, 108)

They further clarify each of the key terms, so, for instance, "motivational state" means "a goal-directed psychological force within an organism" that has four features. First, "goal" means that the organism desires to change something in its experienced world. Second, "a force of some magnitude exists, drawing the organism toward the goal." Third, if the route to the goal is blocked, alternative routes will be sought. Fourth, "the force disappears when the goal is reached" (Batson and Shaw 1991, 108). Another key term, "ultimate goal," means that the goal must be an end in itself, not an intermediate step to something else. If the goal were merely intermediary, then when a barrier arose, alternate routes would be sought that bypassed the intermediate goal. Furthermore, in the case where the ultimate goal was reached without the intermediary being reached, the motivational force (of the intermediary) would disappear. Yet, an ultimate goal cannot be bypassed in these ways. Finally, the authors clarify what increasing one's own or another's welfare means:

> Increasing another's welfare is an ultimate goal if an organism (a) perceives some desired change in another organism's world and (b) experiences a force to bring about that change as (c) an end in itself and not as a means to reach some other goal. Increasing one's own welfare is an ultimate goal if an organism (a) perceives some desired change in his or her own world and (b) experiences a force to bring about that change as (c) an end in itself. (Batson and Shaw 1991, 108)

The clarifications of these terms leave much common ground between altruism and egoism: "Each refers to goal-directed motivation; each is concerned with the ultimate goal of this motivation; and, for each, the ultimate goal is increasing someone's welfare" (Batson and Shaw 1991, 108). But now, with the above clarifications and recognized commonalities, the question can be sharpened: Is our own or another person's welfare the ultimate goal?

Making the case for altruism, Batson and Shaw point out that *self-sacrifice* is not a necessary component of altruism. This distinction is important because sociobiologists often include self-sacrifice in their definitions. We can adjudicate between the two definitions in favor of Batson and Shaw, since they rightly argue that to speak of self-sacrifice shifts the focus from motivation to consequences. Of course consequences, like behavior, can be more directly observed and more easily measured than motivation. Ease of access, however, should not be allowed to prejudice the truth of the question. A good experimental trial works out ways of inferring goals and motivations from observed behavior.

As an example of discerning a person's ultimate goal, Batson and Shaw tell a story of "Frank and Suzie." Frank and Suzie work together, but Frank, who is financially well-heeled, is described as homely and Suzie as music-loving. When one morning Suzie begins to show Frank unusual attention, Frank cannot decide whether Suzie is really interested in him or just trying to get him to take her to a concert that weekend. In other words, Frank is wondering about Suzie's motivation and her ultimate goal. Frank can rightly wonder whether he is an intermediate step or the ultimate goal and lacks sufficient information to decide the question. If, however, Suzie happens to receive two concert tickets from her father, then coolly ignores Frank as she walks past him on her way to invite John, then Frank can conclude with reasonable certainty (and sadness) what her ultimate goal and motivation were (Batson and Shaw 1991, 109-10). Batson and Shaw report on over twenty experiments that employ experimental variations of such Frank and Suzie scenarios, which are set up to test egoistic explanations against the empathy-altruism hypothesis: "Results of these experiments have consistently patterned as predicted by the empathy-altruism hypothesis" (Batson and Shaw 1991, 114). In contrast to the imperial claims of selfish-gene theory, these experimental results show that, at least for some subjects tested, the ultimate goal is altruistic. Following Batson and Shaw, we can say that a pluralistic explanatory model, one that includes altruistic as well as egoistic motives, is required to account for the actual evidence.

Batson's various experiments and Batson and Shaw's convincing account of that work should give real pause to those who would rush to embrace accounts that reduce human nature to such things as Dawkins's "selfish gene." Experimental evidence, Polanyi's analysis of levels, and our instincts all point to a different conclusion. As a would-be universal acid, the neo-Darwinian explanations construe the world as a horror story, but the construal is unjustified.

Neo-Darwinism and Jesus' Love Commands: How Should the Self Be Loved?

Thus far I have tried to recognize the successes of neo-Darwinism and also to show that some prominent neo-Darwinian advocates have been guilty of overreaching. But is there something that neo-Darwinism and theology, particularly Jesus' teachings on love, hold in common? Conjoining two earlier commands of the Hebrew Bible, Jesus proclaims what have become known as the two great commandments: "You shall love the Lord your God with all your heart, and with all your soul, and with all your mind, and with all your strength. . . . You shall love your neighbor as yourself" (Mark 12:30-31; par.).

Given Jesus' qualified affirmation of self-love, theology and neo-Darwinian biology have a point of common interest.

Jesus' affirmation is not free-standing, however, for we should immediately notice that "love your neighbor as yourself" is not the first command but the second. Moreover, the first command is far weightier — we are to love God with all our heart, soul, mind, and strength. No such *all* is given in the second commandment (see Jenson 1999, 94). The second command simply assumes self-love as a given that can be used to measure the way we are enjoined to love others. What kind of self does Jesus advocate? — one that primarily and most intensively loves God and then further qualifies its self-regard with other-regard.

From Jesus' command to love the neighbor as oneself, we can infer that it is God's will that the self flourish and be fulfilled with the deepest sort of happiness. "Love your neighbor as yourself" at once engages us as needy organisms and as more than organisms. It implicitly links biology and its human transcendence in the relationship of love, for no authentic relationship of love is a calculated means to an end, but rather an end in itself. So where the first principle of sociobiology is that the selfish genes, Dawkins's "immortals," must find their way into the next generation, the first principle of the Westminster Confession is, "The chief end of man is to love God and to *enjoy* him forever."[3] Similarly, Aquinas declares that "The ultimate and principle good of man is the *enjoyment* of God" (*ST* II.II.23.7, my emphasis). Rather than removing the self, or destroying it, these Christian views teach eternal self-survival and enjoyment, and they demand that this survival be attended to, for the self and for others. By absurd contrast, imagine a universe where no self sought its own good. Not only biologically, but also spiritually, such a universe is simply incoherent; hence, biology and Judeo-Christian theology can make common cause of the initiations wrought by self-interest.

Christian self-love, however, is not naked egoism. Like all other organisms, humans are rooted in evolutionary, biological origins, which are in turn rooted in contingencies that go back at least as far as the putative big bang. Because we can respond in ways actually counter to our own animal urges, our animality can be part of a nobler, more splendid whole. Our biological nature can be harmonized with a higher nature, although such self-mastery is hardly automatic. Failure to moderate the strong urges of the biological world demotes human life to its animal level. On the other extreme, those who deny the *goodness* of life in the material world repeat the ancient error of the Gnostics. Stephen Pope strikes the balance: "Essential human inclinations

---

3. This juxtaposition was first called to my attention by Jeffrey Schloss. My emphasis.

are to be both fulfilled and transformed in light of human intelligence" (Pope 1994, 54).[4] The heart of the moral life lies in developing consistent habits of preferring and practicing what Aristotle calls the "supremely noble and good" (Aristotle 1962, 1168b30). In Christian thought, bodily pleasures are affirmed, but never at the expense of other persons.

Combining his understanding of the biological with his ordering of love (ordo amoris), Aquinas was quite clear-headed about self-love; he neither vaporizes it in gnostic spirituality nor forces all else into its framework. Aquinas incorporates biology into his arguments, sometimes incorrect biology, but he incorporates it to the point where he might conclude that love of a father is greater than love of a mother (because he erroneously held that the father gives the child the seed and the mother does not contribute a genetic factor). The biology and its ramifications are sometimes wrong, but what is important to note is that the scientific principle, harnessed to his theological commitment, drives the question. Virtuous love is a matter of rightly ordering natural dispositions.

Because natural forms of love give rise to stability, Aquinas affords such love a kind of priority that fits well with the neo-Darwinian notions of kin selection, reciprocal altruism, and even "evolutionarily stable strategies." An evolutionarily stable strategy (ESS) is Maynard Smith's idea of a survival strategy that, once adopted by most members of a population, cannot be improved upon by an alternative strategy (Dawkins [1976] 1999, 69). In short, Aquinas can be used to engage neo-Darwinian biology because he is committed to the notion that natural human affections have moral significance. His insistence that "Grace does not destroy nature but perfects it" (ST I.8.1) is a thirteenth-century invitation to think theologically about the natural world. In something of an anticipation of kin selection and ESS, Aquinas argues that we ought to love those who are more closely united to us, such as family members, even more than we love those who are "better," that is to say, closer to God. He notes that neighbors are often connected to us by a "natural origin" that retains its permanence, whereas virtue may increase or decrease. Furthermore, we love kin and countrymen in more diverse ways, so that the stability of blood relationships gives them preference in such things as providing necessities, invitations to weddings, and the like (ST II.II.26.7-8). Aquinas even places collegial relations under natural law in counseling "to avoid offending those with whom one has to live" (ST I.II.94.2).

While consistently affirming self-love, Aquinas first distinguishes and then ranks different kinds of self-love:

4. I am in many ways indebted to this seminal work.

1. We should love our own bodies (*ST* II.II.25.4);
2. We ought to love our neighbor more than we love our own body (*ST* II.II.26.5);
3. However, even though we should bear bodily harm to protect our neighbor, we should not do anything for the neighbor that would harm our own soul (*ST* II.II.26.4.*ad* 2).

Each case is governed by a healthy sense of self-love. In the case of loving our own body, we are following a basic precept of natural law that has clear resonance with Darwinist thought: "Every substance seeks the preservation of its own being, according to its nature: and by reason of this inclination, whatever is a means of preserving human life, and of warding off its obstacles, belongs to the natural law" (*ST* I.II.94.2). In the case of loving the neighbor more than our own body, at least two things must be said. First, let us reiterate that the *other* receives first mention in "Love your neighbor as yourself." Self-love is implied, virtually assumed as a condition, but other-love is commanded. The second point is even more decisive: sacrificing our own body for the other turns out to be self-love, since such bodily sacrifice is "the perfection of virtue" (*ST* II.II.26.4.*ad* 2). For Jews and Christians, the body counts, but *relationships* of love count even more. Entering into relationships of love is intricately connected to the relationship of love with God. Sustaining and fostering such relationships of *other*-directedness, particularly in the case of bodily self-sacrifice, paradoxically enriches the self far beyond strategic and calculative concern. Finally, in disallowing actions that would harm the soul on behalf of the neighbor, self-love of the eternal variety is again affirmed. Morality is ultimately a pursuit of the good, and the realization of the good is the distinct quest of persons. Fish, ducks, and pine trees struggle to survive; *persons* may struggle to attain the good, even at the cost of biological survival. Every act of love is also an act that intends to promote the good. The good of the body is only to be given up for a greater good, and all good is referred to the possibility of an increasingly realized relationship with God.

The first precept of natural law, "good is to be done and pursued, and evil is to be avoided" (*ST* I.II.94.2), is anticipated in the animal world but can only be fully realized, both in its accomplishment and in its failure, by persons. Wolfhart Pannenberg notes that, in failing to control their own bodies, humans can often be inferior to animals (Pannenberg 1985, 82). Self-love that is directed *only* toward the good of the body is actually a form of self-hatred, for it fails to avail the self of its greatest happiness. There is something strange about the human situation, for, as Aquinas puts it, "The ultimate goal of a rational creature exceeds the capacity of its own nature" (*Compendium theologiae,* 143 [cited in Jenson 1999, 66]). Nature alone is insufficient for human happiness. "He's a real animal" is not said as a compliment. Animality is a human beginning, but not a final destination. Theology shares this with biology — both are about movement. In biology, the survival of inclusive fitness may be understood as selfish, but it already moves the self beyond its own boundaries, strictly considered. In the relationship to God (theology), the self is called to move beyond itself in two interrelated ways: first, as a self-involving movement toward the goodness of God, one that can never be finally settled but that always calls us to become more than we presently are; second, as movement toward, and on behalf of, the neighbor.

Besides joining self-love to love of the neighbor, Jesus warns that undue focus on the self can be ruinous: "For whoever would save his life will lose it; and whoever loses his life for my sake and the gospel's will save it" (Mark 8:35; cf. Matt. 10:39; Luke 17:33; and John 12:25). Jesus' warning is entirely consistent with our thesis that God wants us to succeed (understood in the most noble sense), for Jesus pointedly does not say, "Whoever would save his life will lose it; and whoever would lose his life for my sake and the gospel's will also lose it." It would seem that the spiritual technique of self-love is other-love. The most genuine sort of self-love, self-love of the eternal sort, is paradoxically present in those who increasingly learn to love others. The universal pursuit of biological self-interest faintly anticipates this sort of self-love, but is almost unrecognizably transformed by it. In the strange case of Christian self-love, Darwin's declaration, "Natural selection will never produce in a being anything injurious to itself, for natural selection acts solely by and for the good of each" (Darwin [1859] 1979, 229), does not apply without much re-working.

Moreover, by universalizing the understanding of love, Jesus' teachings further extend the way that self-love is caught up with other-love. When James and John Zebedee ask Jesus to promote them to positions of power, and the other apostles become indignant at them upon learning of the request, Jesus calls them all together and says,

> You know that those who are supposed to rule over the Gentiles lord it over them, and their great men exercise authority over them. But it shall not be so among you; but whoever would be great among you must be your servant, and whoever would be first among you must be slave of all. (Mark 10:42-43)

The normal routines of the Gentiles ("nations" or "peoples") are not to apply. Normal considerations of the self are dramatically reversed.

Jesus' additional teachings on love reinforce the dramatic reversal:

You have heard that it was said, "You shall love your neighbor and hate your enemy." But I say to you, Love your enemies and pray for those who persecute you, so that you may be sons of your Father who is in heaven; . . . For if you love those who love you, what reward have you? (Matt. 5:43-46)

In addition to the unnatural or perhaps supernatural command to love one's enemies, yet another comparison to the normal routine of normal "peoples" is made: "And if you salute only your brethren, what more are you doing than others? Do not even Gentiles do the same?" (Matt. 5:47). The extension of love to those well beyond family and friends, even to actual enemies, creates real dissonance with sociobiology's imperialistic accounts of selfishness.

Jesus' parable of the Good Samaritan (Luke 10:29-37), told in order to define neighbor, reiterates in the strongest possible manner the universalizing tendency of Jesus' teachings. The normal routine is once again reversed as a member of a group detested by Jesus' first-century hearers is depicted as the merciful minister.

Since sociobiologists recognize that many people in many places do practice something like Jesus' commands and do imitate the Good Samaritan, they either need to change the scope of their theory or need to account for such practices. Richard Alexander's deception theory sees the threat and attempts to counter it:

Society is based on lies. . . . "Thou shalt love thy neighbor as thyself." But this admirable goal is clearly contrary to a tendency to behave in a reproductively selfish manner. "Thou shalt give the impression that thy lovest thy neighbor as thyself" might be closer to the truth. (Alexander 1975, 96 [cited in Rolston 1999, 256-57])

The deception theory, which is fairly common among neo-Darwinians, really holds that there is double deception. We must deceive others into thinking that we are loving, ministering Good Samaritans; and, in order to pull this stunt off, we must first deceive ourselves; for only if we really believe that we intend to help others can we be credible enough to receive the social rewards of good reputation and its attendant benefits.[5]

---

5. The double deception theory is critiqued by Rolston 1999, 249-80; and earlier, by Jeffrey Schloss, "Sociobiological Explanations of Altruistic Ethics: Necessary, Sufficient, or Irrelevant Perspective on the Human Moral Quest," in *Investigating the Biological Foundations of Human Morality*, ed. James Hurd (New York: Edwin Mellen, 1996), 107-45; and Langdon Gilkey, "Biology and Theology on Human Nature: Ethics and Genetics," in *Biology, Ethics, and the Origins of Life*, ed. Holmes Rolston III (Boston: Jones and Bartlett, 1995), 163-90.

Several problems can be seen in the skepticism of the deception theory. First, in violation of Occam's razor, it has to work overtime in order to account for the many human acts of charity to those not near and dear. It really would be simpler just to assume that sometimes an act of kindness is what it appears to be. Second, there is at least some experimental evidence to support the claim that altruism can be genuine (e.g., the work of Batson et al.). Third, religious missionaries commonly take great risks and undergo great expense on behalf of groups who bear almost no genetic similarity to the missionaries. As Rolston points out, the trend of universal religion, which is historically traceable, should have been selected against (Rolston 1999, 319). When they move beyond their proper biological applications, neo-Darwinist explanations become tendentious and unpersuasive.

The best explanations for the best religious behavior are still religious. John Henry Newman contends, "The best preparation for loving the world at large, and loving it duly and wisely, is to cultivate an intimate friendship and affection toward those who are immediately about us" (Newman 1987, 258 [cited in Pope 1994, 134]). Here the self-love that we have developed above is extended indefinitely. Because both of them address the love displayed among close kin, neo-Darwinism and Christian love share some common ground. A real dispute emerges only when neo-Darwinians deny the extension of self-love to others (even unrelated others) and God and attempt to reduce it back into their domain. As biologist Robert Trivers baldly states, "Models that attempt to explain altruistic behavior in terms of natural selection are models designed to take the altruism out of altruism" (Trivers 1971, 35).

By contrast, if we assume that "grace perfects nature," then the biological aspects of neo-Darwinism are consonant with God's desire for our happiness. A qualified self-love is normal, natural, and in many circumstances permissible and desirable. But we have other options. We may learn to love others beyond what any strictly biological theory would predict, and we may do so because we receive "a share of happiness from [God]" (ST II.II.26.2). Like all other agents and organisms, we seek our own good, but we do so with a unique vision of love and friendship, one founded on "the fellowship of everlasting happiness" (ST II.II.23.1).

REFERENCES

Aquinas, Thomas. 1947. *Summa Theologica*. Translated by the Fathers of the English Dominican Province. New York: Benziger Brothers. Parenthetical citations in the text will be abbreviated as *ST*.

————. 1906. *Compendium theologiae, pars prima*. London: Thomas Baker.

Aristotle. 1962. *Nicomachean Ethics*. Translated by Martin Oswald. Indianapolis: Bobbs-Merrill.

Batson, C. Daniel, and Laura L. Shaw. 1991. Evidence for altruism: Toward a pluralism of prosocial motives. *Psychological Inquiry* 2, no. 2:107-22.

Cartwright, John. 2000. *Evolution and Human Behavior: Darwinian Perspectives on Human Nature*. Cambridge, Mass.: MIT Press.

Darwin, Charles. [1859] 1979. *The Origin of Species*. New York: Gramercy Books.

Dawkins, Richard. [1976] 1999. *The Selfish Gene*. New York: Oxford University Press.

Dennett, Daniel C. 1995. *Darwin's Dangerous Idea: Evolution and the Meanings of Life*. New York: Simon and Schuster.

Hare, John. Evolutionary naturalism and reducing the demand of justice. Forthcoming.

Jenson, Robert W. 1999. *Systematic Theology II: The Works of God*. New York: Oxford University Press.

Nietzsche, Friedrich. 1976. *Twilight of the Idols*. In *The Portable Nietzsche*. Translated by Walter Kaufmann. New York: Penguin.

Pannenberg, Wolfhart. 1985. *Anthropology in Theological Perspective*. Translated by Matthew J. O'Connell. Philadelphia: Westminster.

Polanyi, Michael. 1969. The logic of tacit inference. In *Knowing and Being*, ed. Majorie Grene. Chicago: University of Chicago Press.

Pope, Stephen J. 1994. *The Evolution of Altruism and the Ordering of Love*. Washington, D.C.: Georgetown University Press.

Rolston, Holmes, III. 1999. *Genes, Genesis, and God: Values and Their Origins in Natural and Human History*. Cambridge: Cambridge University Press.

Ruse, Michael, and Edward O. Wilson. 1985. The evolution of ethics. *New Scientist* 108, no. 1478 (17 October): 50-52.

Temple, William. 1934. *Nature, Man, and God*. London: Macmillan.

Trivers, Robert. 1971. The evolution of reciprocal altruism. *Quarterly Review of Biology* 46:35-57.

Wilson, E. O. 1978. *On Human Nature*. Cambridge, Mass.: Harvard University Press.

Biology and Purpose: Altruism, Morality, and Human Nature in Evolutionary Perspective

Philip Clayton

Agreements Stated and Unstated

It is useful, in the final pages of this volume, to assess what has and has not been achieved. Where we find clear agreements, these should be underscored; where there are deep disagreements, one wants to know why they occur and how significant they are. I close with a theological reflection on evolution, morality, and purpose.

Sometimes one learns the most by considering what has *not* been said. Which issues have *not* exploded into major points of contention in this volume? Consider these four. First, the authors have not engaged in debate about *whether* evolution has occurred. On religious topics there is great diversity. The scholars obviously disagree on whether there is a God and, if so, what role God has played in helping to bring about specific evolutionary outcomes. Between the lines one also discerns deep divergences on the degree to which God intended, and subsequently acted to bring about, the human species in particular. But none of the authors mounts an attack on the standard claim that life has been evolving on this planet for hundreds of millions of years. In at least one case the acceptance is merely hypothetical: John Hare asks, *If* evolution occurred, would that fact help answer the questions of whether we can be morally good and why we should be morally good? The rest of the authors seem to accept evolution as a given and then ask what does or does not follow from that fact.

Second, no author concludes from the fact of evolution that ethical language has been invalidated or that values can no longer guide human individuals and societies. Evolution is not associated with an *amoral* mind-set. Clearly, the writers disagree on whether evolution is *sufficient* to account for the deepest human values, or whether a source is required that lies completely outside the purview of evolutionary theory (we return to this issue below). But no author attempts to argue from the fact of evolution to the conclusion that no values or morals exist. There are debates about where to find the best explanation for these values, but no one here has maintained that values ought to be "reduced" or explained away.

Third, all authors have accepted a distinction between biological and cultural evolution. Thanks to the evolution of complex symbolic language in *homo sapiens,* it became possible for individuals and cultures to transmit their beliefs about matters of fact and about values to anyone who could understand their language and who could be persuaded of their position. In cultural evolution those who inherit these ethical beliefs and practices do not need to be genetically related to the sources from whom the beliefs came. Moreover, one can now pass on acquired characteristics — say, a new set of ethical beliefs and practices — to one's offspring, making cultural evolution Lamarckian rather than Darwinian. Also, one can hold a false belief that does not survive the selection process without oneself dying in the process; biological mistakes are rather less kindly treated. And the pace of this new kind of evolutionary process is many, many orders of magnitude faster than the process of natural selection through genetic variation and selective retention by the environment.

Again, the authors have drawn rather different conclusions from "the two evolutions." Some understand them as two faces of a single, ultimately naturalistic, evolutionary process, whereas others interpret cultural evolution as God's means for transmitting truths about religious and ethical matters from one generation to another. Nevertheless, the fact that the authors acknowledge these two different types of evolution does represent important common ground.

Finally, since the history of *homo sapiens* can be told only by including the categories of cultural evolution, the authors implicitly agree that at least some unique explanatory categories are required in order to make sense of human behavior. On the question of *how great* is the distinction between humans and other animals, the disagreement is vast. Some hold that humans are created by God and uniquely made in God's image; they possess an eternal soul and are responsible before God in a unique way. Others have centered their research on demonstrating that all or virtually all human behavior can be explained by the same principles that explain animal behavior. Nonetheless, the opposing positions do not simply collapse into unbridgeable dichotomies with no common ground. Those who emphasize the uniqueness of human persons still grant that humans are biological creatures who continue to be influenced by their animal natures, and those who emphasize the continuity of explanation across species still grant that certain human characteristics make us unique among the animals. That this common ground exists is extremely significant: as long as the opposing positions represent points along a continuum rather than diametrically opposed answers to yes-no questions, it is possible to make theoretical progress.

Perhaps most important of all, in these pages authors from both sides of the religious aisle were able to draw both on biological and on religious perspectives. The hypothesis behind this multi-year project was that the study of human morality would profit from the resources of both biology and religion. To the extent that religious scholars have been able to utilize data from the biological sciences in understanding human morality, and biologists have found some convergence between the results of their research and religious perspectives — to that extent we may consider the hypothesis to have been verified.

Strategies of Opposition

That there have been oppositions between the positions will be obvious enough to the reader by this point. The task of a final analysis is not to dismiss some of the options as nonstarters — if that were the case, why publish them in the first place? — but rather to understand the reasons for the disagreements and what one can learn from them.

If one looks closely at the preceding chapters, one notes different strategies being employed in this science-religion dialogue on ethics and evolution. Some differences turn on whether the author derives pro-religious or anti-religious conclusions from the dialogue. The starting point is often similar: the chapters summarize scientific data and theories and then speculate on what might be their significance for religion. But competing conclusions are then drawn: some authors maintain that the data and theories support religious beliefs; others think that the science tends to undercut religious beliefs; and yet others argue that their religious position undercuts the scientific conclusions. (Of course, it is also possible that the scientific data are completely neutral with regard to religious truth claims. This seems to be the position taken by Michael Ruse in his *Can a Darwinian Be a Christian?* [2001].)

We learn most about strategies of opposition by considering those who find incompatibilities between science and religion or, in our case, between the neo-Darwinian understanding of evolution and the values that follow from belief in God. Let's call them "incompatibilists." Consider first those incompatibilists who resolve the conflict in favor of science and against theism. Here, too, there is a spectrum of responses, depending on whether one thinks that biology should disincline one toward theism or, more radically, that biology renders belief in God completely without rational justification.

(None of the authors in this volume explicitly takes this latter position; elsewhere, Richard Dawkins is perhaps its most famous spokesperson; see, for example, Dawkins 1987 and 1998.)

Those who pursue the more moderate approach do not argue for a *logical* incompatibility between biological and religious explanations. Instead, they find more subtle ways in which the biological data can be used to undercut religious explanations. Two in particular deserve mention. One strategy is to argue that the adequacy of strictly biological explanations of human behavior renders religious explanations unnecessary. After all, if one has a perfectly good scientific account of some set of behaviors or beliefs, why would one need to introduce religious entities or causes in the first place? In an updated version of Laplace's famous retort, the biologist might simply respond, "I have no need of that hypothesis."

A second strategy sometimes pursued is to "functionalize" the treatment of human behavior and human moral beliefs, so that no place remains for the kind of truth claims that religious believers typically make. If the only question that remains to be asked is, "What social or biological functions are served by this particular religious belief or behavior?" one never gets to the question of whether it is really true.

Both strategies can be found in the writings of David Sloan Wilson, whose position in *Darwin's Cathedral* (2002) is frequently cited in these pages. At times Wilson makes use of the first strategy: as the power of explanations in evolutionary psychology increases, the need for any other kind of explanation, and in particular the need for explanations in terms of divine agency, is decreased. But he also employs the second strategy: once the social-biological functions of Calvin's religious beliefs have been detailed, the beliefs have been fully explained. For example, no grounds remain for raising the question of whether some of the beliefs might actually be true of metaphysical entities or realities such as God.

Analogous strategies are employed by the "incompatibilists" who resolve the conflict in favor of religious belief and against science. Some authors argue for a strong incompatibility: religious explanations are necessarily in tension with biological explanations. The tensions between biology and Christianity are, they maintain, as great as Dawkins thinks they are; it's just that the reasons for accepting Christianity are stronger than the reasons for accepting the biological explanations. Incompatibilists of both types appear to work with the assumption that religion-science comparisons involve a "zero sum" game: the greater the adequacy of theological explanations, the more suspect scientific explanations become, and vice versa. To the extent that scientists are able to account for species development or behavior in biological terms, *to that same extent* religious accounts of the world will be undercut. No one explicitly argues this position in this text. But it would be interesting to explore to what extent certain of the authors implicitly make this assumption.

Another type of argument used by religious incompatibilists, which is related but not identical to the previous one, seeks to point out limitations or flaws in biological accounts of behavior. There is a suspicion — possibly justified — that biological accounts of morality tend to undercut theological accounts (or perhaps that they do so intrinsically). The goal of Christian thinkers, it is then assumed, should be to reveal all the ways in which biological accounts of behavior are inadequate. This may involve either demonstrations that the biological explanations are not really adequate to the data or, if they are, that the biologist has illicitly extrapolated beyond the theory's sphere of validity, drawing conclusions beyond the domains in which the theory is actually valid. Thus, for example, Holmes Rolston argues that theories of altruism that are based on the genetic transmission of behaviors, and in particular the *constraints* on altruism that arise in these contexts, no longer hold when altruistic values are culturally or religiously transmitted. (Joseph Poulshock's essay points in the same direction.) Similarly, John Hare argues that descriptive accounts of moral behavior cannot pass as genuine positions in moral philosophy.

Strategies of Mediation

In the last paragraphs we have concentrated on areas of disagreement, of alleged incompatibility. One should note, however, that many of the authors in this text are compatibilists, at least concerning large areas of the "ethics and evolution" debate. For compatibilists, scientific and religious theories can contribute together to a fuller understanding of the phenomena of human moral beliefs and behaviors. In the remainder of this reflection we explore a broadly compatibilist strategy.

Suppose that one takes as her goal to develop the most adequate possible explanation of ethical beliefs and practices using the terms and theoretical resources of both biology and theology. On this view, which is also my own, one does not worry, at least initially, about theoretical over-determination, that is, that by using several different theoretical frameworks one might come up with more than one adequate explanation of some set of data. The goal of this approach is to produce the most powerful explanations that one can possibly produce, and there is nothing wrong with working on multiple fronts at the same time. Such an approach, which is utilized by many of the writers in this book, does indeed present one at some point with the task of integrating competing theoretical explanations. The integration, on this view, must be achieved using the terms of a third discipline, so that there is no question of the reduction of one explanatory system to the other. It turns out — and I think this is the moral regarding many of the questions in this volume (more on this below) — that *much more* of both sets of disciplines can be retained than one might have expected. Much of biology can be right in explaining human behaviors, and much of religious language can be retained for formulating matters of ethics, morality, and ultimate purpose. When one encounters areas of conflict, it is often possible to detect where one or the other theory has overstepped its bounds, extrapolating further from the data than is warranted or making assumptions that are not necessary to the field in question. In cases of genuine conflict, the disagreements are more often philosophical than directly scientific or religious. In this case, the philosophical alternatives must be clearly formulated and reasons for or against a particular interpretation developed. One may not achieve agreement among all the discussion partners, but one will at least have identified where the (philosophical) issues lie.

In order to present a clearer picture of this approach, I close this conclusion to the volume with a brief essay in philosophical anthropology. Because it involves an understanding of human nature and morality that includes the religious dimension in a significant way, the resulting position is most naturally interpreted as a contribution to *philosophical theology*. Methodologically, these few pages should be classified as *phenomenological*, since they draw not only from the biological data but also from the experience of what it is like to be a human being.

On Human Nature

We turn now to the synthetic questions that arise naturally within the topic of "evolution, ethics, and purpose." It seems appropriate, given such a task, to draw on the discipline of philosophical theology. (One could also say "theistic metaphysics," except for the frightening sound of the term!) Or, to say the same thing in different terms, these pages seek to employ the more constructive tools of the science-religion debate in a quest to formulate some areas of common ground and potential agreement that seem to arise out of the previous chapters. Whatever one calls it, the goal of this closing exercise is to take the best results of science and (in this case) some of the core beliefs from theology, and to see whether one can think the two fields together into a unified account. Call it *the compatibilist hypothesis.*

Such an account will necessarily weave together facts and values — not arbitrarily, one hopes, but under the control of the scientific studies and guided by insights from the theistic religious traditions. As a *Leitfaden* or red thread, I suggest using *the experience of being a human person* to guide the reflection. The guiding question is, What are the core phenomena of human experience, as informed by both science and faith?

A few clarifications are needed at the outset. First, it's undoubtedly true that the union of *all* current scientific conclusions and *all* widely shared Christian beliefs is not a consistent set. Thus one should speak, more accurately, of integrating the best results of science with the more fundamental beliefs of Christianity. There are criteria for this selection process, which I trust will be visible enough in the course of the treatment. Please note, second, that the results of this brief exercise in philosophical theology do not need to *replace* either the science or traditional religious beliefs ("confessional theology"). Philosophical theology need not be a direct competitor to either endeavor. Think of the project differently: *if* one were to look for a systematic answer, a systematic theory of human nature, which reflected the union set of biology and theism, what would it look like? My hypothesis is that only from the standpoint of such an anthropology will we be able to answer the hard questions of "Evolution and Ethics: Human Morality in Biological and Religious Perspective." Finally, I rely heavily on the work of the scientists, philosophers, and theologians whose work precedes the present chapter and on others not represented here. Just as I have minimized note citations in the interests of an approachable and accessible presentation, I have not always summarized the range of empirical and theoretical evidence that stands behind particular claims. Nonetheless, it remains basic to the method presupposed here that I would accept the obligation to list evidence, to hear counter-evidence, and to modify the assertions as a result.

Embodiedness

As humans, we are essentially located in a body. An animal body. This body has very high genetic similarity to the bodies of other higher primates. Phenotypically, we thus have deep similarities: our visual apparatus is similar to the chimps (thus presumably our visual experience is similar); our stomach sensors are similar (thus presumably our experience of hunger is similar); our sexual arousal hormones and sexual organs are similar (thus presumably our experience of sexual arousal is similar); our process of birth and nursing is similar (thus presumably some of the experiences of mother and baby are similar).

Bodies have a history. Your genome is a record of the evolutionary history that brought about *homo sapiens*. The hungers your body feels reflect an otherwise long-since forgotten context of evolutionary adaptation. And bodies deeply affect the type of experience that we have. We *may* be free to act in one way or another in response to these experiences. But we cannot control the input — say, the message that the damage sensors send to the brain — or the sensation of pain that is produced.

Likewise, we have pulls on our behavior — appetites, drives — from multiple sources. Bodies drive us toward drink, food, and sex. They need exercise and sleep. The limbic system releases hormones in the body, which create moods and emotional states; such states in turn create powerful dispositions to behave in one way or another. The neocortex then responds to these inputs. *How* it responds is a product of how the brain has been formed by early experience and how it has been trained by its environment, including especially the inputs from those in our social community. Finally, reflection and reasoning have their roots in neocortical activity. The structure of the neocortext influences how we think and how well we think.

As a nonreductionist, I argue that the drives to reason cannot be fully understood without including the experience and the rules of reasoning (cultural and logical rules). But the full truth about reasoning is not stated until we also acknowledge that reasoning would not occur apart from the precise neocortical functioning on which it depends. What we reason *and how we reason* is deeply influenced by the brain and central nervous system that we have. Thus the neocortex is linked to drives of its own: to understand, to resolve cognitive ambiguities, to obtain new and novel data, to vary existing ideas and concepts. Thus even our higher-order drives — including our drives for novelty and creativity — bear the marks of our genetic origins and evolution.

Temporality

Each of the bodily systems so far described has a history, a context of evolutionary origin. In this sense, time is basic to human being. We are products of our phylogenesis, of how our species came to be. Indeed, each particular individual is a product of the unique facts of her particular ontogenesis, of the history of her body, her brain, and her psyche from her conception onward.

We are a conjunction of histories: of biological history, of cultural history, of the unique history of our body and psyche. Human nature can no more be understood in abstraction from the history of emergence of our species than your friends and family can understand you in abstraction from your personal history, which has formed you to be the particular individual you are.

Contingency

We need constant inputs from the environment: air, water, food, warmth, and shelter. Remove the required inputs and we die: without air, in minutes; without water, in days; without food, in weeks. We also have vast and complicated psychological and social needs, to which I return below. Needs of this "higher-order" type are more difficult to specify: what is a need and what is merely a want, a desideratum for the organism to thrive and experience fulfillment? Still, the human need for love, even if more amorphous than our need for food or water, is no less a driving force in our make-up.

Moreover, we *know ourselves* as dependent. In addition to the list of concrete needs, we also know that our very continued existence is contingent. We could be killed by our physical environment (an earthquake or tornado) or by each other (a traffic accident, a random shooting). Most adults know of someone who "just keeled over and died one day." Women often speak of a feeling of vulnerability, and men are vaguely aware of the aggressive potential of other males. Thus our experience of the world is an experience of radical contingency.

"Weltoffenheit"

The famous philosophical anthropologist Arnold Gehlen defined human nature in terms of the *Weltoffenheit* or "openness to the world" of the human animal (Gehlen 1988). We don't have a given environment but are open to arbitrarily many data from our surrounding world. Much less of human behavior is determined by instinct than is the case with any other animal on the planet. Instincts influence some of our behavior, but they do not determine human choices. In comparison to other animals humans are "biologically unspecialized"; we construct our own environment to a much greater degree than our animal cousins. Since our behavioral repertoire is much broader than that of even the other great apes, our need for behavioral *selection principles* is much greater. The existence of codes of behavior is thus a virtual mandate; without them, social existence would be impossible for this species.

Instincts create a world for most species; they decide for the organisms which objects, which food sources, and which other organisms are significant. Lacking this inbuilt world-selection principle, we must create our own worlds. We consciously (or unconsciously) select among sets of possible lifestyles, professions, companions, and beliefs. A culture, one might say, is a particular set of recommendations on how a person should choose among the virtually infinite possibilities open to him or her. And a given set of *moral principles* represents a meta-biological means for choosing some types of behaviors over others.

Sense of Self

Here, then, is the crux: we are an animal who has an inner sense of self. We form an internalized representation of "the other"; we have, as one says, a *theory of mind*. This fact gives to the human animal an inner complexity that corresponds to the unique complexity of our central nervous system, *without being identical to it*. It is this complex brain and nervous system that *causes* our inner complexity — even though, I maintain, the world of subjective awareness is neither equivalent to, nor reducible to, the physical structures of the brain.

In particular, humans possess sufficient complexity to reproduce the world of their experience using something like closed-circuit feedback loops. We regularly replay our past experiences and learn from them. In certain awkward situations the process of internal feedback can be so strong that effective behavior in the world is inhibited (a first date, or first attempts at speaking a foreign language). I well remember my first appearance at a major academic conference, for instance, when, in a failed attempt to appear calm, I slowly filled my water glass to the top, over the top, and across the table, soaking my lecture notes and the clothes of the famous philosopher sitting next to me!

There are, of course, more positive uses of this inner feedback. We quickly develop a strong "theory of other minds," attributing to others the pleasures or pains that we ourselves experience. Very young children will smile with pleasure when watching another child perform an action or receive a gift that they themselves enjoy. Such empathy may not be sufficient to constitute "the moral perspective," but it is certainly a necessary condition for any morality. All moral reasoning requires the reasoner to take the perspective of the other and to calculate right action toward her based on what it would be like to be a person in her particular situation.

The Inner World

As part of this capacity, we can anticipate an experience that has not yet occurred, trying out actions or words in our head until we light upon what we think is the most adequate one. (I rewrote the previous paragraph three times before moving on to this one, each time imagining you reading it and struggling to find the most effective way to communicate my thoughts so that you would understand them.)

Yet there are downsides to this inner complexity, since it's not always easy to live with an inner world that constantly re-creates the outer world within oneself. Animals suffer — we can recognize it in the eyes of the sheep or cow being slaughtered. But this is, as some authors have dismissively dubbed it, "dumb" suffering. In most cases, the animal suffers the actual pain inflicted on it, *but not more.* We alone, it appears, are capable of magnifying our suffering far beyond the original stimulus itself. We are experts at "adding insult to injury," at recalling the circumstances of our pain and experiencing the pain all over again. We can enhance the pain of rejection (or the pride of achievement) far beyond the original experience; some of us dwell on it for years, until the imagined experience dwarfs the actual experience. Because we inhabit this subjectively experienced inner world, human joys and pains take on an iterative dimension many times more complex than the "unreflected" world of most (though perhaps not all) animals. The infinite weight, and infinite value, of inner experience plays a crucial role in determining the form of human morality.

Self-Deception

Inner complexity has another downside: self-deception. In any competitive situation, it is to others' advantage to be able to discern the contents of their opponents' "inner world," so that they can better anticipate what actions their competitors are likely to take. Clearly this is true in relationships between predators and prey, but it is also true of the less radical competitions that occur within in-group relations. Whenever individuals gain from the actions of the group, there is the temptation to cheat — to give back to the group less than one receives from it. As a result, those around you have evolved to be experts in ferreting out *your* cheating, your (admittedly fully natural) attempts to gain *from* the community more for yourself and your offspring than you give back to it. *It is as if they can read your mind!* Given others' skill in mind-reading (e.g., detecting your sense of guilt when you cheat), it is to your advantage to sincerely believe in your own innocence. Biologically as well as socially, it's often advantageous to deceive yourself into believing that you are fully innocent, since others are then more likely to believe you as well.

Males and females involved in dating relationships know what it means not always to admit to oneself the true motivations for one's actions. People who play sports and referee their own games know about self-deception

("What?! I committed a foul? Impossible!"). Even philosophers can be experts at it ("*Of course* there are no weaknesses in my argument, although yours, unfortunately, is full of holes!"). And couples in long-term relationships know about the excruciating hard work it takes to overcome the natural tendency toward self-deception.

Sociality

Humans are inherently social. A deeply communal animal, we learn largely by imitation, as Mark Heim's chapter in this volume powerfully demonstrates. Even the inner states that make up our experience in the world are deeply influenced by the environment and can be manipulated by the persons around us (Janov 2000). Depending on how you respond to your baby in your interactions with her, the very circuitry of her brain is altered, some of it in a permanent fashion (for some of the data see Lewis et al. 2000). A child who lacks a positive social environment does not merely become less of a person; she fails to develop the fundamental components of personhood, biologically as well as socially. *Friday's Footprint: How Society Shapes the Human Mind* (Brothers 1997), for example, traces these interconnections at the level of brain development.

Socialization thus plays an enormous role in forming individual selves. A far greater percentage of a human's life is lived in dependence on parents than is the case with any other animal, and as the parental role diminishes, friends and work colleagues step in as "socializers" in their place. The age at which humans are accepted into society as fully functioning adults is getting later and later. Whereas once it occurred in the early teens, the existence of the college years as a sort of "psycho-social moratorium" (Erik Erikson) has now extended the date of full adulthood well into the twenties, if then.

Culture

Physics and chemistry describe the structure of the physical world around us, and biology describes the living worlds of our body and our ecosystem. But this interpersonal world that we inhabit is only partially grasped by describing the biology of the agents who inhabit it. The world of sociality is also the world of culture.

Harold Morowitz, in his recent book on the ladder of emergence from the quantum world to spirit (Morowitz 2002), describes a process of exploding complexity. Thanks to our complexity, each individual *homo sapiens* faces an extremely large number of possible behavioral responses to a given stimulus in her environment. Two, three, four, or a classroom full of *homo sapiens* produces a combinatorial explosion — as any teacher who has ever tried to prepare a "lesson plan" will testify. If a given agent had to calculate her way through all these possibilities, she'd never be able to carry out an action.

Culture is thus, in Morowitz's terms, a "pruning algorithm"; it takes a (somewhat) arbitrary set of conventions or instructions for action and labels them "the natural thing to do." You don't have to decide whether to come to a lecture clothed or naked; in fact, the number of clothing choices available to you is rather small — relative to all the things humans around the world do or could wear. (It's even smaller if you are a male.) After the lecture, our particular culture prescribes for you a few "proper" ways to announce your intention to ask a question; you don't throw a rock onto the stage, or send your "second" to negotiate with the speaker's "second." Cultural expectations determine the range of how long your question may be (a few seconds to a few minutes, and longer if you are a "senior scholar," but certainly not an hour!). Culture also specifies appropriate actions to take when you disagree with the speaker's response: no matter what she says, you probably won't scream, or pound your hands on your chest, or run at her with a machete (one hopes).

Cultures form a nested hierarchy. My teenager is American by culture, and Californian by culture, and Christian by culture. But she also belongs to some "foreign" cultures that those over the age of thirty find all but impenetrable. Indeed, her world of cliques and subcliques at high school is so complex that an army of ethnologists might despair of ever grasping it — even though as a seventeen-year-old she navigates her way through it with relative ease. This complexity is not arbitrary (or at least not completely so). A key function of cultures is to distinguish in-group from out-group. This is vital if we are to know who are the friends we can trust and who are those from whom we should protect ourselves. The greater the (perceived or actual) environmental danger, the more important is this function. And culture is extremely responsive to new needs. If the environment changes, a culture can change much, much faster than the human genome can change. If the changes made by one group are adaptive, it has a much better chance to survive and thrive than others do.

Culture is so pervasive in its effects that it's no longer fully true to say that we inhabit a biological world. We do, of course; and our behaviors are constrained by our biology in far more ways than we realize. Yet we — humans in community — are not *reducible to* the biological world, and we are not explainable solely in its terms. We participate in the creative openness of an evolving world of culture, history, and ideas. This fact is crucial for an understanding of the phenomena of human nature, morality, and religion.

Morality

Of course, values are expressed whenever there is an end that an organism selects and strives for. But are we not also moral in a stronger sense? Thanks to neurological structures such as mirror neurons, we experience within our bodies what we see happening to others around us. We smile when another smiles with happiness; we cringe when another experiences pain. (If you're not sure about this, try watching skateboarding videos with the teenager in your household.) Most importantly, our large neocortex allows us to have a sense of self: we know that the one hurt by our actions experiences the unpleasantness of pain as we ourselves do.

This knowledge makes our actions moral or immoral in a deeper sense than is the case for our cousins, the other higher primates. For when you know that your action harms another, and you know that she is a subject like you who experiences pain as the result of your action, yet you commit the action nonetheless, you become *responsible* for that action in a new way. At this moment *the sense of moral responsibility* is born; alone among the animals of this world it is our glory, and our burden. Because we are uniquely free, we are morally responsible in a unique way.

Freedom

There are numerous ways in which humans are not free. Drugs can change behavior. Social or cultural reinforcement can make behaviors more probable. The repetition of a behavior can increase the future probability of its recurrence; hence *habits* can change behaviors.

But individuals can also initiate behaviors based on factors idiosyncratic to themselves. My two-year-old, for reasons known only to her, used to move around the family room, carrying out a ritualized activity in four different corners (hugging a doll, banging a pot), and then repeating the whole pattern over and over. This "habit" built patterns that in turn may well influence later behaviors. (What is she likely to become: an acolyte, lighting and unlighting candles? a CPA, computing columns of figures over and over?) Is freedom indispensable for explaining idiosyncratic and improbable actions — actions that later become habits, cognitive patterns, and perhaps core personality traits? I urge a "yes" answer.

Contemporary philosophy offers two main options for defining freedom. The first is "libertarian" or counterfactual freedom: free agents might have acted otherwise, even if all the causal influences on them were identical. The second is "compatibilist" freedom. Perhaps every one of our "choices" is itself the product of a chain of internal or external causes. As long as the individual does not will *not* to perform the behavior she engages in (a desire which itself is the product of causes), then the action counts as free. "Compatibilist" freedom is fully compatible with scientific explanations, since the causal lines remain unbroken and each action is causally determined.

Which position is preferable? Surely on many occasions we face a panoply of possibilities for action. Among many other factors our brain structure, evolutionary history, environmental conditioning, hormonal balances, and habits all affect the probability of any given action occurring. In general, presumably, we act in accord with the strongest probability, the strongest behavioral disposition. Does this fact spell the end for human freedom? Not necessarily. We do not *know* that all actions are determined by whatever happens to be the strongest disposition, for perhaps humans do not always carry out the action with the strongest dispositional "tug" on them. One might combine this possibility with a second consideration, which is supported by the phenomenology above: sometimes it is *inner reasons* — moral or rational reasons — that turn us away from the (otherwise) strongest tug and compel us to a different decision or course of action. An adequate understanding of an agent's action will often include an analysis of the reasons that she gives for her action. For this reason, explanations are required *on the level of rationality and morality and not merely in terms of underlying causes.* For example, we've noted that ingroup and out-group labels predispose us to trust some and distrust others. If biological and cultural predispositions are the last word, then Peter Richerson's and Robert Boyd's exhortation to move beyond cultural boundaries is nonsense. But if moral reasons sometimes influence actions (and assuming that moral reasons are not always merely summaries of reigning cultural predispositions), then perhaps humans can indeed choose to act differently based on the force of the better argument or the higher moral code.

The experience of agents in the world, as we have seen, is the experience of reasoning, of recognizing others as persons similar to ourselves, of experiencing moral oughts and living in light of them. The understanding of freedom that corresponds to such phenomena is *agential freedom* — freedom for which *the agent's own choice* is the sufficient cause for at least some of her actions. To act freely *is* to act on the basis of purposes — to exercise the sort of intentional, teleological action that René van Woudenberg describes in his chapter. I believe this emergent capacity is both a product of evolution *and* a sign of the image of God in humanity. As the product of evolution, freedom indicates a greater richness and potential in the evolutionary process than is often acknowledged. As a sign of the *imago Dei*, purposive freedom suggests the possibility of divine purposes that may underlie the flow of history as a whole. If the one phenomenon of human freedom in fact reflects both dimensions, then it is possible to link these two sources — what biological evolution can produce and what God may purpose — in a close and mutually reinforcing way.

Altruism or Love

With altruism we reach the crucial question for religious ethics. I will suggest that one cannot develop an adequate account of altruism, morality, *or* human nature without the strong notion of agent-based freedom just discussed.

Darwin first suggested in 1871 that altruistic behaviors on the part of individuals might be compatible with evolutionary biology. Advances in understanding since the sixties have provided many of the details of the answer. Enough has been said in this volume about the evolutionary dimension of natural or reciprocal altruism that further comments would be redundant. Universal altruism is a different matter, however. It involves the *decision* to act apart from, or against, any considerations of survival advantage for self, friends, or kin. I follow the definition put forward by Thomas Oord (this volume): "to love is to act intentionally, in sympathetic response to others (including God), to increase overall well-being."

If the notion of freedom developed in the previous section is correct, one can say that an individual is free to choose to act in a universally altruistic manner — even if her biological drives or social acculturation should incline her against it. At any given moment I *could* live the life of a saint; hence for every moment that I don't, I am responsible before myself and before God. Moreover, one can choose in the present to engage in actions that increase the *likelihood* that one will act in a saint-like manner in the future. For example, one can choose to endorse a set of beliefs that supports universal altruism. Or one can join a religious community that seeks to live according to this value, such as Buddhism or Christianity (among many others).

Some authors have insisted that there would be some problems if universal altruism were universally practiced. Socialization for sympathy might be weakened, and the continued existence of *homo sapiens* might even be threatened. (Of course, greater levels of altruism would also *alleviate* some problems!) Nonetheless, there is no contradiction between the *pursuit* of a life of

333

universal altruism (or agape) and biology. Interestingly, Christian theologians have long advocated a life of agape without ever assuming that it would or could be fully actualized in this world. The only way to imagine the universal practice of agape is to postulate "a new heaven and a new earth" (Rev. 21:1).

Altruism and Human Nature

To advocate an ethics of universal love immediately raises the question of human nature. How great is the contradiction, if contradiction there is, between our genetically pre-given drives and these high moral aspirations? Certain religious traditions, such as Reformed Christianity, emphasize a strong sense of sin and the need for redemption: the love ethic could be achieved only with divine help. Others place less emphasis on fallenness and hence are more optimistic about the human capacity for culture-transcending moral behavior. In either case, the altruistic struggle is intimately linked to the freedom question: will one act in a manner different from one's selfish (or nationalist) inclinations?

Does the fact that we struggle mean that acts of altruism are always *counter* to human nature? I think not, and this for several reasons. First of all, it's a part of our nature to be free, reasoning agents; to exist in this way is an evolved characteristic of human being. A complete theory of human persons must therefore include reasoned moral judgments and the sense of responsibility, both of which are components of other-regarding behavior. Moreover, as this volume has shown, altruism has a place in nature, for sometimes the biological mandate is to act self-sacrificially. Finally, if one holds the Christian assumption that humans were created to act in a loving manner, one cannot at the same time assert that altruistic acts are counter to human nature. Indeed, on the Christian hypothesis, altruism should be the fullest expression of our created human nature.

Altruism and Religiosity

There is sufficient anthropological evidence to conclude that a religious response is basic to the experience of most of humanity in the world. Of course, this fact does not prove the truth of any particular religious tradition, for it is also amenable to biological explanation: we have a brain that produces a sense of openness, of contingency, of wonder and awe at our surroundings, and these neurologically based experiences incline humans toward religious responses to the world. (One thinks of the research of Ramachandran on the functions of the lower temporal lobe.) Any being that can run scenarios in its head of "how things might have been" must have an advanced sense of "could-have-been-otherwise," of contingency. It's not a long step from the awareness of contingency to the idea of a being who is not contingent, who does not, like us, have to die, who is not, like us, morally imperfect. For that matter, the religious sense could be interpreted in exclusively cultural terms as well. Part of culture is telling the story of the group's origins and values. Such a story should also explain the origin of its cultural practices and justify them in some way. Religious narratives and religious cosmogenies serve this function. God or the gods serve to justify one's own practices and morality.

Yet we are no more compelled to explain religious belief and practice in terms of its underlying biological and cultural functions alone than we were compelled to explain consciousness, freedom, or morality in such terms. All four of these phenomena are amenable to treatment in terms of underlying causes and functions; yet no science has demonstrated that they are "nothing but" these underlying causes, and phenomenological study suggests that each has an integrity at the level at which it is experienced. To treat all four phenomena in light of the scientific knowledge we have of them, yet without reducing any one of them to some set of underlying causes, is the core of what I above called "the compatibilist hypothesis." On this view, which I find supported by the approach and arguments explored in these pages, religion serves a variety of biological, psychological, and cultural functions — and is also something more than the sum of these various functions. The phenomenology of religious experience suggests an integrity to this level of explanation that resists reduction into its component parts. And religious beliefs themselves have an explanatory power for answering core metaphysical questions that fills in a hole left by all lower-level explanations. One cannot make sense of "the purpose of the whole" except by using explanatory terms that make reference to the whole. No wonder, then, that biological explanations do not allow for statements about "the purpose of evolution." If there *is* such a purpose, the use of universal or cosmic terms — and that means metaphysical terms such as "God" — will be necessary to formulate hypotheses about it.

Conclusion

Developments in biological theory such as evolutionary psychology have shown that evolution and ethics are not unrelated. At the same time, the treatments in this volume have also shown that the evolution-ethics axis does not exclude religious belief and religious explanations. In the end, the religious level nicely supplements the biological contribution in comprehending human morality.

Numerous theorists have warned that the understanding of human flourishing would be truncated if we fail to provide a *comprehensive* theory of human nature. This brief closing exploration has shown that a complete anthropology can include both biology and freedom. To include freedom, I have argued, is to include morality, that is, to include both the ideal and the possibility of altruistic action in the strong sense of universal altruism. Finally, the entire complex can be conceived against the backdrop of divine purpose — an overall creative intent by God in history to accomplish certain goals. The synthesis of biology, morality, and theology is not mandated by the empirical evidence (how could it be?), though it is supported by arguments such as the one sketched in these pages. In the end, I suggest, the picture yielded by combining biological *and* religious perspectives on human morality is richer than the picture produced by either one of these perspectives alone.

REFERENCES

Brothers, Leslie. 1997. *Friday's Footprint: How Society Shapes the Human Mind.* New York: Oxford University Press.

Dawkins, Richard. 1987. *The Blind Watchmaker: Why the Evidence of Evolution Reveals a Universe without Design.* New York: Norton.

————. 1998. *Unweaving the Rainbow: Science, Delusion, and the Appetite for Wonder.* Boston: Houghton Mifflin.

Gehlen, Arnold. 1988. *Man, His Nature and Place in the World.* Trans. Clare McMillan and Karl Pillemer. New York: Columbia University Press.

Janov, Arthur. 2000. *The Biology of Love.* Amherst, N.Y.: Prometheus.

Lewis, Thomas, et al. 2000. *A General Theory of Love.* New York: Random House.

Morowitz, Harold J. 2002. *The Emergence of Everything: How the World Became Complex.* New York: Oxford University Press.

Ruse, Michael. 2001. *Can a Darwinian Be a Christian? The Relationship between Science and Religion.* Cambridge: Cambridge University Press.

Wilson, David Sloan. 2002. *Darwin's Cathedral: Evolution, Religion, and the Nature of Society.* Chicago: University of Chicago Press.

List of Contributors

Larry Arnhart is Professor of Political Science at Northern Illinois University. His books and articles cover a variety of topics related to political philosophy, biopolitical theory, biotechnology, and evolutionary ethics. Arnhart's most recent book is *Darwinian Natural Right: The Biological Ethics of Human Nature.*

Christopher Boehm is Director of the Jane Goodall Research Center and Professor of Anthropology and Biological Sciences at the University of Southern California. His research interests include egalitarian humans, wild chimpanzees, moral behavior, and the evolution of political and social behavior. Boehm is the author of *Blood Revenge* and *Hierarchy in the Forest* and, among other grants and awards, has been the recipient of a Simon J. Guggenheim fellowship.

Craig A. Boyd is Professor of Philosophy at Greenville College (IL). He has published articles in *Zygon, Journal of Religion and Science, The American Catholic Philosophical Quarterly,* and *The Modern Schoolman.* Boyd's areas of interest include St. Thomas Aquinas, natural law morality, divine command theory, and evolutionary psychology.

Robert Boyd is Professor of Anthropology at the University of California, Los Angeles. In addition to a number of important publications with Peter Richerson he is the coauthor with Joan Silk of several editions of the textbook *How Humans Evolved* and the coauthor of *Foundations of Human Sociality: Ethnography and Experiments in 15 Small-Scale Societies* with Joseph Henrich and others.

Dr. Michael Chapman is a biomedical researcher in the Department of Cell Biology at the University of Massachusetts Medical School. He is currently the recipient of a NIH fellowship to study the cell biology of cilia and flagella. Chapman has published some 25 articles and textbook chapters on symbiosis, cell biology and evolution, including "Centrioles and Kinetosomes: Form, Function and Evolution" and "Morphogenesis by Symbiogenesis."

Philip Clayton is Ingraham Professor at the Claremont School of Theology and Professor of Philosophy and Religion at the Claremont Graduate University. He is the author or editor of some twelve books in the philosophy of science, philosophical theology, and the science-religion debate. Recent publications include *God and Contemporary Science, The Problem of God in Modern Thought,* and *Mind and Emergence.*

Loren Haarsma is Assistant Professor of Physics at Calvin College. In addition to his research in neuroscience, he has written articles and book chapters, lectured, taught courses, and organized seminar series on the interaction of science, philosophy, and theology.

S. Mark Heim is the Samuel Abbot Professor of Christian Theology at Andover Newton Theological School in Newton Centre, Massachusetts. He has authored and edited books on religious pluralism and Christian ecumenism, among other topics. Heim's course on the relation of science and theology has won several Templeton Foundation awards, including one in 1998 honoring the outstanding courses developed in this field.

David Lahti is a Darwin Fellow in the Organismic and Evolutionary Biology Program at the Morrill Science Center, University of Massachusetts. His recent publications include: "Parting with Illusions in Evolutionary Ethics," "A Case Study in Invasive Species Assessment: The Village Weaverbird *Ploceus cucullatus*," and "Morphological and Behavioural Evidence of Relationships of the Cuckoo-Finch *Anomalospiza imberbis.*" Lahti's current work explores the effects of relaxed selection and its relevance to costs of adaptations, as well as the dynamics of antagonistic co-evolution among bird populations.

Thomas Jay Oord is Professor of Theology and Philosophy at Northwest Nazarene University. He is Academic Correspondent and Contributing Editor for *Science and Theology News* and serves as theologian for the Institute for Research on Unlimited Love. Oord has written or edited a half dozen books, the most recent being *Science of Love: The Wisdom of Well-Being.*

Gregory R. Peterson is Associate Professor of Philosophy and Religion at South Dakota State University. He is author of numerous papers on science and religion, as well as the book *Minding God: Theology and the Cognitive Sciences.* Peterson has been active as a review editor for *Zygon* as well as a chair for the Science and Religion group of the American Academy of Religion.

Joseph Poulshock is Associate Professor at Tokyo Christian University and a Fellow at the Discovery Institute's Center for Science and Culture. His current research concentrates on the topics of group selection, mimetics, the limits of evolutionary theories of altruism, and the parallels between universal grammar and morality. Recent publications include "The Difficulty of Making Infinite Sense" and "Evolutionary Theology and God Memes: Explaining Everything or Nothing."

Peter J. Richerson is Professor of Environmental Science at the University of California, Davis. He and Robert Boyd are the co-authors of *Culture and the Evolutionary Process,* one of the most widely cited books on cultural evolution, and a number of papers and book chapters on the same topic. Their forthcoming book is entitled *Not by Genes Alone: How Culture Transformed Human Evolution.*

Philip Rolnick is Associate Professor of Theology at the University of St. Thomas in St. Paul, Minnesota. In addition to his interest in theology and science, he has published several articles on theological language, including "Analogical Possibilities." Rolnick is currently working on a book on the theology of the person.

Holmes Rolston III is University Distinguished Professor and Professor of Philosophy at Colorado State University. He delivered the Gifford Lectures at University of Edinburgh in 1997-98, published as *Genes, Genesis, and God.* He was named laureate for the Templeton Prize in Religion in 2003.

Michael Ruse is Lucyle T. Werkmeister Professor of Philosophy at Florida State University. Widely recognized as one of the leading philosophers of biology of our time, he is the author of numerous books on evolutionary theory, most recently *Darwin and Design: Does Evolution have a Purpose?*

Jeffrey P. Schloss is Professor of Biology at Westmont College. A former Danforth Fellow, Schloss is recognized as one of the leading authorities on the relationship between biology and religion. His writing focuses on evolutionary and theological understandings of altruism, morality, and purpose; recent projects include *Altruism and Altruistic Love: Science, Philosophy, and Theology in Dialogue* and two pieces on evolutionary psychology in the *Journal of Psychology & Theology.*

René van Woudenberg is Professor of Philosophy at the Free University, Amsterdam. He is the author of seven books in epistemology and metaphysics, including *Ontwerp en Toeval in de Wereld (Design and Chance in the World).* With Terence Cuneo he is co-editor of *The Cambridge Companion to Thomas Reid.*